P9-BJV-799

A Measure of Justice

AN EMPIRICAL STUDY OF CHANGES
IN THE CALIFORNIA PENAL CODE, 1955–1971

This is a volume of

Quantitative Studies in Social Relations

Consulting Editor: Peter H. Rossi, University of Massachusetts,
Amherst, Massachusetts

A complete list of titles in this series appears at the end of this volume.

A Measure of Justice

AN EMPIRICAL STUDY OF CHANGES
IN THE CALIFORNIA PENAL CODE, 1955–1971

RICHARD A. BERK
Department of Sociology
University of California
Santa Barbara, California

HAROLD BRACKMAN
Urban Policy Research Institute
Beverly Hills, California

SELMA LESSER
Urban Policy Research Institute
Beverly Hills, California

ACADEMIC PRESS New York San Francisco London 1977
A Subsidiary of Harcourt Brace Jovanovich, Publishers

ACADEMIC PRESS, INC.
111 Fifth Avenue, New York, New York 10003

United Kingdom Edition published by
ACADEMIC PRESS, INC. (LONDON) LTD.
24/28 Oval Road, London NW1

Library of Congress Cataloging in Publication Data

Berk, Richard A
    A measure of justice.

    (Quantitative studies in social relations series)
    Bibliography: p.
    Includes indexes.
    1.   Criminal law—Research—California.   I.   Brackman,
Harold, joint author.   II.   Lesser, Selma, L., joint au-
thor.   III.   Title.
KFC1100.B47   345'.794'0072   76-2941
ISBN 0–12–091550–2

To Peter H. Rossi

Contents

III   Quantifying Legislative Change   115

IV   Trends in the Penal Code Affecting Actors in the Criminal Justice System   135

List of Figures

List of Tables

Preface

WE HAVE TRIED TO WRITE a book for a wide range of potential readers: social scientists, practicing lawyers, legal scholars, criminal justice officials, and legislators. Satisfying such a diverse group is not easy. Specialists in California history and politics may wish for greater detail, while wider audiences may find the material somewhat parochial. Our statistical discussions have been abbreviated and "popularized"—a fact that quantitative social scientists may find objectionable. Our attempts at broader theoretical analysis may seem dry and academic to some, insufficiently elaborated to others. Our only defense is that we are acutely aware of these tensions and have tried to strike an optimum balance.

The study was begun in the summer of 1971 under the auspices of the Urban Policy Research Institute.* The need for a new approach to an understanding of the politics of the criminal law was first voiced by Mae Churchill, the Institute's Director. Using the Penal Code of California as a vehicle for addressing these concerns emerged in discussions between her and Peter H. Rossi, then of Johns Hopkins University. To both of these persons we are indebted.

The qualitative political history of the changes in the Penal Code is primarily the work of Harold Brackman. He profited from the openness and candor of numerous individuals and organizations—among them: Thomas Carroll of the Assembly Office of Research; Rowan Kline, formerly Administrative Assistant to Assemblyman Allan Sieroty; Senator Lou

---

* Then known as the Institute on Law and Urban Studies of Loyola University School of Law.

Casanovitch; former Assemblyman Charles Conrad, then Chairman of the Assembly Committee on the Judiciary; Dr. A. C. Germann, California State University, Long Beach; the Los Angeles County Sheriff's Department, especially Sergeant Rick C. Wallace of the Civil Division; the Sacramento Office of the California Peace Officers' Association; the Pasadena Staff of the Friends Committee on Legislation; and the Los Angeles Office of the American Civil Liberties Union.

The coding of legislative change was designed and supervised largely by Selma Lesser. She also provided editorial continuity, coordinating innumerable manuscript revisions. Finally, she solicited comments from critical but sympathetic readers in the Institute, including especially Mae Churchill; Steven P. Erie, now at the University of Southern California; and Joseph G. Woods, currently in the office of the Solicitor General, Ottawa, Canada.

As for the coding itself, the authors wish to express their gratitude to the young lawyers who approached with enthusiasm and respect the task of scaling legislative revisions for impact on the criminal justice system: Steve Axelrod, Jay A. Bloom, Ralph Boroff, Judith Fry, James Kline, Michael A. Ozurovich, Beverly Rickard, Thomas S. Sorter, and Rolf Wheeler—all recent graduates from law schools of the University of California. In addition, the authors wish to acknowledge their considerable debt to the criminal justice professionals who took time from demanding schedules to assist in the verification of the coding procedure by actually scaling a sample of legislative revisions from the vantage point of seasoned professionals: Judge Arthur L. Alarcon and Judge Kathleen Parker, Superior Court, Criminal Division, Los Angeles County; David A. Kidney and Wilbur F. Littlefield, Public Defender's Office, Los Angeles County; and William Hobbs and Florence Linn, Office of District Attorney, Los Angeles County. Their interest and active cooperation added an important dimension to the validity of our research. Finally, Alana Emhardt and Betty Dameron responded generously as research assistants in systematizing the endless details associated with legislative history and roll-call data.

The statistical analyses and preliminary drafts of all but Chapter II are the work of Richard Berk, then of Northwestern University. He benefited enormously from the advice of Gerald Goldstein of Northwestern's Economics Department who gave consistently sound counsel on appropriate statistical procedures. His ability to distinguish necessary techniques from statistical ostentation reflects a wisdom that is all too rare among quantitative social scientists. In addition, Frederick Dubow of Northwestern's Sociology Department provided guidance through a maze of references and contributed important insights from the sociology of law. Finally, numerous conversations with Arnold Feldman, also of Northwestern's Sociology Deparment, helped enormously in at least raising the larger theoretical issues. These fine colleagues deserve special mention, but we are obviously responsible for such flaws as may remain in the manuscript.

The statistical work was greatly facilitated by Peter Li and Karen Brenner, who coded the *Los Angeles Times*. Michelle Galodetz and Robert Nelson helped tame the CDC 6400 at the Vogelback Computer Center.

Once the main ideas of the manuscript were organized and preliminary drafts prepared, Peter H. Rossi, John P. Heinz, and Stanton Wheeler stimulated rethinking the text. Considering their extremely busy schedules, we are especially grateful.

Finally, we want publicly to acknowledge our debt to one another. We are three people from disparate disciplines, divergent backgrounds, and different generations. The gaps to be bridged were temperamental as well as intellectual, and distance added to the challenge, since during the lengthy period this work was in progress one of us was in Evanston while the other two were in Los Angeles.

Though Berk as senior author exercised final authority, different chapters reflect our varying contributions. Chapter II, with its case studies in political history is very much Brackman's own, whereas Lesser made her largest contribution to Chapters III through V and their quantitative mapping of Penal Code trends. Chapters VI through IX, on the other hand, are the senior author's: They apply more advanced techniques of quantitative analysis and present broader theoretical models for explaining sociopolitical change.

In the active exchange of ideas, each of us has grown; and the manuscript, we believe, reflects this growth. If we are right about this, we also have the privilege of claiming that, as collaborations go, ours has been a success.

I

Sources of Criminal Law: An Overview

Introduction

THE SURVIVAL OF NATION-STATES depends fundamentally on an ability to regulate the behavior of their citizens. Taxes must be collected, soldiers provided for the common defense, and public order maintained. Unless the nation-state is fully prepared to meet all disruptive behavior with brute force, responsiveness to national exigencies must be accomplished by alternative means. It is here that the role of law is especially critical. To the degree that the law is widely regarded as legitimate, citizens will more readily comply with the imperial priorities reflected in its content, while troublemakers and malcontents may justly be subjected to institutionalized sanctions. Moreover, citizen disputes can be routinized to reduce some of their more unacceptable consequences. Although "domestic tranquillity" is never fully achieved, the government itself may come to possess a near monopoly on the use of physical coercion. As Weber observed, the state is a "relation of men dominating men" supported by "legitimate violence."[1] The law—especially the criminal law—defines what kinds of violence will be prohibited, what kinds of violence will be tolerated, and even what kinds of violence will be encouraged.

The United States is no different from other nations in its dependence on law. At virtually every level of government organization, legal codes

1

exist serving a wide range of purposes. Our particular concern will be the law surrounding "criminal" behavior as written in Penal Codes at the state level.

There is a variety of issues about the content of particular state Penal Codes one might address: the ideals the Codes perhaps embody, the organized interests they may represent, the processes by which they are written, and their presumed impact on the broader community. To some degree we hope to touch on all of these issues, although a few will be considered in far more depth than the rest.

Our vehicle is the Penal Code for the State of California. We have considered its changing content from the year 1955 to the year 1971, using both traditional methods of historical research to examine over a score of controversial bills and more recent statistical techniques capable of analyzing the nearly 700 substantive revisions legislated during this period. Not only will longitudinal trends be described but a variety of causal forces shaping the Code will also be suggested. Did the unrest of the 1960s, for example, affect California's criminal law? And, if so, how did the legislature of the nation's largest state respond: with remediation or repression? We will attempt to answer such questions.

We began this research in 1971 moved by growing anxieties about the law-and-order backlash of the late 1960s. Organizations, typically left of center, were predicting that 1984 was about to arrive 10 years ahead of schedule. Conservative interests were proclaiming the need to purge the country of deviants and dissidents while returning to the fundamental values of moral purity, hard work, and respect for authority. Since the criminal law was one avenue through which contending parties could advance their agenda, the California Penal Code seemed a useful place to examine the burgeoning conflict and its potential consequences.

Though the trends of the late 1960s by themselves were our initial concern, it soon became clear that any analysis of recent events could not be effectively undertaken without a comparative perspective. Current content of the criminal law was not especially informative unless juxtaposed to some standard. Thus, knowledge about the penalties for drug use, for example, held limited interest unless viewed in some normative context, with standards generated by sources outside the law (such as social science), or contrasted to sentences at other points in time and/or from other bodies of criminal law. In the first case, one might ask if the law was consistent with some notion of "justice." The second might involve social science findings about the effects of criminal law on society. In the third case, current content of the Penal Code could be compared to the Codes of other states or of California in years past.

Despite some plausible arguments for the first strategy,[2] we discarded a normative approach because we could find no clear and widely accepted values to use as a standard. Though there is probably considerable agreement that laws should reflect such qualities as universalism, justice, and due process, in practice these terms can have so many different and often contradictory meanings that they fail as a metric. Black captures one dimension of our concern when he states: "When legal reality is compared to an ideal with no identifiable empirical referent, such as 'the rule of law' or 'due process,' the investigator may inadvertently implant his personal ideals as society's legal ideals."[3]

The idea of using social science findings on the effects of criminal law was also discarded. It would have been most informative, for instance, had we been able to compare the intent of new laws governing the use of credit cards with their actual impact on potential felons, but such data were not available. Only recently, through the work of such researchers as Becker,[4] Schur,[5] Lindesmith,[6] and Lemert,[7] have we begun to understand some of the consequences of criminal law for the nature of deviance. Similarly, the ways in which criminal law supports or undermines the social structure of a society is just beginning to be explored (see Chambliss,[8] Garnsey,[9] Erikson,[10] Jeffrey[11]). In short, the consequences of criminal law are not sufficiently clear to provide a useful evaluative standard.

Given the problems with normative and social science criteria, we settled on longitudinal patterns as a basis for comparison. Hence, our study will not emphasize how the criminal law relates to some external metric but, rather, how the law evolves over time. For example, we will examine whether or not the California Penal Code was shifting the adversarial balance within the criminal justice system and, if so, whether the shift tended to favor the prosecution or the defense.

Some Broader Theoretical Issues

Though this book will focus primarily on historical events in the State of California, we believe our findings have bearing on several larger issues, particularly the underlying sources of the criminal law. Durkheim, for example, clearly represents the view that law evolves from culture and is typically consistent with it: "Normally, custom is not opposed to law, but is, on the contrary, its basis."[12] This position, which for the purposes of the present discussion we identify under the rubric of "incipient law,"* has been popular with many scholars, who have proposed a variety of defini-

---

* We are grateful to Fredrick Dubow for extricating us from a terminological swamp by suggesting the term "incipient law."

tions of the relevant legal "culture" and mechanisms by which "culture" becomes formalized into law.

In an influential book, Hart emphasizes the foundational role of "custom," which he calls the "primary rules of obligation":

> If a society is to live by such primary rules alone, there are certain conditions which, granted a few of the most obvious truisms about human nature and the world we live in, must be clearly satisfied. The first of these conditions is that rules must contain in some form restrictions on the free use of violence, theft, and deception to which human beings are tempted but which they must, in general, repress if they are to coexist in close proximity to each other.[13]

Given these primary rules, Hart argues that "secondary rules" develop, without which modern complex societies would be impossible. For our purposes, the importance of Hart's position is his emphasis on primary rules as underlying criminal law, with the result that citizens feel internally motivated to conform. In Hart's terms, they feel an "obligation" not to violate the law.

In many ways Fuller takes a position similar to Hart's, but he tries to locate the foundations of law more concretely in the details of human interaction and in the "customary" law underlying the "ordinary" or "enacted" law:

> The phenomenon called "customary law" can best be described as a *language of interaction*. To act meaningfully, men require a social setting in which the moves of the participating players will fall generally within some predictable pattern. To engage in effective social behavior, men need the support of intermeshing anticipants that will let them know what their opposite numbers will do, or that will at least enable them to gauge the general scope of the repertory from which responses to their actions will be drawn.[14]

It is these "stable interactional expectancies" that form the foundations of criminal law.

A final, widely shared statement of the incipient law position can be found in Bohannan, who stresses: "Law may be regarded as a custom that has been restated in order to make it amenable to the activities of the legal institutions."[15] Certain forms of human interaction are institutionalized into custom, of which a part is then "reinstitutionalized" into law. This is the so-called "double institutionalization" process. Hence, law builds on custom, though Bohannan acknowledges that there is often a tension between the two.

As one contrast to the incipient law position, some scholars have argued that law is simply an instrument of the powerful. Rather than reflecting the basic culture or custom of citizens, law is a tool for rulers. Thus Diamond states:

> It is apparent that the contradictory transition from customs to specified law, "double institutionalization," if you will, *is by no means the major source of law.* Whether the law arises latently, in confirmation of previous usage, or through the transformation of some aspect or custom, . . . neither circumstance brings us to the heart of the matter. For we learn by studying intermediate societies that the laws so typical of them are *un-precedented*; they do not emerge through the process of "double institutionalization." They arise in opposition to the customary order of the antecedent kin or kin-equivalent groups; they represent a new set of social goals pursued by a new and unanticipated power in society. These goals can be reduced to a single complex imperative: the imposition of the interrelated census–tax–conscription system. The territorial thrust of the early state, along with its vertical social entrenchment demanded con-scription of labor, the mustering of an army, the levying of taxes and tribute, the maintenance of a bureaucracy, and the assessment of the ex-tent, location, and numbers of the population being subjected. These were the major direct or indirect occasions for the development of civil law.[16]

Quinney takes a somewhat similar view in his analysis of the criminal law in American society, identifying it as "an arm of the ruling class." Law is neither a reflection of custom nor a series of compromises between di-verse, equally matched interests. Thus, Quinney discards both the "incip-ient law" perspective and the pluralist tradition:

> First, my perspective is based on a special conception of society. Society is characterized by diversity, conflict, coercion, and change, rather than by consensus and stability. Second, law is a result of the operation of interests, rather than an instrument that functions outside of particular interests. Though law may control interests, it is in the first place created by inter-ests. Third, law incorporates the interests of specific persons and groups; it is seldom the product of the whole society. Law is made by men, repre-senting special interests, who have the power to translate their interests into public policy. Unlike the pluralistic conceptions of politics, law does not represent a compromise of the diverse interests in society, but supports some interests at the expense of others. Fourth, the theoretical perspective of criminal law is devoid of teleological connotations. The social order may require certain functions for its maintenance and survival, but such functions will not be considered as inherent in the interests involved in formulating substantive laws.[17]

As is true of most complex questions, "either/or" resolutions to the controversy are unsatisfactory. While most current law is created from above, it is also clear that no regime can enact law while totally ignoring the customs of the society. First, the legitimacy and, hence, enforceability of law depend to some important degree on its consistency with normative notions of justice. Second, the members of ruling groups are themselves products of society and share some of the normative biases and blind spots of average citizens. Third, the enactment process is in part a function of the prevailing societal institutions, which in turn reflect the fundamental structure of society. This structure affects both the institutions and the customs and, therefore, must produce certain parallels between the two. Since the customs and institutions are related, law emanating from societal institutions must correlate to some degree with custom. Weber, for example, recognized these complexities when he noted that law can emerge from different (though often related) processes including the formalization of "consensual understandings," decisions by judges, edicts by rulers, pronouncements by charismatic figures, votes by legislatures, and rulings by legal experts.[18]

An Alternative Approach

Weber's eclectic perspective underlines the need to approach the development of law in a more subtle manner. One strategy might begin by breaking down a society's laws into categories suggesting different developmental processes. To take a distant instance, DuBow, in a study of legal institutions in Tanzania, distinguished between law based on local custom, law retained from the colonial regime, law imposed by the emerging state for the maintenance of a national government, and law reflecting offenses of such a serious nature that they violated local custom and the state's need for order.[19] Each type of law reflected somewhat different mixes of custom and imposition from above.

Our data from the California Penal Code are unfortunately, not easily amenable to such a reconceptualization. The primary problem is that perhaps only in nations experiencing fundamental societal rearrangements can one conveniently place laws into categories implying very different roots. Such distinctions are muddy under normal circumstances when over many years numerous complementary and competing factors have shaped Penal Code content. What may begin as imposed law, over time may gain wide legitimacy. Alternatively, a law originally enacted in response to popular sentiments may eventually become the oppressive tool of a narrow elite.

In the face of these difficulties, we shall proceed more inductively by initially stressing observed relationships and later trying to put the pieces together. Nevertheless, as in any coherent analysis, some organizational form must be applied, and ours builds on four types of factors presumedly shaping the criminal law.

1. Social structure
2. Values and beliefs
3. Bureaucratic interests
4. Legislative processes

"Social structure" refers to the content of and relations between the fundamental building blocks of a society and, in practice, includes such indicators as governmental form, economic organization, and demographic mix. "Values and beliefs" include the moral, political, and scientific ideas that make up a society's world view. "Bureaucratic interests" refers to the attempts by formal organizations to enhance their power and fulfill their goals. Finally, "legislative processes" addresses the "nuts and bolts" activities (e.g., committee work and lobbying) that occur within lawmaking bodies enacting the criminal law.

The Role of Social Structure

Most empirical studies of the forces shaping criminal law have analyzed more than one of the four types of variables identified above. Yet some researchers have emphasized a single factor over others. In the case of social structure, Chambliss, for example, has argued that the development of vagrancy laws in England was originally based on the need to "force laborers (whether personally free or unfree) to accept employment at a low wage in order to insure the landowner an adequate supply of labor at a price he could afford to pay."[20] Later, as economic and demographic changes made cheap farm labor far less problematic, the law was rarely applied. However, as England moved to an economy based on commerce, vagrancy laws were resurrected and given new teeth to "facilitate the control of persons preying upon merchants transporting goods." By controlling the "dangerous classes," the safety of commerce was ensured. Though Chambliss's work is an outstanding instance, other researchers have emphasized structural factors affecting the criminal law. For example, Hall analyzes the genesis of the crime of theft in much the same way that Chambliss approaches vagrancy.[21] Garnsey argues that much of Roman law evolved as a means to protect the interests of Roman aristocrats.[22]

Diamond cites a variety of anthropological studies supporting his contention that the emergence of nation-states required the imposition of regulatory laws to ensure the hegemony of ruling interests.[23] Finally, Nelson examines the changing activities of the criminal justice system in Massachusetts from colonial times through early nation-building efforts and concludes that moral underpinnings were replaced by political imperatives, making "the state" vitally interested in bringing criminals to justice.[24]

Some thinking on structural factors shaping the criminal law has drawn extensively on prior theory specifying the most significant aspects of social structure. In particular, various brands of Marxian analysis have focused upon the "means of production" and upon the "ruling class," that results. Probably the earliest lengthy analysis from this perspective was undertaken by William Adrian Bonger at the turn of the century; but more recently Miliband,[25] Quinney,[26] Platt,[27] Taylor, Walton, and Young,[28] and others have adopted somewhat similar approaches. In essence, all have argued that in capitalist societies, the criminal law (and criminal justice system more generally) is forged from ruling-class interests to help stabilize societal contradictions and control the working class (variously defined). Two kinds of mechanisms are commonly emphasized. First, the entire social fabric under the capitalist mode of production—economic institutions, government, ideological perspectives, and so on—favors an economic elite and their agents. Societal arrangements so benefit big business that even without conscious, organized conspiracies, the ruling class will tend to dominate (although in a stochastic manner). Put most simply, it is like playing roulette against the house. Over the long run, it is perfectly clear who will win despite the game's unfettered progress and the fact that an individual gambler will win from time to time. Second, viewed solely as an interest group, ruling class members also benefit from unusual political and economic resources which make them especially formidable opponents. To push our earlier metaphor, not only are the odds structured in their favor, but they have the financial backing to take advantage on the long-run probabilities.

One can sympathize with this view and yet agree with critics who note that up to this point, a Marxist theory of criminal law is but a promising idea. Whatever the value of the broader theoretical perspective, much "critical criminology" is shot through with nonverifiable assertions, functionalist tautologies, and/or conspiracy theories, almost ignoring social structure. Quinney's theoretical work, for example, occasionally lapses into sterile polemics and vacuous formulations. Class imperatives are alleged to "explain" everything in a totally nonstochastic manner, with the details and mechanisms unspecified. The result is an almost mystical explanation of the sources of criminal law.

The Role of Values and Beliefs

The role of values and beliefs has also received a good deal of attention. Radzinowicz, for example, argues that the kinds of sentences attached to criminal offenses can be understood through the dominant philosophical perspectives of various historical periods. During the eighteenth century, the philosophies of Rousseau, Voltaire, Montesquieu, and Diderot inspired an "enlightened" faith in scientific social engineering that in turn shaped Beccaria's "liberal" view of law and penal reform. Though a rather complex cluster of ideas, the liberal position rested on the premise that a "potential offender was . . . an independent, reasoning individual, weighing up the consequences of crime and deciding the balance of advantage."[29] Hence, the deterrent aspects of punishment were paramount. In the nineteenth century, this "liberal" view was challenged by more "deterministic" theories: social and psychological factors so influenced individuals that frequently a "free" choice to engage in crime or not, was nonexistent. This implied that sentencing should reflect rehabilitation, rather than deterrence.

On the American scene, Haskins, in his research on the law of colonial Massachusetts, also stresses the role of values and beliefs—in this case three dominant strands of seventeenth-century Puritan thinking: First, criminal law should reflect God's natural law, which was instilled in the soul of man and could be immediately comprehended. Second, criminal law should also be responsive to God's positive law, which though not ingrained in man's being was revealed in the Bible. Finally, law could include rules enacted by man that were logical extensions and applications of God's law.[30]

Studying more recent events, Sutherland emphasizes the importance of beliefs in the diffusion of sexual psychopath laws. However, rather than the general philosophic mood, he stresses how popular feeling can interact with professional opinion to revamp the criminal law.[31] Widespread hysteria caused by a few heinous sexual assaults (especially on children) was apparently one critical factor in the passage of state laws affecting violent sexual offenses. In addition, professional endorsements of psychiatric treatment were instrumental in codifying the indeterminate sentence, during which the criminal was to be rehabilitated.

In short, there is considerable evidence that the belief systems of relevant actors, and the dominant views of given historical periods, do contribute to the content of criminal law. Indeed, in most instances they may function at least as necessary conditions. Our quarrel with such approaches mirrors the criticism of Taylor *et al.*, who argue that belief systems must ultimately be linked to fundamental structural variables.[32] While the nature of such associations, and their causal ordering, is problematic, it is still clear that the beliefs and values of a society do not constitute the full story.

The Role of Bureaucratic Interests

Though not ignoring values and beliefs, several investigators have recently examined the role of bureaucratic ambition as a factor shaping criminal law. Lindesmith, for example, argues that the Federal Narcotics Bureau has continually lobbied to increase its role in determining drug offenses and consciously subverted the intent of several important court decisions that in effect would have decriminalized many drug-related crimes (e.g., by making heroin available to an addict by means of a doctor's prescription).[33] Becker offers a similar explanation for the role of the Federal Narcotics Bureau in the criminalization of marijuana use.[34] To take a final example more distant in both time and space, Currie analyzes the control of witchcraft in Renaissance Europe as a "form of deviance . . . created and sustained largely through the efforts of self-sustaining bureaucratic organizations dedicated to its discovery and punishment, and granted unusual power."[35] Though the prosecution of witches was originally based in religious notions prohibiting collaboration with the Devil, witch trials became a big business (especially on the Continent), in which the property of those convicted could be confiscated by the courts. Many church officials, court administrators, and court personnel (such as executioners) grew wealthy by convicting large numbers of well-to-do citizens. In addition, the confiscation of property sustained the bureaucratic apparatus and provided motivation to expand its operations. When, eventually, many countries outlawed confiscation as part of the inquisitional process, the prosecution of witches virtually disappeared.

Few would question the importance of bureaucratic interests in shaping the criminal law. Modern societies especially are organized in part through bureaucratic structure, and the criminal justice system in particular is a cluster of cooperating and competing organizations. Since the Penal Code is clearly one critical avenue by which any one of these groups could further its aims, organizational interests are an important explanation of criminal law content. Critics of bureaucratic explanations do not deny these facts. Rather, they argue (1) that the organizational interests are but superficial indicators of the "real" guiding powers of society, (2) the details of bureaucratic in-fighting obscure larger patterns, and (3) that the larger patterns reflect, not pluralism, but dominance by powerful elites. We are keenly sensitive to such criticisms and will be considering these issues throughout the manuscript.

The Role of the Legislative Process

By far the largest body of research about factors affecting law (though rarely criminal law) comes from the many studies of the American legislative process. Typically building on the debatable pluralist assumptions of

American political science, these studies examine in great detail political parties, legislative structures, parliamentary procedures, and the role of lobbies. (The literature is vast and is briefly summarized in Appendix 1.1.) Despite the diversity of geographical settings and substantive issues with which these studies deal, four general conclusions can be abstracted: First, all stress the necessity of looking beyond the formal mechanisms of bill passage in order to understand the shaping of the law. In the politics of criminal lawmaking as in the operation of bureaucratic organizations, informal "structure" is often more important than formal. Second, this literature emphasizes the crucial role of competing groups and individuals. Invariably, one reads about contending lobbies, legislative committees, party leaders, and members of the executive branch. Given these factions, legislative activity cannot be understood except in the context of "horse-trading." Third, the competitive process of bill passage seems so to dominate the scene that original legislative intent is often severely diluted. Some observers have praised this process as a useful instrument of moderation. Finally, even with its ambiguities, ideological assumptions, and lack of structural considerations, probably no approach to bill passage has yet been developed that would provide a better framework for viewing the *details* of the lawmaking process.

For the data examined in this book, one legislative study particularly stands out in its relevance and clarity. In 1969, Heinz, Gettleman, and Seeskin published a case study of the Illinois legislature addressing the processes by which several important criminal justice bills were handled.[36] Of special interest is their conclusion that criminal justice legislation typically involves an "agreed bill" process in which the important decisions are made exclusively by negotiating lobbies and a few members of the relevant legislative committees. Debates on the floor of the legislature, when they occur, are largely window-dressing for negotiations that have already been concluded. The votes in upper and lower houses are typically near unanimous—the official stamp of approval for actions undertaken in proverbial "smoke-filled" rooms. In other words, even for relatively controversial bills, the legislative processes in Illinois really takes place outside the public view and involves groups representing a rather narrow range of interests. These conclusions will be measured against our California data.

An Eclectic Approach

Our discussion of the four general kinds of factors shaping criminal law should not be construed as arguing that these factors operate in isolation from one another. Indeed, some of the best research has demonstrated how they interact. In what has become a classic analysis, Anthony Platt has shown how in Illinois the development of laws and courts responsive to the "deviance" of juveniles came about through all of the basic factors we have discussed.[37] Juvenile delinquency was "invented" in part through a realization by elite economic interests that the children of recent immigrants had to be controlled and properly socialized. Besides this attempt to transform "delinquents" into "useful citizens" (i.e., reliable employees), the "Child Savers" movement was fueled by a growth of legal and correctional bureaucracies. Further, the movement and its institutions created activities for upper-class women compatible with Victorian conceptions of the feminine role. Thus, it might be argued that these women responded to their own oppression by "oppressing" working-class children. Finally, catalyzed by the popular belief in the importance and possibility of rehabilitation, the structural, ideological, and bureaucratic factors converged on the political arena. Here, a variety of compromises eventually determined the final shape of the juvenile criminal justice system.

Platt illustrates the eclectic perspective we favor. In addition, this approach suggests a broader preliminary perspective for studying criminal law.

In brief, we would argue that structural, attitudinal, and bureaucratic factors interact to produce not only organized interests and perceptions of how those interests should be furthered, but also shared understandings even among contending parties about the "rules" by which political conflict may be undertaken. Thus, business executives, perhaps organized under the banner of local Chambers of Commerce, might agree that retail enterprises require greater protection from shoplifters and consequently, might favor stricter penalties for theft. In addition, they might also understand that the "proper" way to affect such change is through their legislative lobbyists. Note that under alternative "rules," they could have tried to approach legislators directly themselves. Similarly, groups such as the John Howard Association (an organization supporting prisoner's rights) while fundamentally differing in intent, might also work through their lobbyists.

Equally important, structural, attitudinal, and bureaucratic factors determine the resources combatants may bring to the conflict: money, favors, votes, labor, and so on. These are obviously critical to who wins and who loses although clearly not the only considerations. The overall result for our study is that various interests with different chances of success, a priori, converge on the state legislature where the criminal law is actually forged.

While the above perspective is certainly not new, there are several implications worthy of special emphasis. First, we are consciously taking a stochastic view in which while some sets of interests may be *systematically* favored (by the "rules" of the conflict, their resources, etc.), they do not totally dominate every outcome. In other words, although some groups may win more than their "fair share," they do not win all the time. Second, our perspective implies that if particular groups feel they are at a disad-

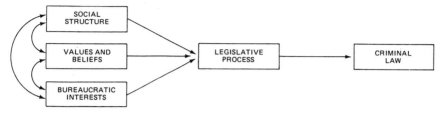

FIGURE 1.1 Sources of the criminal law

vantage they have several options: muster more resources, try different "legitimate" means to further goals, and/or attempt to change the "rules" of the conflict. Moreover, these strategies may well tend to be initiated in that order. If the first fails, the second is tried; if the second fails, the third is tried. Finally, the content of specific Penal Code alterations will be of different salience to different groups. This means that one might observe something approximating "pluralism" for some legislative issues, and something approximating "elite models" for others depending on the groups that are involved. Thus, the critical question becomes which kinds of issues tend to follow which types of political processes. Perhaps the really "important" questions are dominated for example, by a small group of "ruling class" elites? That is, economic elites typically determine the major substantive content of the criminal law while numerous equally matched pressure groups haggle over the details. Alternatively, the criminal law may be largely peripheral to the interests of an economic elite and consequently the criminal law is left in the hands of contending lobbies.

To summarize, our analysis will involve a detailed examination of 15 years of California legislative history. With the changing content of the Penal Code as the primary phenomenon to be explained, standard historical analysis will be blended with statistical procedures. Variables reflecting diverse factors will be employed, with the hope of revealing the kinds of influences that were important and which of them were more important than others. At the most general level we shall be exploring the sources of criminal law, attempting at the same time to place this exploration within the more eclectic framework we have identified above and that will be elaborated as we progress.

Some Comments about Research Methods

Our research design draws from much of the literature cited above. However, there are some important differences in emphasis and techniques that should be highlighted. First, studies of state legislatures have usually been undertaken by political scientists in the pluralist tradition who tend to emphasize the *internal* workings of the legislative process far more than the impact of external forces. Thus, a study by Buchanan[38] focuses on partisanship; a study by Crane stresses roll-call votes; while a study by Wahlke and associates[39] emphasizes the activities of various kinds of legislators, such as "formal leaders" and "experts," whose roles are defined *within* the legislative process. Our analysis will look both at internal variables and at those that impinge from the outside. The quantitative analysis will be especially concerned with links between legislation and outside forces.

Second, while prior efforts have usually analyzed factors surrounding relatively few pieces of legislation, the data for our *qualitative* analysis include over a score of significant bills, while the data for our *quantitative* analysis reflect nearly 700 revisions in the California Penal Code. We have tried to combine some depth with much broader coverage. One clear advantage of this strategy is an increased ability to generalize. Even should generalization not be feasible however, the substantive description we are able to provide of such a large number of revisions is valuable in itself.

Third, what may be most original in the analysis will rest on statistical procedures. The nearly 700 revisions will be quantified through a coding procedure that makes the legislative changes amenable to statistical manipulation. Though statistics are certainly no panacea, they often facilitate analyses that are impossible to achieve through qualitative techniques. We would not argue that statistical insights are necessarily better, only that they are sometimes somewhat different. For example, it would not be feasible to analyze such a vast number of Penal Code changes without statistical data reduction, and a qualitative approach would necessarily limit the range of revisions and consequently the kinds of analyses that could be undertaken. In addition, the use of statistics provides a number of tools whose function is not simply to reduce data to manageable proportions but also to unlock complex processes through concepts and techniques available only through mathematics.

Fourth, there has been considerable debate about the comparative methodological merits of qualitative and quantitative approaches to social science data. "Qualitative" historians like Schlesinger have argued that "almost all important questions are important precisely because they are not susceptible to quantitative answers."[40] "Quantitative" historians like Thernstrom answer this charge by arguing for the utility of statistical techniques despite some practical limitations.[41] Similar debates have occurred in sociology, though quantitative–qualitative issues are often obscured and overlaid with other methodological questions. Researchers as diverse as Goffman, Becker, and Garfinkel have been interpreted as the advocates exclusively of "soft" methods (sometimes to their discomfort). In contrast, Blalock, Coleman, Duncan, and others have been used as standard-bearers of the "hard" techniques. Actually, careful thinkers from both sides admit to the utility of a variety of methodologies, especially when the method is dictated by the research problem. Further, recent research trends have increasingly emphasized the notion of "triangulation," in which quality research is best generated by a variety of measures and a variety of methods.[42] This monograph will present findings from traditional historical analyses blended with extensive statistical material. We hope to demonstrate that a more varied approach, in which skills from several social science disciplines are employed, produces a more plausible picture than do results based on a narrower range of methods.

Some Anticipatory Rejoinders

We suspect that much of this monograph will be controversial. Some scholars will be skeptical of quantifying legislation. They may feel that the application of numbers so abstracts and distorts the "real" content that any analysis is fatuous. Despite such critics, we think a convincing case for our quantification can be made. The statistics remain close to the data, and, though many of our measures appear superficial, the apparent superficiality produces provocative and subtle results. In addition, qualitative archival data are presented to flesh out bare statistical bones and to reconcile what at first glance appear to be contradictory findings.

Some practitioners in the criminal justice system may be skeptical because they will not see how global and "superficial" quantitative measure can meaningfully describe their varied and complex day-to-day activities. Our rejoinder is that we are not trying to detail daily events in the legislature or in the criminal justice system. We are taking seriously a line sometimes attributed to Tukey, who argues that "anything worth doing is worth doing superficially." In other words, broad brush strokes of general patterns and trends are discussed with the hope that they might supplement, *not replace*, research methodologies that deal in more detail with the events with which we are concerned. As for the quantification per se, it is not in fact true that one can say anything one wants to say with statistics. Where subjective judgments influence our statistics we alert the reader. Where possible, analyses close to the raw data are presented so that the reader is free to accept or reject our conclusions. Finally, to take refuge in the sweeping assertion that the quantification of legislation automatically produces serious artifacts is at best a "cop-out." Should suspicions of artifactual results surface, the burden is on the reader to specify in his/her mind exactly what the artifacts are. We have tried to consider carefully the problems raised by potential statistical artifacts, and we hope the reader will do the same before making an evaluation.

The substance of our findings may also be controversial. Though we freely admit that we may have our biases, we have tried to approach the study with open minds. We did not set out to prove that, for example, public opinion is of dubious relevance to the passage of law-and-order legislation. Our initial hunches should not be confused with axe grinding. As with the quantification, a reader who is suspicious must do more than make a blanket challenge of bias. Specific examples, and their implications, must be specified.

An Overview of the Volume

The next chapter discusses "qualitatively" the politics of criminal law-making in California. We analyze the history of critical bills drawn from 11 consecutive sessions (1955–1971), the criteria for "critical" being that the bill generated substantial conflict among the criminal justice lobbies and legislative actors with whom we are most concerned. This allows us to identify the interplay of wider forces that gave each session its distinctive character. Thus, while the Heinz, Gettleman, and Seeskin study focuses on a single legislative session (in Illinois) and a short period in historical time, this study offers a qualitative analysis that encompasses a full decade and a half of immensely significant social and political change in California. At the very least, Chapter II should provide useful grounding for the statistical presentation in the chapters that follow.

After Chapter III, in which the quantitative methodology is detailed, Chapters IV and V present a survey of Penal Code trends from 1955 to 1971. The emphasis here is on graphic description, rather than analysis. These trends ultimately become our most important dependent variables. Chapters VI and VII examine predictors and causes of Penal Code trends and are perhaps the pivotal empirical chapters in the book. Chapter VIII discusses some possible consequences of changes in the Penal Code through the "filtering down" of revision effect in the criminal justice system. Finally, Chapter IX summarizes the findings, draws some conclusions, and tries to place the study in a broader theoretical context.

To anticipate a bit, the following kinds of questions will be addressed: Is there any evidence that the 1960s were marked by significant increases in criminalization and longer prescribed prison sentences? To what degree did legislation favor prosecutorial prerogatives over rights of the accused? How important are crime rates, the American Civil Liberties Union (ACLU), and public opinion in shaping the Penal Code? Were the Democrats really soft on crime? Did conservative Republican triumphs automatically translate into law-and-order victories? Did changes in the Penal Code seem to make any difference in the activities of the criminal justice system or was the legislative process merely a lengthy ritual?

Appendix 1.1: A Brief Summary of Research on the American Legislative Process

The literature on the American legislative process is enormous. Many scholars have focused on the national scene and relationships between political interests and congressional legislative activity. Important domestic issues have been addressed in such works as Dudman's on the dynamics of the political right,[43] Marris and Rein's on the War on Poverty,[44] Kohlmeier's on regulatory agencies,[45] Lowi's on dissent,[46] and Ridgeway's on ecology.[47] Criminal justice per se is also the subject of a growing, though not yet especially large, body of literature. Odegard's study of prohibition politics pioneered in the field.[48] Gusfield[49] and Edelman[50] have since reexamined this and related "symbolic crusades." Other areas have been illuminated by Roby's work on prostitution,[51] Becker's study of marijuana laws,[52] Lindesmith's on the criminalization of drug addiction,[53] and those of Harris[54] and Platt[55] on riot control. Worthy of a final mention are Stone's explorations of congressional roll calls on criminal justice issues, the first systematic attempt to analyze overall voting patterns.[56]

At the state and local level there is also substantial work. In the case of California, the broad interplay between economic interests, political party structure and ideology, and legislative institutions in the shaping of public policy is illuminated in major studies by Barrett,[57] Rusco,[58] Buchanan,[59] Price,[60] Hincker,[61] Cannon,[62] and Rogin and Shover.[63] Kelly,[64] Pitchell,[65] Gregg,[66] and Deutsch[67] have analyzed the political impact of the state's traditionally powerful newspaper empires as well as of its newly influential public relations firms. The evolution of ideologically opposed coalitions of law enforcement and civil rights–civil liberties groups is charted by Carney,[68] Vose,[69] Kenney,[70] and Casstevens.[71] Other group and institutional actors playing important criminal justice roles are the subject of Gilb's scholarly monograph on the California State Bar,[72] Eaton's on the state's penal bureaucracy,[73] Sax's on California crime commissions,[74] and Funston's on the California Supreme Court.[75] Specific criminal justice issues at stake in California are the focus of Sutherland's analysis of the diffusion of sexual psychopath laws,[76] Westin's essay on "Bookies and 'Bugs' in California,"[77] ten Broek's study of the punitive assumptions underlying the state's welfare laws,[78] Blum and Funkhouser's imaginative exploration of legislative attitudes toward approaches to the drug problem,[79] and Leigh's detailed examination of the shaping of the state's antipornography laws.[80] These references constitute no more than a highly selective list of the voluminous material dealing with California politics and criminal law-making, some of which will be cited in the References to Chapter II.

REFERENCES

1. H. H. Gerth and C. Wright Mills, *From Max Weber: Essays in Sociology* (New York: Oxford University Press, 1958), p. 78.
2. Philip Selznick, "Sociology and Natural Law," *Natural Law Forum*, Vol. 6 (1961).
3. Donald Black, "The Boundaries of Legal Sociology," *Yale Law Journal*, Vol. 81 (May, 1973), p. 45.
4. Howard S. Becker, *The Outsiders: Studies in the Sociology of Deviance* (Glencoe, Illinois: The Free Press, 1963).
5. Edwin M. Schur, *Crimes without Victims* (Englewood Cliffs, New Jersey: Prentice-Hall, 1965).
6. Alfred R. Lindesmith, *The Addict and the Law* (New York: Vintage, 1965).
7. Edwin M. Lemert, *Human Deviance, Social Problems, and Social Control* (Englewood Cliffs, New Jersey: Prentice-Hall, 1967).
8. William Chambliss, "A Sociological Analysis of the Law of Vagrancy," *Social Problems* Vol. 12, No. 1 (1964), pp. 135, 139.
9. Peter Garnsey, "Legal Privilege in the Roman Empire," *Past and Present* Vol. 31 (1968).
10. Kai T. Erikson, *Wayward Puritans: A Study of the Sociology of Deviance* (New York: Wiley, 1966).
11. Clarence Roy Jeffrey, "The Development of Crime in Early English Society," *Journal of Criminal Law, Criminology, and Political Science*, Vol. 47 (March–April, 1957).
12. Emile Durkheim, *The Division of Labor in Society* (New York: Free Press, 1933), p. 65.
13. H. L. A. Hart, *The Concept of Law* (Oxford: Clarendon Press, 1961), p. 89.
14. Lon L. Fuller, "Human Interaction and the Law," in *The Rule of Law*, ed. Robert Paul Wolff (New York: Simon and Schuster, 1971), p. 173.
15. Paul Bohannan, "The Differing Realms of Law," in *Law and Warfare*, ed. Paul Bohannan (New York: Natural History Press, 1967), p. 47.
16. Stanley Diamond, "The Rule of Law in the Order of Custom," in *The Rule of Law*, ed. Robert Paul Wolff (New York: Simon and Schuster, 1971), p. 126.
17. Richard Quinney, *The Social Reality of Crime* (Boston: Little, Brown, 1970), p. 35.
18. Max Weber, *Max Weber on Law in Economy and Society*, trans. Max Rubenstein (Cambridge, Massachusetts: Harvard University Press, 1954), Chapter 5.
19. Fredric L. DuBow, "Justice for the People: Law and Politics in Lower Courts in Tanzania" (unpublished Ph.D. thesis, University of California, Berkeley, 1973).
20. Chambliss, "A Sociological Analysis," p. 139.
21. Jerome Hall, *Theft, Law, and Society* (Indianapolis: Bobbs-Merrill, 1935).
22. Garnsey, "Legal Privilege in the Roman Empire."
23. Diamond, "The Rule of Law in the Order of Custom."

24. William E. Nelson, "Emerging Notions of Modern Criminal Law in Revolutionary Era. An Historical Perspective," *New York University Law Review*, Vol. 42 (May, 1967), pp. 450–482.
25. Ralph Miliband, *The State in Capitalist Society* (New York: Basic Books, 1969).
26. Quinney, *The Social Reality of Crime; idem, Critique of Legal Order: Crime Control in a Capitalist Society* (Boston: Little, Brown, 1974).
27. Anthony M. Platt, *The Child Savers: The Invention of Delinquency* (Chicago: University of Chicago Press, 1969).
28. Ian Taylor, Paul Walton, and Jack Young, *The New Criminology* (New York: Harper and Row, 1973).
29. Leon Radzinowicz, *Ideology and Crime* (New York: Columbia University Press, 1966), p. 12.
30. George Lee Haskins, *Law and Authority in Early Massachusetts* (New York: Macmillan, 1960).
31. Edwin H. Sutherland, "The Diffusion of Sexual Psychopath Laws," *American Journal of Sociology*, Vol. 56 (September 1950), pp. 142–148.
32. Taylor, *et al., The New Criminology.*
33. Lindesmith, *The Addict and the Law.*
34. Becker, *The Outsiders.*
35. Elliot P. Currie, "The Control of Witchcraft in Renaissance Europe," *Law and Society Review*, Vol. 3, No. 1 (1968), p. 355.
36. John P. Heinz, Robert W. Gettleman, and Morris A. Seeskin, "Legislative Politics and the Criminal Law," *Northwestern University Law Review*, Vol. 64 (July–August, 1969), pp. 277–356.
37. Platt, *The Child Savers.*
38. William Buchanan, *Legislative Partisanship: The Deviant Case of California* (Berkeley: University of California Press, 1963).
39. John C. Walke, John P. Heinz, William Buchanan, and LeRoy Ferguson, *The Legislative System: Explorations in Legislative Behavior* (New York: Wiley, 1962).
40. Arthur M. Schlesinger, "A Humanist Looks at Empirical Social Research," *American Sociological Review*, Vol. 27 (December, 1962), pp. 768–771.
41. Steven Thernstrom, "Quantitative Methods in History: Some Notes," in *Sociology and History: Methods*, ed. Seymour Martin Lipset and Richard Hofstadter (New York: Basic Books, 1968), pp. 59–78.
42. Norman K. Denzin, *The Research Act: A Theoretical Introduction to Sociological Methods.* (Chicago: Aldine, 1970).
43. Richard Dudman, *Men of the Far Right* (New York: Pyramid, 1962).
44. Peter Marris and Martin Rein, *Dilemmas of Social Reform: Poverty and Community Action in the United States* (New York: Atherton, 1967).
45. Louis M. Kohlmeier, *The Regulators: Watchdog Agencies and the Public Interest* (Springfield, Illinois: Charles C. Thomas, 1964).
46. Theodore J. Lowi, *The Politics of Disorder* (New York: Basic Books, 1971).
47. James Ridgeway, *The Last Play: The Struggle to Monopolize the World's Energy Resources* (New York: E. P. Dutton, 1973).
48. Peter H. Odegard, *Pressure Politics* (New York: Columbia University Press, 1928).
49. Joseph R. Gusfield, *Symbolic Crusade: Status Politics and the American Temperance Movement* (Urbana: University of Illinois Press, 1963).
50. Murray C. Edelman, *The Symbolic Uses of Politics* (Urbana: University of Illinois Press, 1964).
51. Pamela A. Roby, "Politics and Criminal Law: Revision of the New York State Law on Prostitution," *Social Problems*, Vol. 17 (Summer, 1969), pp. 83–108.

52. Becker, *The Outsiders*.
53. Lindesmith, *The Addict and the Law*.
54. Richard Harris, *The Fear of Crime* (New York: Praeger, 1969).
55. Platt, *The Child Savers*.
56. Clarence N. Stone, "Congressional Party Differences in Civil Liberties and Criminal Procedure Issues," *Southwestern Social Science Quarterly*, Vol. 47 (September, 1966), pp. 161–171.
57. Edward Barrett, *The Tenney Committee: Legislative Investigation of Subversive Activities in California* (New York: Cornell University Press, 1951).
58. Elmer Ritter Rusco, "Machine Politics, California Model: Arthur H. Samish and the Alcoholic Beverage Industry" (unpublished Ph.D. thesis, University of California, Berkeley).
59. Buchanan, *Legislative Partisanship*.
60. Charles M. Price, "Voting Alignments in the California Legislature: Roll Call Analysis of the 1957–1959–1969 Sessions" (unpublished Ph.D. thesis, University of Southern California, Los Angeles).
61. Richard G. Hincker, "The Speakership of the California Assembly: Jesse Unruh, Fifty-Fourth Speaker" (unpublished M. A. thesis, San Jose State College, California, 1966).
62. Lou Cannon, *Ronnie and Jesse: A Political Odyssey* (Garden City, New York: Doubleday, 1969).
63. Michael Paul Rogin and John L. Shover, *Political Change in California: Critical Elections and Social Movements, 1890–1966* (Westport, Connecticut: Greenwood, 1970).
64. Stanley Kelly, Jr., *Professional Public Relations and Political Power* (Baltimore: Johns Hopkins Press, 1956).
65. Robert J. Pitchell, "Influence of Professional Management Firms on Partisan Elections in California," *Western Political Quarterly*, Vol. 11 (June, 1958), pp. 278–300.
66. James Erwin Gregg; "Newspaper Editorial Endorsements; Their Influence on California Elections, 1948–1962" (unpublished Ph.D. thesis, University of California, Santa Barbara, 1964).
67. Eadie F. Deutsch, "Judicial Rhetoric as Persuasive Communication: A Study of The Supreme Court Opinions in the *Escobedo* and *Miranda* Cases and the Responses in the California Press" (unpublished Ph.D. thesis, University of California, Los Angeles, 1970).
68. Francis M. Carney, "Methods of American Civil Liberties Union of Northern California" (unpublished M.A. thesis, Stanford University, 1949).
69. Clement E. Vose, *Caucasians Only: The Supreme Court, the NAACP, and the Restrictive Covenant Cases* (Berkeley: University of California Press, 1959).
70. John P. Kenney, *The California Police* (Springfield, Illinois: Charles C. Thomas, 1964).
71. Thomas W. Casstevens, *Politics, Housing, and Race Relations: California's Rumford Act and Proposition 14* (Berkeley: Institute of Governmental Studies, University of California, 1967).
72. Corinne L. Gilb, "Self-Regulating Professions and the Public Welfare: A Case Study of the California State Bar" (unpublished Ph.D. thesis, Radcliffe College, 1956).
73. Joseph W. Eaton, *Stone Walls Do Not a Prison Make: The Anatomy of Planned Administrative Change* (Springfield, Illinois: Charles C. Thomas, 1964).

74. Richard Milton Sax, "California Crime Commissions: A Comparative Analysis" (unpublished Ph.D. thesis, University of California, Berkeley, 1969).

75. Richard York Funston, "The Traynor Court and Criminal Defendants' Rights: A Case Study in Judicial Federalism" (unpublished Ph.D. thesis, University of California, Los Angeles, 1970).

76. Sutherland, "The Diffusion of Sexual Psychopath Laws."

77. Alan F. Westin, "Bookies and 'Bugs' in California," in *The Uses of Power: Seven Case Studies in American Politics* ed. Alan F. Westin (New York: Harcourt Brace & Co., 1962), pp. 117–171.

78. Jacobus ten Broek, "California's Dual System of Family Law: Its Origin, Development, and Present Status," *Stanford Law Review,* Vol. 16 (March, 1964), pp. 257–317, Vol. 16 (July, 1964), pp. 900–982, Vol. 17 (April, 1965), pp. 614–682.

79. Richard H. Blum and Mary Lou Funkhouser, "Legislators on Social Scientists and a Social Issue: A Report and Commentary on Some Discussions with Lawmakers about Drug Abuse," *Journal of Applied Behavioral Science,* Vol. 1 (January–March, 1965), pp. 84–112.

80. Peter Randolph Leigh, "The Implementation of Obscenity Decisions in the State of California" (unpublished Ph.D. thesis, University of Southern California, 1969).

II

Trends in the Penal Code
from 1955 to 1971:
A Qualitative-Historical Analysis*

Introduction

WHILE THIS STUDY WILL CHART trends in the California Penal Code from 1955 to 1971, the underlying theme is the sources of criminal law. As the most immediate and direct cause of Penal Code alteration, the legislative process will be of critical interest and an appropriate starting point for empirical analysis. Clearly, proposals that fail in the state legislature cannot become state law.

The longitudinal data presented in this chapter are in the main qualitative and will be examined at several different levels. Most superficially, we shall describe the formal steps by which bills become law. (See Table 2.1.) Without this structural understanding, later, more complicated analyses will be difficult to follow.

Beneath the formal procedures lie a variety of more subtle processes, which must also be described. We will find, for example, that even for the controversial bills discussed, votes on the floor of the legislature are largely window-dressing for critical decisions made elsewhere. Hence, the rhetoric of "debate" is often a public relations gesture for the folks back home and not a really serious attempt to sway the opinions of fellow legislators.

---

* This chapter is based primarily on research and drafts by Harold Brackman.

TABLE 2.1

A Bill Becomes a Law

Summary of Major Steps Involved

1. Bill introduction and first reading.
2. Referral to committee (in 1955, thirty calendar days had to elapse after introduction before the bill could be considered by committee).
3. Committee consideration.
4. Committee recommendation.
5. Second reading (floor debate with possibility of proposed amendments).
6. Third reading.
7. Vote.
8. Repetition of above steps in the other house of the legislature.
9. Conference committee consideration in the event of disagreement between the two houses of the legislature and subsequent recommendation.
10. Final vote.
11. Submission to the Governor for signature.
12. Governor may:
    a. Sign the bill into law.
    b. Permit it to become law without his approval (which will happen if he does not sign it within twelve days).
    c. Veto the bill. (Through 1966, vetoed measures were reconsidered by the legislature in a separate veto session which was convened on the Monday after the thirty day recess following each regular session. Since 1966, veto actions have taken place within regular legislative sessions.)

The closed-door negotiations that usually determine the outcome of legislative conflict are important not only in themselves but as indicators of contending interests. A careful consideration of contested issues will reveal who stands to gain and who stands to lose, and also will allow us to begin moving back along the causal chain to organized pressure groups and the more ill-defined "public." In a sense, we will start with proposed Penal Code revisions and work backward to more distant causes for these proposed revisions. At each step we will be addressing the sources of criminal law, but the causes will be less proximate. Along this route the roles of social structure, ideology, and bureaucratic growth will be considered.

The data base for this chapter, though deriving in part from interviews, is largely archival: newspapers, organization newsletters, interest group propaganda, committee transcripts, and a variety of secondary source material. Its mode of analysis is primarily qualitative and well within the mainstream of contemporary historical methodology. As such, it has both the strengths and weaknesses of qualitative historical analysis. On the positive side, its rich detail will provide an excellent "feel" for the issues and an overall "gestalt" of the Sacramento scene. Equally important, we will be able to trace a series of longitudinal processes and at least be reasonably certain what happened after what. In other words, if causality is to be inferred, the requisite time ordering will be clear. Further, to the degree that a complex sequence of events can be explained parsimoniously, causal explanations will emerge with the strength of a processual analysis.

On the negative side, we should acknowledge some of the problems associated with conventional historical analysis. First, the data base will represent a purposive sample, constrained by feasibility. In our investigation, the universe of potential material is not accessible, and the access we did achieve involved a variety of nonprobability processes. Hence, some important events may have been ignored or underrepresented, with inappropriate weighting a possible consequence. When we find, for example, a critical role for organized lobbies, it may have more to do with the regular publication of a newsletter than "real" legislative impact. More fundamentally, since it is elites who are more likely to leave behind artifacts of their activities, their salience is to some unknown degree built in. (Indeed, the whole analytical process may approach circularity: A group is called elite because it is visible, from which one infers that it is "visible" because it is elite.)

Second, it is difficult to specify the data reduction techniques used to get from the extensive primary source material to a coherent narrative. The analytic methodology is not easily explained, and, hence, it is hard to imagine what a "replication" would entail. The inability to specify the steps necessary for a replication mean that it is difficult to judge to what degree our conclusions stem from our methodology or from the data. While we believe that our analysis builds on sensible and "obvious" historical procedures, this contention is not subject to exact proof. For example, it would seem reasonable to interpret policy pronouncements from official lobby newsletters as organizational consensus. Nevertheless, one might find that such statements reflect the views of some dominant faction within the lobby, rather than those of the rank-and-file membership. Such problems are inherent in *all* empirical work, but they are exacerbated to the extent that the methodology is less explicit.

Third, just as the step from data to narrative is problematic, so is the step from narrative to conclusions. Once again, it is difficult to specify a formal methodology. Consequently, our conclusions derive from a complex and irreducible mix of "objective" facts and analytic processes. At best we can argue that our conclusions represent a parsimonious interpretation. Yet the real possibility of a still more parsimonious view exists, and the possibility of potential spuriousness in causal explanations remains.

Fortunately this is our first empirical chapter. As we later turn to our quantitative material, we make an effort to compensate for many of the limitations in the qualitative analysis. On the other hand, the very real vulnerabilities in the quantitative data will be shored up with the data presented in this chapter. In the end, the two data sets, collected independently, will inform each other, and a more complete and rounded picture should emerge.

With these caveats in mind, we are ready to proceed. The chapter is organized into 13 sections, 11 of which contain a case study drawn from a particular session of the California legislature. After a brief "overview" of the history of the legislative process in California, each section typically uses the history of one Penal Code revision to highlight significant characteristics of that legislative session. While we would not argue that through one bill one can learn all there is about a given session, the bill was selected as representative of the most salient concerns of that period in the area of criminal lawmaking. The major exception to this approach is the 1955 session, where a range of bills is collectively considered to introduce the reader to "typical," rather than "significant," processes. The final section draws together important trends and suggests tentative conclusions.*

The Sacramento Battleground—An Overview

Since 1849, when the first session of the California legislature was derisively christened "the Legislature of a Thousand Drinks," interest groups have played a dominant role in state politics. At the turn of the century, vast political power rested with the Southern Pacific Railroad, still at the height of its economic dominance. While Progressives before World War I managed to slay the "railroad octopus," the subsequent interest group vacuum was gradually filled. The 1930s and 1940s saw the growth of a multiindustry lobbying empire presided over by Artie Samish, notorious as the "Secret Boss" of the legislature.[1]

The Samish era ended in 1950. However, the end of cross-filing,† coupled with the resurgence of party organization, still left a critical role for well-organized and heavily financed business lobbies. As Jesse M. Unruh, Speaker of the California State Assembly, noted several years later, "money is the mother's milk of California politics."[2]

As the administrative arm of California's state government grew, some industries supplemented their lobbying activities with concerted attempts to "settle down" within such friendly statewide regulatory agencies as the Public Utilities Commission. Yet, this more subtle strategy did not reduce

---

* The reader who wishes to anticipate our summary and conclusions should turn to Table 2.3 in the final section of this chapter. Table 2.3 also can be used throughout as a prop to help keep the California chronology in proper perspective.

† Cross-filing allowed candidates to run in the opposition party's primary, in which a victory at that time obviated the necessity of facing an opponent in the general election.

traditional attempts to shape legislation. Indeed, by the late 1960s, corporate giants controlled most of the more than 500 registered lobbyists who admitted spending over $3 million a year (excluding campaign contributions) to influence legislation.[3]

Despite the continued salience of big business lobbies, the past two decades have seen the legislative process in California gradually open up a greater diversity of interests.[4] A wide range of professional organizations and "cause" lobbies began to play important roles, with the State Federation of Labor and the Senior Citizens' Lobby early pioneers. By the late 1950s, the State Federation of Teachers, profiting from post-Sputnik anxieties, had become one of the most effective lobbies in the state. About the same time, criminal justice lobbies also became highly visible. Though they were all founded in the 1920s, it was not until the 1950s that the California Peace Officers' Association (CPOA), the American Civil Liberties Union (ACLU), and the State Bar of California began to participate continuously and as independent actors in the legislative process.[5]

Traditionally, the legislature had been vulnerable to aggressive lobbyists because California had lacked the strong parties that, in the other states, buffered the legislative process from insistent pressure groups. But a history of weak party organization also had a countervailing effect. It forced the legislature, almost in "self-defense," to emulate the United States Congress by giving its committees considerable power. Only these committees saved the legislature from drowning beneath the flood of proposals, averaging about 5000 bills a session, that deluged the legislature during the 1950s.[6]

However, the strong committee system could not always protect the legislative process from undue meddling. During the Samish era, committees were easily packed. Not until the 1960s did higher salaries (increased almost 10-fold from the $3000 level of the late 1940s) and heightened legislative professionalism markedly free committee members from Samish-style control.[7]*

The increased independence of legislative committees somewhat "democratized" lobby influence but did not decrease its overall influence. Thus the Judiciary Committees of both houses pushed through a law enforcement–sponsored ordinance against slot machines that the Samish-dominated Assembly Committee on Public Morals had killed before the 1950s. Similarly, the State Bar was no longer dependent on Samish's goodwill for legislative approval of its recommended judicial appointments; it began to exercise independent influence. "Professional" interests were taking

---

* Committee independence was further encouraged by the introduction of staff consultants and student interns, who provided systematic information. Accelerating in the 1960s, these support services employed 1500 people by 1971.

precedence over economic interests, but they were "interests" nonetheless.[8]

At the same time that committees were gaining more resources and the impact of new interest groups was beginning to be felt, anemic party organizations were slowly being revitalized. The end of cross-filing in 1959 (undermined already in 1954 by the introduction of party designations for primaries) helped to reshape the nonpartisan culture of earlier years. The rise of Democratic partisanship under Assembly Speaker Jesse M. Unruh and subsequent Republican resurgence under conservative Governor Ronald Reagan heightened the trend. Rather than undercutting legislative professionalism, however, partisanship overlaid it. By the end of the 1960s, the California legislature had come a long way from the Samish era.[9]

In broad terms, then, legislative activity in California from 1950 through 1970 was marked by three trends within a long tradition of interest group politics. First, corporate groups were joined in Sacramento by new lobbies, including professional and "special cause" organizations. Second, the resources and independence of legislative committees grew markedly. Third, partisan politics emerged as a potent force reshaping all facets of the legislative process. Overall, these general trends—coupled with shorter cycles in public mood, political leadership, and important societal events—greatly complicated the processes surrounding legislative activity. It is such complexity, focused specifically around Penal Code legislation, that will be addressed in detail in the rest of this chapter.

1955: "Typical" Processes in Criminal Lawmaking—A Composite Portrait

If one were to look for a tranquil moment amidst postwar upheavals, 1955 is as close an approximation as could be found. The hysteria of the McCarthy years had largely subsided, while still ahead were the anxieties induced by Hungary and Suez, by Sputnik and the 1958 recession, and finally by Vietnam and the unrest of the 1960s. An incipient era of good feeling suffused the state, while Governor Goodwin J. Knight, a middle-of-the-road Republican, carried on in the Earl Warren tradition of "bipartisan" appeals and "low-key" political leadership.[10]

1955 was also the last year in which the Republican Party in California enjoyed the clear-cut legislative majorities (48 to 32 in the Assembly and 23 to 17 in the Senate) that it had come to take for granted. There were already hints that growing support for the Democratic Party would soon threaten Republican control. Yet in 1955 the Republican Party, having managed to reverse defeats of the Depression era, still profited from the appeal of Earl Warren's "modern Republicanism."[11]

Yet the very dominance of this amorphous Republican ideology made it difficult to distinguish meaningfully between Democrats and Republicans. Like Warren's, Knight's popularity had little to do with party label, and salient issues in the state legislature still cut across party lines. The gradual phasing out of cross-filing plus grassroots Democratic campaigns designed to strengthen party loyalties were to change this nonpartisan style by decade's end.[12] In 1955, however, partisanship still had little legislative substance.

The key force in the 1955 State Assembly (the legislature's most important law-originating branch) was "the Lincoln Coalition," the outgrowth of a group that had toppled Artie Samish from power a few years before. Despite (or because of) this leadership, the session proved rather bland. After a heated contest in which the coalition leader, Republican Luther H. "Abe" Lincoln, became Speaker, little was produced of interest. None of the major issues—alcoholic beverage administration, state water development, and disposal of tidelands oil revenue—were conclusively addressed. Avoidance of major controversy was even more apparent in the field of criminal lawmaking. Bills were introduced on two major criminal justice issues, abolition of capital punishment and legalization of wiretapping, but in both cases the legislation was largely a trial run for later, more serious efforts. Neither of these bills advanced far enough to be considered on the floor of either house.[13]

Of the Penal Code bills introduced in 1955, 65 (or 40%) were signed into law. This was a higher percentage than succeeded overall: Only 2000 of nearly 5500 proposals involving other codes ever made the statute books. Significantly, the State Bar felt that only 6 of these 65 "successful" Penal Code bills should be included in its survey of "significant" legislation affecting criminal law. Two enactments provided for compensation of court-appointed counsel.[14] The other four involved the verification of pleas,* the presumption of legitimacy,† the prosecution of public nuisances, and the toughening of laws governing checks written without sufficient funds.[15] Using different criteria for significance, several other bills could be added to the list, among them: AB 1505, allowing time off for good behavior for county prisoners; AB 2285, restoring the felony penalty for escapes from county jails; and AB 3508 and 3511, slightly reducing penalties for weapon offenses.[16] Yet, regardless of which criteria are used, the 1955 session made no major changes in the California criminal law.

It is important to emphasize that most of the bills passed by even the most "epochal" sessions usually consist of "innocuous" and "minor" en-

---

* That is, they amended those provisions whereby the party pleading establishes the truth of what he has set forth.

† Before this amendment, legitimacy was presumed for purposes of child support even if the wife lived apart from her legal spouse and bore children by another man.

actments. In this sense, the 1955 legislation was typical of what Benjamin Gross characterizes as "minute insertions" in a long-standing legislative framework, and what William Buchanan calls "chuck hole legislation."[17]

The internal legislative processes in 1955 were regulated by a 1912 constitutional amendment dividing the sessions into two parts. In January of odd-numbered years, the legislature convened for a 30-day period during which bills could be freely introduced. This was followed by a 30-day recess after which the legislature reconvened to act upon the bills submitted during January.* The constitutional recess often caused proposed legislation to be written hastily in order to beat the introduction deadline (after which no proposal could be introduced in either house without consent of three-fourths of the membership). But it also gave interest groups time to examine carefully bills affecting their special concerns. During the February 1955 recess, for example, the CPOA decided that of the 5400 bills titled, digested, and numbered in January, more than 700 potentially "affected law enforcement." Three-fourths of these 700 bills proposed changes, not in the Penal Code, but in the Codes of Civil Procedure, Government, Health and Safety, and Labor. This analysis, however, will focus only on Penal Code bills.[18]

Before a legislative rule change in 1963 forbade the practice, many bills indicated on their title page "by the request of" whom they were introduced. These designations constitute one source of the estimates that follow.† Some 40 of the 160 Penal Code bills were the handiwork of the "law enforcement lobby"—namely, the CPOA, the California State Sheriffs' Association, and the California State District Attorneys' Association. Various civil liberties groups and the State Bar, the other two "criminal justice lobbies" active in California, together accounted for no more than 20 bills. About the same number originated with private citizens and individual legislators. But *governmental bodies*, local as well as state, were the single most important source of proposed legislation, accounting for about one-half of the Penal Code bills introduced.[19]

The executive branch was far and away the most important government

---

* Rules of the legislature were subsequently amended so that the period during which bills could be introduced was extended up through the first Friday following the Easter recess of a regular session. However, no bill could be heard by any committee, or acted upon by either house, until 30 calendar days had elapsed following the date the bill was first introduced. California Constitution, Art. IV, Sec. 3 (a) and Sec. 8 (a). In 1973, after the terminal year of this study, the ground rules were again revamped.

† Reports on bill sponsorship published in the journals of the various criminal justice lobbies constitute the other major source of information. There are some bills, however, whose origins cannot be determined on either basis; this is why exact figures on sponsorship, especially for a session as long ago as 1955, are impossible.

source of these new proposals (usually involving no more than a technical revision needed to clarify a bureaucrat's authority). This was two decades ago, when the legislature had only begun to develop its present capabilities for originating innovative and far-reaching proposals. Nevertheless, the proportions for 1955, heavily weighted toward "public" rather than "private" and "executive" rather than "legislative" input, would hold up almost as well in 1972.[20]

When the 1955 session reconvened in March, all bills that had been "read" for the first time in their house of origin and assigned to an appropriate committee were subject to hearings.* For criminal justice legislation, hearings took place before the Judiciary Committees† of the Senate or the Assembly. Traditionally, author control was honored to the extent that a legislator had considerable leeway in determining when "his" bill would be heard. However, committee decisions, especially those rendered by the powerful Judiciary Committees, were almost always impossible to overturn. Further, since committee debates were rarely recorded and no roll-call votes were taken,‡ bills were vulnerable to negative committee votes hidden from the public view. A legislator could vote against a bill and suffer no adverse publicity. Moreover, he could avoid even this minimal risk by being absent since a "no" vote and an absence amounted to the same thing under a system that required a majority of the full membership to *approve* a bill for it to clear committee.[21]

The one out of two bills that overcame committee hurdles usually had smooth sailing thereafter. After being read a second time before the full house, amendments "suggested" by the committee and agreed to by the author were likely to be quickly adopted by the larger legislative body. For example, AB 2285 proposed restoration of a felony penalty for escape from a county jail. Despite widespread outside support, the bill would have died in the Assembly Judiciary Committee had not law enforcement spokesmen agreed to amendments making the offense an "alternate misdemeanor" rather than a "straight felony." One day after the second reading on the floor of the Assembly, the way was cleared for a third reading and a final roll-call vote. After repeating essentially the same process in the Senate, the bill was sent to the Governor for his signature.[22]

---

* See Figure 2.1 for procedural steps in bill passage.

† In 1959 the Assembly Judiciary Committee was divided into civil and criminal components. The component concerned with criminal matters was designated the Assembly Committee on Criminal Procedure (renamed in 1971 the Assembly Committee on Criminal Justice). In the Senate, the Judiciary Committee continued to consider both civil and criminal matters.

‡ Not until 1972 were roll-call votes publicly tabulated in both the Assembly Committee on Criminal Justice and the Senate Judiciary Committee.

While the 1955 session reveals the "typical" steps of Penal Code enactment, more recent legislation, though still largely reflecting the "agreed bill" process, reflects the impact of additional factors. One can gain some detailed understanding of recent trends using Buchanan's summary description of the California legislative environment in the middle and late 1950s as a benchmark:[23]

1. The vast number of bills
2. The essential part played by the author
3. The open committee hearing and the overt role of lobbyists in decision making
4. The "automatic calendar,"* which ensures some consideration of every bill for which the author has requested it
5. The unimportance of the floor vote
6. The unpredictability of the outcome of any given issue, depending as it does upon the actions of certain members, who remain until the last essentially free agents
7. The irrelevance of political parties.

This characterization was only partly appropriate for later years. Legislative sessions still produced a vast number of bills. And the bill's author was still responsible for the strategic steps necessary for final passage. In addition, the "automatic calendar" and open committee hearings with active lobbyists continued to prevail. However, committees gained additional power. Committee recommendations, especially when they were the product of the legislature's new, high-powered research machinery, became not merely influential but decisive. Another important change was the increasing impact of political parties. Where Buchanan stresses the minimal relevance of party affiliation in 1957, our study will reveal the growing influence of partisanship in the field of criminal lawmaking. Party composition in the powerful criminal justice committees has become especially crucial with reference to bills that reflect basic ideological assumptions about due process and the causes of crime. These and other changes will emerge as we focus on the post-1955 sessions.

Yet, precisely because of this chapter's emphasis on controversy, it must be emphasized again that during the 15 years under consideration only a small percentage of the bills enacted reflect serious political or ideological conflict. Even considering the 579 substantive bills identified by the Cal-

---

* Introduced in 1959, the automatic calendar formalizes and expedites the handling of noncontroversial bills by putting them on a special legislative "track" that leads smoothly and quickly to passage.

ifornia State Bar's *Review of Selected Code Legislation* and included in our quantitative analysis, 79% were the result of unanimous votes, 14% reflected dissenting votes of four or less, and only 7% of the bills were passed with five or more legislators dissenting. Throughout the entire period 1955–1971, during which 1158 roll calls were registered on the bills analyzed in this study, only 31 roll calls involved a negative vote from the floor of 25% or more of the legislators voting.[24] Therefore, the fury of post-1955 ideological struggles over law and order actually occurred in a legislative environment in which bureaucratized procedures regulated by criminal justice "experts" generated vast numbers of dull, unspectacular bills. Subsequent sections of this chapter, by emphasizing dramatic confrontation, will highlight the volatile dimension. In contrast, Chapter IV will take up where this chapter leaves off by tracing trends in the routine, pedestrian Penal Code revisions that are truly "typical."

1957: AB 1857, The "Easy Arrest" Bill[25]

AB 1857 was the opening shot in a still continuing campaign by California law enforcement to overhaul the state's arrest laws. As originally drawn, the bill's omnibus provisions (which affected 16 subsections of the Penal Code) proposed "codification" and "modernization" through total restructuring of the prearraignment criminal justice process.[26] Two interrelated sections abrogated the common-law right to resist illegal arrest and immunized the peace officer from civil liability when "acting within the scope of his authority."[27] Other changes included relieving arresting officers of the obligation to produce an authorizing warrant, broadening their authority to search for weapons while making an arrest, and sanctioning "release without charge" as an alternative to formal booking.[28] Critics labeled the original AB 1857 the Easy Arrest Bill, objecting most to those sections that added to the power of arrest an entirely new statutory authority to detain a suspect for up to 2 hours for purposes of investigation and identification:

> Sec. 13 Section 832 is added to the Penal Code to read:
> a) A peace officer may stop any person whom he has reasonable cause to believe is committing, has committed, or is about to commit a public offense and may demand of him his identity, address, and the reasons for his presence there.
> b) Any person so questioned who fails to reasonably identify himself or explain his reason for being there may be detained and further questioned and investigated.

c) The total period of detention provided by this section shall not exceed two hours. The detention is not an arrest and shall not be recorded as an arrest in any official record. At the end of the detention, the person so detained shall be released or be arrested for a public offense.[29]

For our purposes, the mixed fate of this bill is interesting for two reasons. First, the bill originally evolved from a long-standing collaboration between the California Peace Officers' Association and the Attorney General's Office. Since the 1930s when Earl Warren was Attorney General, this office had frequently served as the law enforcement lobby's political arm. By the 1950s however, this critical alliance was experiencing severe strains.

Second, the battle over AB 1857 also engaged civil liberties groups and the California State Bar in ways that illuminated the basic power relationships between all the state's chief criminal justice lobbies in 1957. The civil liberties and law enforcement lobbies, which already were beginning to see themselves as antagonists in a zero–sum game, fought the first of the bitter battles that have become an ongoing characteristic of California politics in the criminal justice field. The State Bar, with interests of its own, typically played a less polarized role, sometimes acting as broker and sometimes giving support to one side or the other to break deadlocks.

To its sponsors, the Easy Arrest Bill seemed "a modest proposal," a long overdue attempt to "modernize" the state's 85-year-old laws of arrest. Compared to the views of such hard liners as Los Angeles Police Chief William H. Parker, AB 1857 was indeed rather restrained.

> As I approach the close of 29 years of police service, I am more convinced than ever that the police are the low men on the totem pole of the machinery of criminal justice in the United States. . . . Rarely, [however,] does the machinery of criminal justice go into operation until an arrest is made by a police officer. . . . [Despite this truth,] a dangerous custom has arisen in America in which the hapless police officer is a defenseless target for ridicule and abuse from every quarter. . . . This is a situation long sought by the Masters in the Kremlin. . . . The welfare of the United States demands that the police assume a new and different relationship to our employers, the people [for] the future of America may well rest in the hands of the police service.[30]

Law-and-order advocates like Parker were reacting in particular to *People v. Cahan* (44 Cal. 2nd 434), a 1955 decision of the California Supreme Court, which barred the admission of illegally obtained evidence. Yet, the ruling's substance nettled them less than its language, characterizing law enforcement methods as "brutal," "shocking," and "intolerable."[31] Singled out for special judicial criticism were recent innovations in electronic surveillance that were a special source of pride to California's law enforcement elite. In short, Parker's notions of police professionalism were being officially challenged.[32]

From the law enforcement perspective, an assault on the *Cahan* decision became the top legislative priority.* Significantly, however, the original CPOA-sponsored Senate bill proposing an outright reversal of *Cahan* was aborted in the Senate Judiciary Committee before it reached the floor. Attorney General Edmund G. "Pat" Brown, a moderate Democrat, effectively killed the bill by not actively supporting it.† This new schism in law enforcement ranks set the stage for the CPOA's later legislative interventions, independent of the Attorney General's Office. It was a painful lesson of how important its earlier alliance with the Attorney General had been.[34]

For civil liberties forces, Brown's nonsupport of the Senate bill was vital. Though the bill was drafted 6 months prior to its January introduction, civil liberties forces led by the Friends Committee on Legislation (FCL), the ACLU, and the National Association for the Advancement of Colored People (NAACP) were slow to mobilize.[35] Law enforcement interests had seized the initiative and might have won had Brown given the support they had come to take for granted.

During the 6 months of the 1957 session, AB 1857 became a subject of inflammatory rhetoric. Opponents branded it "Hitlerian," while supporters dramatized their cause with a special showing of a *Dragnet* episode and argued that AB 1857 was the only alternative to the "skyrocketing California crime rate."[36]

Actually, these public debates were but a smoke screen for the crucial private bargaining process that really determined AB 1857's fate. Moreover, this process did not even take place within the confines of the legislature. The key arena was the State Bar, which stood between civil liberties and law enforcement combatants.[37]

---

* The Cahan decision itself contained ambiguities that almost invited a challenge. For the State Supreme Court had defended the exclusionary rule as a judiciously created, rather than constitutionally mandated, requirement, subject, therefore, to modification by legislative action.[33]

† A consensus of law enforcement opinion had been forged during the 1930s by Earl Warren, the man who had been California law enforcement's leading patron before he became its *bête noire*. Elected district attorney of Alameda County in 1926, Warren gradually coordinated the lobbying activities of the state's district attorneys with those of its police chiefs and sheriffs. He then served as executive secretary of the CPOA, as well as president of the State District Attorneys' Association, before winning the California attorney generalship in 1938. Brown, who succeeded to the office a dozen years later, benefited from the CPOA-spearheaded purge of Attorney General Fred N. Howser, a conservative Republican. Howser had compromised both the law enforcement lobby and its political arm through his liberality toward big-time gamblers.

Bar associations traditionally are "natural" battlegrounds for defense and prosecution agenda. Yet in California in 1957 the State Bar's preeminence was also a consequence of the as yet unchallenged belief that vital legislative decisions affecting the criminal justice system *ought* to be made by legal experts. This "elite" model would soon change, as police militancy and law-and-order sentiment began to define law enforcement as a political question and as the due-process controversies forced civil liberties groups to broaden their involvement. But in 1957 neither side was quite ready to explore the possibilities of transforming criminal justice debate into a phenomenon of mass politics.[38]

In the ensuing struggle, law enforcement advocates, led by James Francis Coakley,* put top priority on "capturing" the Bar's Committee on Criminal Law and Procedure. In 1954, while not calling for the introduction of the exclusionary rule in the state, the Bar Committee nevertheless had antagonized California law enforcement by echoing the Supreme Court's criticism of law enforcement for its "shocking and . . . inexcusable violations." Now, however, the law enforcement point of view was pressed with enough vigor for the majority of the Bar Committee to endorse the Easy Arrest Bill.[39]

The victory proved short-lived. In March 1957, in an almost unprecedented action, the Bar's Board of Governors overrode its Committee's recommendation and instructed its representative in Sacramento to testify against the detention provisions of AB 1857. Much of the responsibility for this reversal belonged to Bar President Joseph H. Ball, a prominent Southern California attorney sometimes identified with civil libertarian positions. Also important were the attitudes of old-fashioned, court-revering conservatives, who found the Easy Arrest Bill too "radical" a departure from past practices.[40]

Bar opposition did not prevent the hard-line Assembly Judiciary Committee from approving the bill by the end of May. But pressure from the Bar did double the 10 votes that the civil liberties forces alone would have been able to muster among liberal Democrats in the Assembly. The result was a moderately partisan "conflict roll call" of 42 to 20, unusual for a legislature in which the "agreed bill" process remained the norm and over 70% of the roll calls were unanimous.[41]

Once AB 1857 reached the more liberal Senate Judiciary Committee, the Bar carried the day; "major surgery" was performed, and the authority to detain for up to 2 hours was removed. In this watered-down form the bill was passed by the Senate, repassed by the Assembly without significant

* Alameda County District Attorney and long-time chairman of the Law and Legislative Committee of the State District Attorneys' and Peace Officers' Associations.

opposition, and signed into law by the Governor in the waning days of the 1957 session.[42]

Together with a Senate bill broadening the grounds for search warrants, diluted AB 1857 was the major legislative gain for law enforcement interests in 1957.[43] But they also achieved a "negative triumph" by defeating liberal initiatives in the areas of individual privacy and electronic surveillance. Such law enforcement victories were in no sense final, and the major issues of the 1957 session continued to generate passionate controversy before the courts and in the legislature. Further, by 1959, when the next session convened, a new balance of power had emerged in Sacramento, putting initiative on criminal justice matters into other hands.

What can be abstracted from the analysis of AB 1857? First, of course, is the recurrent conflict between law enforcement and civil liberties forces.

Second, while both camps felt intensely about the issues, the controversies involved far more than competing ideologies. Law Enforcement interests were heavily committed to an ongoing criminal justice establishment, which meant that battles were being fought over substantial bureaucratic stakes. Recall that the *Cahan* decision was viewed not only as ideologically distasteful but as an attack on practical day-to-day police and prosecutorial activities. In contrast, the civil libertarians seemed more directly motivated by ideological concerns unconnected with any particular sector of the criminal justice system.

Third, the elite nature of the legislative process was highlighted. Implicit in this procedure was the exclusion of the general public. They did not effectively support any particular lobby, nor did they directly participate in negotiations. Moreover, the vast majority of elected representatives had little input into the process, acting even in this instance largely as a collective rubber stamp for decisions made in committee.

Fourth, there was only modest evidence of partisan politics. Committee members were able to vote according to their ideological predispositions and interest group alignments, with little pressure to conform to a party line or program.

Finally, while the committees were an important arena of legislative activity, AB 1857 originated with the lobbies and the executive branch. This was typical of the 1950s when legislative initiative rarely rested with California's elected representatives.

1959: AB 342, The One Telephone Call Bill[44]

The 1959 legislature opened with the Democrats controlling both houses for the first time in the century, with margins of 47 to 33 in the Assembly and 28 to 12 in the Senate. Equally unprecedented was the hospitality shown for "liberal" legislative programs. Enactments included increased social insurance and unemployment benefits financed by higher corporate taxes, expanded state aid for public schools, a master plan to speed the growth of higher education, and a comprehensive state water plan involving the sale of $2 billion in bonds. Much of the responsibility for this liberal offensive belonged to Edmund G. Brown, elected Governor in 1958 in a 1-million vote landslide. Under his election slogan of "responsible liberalism" he submitted 40 major bills to the legislature, 35 of which were ultimately successful.[45]

Though the major thrust of these liberal reform measures were social and economic, the legislature did not ignore civil rights and civil liberties. The establishment of a Fair Employment Practices Commission (FEPC) was the culmination of a 20-year struggle by California civil rights advocates. Less dramatic but no less pleasing to civil libertarians was a covey of liberal enactments in the field of criminal justice. However, to the surprise of many, only one of these survived Governor Brown's blue pencil. This lone survivor was AB 342, a modest advance for the rights of arrested citizens known as the One Telephone Call Bill. Tracing its history provides an excellent means of exploring both the sources and the limits of liberal impact on the criminal justice lawmaking process.[46]

AB 342 was one of a half-dozen bills designed to regulate arrest practices. The package, as introduced by Republican Assemblyman Louis Francis, in essence would have provided a new definition of booking, requiring that a person placed in custody be either released or formally charged within 3 hours.[47] In addition, the proposed legislation granted such a person the right to make up to three telephone calls immediately after being booked. Both stipulations were backed by misdemeanor penalties for arresting officers who failed to comply.[48]

Francis's sponsorship of AB 342 involved elements of political paradox. Other major bills under his signature were antipornography and antisubversive measures, supported most enthusiastically by conservative forces. However, this apparent contradiction reflected the fluid ideological alignments prior to the heightened polarization of the 1960s.[49]

No such contradictions troubled Democrat John O'Connell. In his liberal-dominated Assembly Committee on Criminal Procedure, AB 342 was in sympathetic hands. Yet, more than ideology lay beneath the bill's support. The nucleus of the Committee's 7 to 3 majority of liberal Democrats had served from 1957 to 1959 on a Subcommittee on Constitutional Rights. O'Connell also headed this subcommittee, which had examined arrest law, vagrancy statutes, and the question of arrest records. The hearing transcripts and staff reports provided the raw material from which a program of "progressive" criminal justice legislation could be wrought.[50]

Nothing much would have come of this preparation, however, had not the 1958 elections and the 1959 legislative reorganization freed the parent Assembly Judiciary Committee of the conservative majority that had dominated it in 1957. The election, which the Democrats won with a state platform lauded by the ACLU, had a profound and obvious impact. More subtle was the effect of the Judiciary Committee reorganization. In order to rationalize the operation of the overworked committee, it was divided into civil and criminal divisions. Probably unintended was the resultant self-selection of committee members, forced to choose between criminal justice and civil concerns. Conservative and corporation-minded lawyer–legislators of both parties gravitated to the new Judiciary Committee; more liberal legislators preferred the newly formed Committee on Criminal Procedure.[51]

The law enforcement lobby reacted to the liberal transition with outspoken hostility. William O. Weissich, District Attorney of Marin County, characterized the committee as "packed . . . for the most part [by] eggheads or do-gooders" who looked "down their noses" at law enforcement spokesmen and made them feel "like pariahs."[52] J. Frank Coakley, Oakland's District Attorney, took a more "political" view of his experiences with O'Connell's group:

> I sometimes thought that probably the propaganda campaign of the International Communist Movement had considerable to do with it. . . . This is something for us to think about. I think the climate that we find in the legislature and other quarters, [is] motivated indirectly to a certain extent by this propaganda which has seeped up from the out-and-out card carrying Commies, to the pinkos, parlor pinks, phony liberals, the eggheads and the do-gooders, and we have got to face it and ought to do something about it because it affects our work in many, many ways.[53]

Previously, public villification of this kind was reserved for civil liberties zealots outside the legislature. One leading target was A. L. Wirin of the ACLU,* who was once characterized by Chief Parker as "a brilliant man from Russia who went through Harvard in three years and who has been identified with the defense of Communists in practically every action that he has been involved in ever since." By the late 1950s, however, such criticism was sometimes directed at liberal Democratic politicians inside the

---

* In 1959, the ACLU in California had 10,000 members and a budget exceeding $100,000. Yet lobbying within the legislature ranked so far below action in the courts that neither of its California branches retained a full-time Sacramento lobbyist. Coleman Blease, in 1959 legislative representative of the FCL, was not hired away by the ACLU of Southern California until 1961.

legislature as well. Still, this was low-keyed compared to the rhetorical warfare of the 1960s.[54]

Though law enforcement's legislative influence was at a nadir in 1959 (its only significant victory being the establishment of a Commission on Peace Officer Standards and Training), the lobby's power within the executive branch remained significant. O'Connell's proposed repeal of the state's 87-year-old vagrancy law (opponents labeled his bill "the Beatnik's Bill of Rights"), as well as his attempt to mandate the use of arrest warrants wherever "practical and feasible," fell victim to law enforcement-generated vetoes by "responsible liberal" Governor Brown. A 3-hour booking requirement, which was the cornerstone of arrest revision, met a similar fate.[55]

But Governor Brown's justification for refusing to sign the measures did nothing to bolster law enforcement confidence in his future course. While vetoing the vagrancy repealer as failing to provide sufficient alternative authority for "police control of certain dangerous conduct," he praised its "laudable objective" of eliminating vagrancy as a crime of status. This suggested that he would sign a statute rewritten to satisfy his limited objections. (He signed such a bill during the 1961 session.)[56] And, though he vetoed as "administratively unworkable" and too expensive, bills providing for more than three telephone calls at public expense, he signed AB 342 after an amendment deleted public financing of such calls.[57]

Possibly most significant in the history of AB 342 is the role of Governor Brown. His prosecutorial background as San Francisco's District Attorney and California's Attorney General left him sympathetic to the *pragmatic* arguments against due-process reform advanced by such groups as the CPOA. On the other hand, he harbored no *principled* objections to civil liberties legislation of the kind that his predecessor, Governor Goodwin Knight, had vetoed as an "unreasonable interference with law enforcement."[58]

Thus, at a time when control over the increasingly partisan legislative process was passing into the hands of civil liberties–minded Democrats, the executive branch was moving away from its traditional ideological alliance with the law enforcement lobby. Suffering from the continued inability to win the potent legislative backing of the State Bar, law enforcement advocates now stood doubly isolated from traditional "elite" sources of support. Hence, the search for new support, as well as the attempt to reconstitute old alliances, became the paramount concern of the CPOA as it emerged from the "debacle of the 1959 session." The leadership eventually concluded that an issue had all along existed that, properly focused, could restore their fortunes. Drug abuse was to be their savior and "Make 1961 Fight Narcotics Year" was to be the banner under which they would regroup.[59] Dramatic as was the issue itself, the change its choice foreshadowed in the nature of California criminal justice politics was even more so. The CPOA was about to "go public."

To summarize, 1959 was the year in which liberals first seized the initiative in criminal justice legislation. This was largely a result of changes within the legislature and not of any heightened role for the civil liberties lobby. In contrast to 1955 and 1957, a Democratic-controlled legislature was not only more attuned to the rights of citizens but more inclined to initiate Penal Code change. This more activist stance took much of the play from law enforcement advocates, who had earlier been able to set legislative agenda as well as channel significant aspects of the outcome. Had partisan politics been more salient, Governor Brown might have supported the Democratic legislative cohorts more fully and law enforcement interests could have been dealt much more telling a blow. This possibility for the future was not lost on the CPOA.

1961: AB 9 and SB 81, The Regan–Dills Drug Control Acts [60]

Prior to 1961, only three sharply focused criminal justice issues had ever generated the kind of enthusiasm out of which new political realities could be forged. The Sexual Psychopath Law passed in 1950 by a special session of the California legislature is an example of the impact of one such issue. A second, no less powerful, concern was capital punishment. Despite later replays, the controversy reached a dramatic climax in 1960, the year convicted rapist Caryl Chessman was executed.[61]

The drug problem was the third politically potent issue, erupting early in the decade and then again at its close. Between 1951 and 1954, grassroots demand to impose the death penalty for selling drugs converged with hard-line pressure from the Federal Bureau of Narcotics. As a result, the legislature increased sentences across the board. From 5 years to life became the new maximum for offenders convicted of the sale or distribution of narcotics (including marijuana).[62]

By 1959, popular clamor for punitive measures was again on the rise, especially from Southern California, where 80% of the state's narcotics arrests were made. Local Elks Lodges circulated an antidrug petition and with a million signatures precipitated the introduction of numerous punitive bills. The most draconian proposed a 30-year *minimum* sentence for pushers, and the death penalty for anyone selling drugs to a minor. For good measure, the alternative misdemeanor sentence for marijuana possession was to be eliminated.[63]

Though the package failed in 1959, parts were reintroduced in 1961 as AB 9. An examination of AB 9 and its companion bill SB 81 (a "civil commitment" statute) reveals critical new factors shaping the politics of California criminal lawmaking.[64]

The fate of antidrug bills in 1961 must be viewed against the backdrop of their failure in 1959. Then, complicated political infighting within the criminal justice establishment had undermined the unified front essential for such controversial legislation. Harry Anslinger of the Federal Bureau of Narcotics and his allies in the California drug enforcement apparatus favored, in principle, increasing criminal penalties. Harsher sentences symbolically affirmed the importance of narcotics agents, while increasing their leverage in bargaining with violators willing to turn informer. However, as criminal justice professionals, they also viewed some of the Elks proposals as "hysterical" and "overenthused." Anslinger's bureau, moreover, had to move cautiously because its battle with the United States Department of Justice—ultimately a losing one—was already taking a heavy toll. Politically this meant that the CPOA, led by police chiefs and prosecutors rather than by narcotics agents, would have to provide the lobbying muscle.[65]

During the 1959 legislative session the CPOA took some tentative steps toward the antidrug campaign. Its major attack on the *Cahan* decision had been legislation that sought to exempt narcotics cases from application of the exclusionary rule. Similarly, a companion bill attempted to reverse the California Supreme Court's *Priestly* decision (50 Cal. 2d 812 [1958]), which required disclosure of the identity of narcotics informants.[66]

Significantly, neither measure proposed increased penalties. Further, rather than merely ignoring legislation proposing tougher penalties, the CPOA had worked efficiently behind the scenes to *secure its defeat*. They feared that increased penalties would reduce conviction rates; but they conducted this campaign discreetly so as not to antagonize ideological allies.[67]

Why did the CPOA later reconsider its position and join "the punitive vanguard"? As early as 1958, William B. McKesson, Los Angeles County's District Attorney, was suggesting the need to "capitalize on what I hope may develop to be a general feeling among the public that if they want the narcotics law enforced, they have got to give law enforcement some adequate tools to do it with."[68] Growing political isolation and severe law enforcement defeats in 1959 painfully demonstrated that this "general feeling" could not be exploited by an antidrug program that failed to cater to the popular concern about penalties. This realization, more than any principled conversion to a more punitive ideology, explained the CPOA reversal. Their new stance was underscored when San Francisco District

Attorney Thomas Lynch openly called upon the CPOA "to be in the van . . . in Sacramento in 1961 . . . of the people who demand stiff penalties."[69]

The CPOA's change of mind about drug penalties went hand in hand with a broader and even more far-reaching change in strategy. In previous years, various interests had from time to time taken their case to criminal justice outsiders: the media, business groups, and the public. Nevertheless, the elite process of criminal lawmaking was the rule and actions running counter to it were generally considered bad form. By the early 1960s, however, the tide was clearly running against law enforcement priorities. The Governor's Mansion was in liberal hands, the Attorney General's Office was no longer a reliable ally, key legislative committees were dominated by civil liberties sympathizers, and the legislative atmosphere in both houses did not look promising. Even the State Bar, sometimes sympathetic in the past, now seemed increasingly unresponsive to law enforcement interests. Clearly, a change in tactics was necessary if still greater defeats were to be averted.

In essence, the rules of the game had to be altered. The CPOA and its allies, desperately needing new supporters, energetically began to take their case to the media, various business organizations, and the public at large. This was not only an escalation in effort and scope but a rearrangement in the politics of criminal lawmaking. While parts of this strategy had been tried before, they had never been applied as a well-coordinated package that, in turn, was the central component of a sweeping political offensive. Coupled with growing partisanship, this was the beginning of the polarization that was to characterize the politics of the 1960s.

The new approach soon produced positive results for the CPOA and its allies in the form of extensive media backing. The Hearst papers in San Francisco and in Los Angeles were favorably disposed toward the new antidrug campaign, which resonated with their criminal justice positions. Since the mid-1950s, the Hearst chain had been campaigning on its own for just such a law enforcement priority as legalized wiretapping. But adding their voices to the Hearst papers after 1960 were such other conservative dailies as the *Oakland Tribune* and even the increasingly moderate *Los Angeles Times*.[70]

Efforts to win over the media were highlighted by such innovations as newspaper–police forums:

> One of the best recent jobs of crime reporting, anywhere, evolved from the forum conducted May 12 by the editorial staff of *The Oakland Tribune*. Six crack newspapermen faced the panel of top law enforcement officers of Alameda and Contra Costa Counties . . . asking direct ques-

tions about the surge of violence in Bay Area Streets. They got direct answers, too—enough to fill more than two full pages in *The Tribune's* Sunday edition, so more than half a million subscribers got a comprehensive picture of the Bay Area's crime problem and learned that each of them has a part in its solution.[71]

Large newspapers were not only public relations vehicles but economic institutions with political impacts of their own.[72] The same consideration dictated the cultivation of politically influential Chambers of Commerce. Also as far back as 1958, strained relations with the State Bar had led Oakland District Attorney J. Frank Coakley to suggest that "big business" might provide an alternative source of prestigious support for CPOA programs:

> Now why did I say we can use the Chamber of Commerce? I will give you a reason why: When big business is looking around in the West here to locate a big plant, and that goes also for big government, Uncle Sam, when he is looking around to locate a big base, they are interested in various things—the labor supply, of course, and climate, and also other factors—but one of the factors which they look at is "What kind of law enforcement exists in the particular areas which we are considering?"[73]

By 1960, law enforcement interests translated these tentative reflections into a series of presentations before business influentials. One such "forum" was described by liberal journalist Loren Miller in these terms:

> [Los Angeles] Police Captain Edward M. Davis . . . went before a Chamber of Commerce group to paint a lurid picture of hordes of "heroin peddlers" and other criminals standing applauding the misguided—and worse—proponents of the review board idea. He found it significant that some of the sponsors are "also seeking clemency for Morton Sobell, convicted associate of atom spies Julius and Ethel Rosenberg."[74]

In one sense these offensives against drug abuse were all too effective. The issue itself seemed to touch people across the state, and extensive media coverage encouraged a perception of crisis. The public's concern was not lost on politicians who, no less than the CPOA, recognized political potential in the drug "menace." Coupled with growing partisanship, such widespread interest made it increasingly difficult to play both sides of the political street, and the CPOA, among others, was being forced to choose sides. By the end of 1961, it was becoming clear that the issue and the lobby shared an ultimate trajectory leading into the Republican party.[75]

Assemblyman Bruce Allen of San Jose was probably the most important Republican "pioneer" who "staked out" crime in general and drugs in particular as GOP issues. While chairman of the Assembly Judiciary Committee during the 1957 session, he appointed himself head of a long-lived Judiciary Subcommittee on Rackets. The Committee issued its final report in 1959, which Allen used as a partisan challenge to the Democratic Governor and Attorney General. He blamed them for legal "loopholes" through which "admittedly guilty thugs, hoodlums, and gangsters" had escaped, and he took special aim at due-process reforms allowing addicts to be released "too quickly for police to take advantage of their withdrawal pains to extract confessions."[76] Governor Brown challenged the 1959 report as "a waste of the people's money" and "completely irresponsible."[77]

In 1960, Allen returned to the attack. By this time drug abuse was becoming a Republican issue. Backed by the *Republican Whip* (the house organ of the Republican State Central Committee), Allen supported a demand for a special legislative session to combat "the drug menace." When this tactic failed, he used the 1960 special session on capital punishment to introduce three bills specifying the death penalty for selling drugs to minors. When these bills lost, the Democrats hoped, no doubt, that the Republican antidrug crusade was over. They were soon disappointed. First out of the gate in 1961 was to be Allen's AB 1, a reprise of his earlier get-tough-on-drugs legislation.[78]

Meanwhile, Governor Brown was having troubles of his own. He lost substantial public support over the Chessman case, which made him even more vulnerable to growing pressure "to do something about drugs." Nearly a year earlier, he had reluctantly appointed a Special Study Commission on Narcotics. Chaired by Harry M. Kimball, a product of the drug enforcement bureaucracy, the Commission prevailed on Brown to incorporate some constitutionally questionable search-and-seizure recommendations in his 1961 legislative program. But its chief contribution to the antinarcotics trend has been its advocacy of compulsory hospitalization and mandatory outpatient treatment of addicts.[79] More on this later.

The stage was now set for the 1961 legislative session. Feeling cornered, law enforcement groups had taken their case to the media, business interests, and the public. Drug abuse—always a popular issue—was becoming a Republican issue as well. At the same time, the Chessman case had weakened Brown and his fellow Democrats so that liberals, so effective in the 1959 session, were on the defensive.

The first Assembly bill introduced (AB 1) was Bruce Allen's measure specifying the death penalty for selling drugs to minors. Thirty-five penalty-increasing measures flooded the Assembly in the weeks that followed. The antidrug crusade was, if anything, gaining momentum.[80]

The Senate was soon to be involved in more subtle issues. Involuntary civil commitment for narcotics addicts had been supported in sophisticated law enforcement circles since its experimental introduction at Chino in 1959. It was also enjoying some vogue among liberals who felt that addiction should be treated as a disease, not a crime. But the state's law enforcement establishment recognized far more quickly than did most liberals that such proposals as "compulsory treatment" were, despite rehabilitative claims, quite compatible with a "police approach" to addiction. Indeed, even Chief Parker of the Los Angeles Police Department was willing to tolerate their passage. Consequently, the CPOA did nothing to discourage Governor Brown when he later had such a proposal grafted onto SB 81, originally a simple addict registration act.[81]

SB 81 was but one of four interrelated Senate bills introduced at the behest of law enforcement interests. Edwin J. Regan, chairman of the Senate Judiciary Committee, also authored these other bills, calling for reversal of *Priestly* (SB 80), repudiation of *Cahan* (SB 82), and increasing drug penalties (SB 83). Regan's moderate image, key chairmanship, and considerable prestige within the Democratic senatorial establishment made him an ideal spokesman for law enforcement's legislative offensive.[82]

In a reversal of past history the CPOA did not do as well in the executive branch. Despite Brown's interest in SB 81 (civil commitment), he opposed the rest of the package. In the fall of 1960, the CPOA had set up a new Committee on Legislative Liaison, which still hoped to win over the Democratic Governor and Attorney General. A month before the legislature convened, both were given copies of the Regan bills. But neither Governor Brown nor Stanley Mosk, his successor as Attorney General, gave the kind of support that the law enforcement lobby had once enjoyed as a matter of course. Forced to go ahead without support from the executive branch, the CPOA's fortunes depended on its ability to focus broader pressure on the legislature.[83]

If the liberals were under attack in the usually staid atmosphere of the Senate, it was a good bet that they would fare even less well in the more unpredictable Assembly. In his opening message, Governor Brown had attempted to head off precipitous legislative action through a promise that later he would introduce his own program to "guarantee that peddlers will no longer feel that the penalty is worth risking because the crime is so profitable." This strategy collapsed midway through February; administration supporters were defeated on the floor of the Assembly when they tried to reassign two penalty measures (AB 9 and AB 271) to the liberal Criminal Procedure Committee. Had the bills been reassigned, they would have died in this already famous graveyard for conservative bills.[84]

AB 9 and AB 271 were, instead, placed in the hands of the friendly Public Health Committee. They were the eclectic creations of Democrat Clayton Dills, who drew both his inspiration and his cosponsors from a wide variety of partisan and ideological sources. Like SB 83, AB 9 eliminated the existing alternate misdemeanor sentence for drug offenses; state prison terms were uniformly substituted. The only real difference between the Senate and Assembly bills was that Dills's imposed additional restrictions on the power to grant probation. But AB 271 was even more draconian, eliminating lesser sentences and increasing maximum ones. Before February was out, the Assembly passed both by overwhelming margins (AB 9 by 69 to 11, and AB 271 by 54 to 25), with liberal Democrats, mostly from Northern California, providing most of the opposition.[85]

These votes constituted one of the most humiliating defeats of Governor Brown's first administration. Yet, had he been given to philosophizing, he could have found a certain solace in the dilemma created for law enforcement interests. The prosecutorial wing of the CPOA was appalled by the prospect of obtaining convictions under the merciless provisions of AB 271. AB 9, though less objectionable, reduced the probation-granting authority enough to give pause even to narcotics agents, who were in the habit of using a promised intercession with the judge as a device for recruiting informers. These fears help to explain why the CPOA maintained an embarrassed neutrality during the Assembly debates on both measures.[86]

No less problematic for the CPOA was the fate of their own penalty measure in the Senate. Administration supporters in the Senate Judiciary Committee, backed by the considerable influence of the State Bar, mustered a 1-vote majority to amend Regan's SB 83. All the restrictions on the granting of probation were removed. Consequently, the law enforcement lobby was faced with a Senate penalty bill it considered too liberal and two Assembly bills it considered too harsh.[87]

Law enforcement interests swiftly counterattacked in the Senate, and their efforts, plus considerable Senate resentment over gubernatorial arm-twisting, caused Regan's bill to be reamended to original form before it passed. But the CPOA victory, though sweet, was short-lived. By April, when SB 83 finally reached the Assembly, antidrug sentiment had reached such heights that the Public Health Committee rewrote the bill. Its new form was even more restrictive on probation than the unacceptable Assembly bill.[88] Faced with the prospect of this legislative disaster, both the Governor and the CPOA quickly adopted the "lesser evil" argument and reconciled themselves to Dills's AB 9. Passed by the Senate and signed by Governor Brown, it became law immediately, thereby defusing the sentiment in the Assembly for more extreme action.[89]

In contrast, SB 81, the hybrid "registration–rehabilitation" measure, passed with little serious opposition. Its interesting blend of liberal and law enforcement ideology, plus scant knowledge of what its effects might be, undermined potential controversy. SB 80 and SB 82 were not so fortunate. Together they had compromised a law enforcement "one-two punch" aimed at knocking out the *Priestly* and *Cahan* decisions. Both ultimately died in the Senate Judiciary Committee. Governor Brown threatened vetoes if they passed unamended, while the law enforcement lobby refused to accept the drastic amendments that the administration forces proposed.[90]

During these battles, Brown was not without interest group support. His coalition included not just the State Bar but also liberal activists allied with Americans for Democratic Action and the California Democratic Council. In a limited way, the ACLU also got into the act. They had remained neutral on Dills's proposed legislation as well as on SB 83, using the justification that penalties per se involved no civil liberties issue. In addition, they were so reassured by the emphasis on rehabilitation that they failed to oppose the compulsory civil commitment provisions of SB 81. Rather, Coleman Blease, the Southern Branch's newly hired full-time lobbyist, was ordered to devote all his energies to defeating SB 80 and SB 82.[91]

It should be emphasized here that the civil liberties lobby owed its modest defensive effectiveness to acting as an integral part of a liberal political coalition presided over by a sympathetic Governor. Both coalition and leader had shown remarkable resilience during a session deluged with antisubversive measures (the most introduced since the Korean War) and antinarcotics legislation.[92] By the end of the 1961 session, Brown was counterattacking with a boldness which clearly demonstrated that the broader law-and-order issue which was to demoralize his second administration had not yet erupted:

> In Los Angeles County . . . we have had continuing bad law enforcement due to political law enforcement officers. . . . They have blamed the judges, they have blamed the legislators, and they have blamed the Governor for their own inadequacies.[93]

Just after the 1961 legislature adjourned and just as Governor Brown was preparing for another gubernatorial campaign, the U.S. Supreme Court handed down the historic decision in *Mapp* v. *Ohio* (367 U.S. 643 [1961]). The decision seemed to vindicate California liberals by federalizing the exclusionary rule as a means of ensuring the national implementation of the Bill of Rights. *Mapp* v. *Ohio* marked a rapid acceleration of the due-process revolution and set the stage in California for a further intensification of the political and constitutional struggle over criminal justice issues.[94]

But these issues were now being phrased in terms unknown several years earlier. Law enforcement interests were increasingly tied to Republican interests. Civil liberties became a Democratic issue. Further, these coalitions were being forged outside the professional–elite model of criminal justice legislative process that had prevailed in years past. One important consequence was that as more parties became involved and as the issues became more polarized, it was more difficult for law enforcement interests to contain the issues they helped generate. The strategy of taking their case to the media and business interests, and indirectly to the public, had wrought changes that were beyond their expectations as well as beyond their control. Soon this participation was to widen even further. Criminal justice was about to be injected, albeit tentatively, into statewide elections. Law and order was starting to emerge, not just as a partisan issue, but as a partisan issue to be taken to the people in a pivotal gubernatorial campaign.

1963: AB 2473, The Burton Antibugging Bill[95]

In 1962, state elections set the stage for the 1963 legislative session. Democrats not only wrote Richard Nixon's apparent political obituary by reelecting Brown; they increased their margins in both houses. The victors won 27 of 40 Senate seats, while falling only 2 votes short of a two-thirds control of the 80-seat Assembly. Yet these increased legislative margins reflected more than the party's popular appeal. They were also a tribute to skillful gerrymandering by Jesse M. Unruh, who was elected Speaker of the Assembly in a special postsession election in 1961.[96]

For this and other reasons the election brought ambivalence for civil liberties groups. Their efforts were increasingly defined in partisan terms as they found themselves firmly wedded to the political fortunes of Democrats. This raised important ethical and strategic questions about their role. A second cause for concern was the victory of conservative Max Rafferty in the statewide contest for the nonpartisan but ideologically sensitive office of Superintendent of Public Instruction. No such worries, however, detracted from their enthusiasm over Governor Brown's victory—a victory that was all the more comforting for civil libertarians because the crime issue injected into the campaign by the Republicans had failed to ignite.[97]

In his presidential campaign of 1960, Nixon had so ignored the crime issue that the word does not appear in the index of his speeches. As California gubernatorial candidate, however, he occasionally paid attention to the advice of his party's would-be crime busters. Thus, he promised to "make California the first state in crime prevention" and faulted the Brown administration for its squeamish refusal to support the death penalty for "big-time dope peddlers":

> What is the record of the present state administration? Instead of being first in prevention, California is now first in crimes committed. Today,

according to the FBI, there are more major crimes in California than in
New York, Pennsylvania and New Jersey together—states whose combined
population is twice as large as California.[98] *

Yet Richard Nixon's own refusal to make crime the pivotal theme of his
campaign may have prevented it from catching fire. He relied on a private
poll showing "a very strong feeling (especially in California) that America
is threatened from within by Communism as much as from outside." This
accounts for the greater play he gave to a stale proposal for public school
"indoctrination against Communism" than to "the crime problem." [100]

Indeed, even Nixon's appeal to anti-Communism was halfhearted. In
1962, antisubversion still had enough political appeal, at least in Southern
California, to qualify for the ballot in the form of the Francis Amendment.
Ultimately defeated by a million votes, it would have given grand juries
sweeping power to stigmatize and penalize any group they chose to define
as "Communist" or "subversive." Nixon, the "mature" and "moderate"
statesman, competed with Brown in his denunciations of such "Birchite
extremism." The result was a significant alienation of the most dynamic
element in his party, especially the grass-roots activists who were to win
the Republican primary for Barry Goldwater in 1964 and help win the state
for Ronald Reagan in 1966. In 1962 they worked instead for conservative
Assemblyman Joseph Shell in the Republican gubernatorial primary† and
then largely sat on their hands during the general election campaign.[101]

The same internecine warfare racked the Republican legislative dele-
gation all through 1962 and into 1963. Together with the Democratic
gerrymander, squabbles reduced Republican abilities to articulate crime as
a partisan issue. Yet beneath this surface strife a process of party renewal
was already under way that eventually produced a whole new generation of
Republican crime fighters. Among them were Assemblyman George Deukmejian and State Senator Robert Lagomarsino, both from Southern California, who in 1963 began earning their stripes in the most partisan session
the California legislature had yet seen.[102]‡

* However, Governor Brown demonstrated that, as late as 1962, a liberal politician
could still put a comforting gloss on crime statistics. He noted that for the preceding
twelve months crime showed declining rates of increase, especially for crimes of
violence.[99]

† Shell garnered one-third of the vote against Nixon.

‡ During the session's tumultuous finale, the Republicans closed ranks and temporarily denied Speaker Unruh the 2 non-Democratic votes he needed to pass the
budget. This so provoked the Speaker that he ordered a 24-hour lockup of the recalci-
trants. He then pushed through a rules change that, though repealed in 1964,
eliminated the traditional right of the minority party to help elect the Speaker and to
serve as committee chairmen.

Throughout most of the session, Republican disarray allowed the Democrats and their civil liberties allies to monopolize the political and ideological initiative. The controversial Rumford Fair Housing Act, passed after several unsuccessful attempts, was the major liberal triumph. In addition, the legislature's actions on counsel for indigents, the disposition of arrested persons, and rehabilitation of convicted offenders reflected the same liberal thrust.[103]

AB 2473, an antieavesdropping statute introduced by San Francisco Democrat John Burton, is as good an example as any of the session's "autumnal" liberalism. A legislative logjam on wiretapping and bugging had existed for 10 years. It had begun in the early 1950s with a concerted law enforcement campaign to add authority for court-ordered wiretaps to a 1940 statute that already sanctioned police use of dictographic listening devices. In 1957, however, the civil liberties lobby had counterattacked by sponsoring a bill, also introduced by Burton, that outlawed under felony penalty all forms of electronic surveillance by anyone, including police. Although this bill was rejected in 1957, Burton reintroduced it again in the 1959 session. Burton's bill, which seemed on the brink of passage, was amended at the last moment on the Assembly floor. Rather than accept a diluted version, he withdrew it.[104]

The general tenor of the 1961 session ruled out another serious push for antisurveillance legislation until 1963. However, to obtain passage even then, Burton had to accept the "half a loaf" he had rejected in 1959. In its final form, AB 2473 was compromised in its severity and scope by excluding police "authorized by law" and reducing the penalty to a misdemeanor.[105]

The one important provision that Burton did not have to dilute was a landmark in legislative implementation of the due-process revolution. By making evidence obtained in violation of the statute inadmissible in "any judicial, administrative, legislative or other proceeding," he had for the first time put the legislature's stamp of approval on the exclusionary rule as enunciated originally in the California Supreme Court's *Cahan* decision. The civil liberties lobby, which was deepening its legislative involvement to defend and extend such due-process reforms, had convinced a sympathetic legislature that the *Mapp* decision of the U.S. Supreme Court made such a "recognition of reality" inevitable.[106]

The 1963 legislature also had before it a bill that, in the view of its critics, would have circumvented the second major achievement of the due-process revolution. Edwin Regan's SB 392 directly challenged the U.S. Supreme Court's decision in *Robinson v. California* (370 U.S. 660 [1962]), which banned as "cruel and unusual punishment" a California statute criminalizing the medical status of addiction. Regan proposed replacing the "status crime" of addiction with a new misdemeanor penalty for anyone with "reasonable cause to believe himself addicted [or] in imminent danger of becoming addicted" who failed to report to a District Attorney. The bill's failure, along with the defeat of several companion measures, reflected the wane of antinarcotics preoccupations. Despite the later quantum leaps in drug arrest statistics, antinarcotic efforts never again reached the levels of 1961. An issue on which the law enforcement lobby had based its broad political strategy had lost its potency. The Regan bill's demise also revealed the nature of the 1963 legislature's constitutional scruples; these scruples annoyed the law enforcement lobby almost as much as the judicial decisions the legislature had refused to override.[107]

Despite their innovative political tactics begun 3 years earlier, law enforcement interests were clearly on the defensive once again. The broad base of support they sought had not yet materialized. As if sensing an impending catastrophe, Chief Parker only one month before the *Mapp* decision was handed down had warned:

> Our free society would be in danger and our international enemies could possibly destroy us if the judiciary continues to spell out the rules of criminal investigation.[108]

In 1962, mounting nationwide demands for police review boards led him to make another urgent appeal, calling California "the last stronghold of police professionalization" because the men in blue elsewhere had been "beaten to their knees" by "the subversives and other hate groups" that were about to "take the country over." And by 1963 the mutual contempt that characterized Chief Parker's relations with the legislature had progressed (or regressed) to the point where he was "almost tossed out" of a hearing for suggesting that legislative permissiveness was responsible for "flooding the state" with homosexuals.[109]

Compounding the law enforcement lobby's difficulties were the internal organizational problems plaguing the CPOA. Long a model for police organizations, CPOA had more than doubled its membership in less than a decade. By 1963 its ranks included roughly one-fourth of the 25,000 peace officers in the state. Most of this growth, however, was a paper phenomenon produced when smaller cities bought memberships for virtually their whole police forces in order to qualify for the inexpensive false-arrest insurance program the Association offered. By the early 1960s this source of growth was drying up and critics both within and outside the organization were increasingly faulting it as a "prim old maid" too attached to old-fashioned politics. To make matters worse, the grass-roots Peace Officers' Research

Association of California (PORAC)* was generating right-wing splinter groups so extreme that the state law enforcement establishment was embarrassed.[110] But this was 1963. Fortunately for the CPOA, California's political climate changed so radically during the next 2 years that it was able to reassert control over its own law enforcement bailiwick and regain considerable influence in the corridors and committee rooms of the legislature as well. To this dramatic reversal this chapter now turns.

1965: AB 1920, The Mulford Campus Trespass Act[111]

The 1965 legislative session produced in microcosm the stunning liberal reversal that later characterized the national scene. Between January and July of 1965, California's version of the law-and-order controversy emerged to challenge liberalism and the Democratic party. Perhaps even more than the Vietnam War, the law-and-order issue altered political fortunes.

The 1965 session was sandwiched between the two most famous California upheavals of the decade: Berkeley and Watts. The climactic episodes of the Berkeley Free Speech Movement occurred a month before the legislature convened, and aftershocks reverberated through Sacramento for the next several years. The Watts riot of August 1965 did not erupt until after the legislature had adjourned. However, black frustrations and a budding white backlash had already reached such intense levels during the 1964 referendum on California's Fair Housing Law† that the threat of racial strife became one of the palpable fears of the 1965 session.[112]

Yet, campus protest and ghetto revolt might not have become such partisan issues had not the groundwork been laid by Republican law-and-order entrepreneurs. Building in part on the experiences of the 1961 and 1963 legislative sessions, the California Goldwater campaign put an even deeper Republican imprint on the issue. Earlier sporadic attempts to brand the Democrats as soft on murderers and drug pushers now became more systematic. As early as April 1964, for example, the Republican caucus in the Assembly demanded that crime and law enforcement be put on the agenda of that year's Special Session. Governor Brown's refusal to provide an opportunity to legislate against "lawless mobs engaged in sit-in demonstrations, traffic tie-ups, and school boycotts" provoked a stinging reply from

---

* A "mass" police organization of 18,000 members, with a restrictive constitution that had limited it to "bread-and-butter" lobbying.
† The referendum went 3 to 2 against Rumford's Fair Housing Act.

George Deukmejian, the Assembly's most forceful law-and-order advocate. "The only bill dealing with crime that has received the full support of the Governor during the past three years was a bill to declare a moratorium on the death penalty."[113]

Republicans had reason to feel assertive. In the face of the Johnson landslide of 1964, they were able to defeat Pierre Salinger and send the extremely conservative George Murphy to Washington. They also were able to overcome disadvantageous district lines to reelect all 13 of their State Senators and add 3 Assembly seats to the 28 they previously held.[114]

After the election, the Republicans in the Assembly chose a new floor leader, replacing Goldwaterite Charles Conrad with the pro-Rockefeller Robert Monagan. Remarkably soon, however, moderates and conservatives both united around the partisan law-and-order platform forcefully enunciated during the 1964 campaign. By March, Monagan and Deukmejian cosponsored a "Republican-Action Program" that looked backward to Goldwater and forward to Reagan in its affirmation of "toughness" as the solution to "the crime problem." By the end of the session the Republicans were so confident of their direction that they decided to risk adverse publicity by holding up war-on-poverty appropriations. The tactic was aimed at Democratic Speaker Jesse Unruh's efforts to retain moderate amendments written into Republican-sponsored crime bills.[115]

The Democrats, on the other hand, suffered from progressive demoralization. Factional disputes pitted Speaker Unruh against Governor Brown (both eyeing the 1966 gubernatorial nomination) and Unruh against the State Senate (both mired in court-ordered reapportionment).[116] The net effect was to hasten the legislature's drift to the right. When a replacement had to be found for Judiciary Chairman Regan (elevated to the bench by Governor Brown), Donald Grunsky, a conservative Republican, was chosen. As the result of a feud with Unruh, the Assembly Criminal Procedure Committee also lost its Chairman, Gordon Young.[117] All told, these changes made the year 1965 in the eyes of the civil liberties lobby a "debacle" in which "the number of persons in the Capitol whom one could turn even for an honest and straightforward answer as to what was going on had dwindled almost to zero."[118]

It was into this fast-hardening legislative environment that campus disorder was injected. However, of the score of punitive bills introduced (the lion's share by Republicans), only Oakland Republican Don Mulford's law enforcement–sponsored AB 1920 was successful. From the liberal perspective, it represented a lesser evil, greater evils having been avoided through Republican overzealousness as well as strategic Democratic maneuvering.[119]

In the Senate, Republican Jack Schrade of San Diego had gotten the jump on Mulford in the session's opening hours. He introduced a battery of antiuniversity measures that would have imposed a variety of misdemeanor and felony penalties on campus disrupters, while placing ultimate disciplinary authority over both students and faculty with the legislature. Mulford's AB 1920 was so much more modest that it was actually endorsed by university authorities. As a misdemeanor antitrespass statute, it gave the university power to remove nonstudents from campus whenever it appeared that "such person is committing an act likely to interfere with the peaceful conduct of the activities . . . or has entered such campus or facility for the purpose of committing any such act."[120]

Meanwhile, Speaker Unruh and his Senate counterpart, President Pro Tempore Hugh Burns, combined minimum statutory action with bellicose antiuniversity posturing. Burns had stated even before the session began that the Free Speech Movement was the product of "a group of malcontents, silly kids and addle-headed teachers, egged on by Communist stooges." Later, as Chairman of the Senate Fact-Finding Committee on Un-American Activities, he issued a report blistering university officials. Its tone prompted Clark Kerr, President of the University of California, to attack the document as character assassination.[121] *

After the March eruption of Berkeley's Filthy Speech Movement, the rhetoric surrounding AB 1920 became increasingly one-sided and hysterical.[122] Trampling over objections from civil liberties groups, the legislature soon passed the bill and passed it with the two-thirds majority needed to make it an emergency measure. AB 1920 went into effect immediately upon the Governor's signature.[123]

Without exception, all those voting against AB 1920 in either house were liberal Democrats.[124] This pattern reflected a growing punitive, antistudent orthodoxy that gathered impetus from each later campus upheaval. A telling analogy, used by a Senate Committee a few years later, reveals, perhaps unintentionally, some of the thoughts shaping the legislature's stand.

> The committee was appalled that the president of the college, when asked whether in his opinion the college had any responsibility for the creation or maintenance of standards of morality on the campus, replied, in essence, that since studies have shown a person's morals to be established before

---

* Governor Brown's administration, rather than Kerr's, may have been the real target of this campaign. Unruh personally sponsored an Assembly Constitutional Resolution establishing a Joint Legislative Committee on Higher Education. Its explicit investigatory power was likely part of a larger design meant to "protect" the university from more extreme legislative action while making it a political "hostage" in his warfare with Governor Brown. [122]

or at the time they reach college level, he felt that there appeared to be little the college could or should do regarding the moral climate surrounding its students. The committee feels that if this reasoning were carried to its logical conclusion, there would be no reason to attempt rehabilitation in any of the thousand adult corrective institutions.[125]

Overall, the enactments of the 1965 session bore a law-and-order imprint that was quite new to Sacramento. Earlier sessions, such as 1961, had been more punitive in one particular area; none, however, could match the catholicity of 1965. To the Penal Code were added restrictive laws on dangerous drugs, child abuse, assaults on police and prison guards, control of guns and "paramilitary organizations," white-collar crime, and consumer fraud. Indeed, as this list shows, even the session's liberal enactments involved extension of the list of "society's offenders" by criminalizing behavior in such areas as consumer fraud and white-collar crime.[126]

The new legislative mood boosted law enforcement morale. Before the mid-1960s, campus disorder was so far removed from the CPOA concerns that about the only reference in its official magazine was a 1957 defense of the Berkeley police against charges of lax enforcement during "pantie raids." Now, legislators and criminal justice personnel were wedded by a common revulsion toward the Berkeley "outrage." However, translating such unity into the kind of legislation CPOA professionals were seeking remained problematic.[127]

For, though the CPOA derived satisfaction from the legislature's new punitive stance, criminalization and severe penalties were not at the top of the CPOA's agenda. There were already laws aplenty on the books, and heavier penalties could lower conviction rates. Typically, law enforcement interests concentrated on questions of due process and police discretion, which more immediately affected their prestige and power. The legislature's priorities, when it came to dealing with such issues, were different. Consequently, with one modest exception,* the criminal laws enacted by the 1965 session were still tangential to the CPOA's major legislative goals.[128]

The inability of the law enforcement lobby to seize the initiative more effectively had much to do with their continuing internal dissension and financial weakness. These problems had, since 1963, caused them to dispense with the services of a full-time legislative advocate and temporarily to cease publishing an official journal. The political moral was that, in the absence of solid organization, even the most promising issues could be

---

* AB 979, embodying a change defeated three times before, which modified the rules governing the disclosure of informants in drug-related cases in the direction of the anonymity favored by the CPOA.

wasted. However, the CPOA's impact was gradually increasing, thanks to the political dynamic behind law and order. And, as the 1965 session drew to a close, both the law enforcement lobby and the GOP were looking ahead to a law-and-order–dominated campaign that might place both legislative control and the governorship in the hands of the more conservative faction, who had made warring on crime the political stock-in-trade of California Republicans.[129]

1967: SB 85–87,
The Reagan–Deukmejian Penalty Package [130]

Between June 1965, when the "Friends of Ronald Reagan" announced the dawning of a new political star, and November 1966, when the California electorate eclipsed "Pat" Brown's tarnished image beneath a 1-million-vote majority for his opponent, the law-and-order issue moved to center stage of the state's politics. The 18 months of Reagan's gubernatorial campaign witnessed the fusion of a charismatic new personality and a compelling new issue. To the victors, the election was a triumphant moral crusade, to the vanquished a catastrophe in which they failed to prevent a devastating convergence of style and substance.[131]

Liberal Democratic ineffectiveness had two components: a muddled attempt to derail Reagan's personal candidacy and an abject inability to defuse the law-and-order issue. As to the former, Governor Brown's forces eventually recognized, though too late, that the positive Reagan image as a "citizen–politician" would undercut the issue of "inexperience." Hence, they chose to concentrate instead on branding Reagan an "extremist collaborator." But, though Reagan's recent past was heavily-laden with "extreme right-wing" associations (just as his more distant past had been with "extreme left-wing" ones), this strategy also involved a profound misreading of the Reagan movement and of the wider mood of California voters. In 1966, Californians were as bored with charges of Birchite extremism as they had been sated by Red-baiting accusations in 1962. Equally important was the Democratic misreading of Reagan's appeal—a mass conservative and Republican phenomenon, rather than a product of the lunatic fringe.[132]

On the law-and-order issue, the Democrats were challenged by "the jungle motif" that was central to Reagan's campaign:[133]

> Let us have an end to the idea that society is responsible for each and every wrongdoer. We must return to a belief in every individual being responsible for his conduct and his misdeeds with punishment immediate

and certain. With all our science and sophistication, our culture and our pride in intellectual accomplishment, the jungle still is waiting to take over. The man with the badge holds it back.[133]

Governor Brown resorted to three major strategems to counter this law-and-order appeal. First, he made rhetorical concessions to the same hard-line sentiment to which Reagan catered. Beginning as early as 1964, Brown took to lauding California law enforcement for its "quiet and effective" professionalism, which contrasted with "Bull Conner's misuse of dogs and hose in Birmingham." He even went so far as to echo conservative criticisms of the criminal justice innovations of the courts:

> What I want to emphasize is the concern which I share with you and many other citizens over the unsettling and disruptive consequences of the game of judicial "What's My Line?" In it the ground rules are constantly and suddenly changed and familiar principles discarded under the compulsion of newly-found wisdom.[134]

Brown's second strategy sought to defuse law and order's emotional appeal. In essence, he attempted to transform law and order into a value-neutral "technical problem." This may have constituted the political rationale for a "systems analysis and cost effectiveness study" by the Space-General Corporation. It may also have inspired Brown's appointment of a Governor's Interim Committee on Technological Approaches to Criminal Justice.*

Hard-line rhetoric and proposed aids to law enforcement were both embodied in the third leg of Brown's strategy. During a special 1966 legislative session, Brown introduced a concrete program designed to crack down even-handedly on "bigots and Birchers and any advocates of black power." But this strategy, like the others, failed as Brown was whipsawed between competing pressures. Brown quickly had bills introduced increasing the penalties for arson and for assault on, or interference with, firemen; yet he left himself open to withering attack from conservatives by initially refusing to put the general subject of "riot prevention" on the session's agenda. When, in June, the topic was tardily addressed in a Brown-backed "incitement-to-riot" statute, party liberals (who already resented the Governor's stout defense of the Johnson Vietnam policy) joined spokesmen for minority groups to castigate him for signing the measure "under a mood of hysteria similar to when the Japanese were expelled from the state." This legislation, together with Brown's temporizing on open hous-

---

* This was a panel of law enforcement officials charged with the responsibility of deciding "how best to use aerospace technology to fight crime." [135]

ing, was enough to deprive his campaign of idealistic volunteer workers and a large ghetto turnout. It was far from enough, however, to appease conservative Democrats like Mayor Sam Yorty of Los Angeles, who damned the bill as a "fraudulent and impotent measure."[136]

During the 1966 campaign, Reagan relentlessly hammered at Brown's "softness on crime." He blamed Brown for the minor ghetto disorders that punctuated the election year and kept the memory of Watts vividly alive. He blamed Brown for allowing Berkeley to become the scene of sex-and-dope orgies "so vile I cannot describe them to you." He blamed Brown for not signing all the punitive bills passed by the 1965 legislature. He even blamed Brown for the court-ordered delays that had kept the gas chamber at San Quentin shut down since January 1963, thereby creating the need for an "urban renewal project on death row."[137]

Indeed, Reagan used the California Supreme Court as a pivot for his campaign in a way that anticipated the 1968 presidential race. Already under fierce attack for its anticipation of *Miranda* in the *Dorado* case (62 Cal. 2d 338 [1965]), the California Court also invalidated the anti–open-housing referendum, which had carried by more than a million votes. The result was two anticourt crusades, the most important of which sought to remove the four-man majority held responsible for the controversial decisions. Three of these judges were Brown appointees, while one was a holdover from the earlier liberal Democratic regime of Culbert Olson. Not only did the four-man majority survive the November vote of confidence; but the electorate rejected Proposition 16, the "Clean Initiative," which was meant to overturn the court's rulings in the area of obscenity. Nevertheless, anticourt sentiment was growing, and Reagan cleverly managed to exploit it. He gave court critics aid and comfort, but without whole-heartedly endorsing either Proposition 16 or the anticourt campaign.[138]

The election produced an impressive party victory for the Republicans as well as an overwhelming personal victory for Ronald Reagan. With the exception of Attorney General Thomas Lynch (himself less liberal than his Democratic predecessors Mosk and Brown), all the Democratic incumbents holding statewide office were defeated. Had it not been for the gerrymanders of 1961 and 1965, the Republicans almost certainly would have captured the legislature as well, for they also won a clear majority of the statewide vote for Senators and Assemblymen. As it was, the Democrats held tenuous control of both legislative houses: 21 to 19 in the Senate, and 42 to 38 in the Assembly. The precarious nature of this control was demonstrated late in the session, when a special election called to fill a death-created vacancy resulted in a Republican victory and a 20 to 20 senatorial deadlock.[139]

Reagan lost no time in defining the law-and-order thrust of his administration. He appointed the legislature's three prominent Republican conservatives (Senate veterans Grunsky and Lagomarsino and a Senate newcomer, former Assemblyman Deukmejian) to a select committee for drawing up his legislative crime control program. Later, Grunsky and his colleagues sponsored proposals designed to implement the six-point anticrime package that Reagan had introduced.[140]

The 1967 legislature rejected outright bills embodying four of these six points: those calling for tighter pornography laws, state involvement in the regulation of sexual activity, the selective sealing of the arrest records of only those "proved to be innocent," and "merit selection" of judicial appointments. The fifth proposal, a Deukmejian-authored bill creating a California Council on Criminal Justice (CCCJ),* easily won approval, despite some low-key muttering that the council might chart a course toward 1984.[141]

The only components of Reagan's anticrime program that overcame intense opposition were three bills (also introduced by Deukmejian) increasing the penalties for crimes of violence. In their original form, SB 85–87 would have eliminated "five to life" and substituted "straight life" for robbery, rape, and burglary committed with a dangerous weapon. Before reaching the Governor's desk, however, they were subject to multiple amendments as a result of considerable disagreement over the merits of their various provisions.[142]

The Assembly Criminal Procedure Committee proved to be the crucial arena in which the fate of SB 85–87 was decided. Since the early 1960s, when dominated by John O'Connell and a top-heavy liberal majority, the Committee had gradually moved in membership and ideology to a more conservative stance. In 1967, Speaker Unruh, clearly on the defensive, formalized the transition by naming Republicans to 5 of the 10 committee positions and appointing a moderate Republican, Craig Biddle, as chairman. This allowed Unruh to claim that he was giving "the Governor's party" an equal role in shaping the Assembly's response to the "crime problem," while at the same time giving the Democrats the 5 votes needed to bottle up objectionable bills.[143] Lou Cannon describes the result:

> In the first two years of the Reagan administration, this committee killed Republican proposals that would have outlawed distribution of pornography to minors, increased the penalties for narcotics use and for campus trespass, lengthened mandatory minimum sentences for a number of crimes, and "untied the hands" of law enforcement agencies, at least to the degree permitted by the Supreme Court.

* The CCCJ was intended, among other things, to direct funding for technological improvements in the criminal justice system.

But while Democrats were disposing of such "law and order" remedies, Republicans were killing proposals that would have eased penalties for narcotics use, authorized earlier release of prisoners, and imposed gun controls more wide-ranging than in any state. The committee became almost, but not quite, a total exercise in law enforcement and civil libertarian rhetoric rather than in the legislative process.[144]

The passage of SB 85–87 was one of the rare occasions during 1967 in which Democrats buckled under law-and-order pressures. As these bills were being considered by the Criminal Procedure Committee, only one member risked heresy by openly suggesting "the futility" of penalty increases as a means of "stopping the rise in the crime rate." Still, the Democrats forced Deukmejian to accept two major amendments: One preserved the principle of indeterminancy by amending the straight life penalty to 15 years to life; the other narrowed the bill to situations when physical harm had actually been inflicted. In this form, the three bills, having already won Senate approval 25 to 11 (a vote characterized by moderate partisan disagreement), swept through the Assembly. Governor Reagan's enthusiastic signing of these measures might be allowed to pass without mention had Governor Brown not pocket vetoed almost identical legislation in 1965. This transference of veto power from a liberal Democrat to a conservative Republican was probably the single most important change in the legislative balance of power between 1965 and 1967.[145]

Consistent with their traditional priorities, the law enforcement and civil liberties lobbies were at best moderately interested in the Deukmejian bills. While the CPOA supported the bills, perhaps its major contribution to the early Reagan administration was in personnel rather than policy. Edwin Meese III, formerly a Deputy District Attorney and law enforcement lobbyist,* became Reagan's Legal Affairs and Executive Clemency Secretary. Thanks to Meese, the gas chamber at San Quentin was readied for the future, reassuring Birchite Senator John Schmitz, who, though appalled by the administration's overall "breach of faith" with his kind of conservatism, at least had kind words for this "anticrime measure."[146]

As a result of internal divisions, the civil liberties lobby failed to mount as effective a campaign against SB 85–87 as it did against the other major components of the Reagan anticrime package. The FCL opposed the bills on the grounds that "the legislature should not continue to increase criminal penalties without study of [their] effectiveness." Even as late as 1967, however, the ACLU maintained the position that penalty increase proposals per se "do not raise clear civil liberties issues." Neither the national

---

* He represented the CPOA and the District Attorneys' Association.

organization nor the Southern California branch (which often took the lead in such matters) had yet generalized their stance against capital punishment into opposition to lesser forms of "cruel and unusual punishment."[147]

While the Reagan victory and the salience of law-and-order politics were the most visible aspects of the 1967 session, another important institutional dynamic was beginning to develop. In November 1966, California voters had approved a constitutional amendment that tripled legislative salaries and instituted annual sessions. The resulting intensification of the legislative process made intensification of the lobbying process inevitable. The ACLU of Northern California was but one of innumerable organizations that felt compelled to increase its representation in Sacramento. Nor was it alone in having to generate a 25% larger budget in order to cover the additional expense.[148]

Concurrent with the constitutional revision, new lobby groups began to appear in Sacramento. Among the "new allies"* for the ACLU were the State NAACP, the Mexican-American Political Association, the Northern and Southern California Council of Churches, the Association of California Consumers, and such progeny of the War on Poverty as the Federation of the Poor. The impact of this new liberal coalition, however, was counteracted by intensified activity from the law enforcement lobby. By 1968, its forces in Sacramento were being supplemented with manpower "loaned" on a regular basis by the Los Angeles Police Department, by the Sheriff's Departments of Los Angeles County, and by other major jurisdictions.[149]

Thus the 1967 session saw the partial fruition of one trend and the quiet birth of another. Early attempts by law enforcement interests to broaden their political base had mixed with grass-roots reactions to Berkeley, Watts, and rising crime rates. In an atmosphere of disenchantment with liberal social programs, these forces converged on Sacramento to make law and order a polarized and highly partisan political issue. Ronald Reagan personified the new hard line on crime; the process of Penal Code alteration had come a long way from quiet closed-door negotiations among criminal justice professionals. It was not as if backroom deals no longer occurred. Rather, the negotiations now had to include highly charged ideological and partisan considerations. However, if there was a trend away from an elite model of lawmaking at one level, there was an implicitly elitist trend toward legislative professionalism gaining momentum on another. More and more over the next few sessions, a legislature strengthened by growing

---

* They had never before been more than sporadically involved in legislative lobbying.

financial support and independent research staff would begin to take the initiative. Committees would no longer act simply as arenas for negotiation; they would be innovators of criminal justice policy as well.

1968: AB 581, The Sieroty Prisoner Rights Bill [150]

Thanks to a constitutional amendment, the California legislature that convened in January 1968 was the first general session ever to be held in an even-numbered year. This also made it the first session not preceded by an election campaign. Nevertheless, at least in the field of criminal justice, the autumn of 1967 had a profound impact on the upcoming session's legislative direction; for it was then that the Assembly's Office of Research (AOR), on behalf of its Committee on Criminal Procedure, had begun its critical and critically important study of the whole system of criminal law and corrections.

The preliminary report, "Deterrent Effects of Criminal Sanctions,"* was issued in the middle of the 1968 session. It argued that properly focused scientific research could decisively shape legislative responses to crime and other social problems. In particular, with regard to corrections and the need for legislatively mandated prison reforms, the report was devastating:

> The state of California maintains one of the most expensive correctional systems in the nation to implement a penalty policy of entirely unproven effectiveness.[151]

After finding "no evidence that state correctional institutions rehabilitate effectively" and much evidence for "the active nature of the destruction that occurs in them," the study outlined policy alternatives. These were the economic and moral grounds given for decentralizing the system and rationalizing parole procedures:

> The Legislature should direct the Adult Authority to release to parole all offenders at expiration of their statutory minimum parole-eligible period, with the exception of those convicted of . . . specified crimes of serious personal violence and those with histories of professional criminality or habitual extreme violence. The resulting savings in annual prison costs and further capital outlay [should] be appropriated to subsidize local supervision of offenders, increased use of local custody, and improvements in statewide crime control, technical resources and local law enforcement.[152]

* The report was the joint product of the AOR and Social Psychiatry Research Associates of San Francisco, an independent consulting firm.

These conclusions and recommendations forced the state's correctional bureaucracy into a defensive posture. The findings also encouraged liberal critics of the corrections system, who were becoming more vocal in the very midst of the law-and-order 1960s.[153]

The report owed its influence at least as much to the prestige of its source, the Office of Research of the Assembly, as to the plausibility of its arguments. Increasingly, just this kind of expert intervention was transforming the California lawmaking process. For the legislature was no longer satisfied with the passive role of responder to outside pressures from professional lobbies, the executive branch, and, less frequently, citizen groups. Nor were its committees any longer willing to settle for the limited role of referee in the battles between such contending extralegislative interests. So, by the mid-1960s, considerable resources were being committed by the legislature to the research and staff needed for California lawmakers to seize the lawmaking initiative. Because its significance for criminal lawmaking in California was critical, we will briefly review the stages in this process of legislative self-reform.

Caught up in the fervor of Progressive reform, California in 1913 established a Legislative Counsel Bureau to help regulate the flood of meliorative legislation introduced at that time. Subsequently, during the 1930s, the legislature's need for long-range policy studies produced a liaison with the Bureau of Public Administration (later renamed the Institute of Governmental Affairs) of the University of California at Berkeley. Between this reform and the innovations of the late 1950s, major improvements in legislative operations involved not the establishment of additional outside liaisons but the creation within the legislature itself of two effective investigative arms: The Legislative Analyst's Office (1941) and the Legislative Audit Bureau (1955).[154]

Yet the decisive phase of legislative self-improvement did not begin until Jesse M. Unruh assumed the Assembly speakership in 1961. Unruh began modestly by giving each Assemblyman a secretary, an administrative assistant, and a district office allowance for the period between legislative sessions. He then began to recruit new academic assistance. "It is a sad irony," Unruh complained in 1962, "that the closest that some of California's own scientists and scholars come to their own state capitol is 30,000 feet while on flights to Washington to participate in deliberations of the Federal Government." To remedy this situation, he called upon President Clark Kerr of the University of California to help him organize a series of California Assembly Seminars for interested legislators during 1963 and 1964.[155]

Coupled with new staff and academic inputs were the Unruh-initiated reforms in committee operations. First, the number of "automatic" standing committees were reduced. Surviving committees were provided with at least one full-time research specialist to help them respond innovatively in the areas where "the great problems of tomorrow lie." Second, interim committees were encouraged to consider subjects as a whole. The hope was they would develop more comprehensive programs by drawing on scientific input. Third, even the minority caucus was assigned independent researchers.[156] To round things out, the staff buildup and the committee system's new investigative resources were put under the direction of a Chief Assembly Consultant, whose position was the forerunner of the 18-member Assembly Office of Research. The AOR was formed in 1967, initially to coordinate the activities of the lower house's 200 professional employees and to administer an influx of federal grants.[157]

Like many significant institutional innovations, the growth of a more powerful and independent legislature owed much to the personal and political ambition of one man, in this case, Jesse Unruh. In Sacramento they said that while Hugh Burns, the Senate President Pro Tempore, ran the upper house "like a club," Unruh ran the lower one "with a club." Nor could it be doubted that Unruh's political aspirations were a motive for providing the Assembly with an independent policy-initiating capacity to rival the executive branch. From this perspective, the organizational and academic honors that Unruh received for these legislative reforms were just so much icing on the cake.[158]

To the extent that Unruh's innovations reflect an elitist–liberal model of political decision making by experts and technocrats, they could be subject to a searching critique. However, what matters here are their "middle range" or institutional consequences for the criminal lawmaking process in California. To begin, the improvement in bill-drafting and bibliographic services affected routine legislative operations by enlarging the capacity to turn out "chuck hole legislation":

> Routine bills consume a greater deal of time. These include laws regulating manufacturing, commerce and employment in which detail is necessary. They include decisions in borderline cases on the incidence of sales, excise and property taxes. They set the limits of authority for local governments and school systems. Constitutional requirements, ambitious administrators, businessmen seeking a more favorable climate for their particular operations —these thrust a host of decisions upon the legislature. Any one of these decisions seems relatively insignificant, but in the aggregate, they may add up to important policy.[159]

Most of the legislative enactments that find their way into the Penal Code fall within this category. Were it otherwise, our later, quantitative approach to the evolution of the criminal law in this study would be unnecessary.

Unruh's reforms also affected less routine matters, and here the legislature's new ability to transcend a passive role was especially vital. During the Unruh speakership, in-depth committee investigations lasting as long as 3 years bore fruit in a variety of comprehensive enactments. Sophisticated legislative packages addressed social insurance, tax assessment practices, mental patient rights, therapeutic abortion, and clean air. Appealing to growing legislative pride, Unruh and his disciples were able to mobilize majorities across party and ideological lines and to stay several steps ahead of the executive branch in a half-dozen vital areas. In criminal justice, the main target was the state corrections system, and we return to that issue now.[160]

During the 1963–1965 interim, the Assembly Committee on Criminal Procedure, with the help of outside expertise, began its review of the corrections system, the fruits of which were a Probation Subsidy Act and an expanded prisoner furlough program.[161] By 1968, the California corrections system, only recently the epitome of "progressive penology," was under attack from liberals and conservatives alike. This was a startling turnabout from 1964, when the corrections bureaucrats complained only of insufficient financial support. Then, Richard A. McGee, administrative chief of the Youth and Adult Corrections Agency had said:

> At present, [corrections] lacks the glamour of the physical sciences, of rockets to the moon or [even] cores drilled to the center of the earth. It lacks the prestige of medicine and law. . . . And, as you'd expect from all that, it lacks the real American indicator—money.[162]

While money may not have been plentiful, kind words were bestowed in abundance. Indeed, as the 1960s drew to a close, the system's national reputation still was sufficiently intact for a liberal humanitarian like Karl Menninger to praise its "brilliant leadership" for the creation of something approximating an ideal therapeutic community behind prison walls:

> The California corrections system . . . has been far out in the lead among the states, with excellent programs of work, education, vocational training, medical services, group counseling, and other rehabilitative activities. A notable feature is the combination of diagnosis, evaluation, treatment and classification at its hospital–clinic–prison center, the combined Medical Facility and Reception Center at Vacaville. This constitutes a systematic effort along scientific principles to ascertain from collected case history data and from first-hand examination just what the assets and liabilities of the floundering individual are.[163]

From California, however, the perspective by 1968 was quite different. Even before Reagan's election, the state's correctional bureaucracy had begun to respond to growing law-and-order sentiment by instituting "violence control" programs.*

Liberal disaffection further intensified with each conservative Reagan appointment to the corrections bureaucracy.[164] After retirement, McGee himself came to criticize the indeterminate sentence, one of the cornerstones of "reform penology," on the pragmatic grounds that, while ideally allowing for individualized treatment, it was subject to abuse by reactionary administrators. However, the causes of liberal disillusionment went still deeper. Before Reagan took office the evidence already suggested that California's cosmetically packaged experiments in rehabilitation and treatment were at the point of bankruptcy. The mid-1960s produced a harvest of scholarly studies (many either encouraged or even commissioned by the state correctional bureaucracy itself) that found "no significant relationship" between prison rehabilitation techniques and parole outcomes.[165]

In January 1967, these issues were dramatically reinforced when prisoners at San Quentin rioted. It was the first serious disruption in a generation, and one of the worst in San Quentin's 115-year history. James Park, associate warden, described the riot and the more serious disorders that followed as a "new type of prison revolt planned and executed by a mixed group of prisoners, former prisoners, academic penologists, and adherents of various New Left philosophies:"

> The age-old dissatisfactions of the convict were transformed into a well-planned and sophisticated attack on state laws and policies, the operations of the paroling agency, the limitations on legal rights of parolees, the indeterminate sentence, and other issues far removed from the usual minor food grievances.[166]

Civil liberties activists in the state took a more sympathetic view of the turmoil and the grievances that caused it. They gave aid and comfort to a unique civil liberties group, the California Prisoners Union, which emerged from the disorder. Characteristically, the ACLU did not begin to involve itself seriously in the problem of prison reform until prisoners and ex-prisoners provided this lead. Indeed, 1968 was the first year that "parole revocation" and associated due-process violations became a major item on its legislative agenda.[167]

---

* In the early 1960s, "violence control" referred to policies aimed at reducing crime by tightening parole procedures and lengthening sentences. In the late 1960s, the same label was attached to internal programs designed specifically for violent-prone inmates, emphasizing innovative techniques ranging from isolation to controversial psychotherapeutic treatments.

In contrast to the ACLU, the FCL had always been heavily involved in corrections issues. Until the late 1960s, however, it acted almost solely as an uncritical ally of liberal bureaucrats who presided over the system. Indeed, the FCL was so infatuated with "reform penology" during this period that it not only defended the indeterminate sentence but even partly based its stand against capital punishment on the system's claims to have perfected "the science" of rehabilitation.[168] However, by 1968 the FCL also was in the process of assuming a new radical stance toward corrections, attacking the Friends' own traditional reformist palliatives. One radical Quaker manifesto declared:

> It would be naive not to acknowledge the blunders that an uncritical faith can produce. The horror that is the American prison system grew out of an eighteenth century reform by Pennsylvania Quakers and others against the cruelty and futility of capital and corporal punishment. This two hundred year old experiment has failed. . . . More judges and more "experts" for the courts, improved educational and therapeutic programs in penal institutions, more and better trained personnel at higher salaries, preventive surveillance of predelinquent children, greater use of probation, careful classification of inmates, preventive detention through half-way houses, removal of broad classes of criminals (such as juveniles) from criminal to "nonpunitive" processes, the use of lay personnel in treatment —all this paraphernalia of the "new" criminology appears over and over in nineteenth century reformist literature. After more than a century of persistent failure, this reformist prescription is bankrupt.[169]

State legislatures are not in the habit of enacting radical blueprints for institutional change, even when these blueprints are the products of respectable Quakers and even when they are supported by legislative committees. Hence, the 1968 session defeated the most comprehensive design for penal reform. For example, AB 1269, authored by Democrat John Vasconcellos, would have required the Adult Authority to release all nonviolent, nonhabitual offenders at the end of their minimum sentence, or state in writing a weighty reason for not doing so. The dollars saved from the estimated 20% to 40% drop in prison population were to be used to finance parole supervision and improve local law enforcement.[170]

The Governor's Office and the correctional bureaucracy produced a deadlock in the Criminal Procedure Committee that killed Vasconcellos's proposal. One powerful argument was that the Probation Subsidy Program enacted within the Welfare and Institutions Code in 1965 already promised massive economies. This program provided participating counties with funds for local treatment in lieu of prison sentences, and the number

TABLE 2.2

Disposition of Adult Felony Population: 1954–1971[a]

Year	Adult felony defendants	% Convicted	Convicted felons: state prison		Convicted felons: probation[b]	jail
			Number	(%)	(%)	(%)
1954	20,014	87.3	4,902	28.2	45.0	19.7
1955	17,997	85.4	4,141	27.2	44.2	20.6
1956	19,648	85.9	5,105	30.3	43.5	18.4
1957	22,985	85.5	5,502	28.0	45.9	18.9
1958	26,054	86	6,245	27.7	47.4	18.1
1959	26,539	86.4	6,407	28.0	44.5	19.5
1960	28,751	86.3	6,971	28.1	44.3	19.0
1961	32,175	86.9	7,248	25.9	45.2	20.2
1962	31,435	86.7	6,420	23.7	46.3	18.8
1963	33,102	86.3	6,606	23.3	48.9	16.7
1964	32,801	85.4	6,365	22.9	50.8	15.8
1965	36,878	84.2	7,184	23.3	50.8	15.2
1966	37,584	84.9	6,731	21.0	54.6	15.6
1967	41,027	84.6	5,990	17.3	58.7	12.5
1968	47,277	85.6	5,492	13.5	61.9	13.1
1969	59,497	85.0	4,950	9.8	65.9	13.9
1970	59,257	84.3	5,025	10.1	67.7	12.2
1971	65,236	85.9	5,386	9.7	70.4	10.3

[a]Source: Bureau of Criminal Statistics, Department of Justice, State of California. *Crime in California*, 1954–1964 (separate volumes); *Delinquency and Probation in California*, 1954–1961 (separate volumes); *Crime and Delinquency in California*, 1965–1972 (separate volumes).
[b]Straight probation or probation/jail.

of commitments to state prisons during the first year of implementation fell significantly (see Table 2.2). Hence, much of the urgency for Penal Code revision of sentence determination was lost.[171]

Assemblyman Alan Sieroty's* AB 581 fared much better. Called by the sponsoring FCL "the first step" to limit "the absolute authority" of the Department of Corrections and the Adult Authority, Sieroty's measure would have repealed the "civil death" status of convicted felons and granted inmates and parolees the following rights:

* Sieroty of Beverly Hills was a member of the Southern California ACLU Board of Directors.

1. To inherit real or personal property
2. To initiate civil actions
3. To contract
4. To correspond confidentially with any member of the State Bar, or holder of public office
5. To own all written material the prisoner produced during his term of imprisonment
6. To purchase, receive, and read any and all published materials.[172]

In order to obtain passage, however, Sieroty and four fellow Democrats had to make major concessions to the Republican side of the evenly divided Criminal Procedure Committee. Not only were the rights to sue and contract sacrificed, but the confidentiality and freedom-to-read provisions were significantly diluted. Together with a right to censor, prison authorities were allowed, via an amendment, to continue to inspect all mail for "contraband." In this amended form, AB 581 cleared the Senate Judiciary Committee as well as its Assembly counterpart, passing both houses of the legislature with majorities over 60%. However, for the first time since 1957, partisan differences toward criminal justice were translated into votes marked by "significant party division." While the Democrats in each house voted more than 90% in favor, the Republicans voted roughly 2 to 1 against the measure.[173]

Significantly, it was the "swing vote" of "moderate" Republicans that deserved most credit for the passage of Sieroty's bill. The key figure was Craig Biddle, who, though a Republican, was reappointed by Unruh in 1968 to chair the Criminal Procedure Committee. Biddle was so impressed by his committee's study of "Crime and Penalties in California" that he condemned "the arbitrary and unfounded actions" of "quasijudicial" correctional authorities. He also changed his mind about marijuana laws and introduced an ultimately successful bill reducing penalties to what they had been before the antinarcotics hysteria of 1961.[174]

Reagan's signature on both Sieroty's prisoner rights bill and Biddle's marijuana penalty reduction law requires explanation. He signed them quite simply because the law enforcement lobby did not emphatically ask him to veto them. In both cases, amendments removed major objections and made it much easier for the lobby to accept the bills despite their liberal flavor. Further, the corrections bureaucracy was still unable to function smoothly as part of the law enforcement lobby because of its "liberal past" and now, on its own, it lacked the necessary muscle to kill compromise measures granting rights that the courts seemed on the verge of granting.[175]

If there is one lesson to be learned from the 1968 session it is that at least sometimes a legislature can chart its own independent course. While liberalism was clearly on the defensive, the work of the Assembly's Office of Research helped to mobilize Democrats and moderate Republicans against Reagan's regime. The significance of this result deserves stress, since it introduced a critical new factor into the calculus of California politics. However, with upcoming state elections, things were going to get worse for the liberals before getting better. As the 1968 session drew to a close, a contest loomed that would end the Democrats' 10-year domination of California's legislature.

1969: SB 62–63, The Lagomarsino Antiobscenity Statutes [176]

During the first half of 1968, the law-and-order issue had shown an ironic new face. Rather than generating hard-line legislation, the issue so polarized the criminal lawmaking process that uncompromising factions typically cancelled each other out. The result was a session that, except for its crackdown on drunk drivers, did not produce one major piece of legislation whose passage the ACLU considered a serious defeat.[177]

During the second half of 1968, however, legislative infighting gave way to broader election-year politics, and the law-and-order issue again demonstrated an ability to win voters. In 1968, the Republicans not only carried the state for Richard Nixon by 300,000 votes, they also captured nearly 55% of the vote in state legislative races. By a slim majority, the Assembly was theirs.[178]

After the election, party discipline was so pronounced that in January of the new year, no more than a 1-vote margin was needed to ensure a Republican victory in the speakership election. By 41 to 39, Jesse Unruh was replaced by Robert Monagan, the first Republican speaker in more than a decade. Republicans now held the two most powerful political offices in the state.[179]

While Reagan was not up for reelection, the fall's political climate seemed to bolster him as well. The earlier legislative deadlocks could be traced in part to Reagan's midterm slump in popularity and the credibility gap created by his noncampaign for the presidency. But the "third world" student insurgency which, beginning in the fall of 1968, convulsed first San Francisco State and then Berkeley rebuilt substantially the Governor's standing with the voters. After the 1969 legislative session opened, Republican moderates like Monagan, whose desertions had helped produce earlier Reagan setbacks, were less inclined to oppose a party chief enjoying 75% public approval in the polls.[180]

In his campaign to elect a Republican legislature, the Governor had emphasized that a party victory would allow an ideological restructuring of the Assembly Criminal Procedure Committee. Clearly he had good reason for setting his sights on this goal. In 1968, Speaker Jesse Unruh, while maintaining its 5 to 5 partisan complexion, had reinforced Criminal Procedure's function as a graveyard for hard-line legislation. He replaced politically vulnerable Walter Karabian with John Vasconcellos, a liberal Democrat who faced no reelection worries. Stung by the subsequent Republican defeats, H. L. Richardson, Republican State Senator and former Birch Society functionary, accused the committee of having become a creature of the ACLU and a collaborator "in defending left-wing radicals, beatniks, peaceniks, draft dodgers and subversives."[181]

Only two weeks after the November elections, Chairman Craig Biddle of Criminal Procedure told a reporter: "The new session will offer a golden opportunity for law enforcement to get some of their long-sought programs enacted into law."[182] Robert Monagan's elevation to Speaker and Biddle's succession to the second-ranking position of Majority Leader had created the need for a new chairman of the Criminal Procedure Committee. Lawyer Frank Murphy was chosen; though a political moderate, he pledged to let law enforcement have its day. Even more important, the new Republican leadership reduced the committee's membership from 10 to 9, thereby giving the majority party a 5 to 4 margin with which to determine the fate of controversial legislation.[183] A pleased law enforcement spokesman commented:

> The difference this year is not so much that Republicans have control of the legislature but that Alan Sieroty of Beverly Hills has lost control of the Assembly Criminal Procedure Committee. . . . It did not matter where he sat on the Committee. He was its philosophical architect, and he had the votes [to leave] local police bitter and frustrated.[184]

Obscenity and pornography were two issues where Republican dominance soon made a difference. Between 1963 and 1968 the Criminal Procedure Committee had killed 26 major attempts to revamp the state's antiobscenity laws. In 1969, it helped to maneuver through the legislature SB 62–63, the bills that allowed some to claim that they had finally won the legislative war against smut.[185]

Drawn up 2 years earlier in collaboration with the Attorney General's Office and unsuccessfully submitted to both the 1967 and the 1968 sessions, the package was sponsored by Republican Senator Robert Lagomarsino. Lagomarsino, a Reagan intimate, was a law-and-order crusader who had sponsored punitive measures against offenses from kidnap–rape to dognapping. On balance, however, he was a sober and substantial conservative, much too serious to indulge in the antics (such as exposés of the "pornographic contents" of the *Dictionary of American Slang*) which had opened to ridicule earlier antivice crusaders.[186]

The carefully drawn provisions of SB 62–63 indicated an astute grasp of the constitutional issues surrounding obscenity. Most conservative efforts in this area had attempted to assault frontally the U.S. Supreme Court's landmark *Roth* decision (354 U.S. 476 [1957]) by deleting the requirement that obscene matter be "totally without redeeming social importance." Lagomarsino's bills opted for a subtle strategy exploiting the openings for constitutionally defensible changes that the U.S. Supreme Court itself had recently created through its "backlash" decisions in the *Ginzburg* (383 U.S. 463 [1966]) and *Mishkin* (383 U.S. 502 [1966]) cases.[187]

Seizing on the *Mishkin* "variable standard" for judging obscenity, and also on a New York "juvenile obscenity" statute,* SB 62 addressed the sale and distribution of "harmful matter" to minors. As originally introduced, it imposed a misdemeanor penalty on first offenders (a felony for a second offense) convicted of selling or distributing to juveniles such matter, "the redeeming social importance" of which was "substantially less" than its "prurient appeal." Pressure from the civil liberties lobby and fear of judicial interference† led Senator Lagomarsino to accept an amendment. Conviction was made contingent upon proof that the "questionable material" was "utterly without redeeming social importance for minors." Even in revised form, however, the measure allowed jurors to balance literary merit against what they believed "average children" ought to read, and to second-guess booksellers who "recklessly" sold questionable material to a juvenile.[188]

SB 63, in contrast, was aimed at "the adult market." It incorporated the "variable standard" into the law by criminalizing the sale and distribution of "matter which possessed a prurient appeal" only for "sexually deviant groups." Its key provision, however, was a pandering section, an outgrowth of the doctrine of "contextual obscenity" first advanced by Warren in the *Roth* case and then adopted by a court majority in *Ginzburg v. the United States.* This made "commercial exploitation for the sake of prurient appeal" an alternative basis for guilt where conclusive proof that the matter was "utterly without redeeming social importance" could not be had.[189]

---

* *Ginzberg v. State of New York* (390 U.S. 692 [1968]), in which the U.S. Supreme Court upheld the state.

† Unamended, SB 62 was such an explicit departure from the *Roth* formula that it seemed to be inviting a court test case.

The ACLU damned both bills as "extraordinarily dangerous" and an "open invitation for censorship groups to attack books." However, ACLU opposition was undercut by chapter-and-verse citations from the Warren Court supporting the legality of SB 62–63. After amendments had even further buttressed its punative constitutionality, SB 62, California's new "juvenile obscenity" statue, passed virtually without opposition. SB 63, though arousing more controversy, also sailed through in amended form with 3 to 1 margins in both houses. The only Republican in the house voting negatively was Richard Barnes, a totally inflexible legislative crusader unwilling to endorse any measure that could not guarantee absolute purity.[190]

In a study of the refusal of the 1968 legislature to pass almost identical bills, Peter Leigh concludes that the lawmakers tried to avoid the obscenity issue "as if it were a contagious plague." Reagan then branded this "Democratic failure" as a "tragic victory for the purveyors of pornography" and a "shirking of responsibility to the youth of California." In response, the Democrats had pushed an obscenity bill of their own, a narrowly focused measure promising to "crack down" on pornography peddlers loitering about schoolyards. But this died in committee after Republicans contemptuously dismissed it as "an innocuous dirty old man bill." More sweeping legislation passed in 1969 largely because the new Republican legislative leadership made hidden opposition impossible. The obscenity issue was forced into the public spotlight of floor debate and here most of the behind-the-scenes Democratic opposition evaporated.[191]

The Republican floor strategy illustrated in SB 62–63 was in part a reaction to earlier Democratic back-room recalcitrance. One reason for law enforcement's limited success in 1967 and 1968 was an "oppositional psychology," common among minority parties, that gripped the Democrats even before they lost legislative control. Fused with civil-libertarian scruples, it created an obstructionist style and quietly sabotaged the Reagan get-tough-on-crime programs. Had the Democrats been able to continue this strategy after becoming the actual minority in 1968 the deadlock probably would have continued into 1969 and 1970. Yet this did not happen. Though party balance was too even for Republicans to pass controversial bills without bipartisan support, the loss of legislative control prevented Democrats from any longer killing major law-and-order initiatives through cloakroom maneuvers. Faced with the prospect of openly opposing a popular governor and his anticrime program, their united front collapsed.[192]

The CPOA's *Newsletter*, which was now sounding like the house organ of the Republican State Central Committee, reported appreciatively on the Democratic disarray.* Capitalizing on Republican legislative control, the CPOA sponsored over 60 law-and-order bills, three times the number of past years.[193] Many "very significant" bills, and half overall, became law. This was enough for the lobby to characterize the 1969 session as law enforcement's "most successful legislative endeavor."[194] To Coleman Blease, ACLU legislative representative, the session was "lengthy, quarrelsome, and productive of little but regressive measures":

> Individual liberties . . . were stretched or mutilated, as if on the legendary bed of Procrustes, to make them conform to currently hawked notions of law and order.[195]

These divergent assessments were carried into 1970. The civil liberties lobby expected another dismal year. Whereas Sheriff Peter J. Pitchess of Los Angeles County reflected optimistically:

> Law enforcement is currently receiving a great deal of positive attention in Sacramento and there is every indication that this attitude on the part of the Legislature is ascending. Obviously, now is the time to introduce pro–law enforcement legislation with which we may have had difficulty in obtaining passage in the past.[196]

In this traditional sense, 1970 was sure to be another "banner year" for the law enforcement lobby. As the 1960s drew to a close, however, its ambitions were soaring beyond passage of the piecemeal "pro–law enforcement legislation" it had sought in the past. As the new decade opened, it remained to be seen whether the lobby's reach would exceed its grasp.

1970: SCA 24 and SB 857, Law Enforcement's Abortive "Reconstruction of the Criminal Jury System" [197]

The 1970 legislative session opened just as the 1969 session had closed. Republicans were in control, and the law enforcement lobby was emboldened with success. Besides earlier victories surrounding Penal Code

---

* Indeed, on one occasion Democratic legislators futilely pushing a moderating amendment to a successful 1969 bill affecting the disclosure of the identity of narcotics informants had the vote on the amendment expunged from the record so that the "folks back home" would never know that their support for the legislation had ever been less than 100%.

legislation, three additional factors fed a growing law enforcement optimism that would soon inspire an assault on the fundamental right of trial by jury.

First, in the interim between the 1969 and 1970 sessions, the law enforcement lobby helped purge the staff of the State's Penal Code Revision Project. After 5 years, the project was about to offer a blueprint for the first systematic updating of California's substantive criminal law in just under a century. In ordering a mass dismissal, Republican Donald Grunsky, Chairman of the Joint Legislative Committee for Revision of the Penal Code, praised the staff's hard work but damned its drafts as "far too liberal," "visionary," and "ready to legalize pot."[198]

Grunsky's action was the triumphant culmination of a year-long crusade against "ultra liberal law professors" by the California law enforcement establishment. The CPOA had originally been dissatisfied when only two seats on the Project's eight-member Advisory Board were set aside for District Attorneys. While pressuring the 1969 legislature for additional law enforcement representation, the CPOA created its own Penal Code Revision Committee, ostensibly "to evaluate, report, and recommend support or disapproval . . . of suggested changes." Actually, this committee worked energetically behind the scenes to have the Penal Code Revision project "terminated . . . before any final drafts can be presented for consideration." [199] Later testimony on marijuana legalization from Sheriff John Misterly of Sacramento County gives some notion of the hostility liberal academics could generate:

> Dr. Timothy Leary and Angelo Mead (individuals educated far beyond their intelligence) that go out there and advocate its use with no basis whatsoever. Here is a woman that is an anthropologist. She should be dusting off bones in the middle of the African desert somewhere. She is out there hollering to make it legal for 16 year old kids and over. Now, this is stupidity. Timothy Leary, a psycho, if I have ever seen one anywhere. "Make it legal; it is wonderful stuff."[200] *

* This quote should not be taken to mean that Misterly, with a career in narcotics enforcement stretching back to 1942, could not draw upon his wealth of practical experience to make shrewd and discriminating arguments in support of his tough law-and-order views. For example, he scored tellingly in the same hearings against both academics and legislators in favor of such "compromise solutions" as continuing the criminal sanction against marijuana use while reducing the penalty to a "straight misdemeanor." His argument was that, in terms of the realities of criminal law enforcement, the impact of such a reduction would verge on total legalization because misdemeanor arrests made without a warrant are valid only when the offense is committed under the eyes of the arresting officer; this requirement would, of course, make it virtually impossible to make a *legal* arrest for marijuana use "in private."

The ten men on the staff, of course, had little in common with "Angelo" Mead, let alone Timothy Leary. Arthur Sherry, the project director, had been a Deputy District Attorney and Assistant Attorney General before he became a "liberal academic." [201] More sophisticated products of the law enforcement establishment like Edwin Meese (Reagan's Legal Affairs aide) recognized such distinctions. But Meese's evaluation of what universities could then contribute was essentially the same:

[For] several years under the deanship of O. W. Wilson, who later became superintendent of police in Chicago, and is now retired and living in California again, the University of California's Criminology School at Berkeley produced some of the outstanding police executives of the nation. The International Association of Chiefs of Police Headquarters in New York was staffed about 50% by Californians because of this, and they were able to utilize their expertise in advising police departments throughout the country. Recently the new commissioners of the newly formed Bureau of Narcotics and Drug Abuse, formed under the Department of Justice, picked as its commissioner a graduate of the University of California, Jack Ingersoll. Mr. Ingersoll had served in the Oakland Police Department; had been a faculty member at Berkeley; and later on became Chief of Police at about the age of 36 in Charlotte, North Carolina; and was recently promoted to this position as commissioner. This is the quality that we have received in the past and, for some reason, we no longer have those kinds of people being turned out of Berkeley. . . . I think they have fallen down in a number of fields.[202]

While the Penal Code Revision Project was not aborted, its political complexion was totally altered. Grunsky replaced liberal academics with law enforcement professionals unencumbered by scholarly reputations.[203]

A second cause of law enforcement boldness was a growing confidence in technological solutions to crime and unrest; some forms of specialized knowledge and expertise were exempted from the lobby's sweeping hostility toward most contemporary academics. The CPOA, long an advocate of police professionalism and technical innovation, had established a working relationship with the Systems Development Corporation of Santa Monica as early as 1963. This was years before such law-and-order "think-tanks" began to emerge nationally in conjunction with the 1968 Omnibus Crime Control Act.[204]

The Systems Development Corporation (SDC)* was the brainchild of William Herrmann and came to specialize in the "domestic application" of counterinsurgency research:

* SDC had a payroll of over 1000 "datacrats" by the late 1960s.

Terrorism leads to a clampdown and so to charges of repression. The remedy is to split off those bent on destroying the system from the mass of dissenters, then, following classic guerrilla warfare theory, to find means which will win their hearts and minds.[205]

In 1970, Herrmann's words found concrete embodiment in a report he produced as head of Ronald Reagan's Task Force on Riots and Disorders. The report, which soon became a cornerstone in the California "war on crime," was the source of proposals for blanket electronic surveillance, computer data banks, preventive detention, and "emergency power" acts.[206]

The third cause of law enforcement optimism was a growing realization of their grass-roots political power. The dialectic of radical protest and conservative reaction had by 1970 generated unprecedented police militancy. Among the rank and file, this produced a revolt that forced PORAC* to drop both its no-strike pledge and regulation against political endorsements. However, PORAC continued its traditional emphasis on the "bread-and-butter" issues of police salaries and working conditions. In contrast, the CPOA translated the new militancy into heightened political involvement in contests with higher stakes. We turn now to the 1970 legislative session, the arena in which this contest would be fought.[207]

To the law enforcement lobby, the criminal jury system seemed an ideal target. A concerted attack on the jury system would cement the lobby's alliance with the Reagan administration as well as shifting the balance of power within the criminal justice system. How better to insure the support of both fiscal conservatives and law-and-order partisans than to attack a system that was as "inefficient" in its dollars-and-cents operations as it was "uncertain" in its conviction-producing results?[208]

All that was needed was a constitutional opening. The CPOA hoped to produce such a breach by sponsoring Republican Gordon Cologne's SCA 24 and SB 857, a proposed constitutional amendment plus an enabling statute, permitting a 10 to 2 verdict in all criminal cases. Supporters argued that a "reconstruction of the criminal jury system" would eliminate "the log jam created in the Superior Courts of this State through the ever-increasing number of hung juries." Hence, they anticipated the Berger Court which later held that 12-person criminal juries† and unanimous verdicts‡ were not mandated by the Bill of Rights. Reagan strongly supported the proposed constitutional amendment and warned the 1970 State Bar con-

---

* PORAC was a benevolent and mutual benefit organization to which 27,000 of California's 32,000 law officers belonged in 1971.
† *Williams* v. *Florida* (399 U.S. 78 [1970]).
‡ *Johnson* v. *Louisiana* (92 S. Ct. 1620 [1972]).

vention that "the jungle was closing in" because judges and juries had failed to put "their house in order." [209]

Yet all this lobbying proved to no avail. SCA 24 was consigned to interim study by the Senate Judiciary Committee. SB 857 was totally transformed by amendments on the Senate floor, emerging as a statute aimed at disruptive defendants, rather than at jury size. The Assembly Criminal Procedure Committee compounded these disappointments by killing ambitious CPOA initiatives on preventive detention and court-authorized wiretapping.[210]

A key to the legislature's reactions was the changing attitude of the State Bar. Both the Reagan administration and the law enforcement lobby had cultivated the support of the Bar's Board of Governors during the Governor's first 3 years in office. They succeeded to the extent that, in 1968, Herbert Ellingwood of the CPOA also served as the Bar's legislative advocate in Sacramento. The fruits of this collaboration were Judicial Selection Acts which Reagan had introduced for 3 consecutive years. Heartened by the prospect of controlling judicial appointments, the Bar's leadership endorsed the Judicial Merit Plan incorporated in these acts despite the disquieting anticourt rhetoric in which it was packaged.

Supported by the Bar, by efforts of the almost legendary public relations firm of Witaker and Baxter, and even by Standard Oil of California, the Merit Plan had in 1968 fallen just one vote short of the two-thirds needed to pass the Senate. The main stumbling block had been lawyer-legislators who feared (not without reason) that the new selection plan would virtually eliminate their chances for judicial preferment.[211]

In 1969, however, Bar support for this and other law enforcement innovations sponsored by Reagan began to erode. September of 1969 witnessed a "revolt of the masses" by the rank-and-file Conference of Delegates that shattered the Bar's veneer of "conservative unity." The Bar's Board of Governors was forced, if not to "radicalize" their political stance, at least to return to the "politics of dead center." Delegate votes for abolition of the death penalty, decriminalization of marijuana, and legal toleration of private sex acts between consenting adults all demanded of the Board some form of appeasement. In 1970 the appeasement was the Board's "courageous" stand against legalized wiretapping, the law enforcement lobby's top priority for the year. This "unexpected opposition," wrote CPOA lobbyist Carl Anderson, "shocked us all." [212]

By the standards the CPOA had once used to judge legislative success, 1970 was certainly a successful year for the law enforcement lobby. Of the 55 bills comprising the CPOA's "affirmative program," 30 were signed into law, while all major "opposition measures" were either defeated or vetoed. Nevertheless, the surprise that Carl Anderson expressed reflected a more general CPOA disappointment caused by expectations that had outrun achievements.[213]

Anderson's counterpart on the FCL wisecracked that he was unable to characterize the 1970 California legislature. Since Democratic Assembly-man Willie Brown had used the word "disaster" to describe the previous session, there was "no word adequate" for the current one. Yet this remark left unstated an essential point. Even at this high-water mark of law-and-order sentiment, legislators refused to change fundamentally what the ACLU called the "historic character" of the criminal justice system. California's lawmakers were here reflecting the same ambivalence that expressed itself in national polls. A pervasive but amorphous anxiety over crime had failed to translate into mass support for any of the "radical" constitutional departures advanced by the law enforcement lobby.[214]

More fundamentally, the legislature's "conservative" defense of the jury's unanimity rule indicated an underlying difference in priorities even between law enforcement groups and many law-and-order legislators. More attuned to the political ramifications of crime than to the administrative ramifications of enforcement, the legislature responded to the public mood of the 1960s by making criminal law more punitive. The law enforcement lobby, on the other hand, had always placed highest priority not on penalties but on crucial procedural questions that defined "the rules," and thereby the outcome, of the criminal justice process. By late in the decade, the gap was even wider. The lobby's trajectory had led it beyond limited demand for rule revisions to urging a more basic change in the criminal justice system. Here they parted company even with old-fashioned conservatives, who drew the line at such a substantive assault on constitutionally mandated civil liberties.[215]

By the end of 1970, it was becoming increasingly clear to law enforcement interests that far-reaching structural change could be achieved only *outside* the legislature, through statewide initiatives and referendum campaigns. The success of such efforts would depend, however, on the mood of the California electorate. And November 1970 was to bring political results that, despite Ronald Reagan's reelection victory, would severely jolt the state Republican party as well as the law enforcement lobby, casting a shadow over the future of both.[216]

1971: AB 1811, The Vetoed Penal Ombudsman Bill[217]

When 1970 began, the air was heavily laden with predictions that a right-wing ice age was about to overtake California. During the year, Brian Chapman's *Police State* appeared; and though generalizing from European experience, it was not without speculative applications to the American scene:

A regime's deliberate and sustained attempt to harness, for its own un-
avowed purposes, the policeman's innate desire for order, coherence and
form unhinges the virtue and leaves only the vice. The policeman who was
a soldier becomes a hired assassin; he who was a priest becomes a clinical
psychologist; and the one who was an artist becomes a predator.[218]

Such dire predictions overlooked the political constraints within Reagan's
own law-and-order constituency. Despite the extreme "war-on-crime" rhetoric, fundamental movement toward a "police state" (or in any other
direction) was checked by visceral conservatism and a bedrock commitment to fiscal orthodoxy. However, the implicit limits of law-and-orderism
did little to cheer despairing liberals. While facism might not be in the
immediate offing, conservative dominance seemed to be. What liberals
needed was a "good election." [219]

At least partly, the fall of 1970 provided the necessary tonic. Although
Ronald Reagan was reelected by a half-million votes, his margin was only
one-half of the 1966 landslide. Indeed, it even fell nearly a 100,000 shy of
the plurality for Democrat John Tunney, who had been given little chance
of defeating George Murphy, the conservative Republican candidate, several months earlier. And, beneath the surface of Reagan's personal triumph
over Unruh, Reagan's party lay in shambles. Not only did the Republicans
lose their incumbent U.S. Senator, they also lost control of both houses of
the state legislature. During the campaign, both Unruh and Tunney had
attempted to defuse the law-and-order issue by proposing their own programs to fight crime. But the key to Democratic resurgence was the economic reality behind Labor Department statistics showing a state unemployment rate above 7%. Law-and-order concerns had taken a back seat.[220]

The economic issue revitalized liberal Democratic fortunes. They gained
slim but working legislative majorities: 21 to 19 in the State Senate, and
43 to 37 in the Assembly. And though criminal justice was not the dominant campaign issue, the change in legislative leadership had consequences
for the criminal lawmaking process. To begin, the new Assembly Speaker
was Robert Moretti, 34 years old and an Unruh protégé. During his first
2 years of legislative service, Moretti had made peace with rising law-and-
order sentiment by authoring a compromise antiriot bill and by cospon-
soring (with Republican George Deukmejian) legislation creating the
California Council on Criminal Justice. However, on the day-in, day-out
votes, Moretti's overall performance was good enough to win an 88%
approval rating from the FCL.[221]

As Speaker, his appointments to the Assembly Committee on Criminal
Procedure * reflected the same cautiously liberal bent. He followed Unruh's

---

* Renamed in 1971 the Assembly Committee on Criminal Justice.

1967 precedent by appointing Republican moderate Robert Beverly to the chairmanship and was thus able to claim that "the battle against crime and violence is a nonpartisan issue." But whereas Unruh had had to be satisfied with the "veto power" of a 5 to 5 partisan–ideological split, Moretti's appointments gave liberal Democrats a 5 to 4 majority. On several dramatic occasions during the 1971 session, this majority voted out of committee controversial legislation (including the first capital punishment repealer to reach the Assembly floor since 1961) that would otherwise have quietly died.[222]

Proposals for changing the correctional system constituted the largest order of business before the committee. Building since the late 1960s, interest in correctional reform inspired the introduction of nearly 150 separate pieces of legislation in the 1971 session. As in years past, the chief targets were the personnel and policies of the Adult Authority.* One major proposal called for increasing its membership from 9 to 12, another called for streamlining the Authority down to 5. Both, however, captured liberal intent by guaranteeing seats for legal and social-science experts and thereby preventing any future Governor from packing the Adult Authority with law enforcement personnel. Even more far-reaching were proposals laying down guidelines for the Authority's powers over sentencing and parole. One bill, however, stood out in 1971 in its attempt to increase legislative control over the corrections system. This was AB 1811, Republican Frank Murphy's proposal to establish an Office of Ombudsman for Corrections.[223]

Groundwork for AB 1811 had been laid during the previous session, a session whose opening coincided with the deaths of three black Soledad inmates and whose closing immediately preceded the strike–lockup that paralyzed Folsom Prison. In July of 1970 a group of black legislators issued a report on "Treatment of Prisoners at California Training Facility at Soledad Central," which recommended that the legislature:

> create a full-time salaried board of overseers for the state prisons. The Board would be responsible for evaluating allegations made by inmates, their families, friends, and lawyers against employees charged with acting inhumanely, illegally, or unreasonably.[224]

The favorable response to this report by the Criminal Procedure Committee, which in 1970 was still under Republican control, might appear anomalous. But Republicans too saw corrections beset by fundamental problems. Appalled by steadily rising expenditures and incessant demands

---

* The Adult Authority is an administrative arm of the Corrections System with responsibility for implementing the indeterminate sentence statutes and setting parole dates. Members of the Adult Authority are appointed by the Governor.

for larger capital outlays, the 1969 legislature had ordered a study of the fundamental fiscal and philosophical premises of California's prison system. In 1970 responsibility for that study was given to the Assembly's newly created Select Committee on the Administration of Justice, chaired by Minority Floor Leader Craig Biddle. The result was a report titled *Order Out of Chaos*, a devastating critique of California parole practices. Following on its heels was a Committee-sponsored bill demanding sweeping changes, and only the most strenuous lobbying by the Governor's Office prevented the bill from passing.[225]

Still, the pressures for correctional change were too great for either the Governor or the corrections bureaucracy to ignore totally. Admitting that "perhaps the thrust of the seventies should be in the correctional system," Reagan, in his State of the State Message, proposed "an immediate, major, in-depth study of all correctional processes in California." Early in 1971 the report appeared; it called for closing down Folsom and San Quentin as well as thoroughly overhauling prison and parole administration.

Corrections officials were painfully aware of the mounting pressure. As early as the spring of 1970 the Adult Authority had begun to move toward "self-reform," if only to avert legislative initiatives that would drastically curtail its powers. The fruit of this self-reform was the contingency parole plan, promptly granting most new state prisoners a tentative parole date and a program for "earning" release. The FCL had to admit that the plan would "meet the sharpest complaints against the Adult Authority" if carried out effectively.[226]

Though far from ending complaints, the promised parole procedures did reduce criticism to some extent. It was now more difficult to depict the correctional system as a "pathological bureaucracy" incapable of putting its own house in order. But political maneuvering was not the only motivation behind self-reform. As David Rothman remarked:

> It is not just academic students of criminal incarceration who despair of the penal system. Those in charge of the prisons, from wardens and corrections commissioners to state legislators, also share an incredibly high degree of self-doubt, ambivalence, dismay, and even guilt over prison operations.[227]

Hence, by the opening of the 1971 legislative session, bipartisan pressure suggested that major change in California's correctional system was in the offing. However, only a month prior to Attica, California experienced an ugly outburst at San Quentin, in which three prisoners died. While the long-range impact was to add fuel for reform, the immediate reaction was different. San Quentin and Attica had put a new weapon in the hands of the correctional bureaucrats, who now lobbied against major change in the midst of crisis.* This proved so effective that, of the many penal reform measures introduced in 1971, Murphy's Penal Ombudsman was but one of a handful ever reaching the Governor's desk.[228]

The details of the bill had taken shape in the short interim between the 1970 and 1971 sessions, when the Assembly's key criminal lawmaking committee was still called Criminal Procedure and when the Republican Murphy was still chairman. "Perhaps the single most important feature" of the proposal, according to a brief in its favor, was that the Ombudsman would have "no power himself to alter administrative decisions." Rather than "an attack on corrections" it would be a "complement to the present state of the art," a "safety valve" and "fail-safe device" to supplement existing "prison complaint-handling mechanisms (internal grievance procedures)."[229]

Such modest advocacy played a vital role in winning enough conservative Republican votes to ensure passage.† However, opponents who characterized AB 1811 as "bold and sweeping" were closer to the truth. The bill would have created not only an independent investigator of prisoner grievances but a Joint Legislative Committee on Corrections Administration with the Ombudsman as its right arm. Chosen by the Joint Committee, the Ombudsman was to assist it in analyzing correctional operations and recommending legislative changes. Clearly, the potential existed for the Ombudsman to become a counterpart of the Office of Legislative Analyst. As an attempt to monitor and regulate certain day-to-day correctional practices, Murphy's bill constituted a greater challenge to the correctional bureaucracy, and to the executive branch in general, than proposals that called "only" for changing the personnel and policies of the Adult Authority. Hence, it was not surprising that the Governor's Office and corrections officials vehemently opposed the bill, nor that Governor Reagan eventually vetoed it.[230]‡

It was indicative of a general trend that the aspect of the 1971 session (damned by CPOA as "one of the worst in history") the law enforcement lobby could most praise was a string of Reagan vetoes. Law enforcement successes were largely obstructionist; a bill imposing some restrictions on pretrial appellate review was virtually the only major legislation whose

---

* The San Quentin uprising did not occur until well into the 1971 session. However, a bitter struggle over reapportionment delayed the consideration of legislation and hence played into the hands of reform opponents. When corrections reform finally was considered, it was too late.

† The partisan and ideological balance was still too close to allow passage of such significant legislation without bipartisan support.

‡ The Governor's arm twisting got a majority of Republicans, though not a monolithic one, to vote against AB 1811.

passage gave the CPOA any real satisfaction. Its origins, however, constituted further evidence of law enforcement dependence on the executive branch. The primary force behind the bill was Evelle J. Younger who, in November 1970, had won an eyelash victory to become the state's first Republican Attorney General in 20 years.[231]

By wedding their fortunes to those of Younger,* the law enforcement lobby had come full circle. As in the early 1950s they were again very much dependent on the Attorney General's Office for political support. However, they now had a whole range of new political tactics that offered hope of escape from permanent subordination and were not about to accept passively a subordinate role. Thoroughly appalled by the "absolute disinterest" the 1971 legislature had shown in legalized wiretapping, the CPOA began as early as April to prepare a 1972 initiative to take "the fight directly to the people." Within a year, a decision by the California Supreme Court† would rechannel this campaign into an ultimately successful attempt to restore the death penalty. Nevertheless, a broad conclusion seems clear. After a generation of effort, law enforcement interests still were not automatically able to call the tune inside the California legislature.[232]

Ironically, leading civil liberties groups were almost as negative in their assessments of the 1971 session as the law enforcement lobby. The legislature had proved reluctant to challenge openly the public's law-and-order concerns, and gubernatorial vetoes had done the rest of the damage. Yet, while civil liberties were also being ignored at the national level, there were some hopeful signs in California. The social and racial turmoil that had fed the public's preoccupation with law and order had peaked. Law enforcement, guilty of political hubris, was being viewed more skeptically, sometimes even by conservative legislators. Indeed, the entire legislature seemed a bit more sensitive to civil-libertarian and reform-oriented priorities. In short, there was some reason to believe that the passage of the Penal Ombudsman Bill was no fluke and that the pendulum had begun to swing back, however slightly.[233]

Summary and Conclusions

In the early 1950s, California politics was only beginning to emerge from two generations of party anemia. The making of its criminal law remained narrowly circumscribed within an "agreed bill" process that generally prevented wider participation even in major issues. Lacking more than a rudimentary ability to initiate and shape policy, legislators still followed the

* Even Younger was too moderate in his conservatism to have been the CPOA's first choice for Attorney General.

† *People* v. *Anderson*, (6 Cal. 3rd 628 [1972]).

lead of major criminal justice lobbies. The lobbies in turn rarely ventured beyond the traditional elite model of criminal justice lawmaking. Partisan political alliances and appeals for mass ideological support were as yet almost unknown.

But by the decade's end, California had begun to move toward stronger party organization and greater legislative independence. And criminal justice issues were becoming more salient. 1957 saw a first attempt by law enforcement interests to challenge the California Supreme Court and its trailblazing criminal justice rulings. 1959 was characterized by the confident partisanship of the victorious Democrats and the deepening legislative involvement of the civil liberties lobby. 1961 owed its distinctiveness to an eruption of antinarcotics hysteria and liberal reversals. 1963 witnessed a general escalation of conflict over criminal justice issues as the due-process revolution continued to gain momentum. Criminal justice lobbies on each side reacted with particular intensity. 1965, with Berkeley and Watts, was the crucible in which the ideology of law and order really took shape. Capitalizing on this issue, Republicans restored their political fortunes. 1967 and 1968, though dominated on the rhetorical level by law-and-orderism and Reagan Republicans, proved less important for concrete criminal justice enactments than for the polarization of debates about crime. The controversy helped complete the new and highly partisan nature of California's political system. 1969 and 1970 gave Republicans legislative control and witnessed some significant breakthroughs on the law-and-order front. Nothing happened, however, to dismantle the evolving machinery for legislative investigation and policy initiation that was turning out studies and proposals usually pointing in quite a different direction. 1971, the year Democrats regained legislative control, brought a heightened attack on an increasingly defensive correctional system. Law-and-order forces enjoyed a firm grip on the criminal justice bureaucracy through the Executive branch, but at least in the legislative arena, it appeared that the power had peaked. To assist the reader, these and other changes are summarized in Table 2.3.

Several interrelated trends can be abstracted from this chronology. First, consistent with patterns across most legislative areas, criminal justice lobbying opened up to a wider range of groups. The elite or professional model of legislation faded and the negotiation process became far more complicated. Backroom deals were not of less import; rather, there were more dealers, as participants became more diverse. Floor votes, however, still reflected largely the "agreed bill" process.

Second, with wider participation came greater polarization. Two components were involved: partisanship and ideology. After the early 1960s, both parties were able to command significant discipline within committees and on the floor, while party label almost automatically began to carry with

TABLE 2.3

Historical Summary of the California Legislature, 1955-1971

Session	1955	1957	1959	1961	1963	1965	1967	1968	1969	1970	1971
Governor	Knight	Knight	Brown	Brown	Brown	Brown	Reagan	Reagan	Reagan	Reagan	Reagan
Assembly control	Republican	Republican	Democratic	Democratic	Democratic	Democratic	Democratic	Democratic	Republican	Republican	Democratic
Assembly committee control[a]	Republican	Republican	Democratic	Democratic	Democratic	Democratic	Even	Even	Republican	Republican	Democratic
Senate control	Republican	Republican	Democratic	Democratic	Democratic	Democratic	Democratic	Democratic	Republican	Republican	Democratic
Senate committee control[a]	Republican	Republican	Republican	Democratic	Democratic	Democratic	Republican	Republican	Republican	Republican	Democratic
Partisanship	Low	Low	Low	Moderate	High	High	High	High	High	High	High
Law enforcement lobby (LEL) activity	Low	Moderate	Low	High	Moderate	High	Moderate	Moderate	High	High	High
Civil liberties lobby (CLL) activity	Low	Low	Low	Moderate	Moderate	Moderate	Moderate	Moderate	Moderate	Moderate	Moderate
Important legislative issues	None	Easy Arrest package	Regulation of arrest practices	Reagan-Dills drug control package including civil commitment	Many liberal bills, e.g. anti-bugging	Campus disorder; increases in criminalization	Reagan's six point anti-crime package	Prisoner's Rights	Obscenity, pornography	Attack on jury system	Attack on Adult Authority
Important events	*Cahan* decision	CPOA attack on exclusionary rule	Democratic ascendancy; CPOA political isolation	Drug hysteria; public relations offensive; Democrats on defensive; *Mapp* decision	Unruh speaker; Democrats solidify control; drug issue abates; *Gideon* decision	Berkeley; Watts; fair housing at issue; conservative offensive	Reagan victory; law and order initiative; *Dorado* decision	AOR report on corrections; national and state elections	Continuing student strikes at San Francisco State and Berkeley	Police militancy; State Bar defections from CPOA; Soledad murders; Folsom strike	Democrats regain control of legislature; San Quentin riots
Outcome	Inactive session	Small LEL victories	Small CLL victories	Moderate LEL victories	Large CLL victories	Large LEL victories	Moderate LEL victories	Small LEL victories	Large LEL victories	Moderate LEL victories	Draw

[a] Legislative committee to which proposed Penal Code revisions are referred.

it certain positions. Typically, "party lines" were eclectic mixtures of beliefs, often complicated by self-contradictions, but they managed to identify
"good guys" and "bad guys" nevertheless. With good guys and bad guys
came knee-jerk rhetoric, and by the late 1960s legislators often seemed to
be talking more and listening less. One critical consequence was a virtual
stalemate between liberals and conservatives in many areas of criminal
lawmaking.

Third, while wider participation and increasing polarization were "depro-
fessionalizing" the legislative process, reform within the legislature was
slowly introducing a countertrend. As the legislature gained more resources,
there were signs of growth in self-confidence and independence. By the late
1960s, committees had begun to shape policy and take legislative initiative.
Legislators began to see themselves as experts not only on winning elections
but on substantive issues as well. At least part of the time, data replaced
speculation; considered judgments, empty rhetoric. Overall, the legislature
grew in stature and began to demonstrate significant leadership in the criminal justice lawmaking process. Inevitably, this took some initiative away
from lobbies and the executive branch.

Fourth, given the range of contending interests active in Sacramento, it
would be hard to argue that any one party or group dominated the scene
over the 15 years of our study. Parties rose and fell in influence with about
the same frequency as lobby groups. The late 1950s saw Democratic fortunes soar, as Democrats wrested control from the Republicans. The courts
seemed to be ruling in favor of wide-ranging liberal causes, and civil liberties
groups were winning on several fronts. Still, as in the 1961 antidrug campaign, law enforcement interests could counterpunch with effect. By the
late 1960s, Berkeley, Watts, and the law-and-order issue had helped cata-
pult the Republicans into power. And yet, despite the conservative victories,
liberals often held their own. Recall how in 1968 moderate Republicans
and liberal Democrats managed to pass civil liberties legislation returning
some important rights to prisoners. By 1971, the pendulum seemed to be
swinging back somewhat toward the liberals, but the potential for domination by any one group appeared rather slim.

The really important issue is what all this has to do with our primary
question. What is the source of criminal law? In the most immediate sense,
our examination of the California legislature has begun to provide an answer. We have seen a variety of bureaucratic, ideological, and political
forces converge on Sacramento and have noted how such pressures can
shape the evolving Penal Code. What is missing is a more abstract assessment of how this process works and where these outside forces come from.
That discussion will be postponed until more data have been presented.

REFERENCES

1. Totten J. Anderson, "California: Enigma of National Politics," in *Western Politics* ed. Frank H. Jonas (Salt Lake City: University of Utah Press, 1961), p. 97; Leonard Pitt, *The Decline of the Californios: A Social History of the Spanish-Speaking Californians, 1846–1890* (Berkeley: University of California Press, 1971), p. 60; Oscar Lewis, *The Big Four* (New York: Alfred A. Knopf, 1938), *passim*; George E. Mowry, *The California Progressives* (Berkeley: University of California Press, 1951), *passim*; Spencer C. Olin, Jr., *California Prodigal Sons: Hiram Johnson and the Progressive Movement, 1911–1917* (Berkeley: University of California Press, 1968), *passim*; Elmer R. Rusco, "Machine Politics, California Model: Arthur H. Samish and the Alcoholic Beverage Industry" (unpublished Ph.D. thesis, University of California, Berkeley, 1960), *passim*.

2. William Buchanan, *Legislative Partisanship: The Deviant Case of California* (Berkeley: University of California Press, 1963), pp. 28–48; Lou Cannon, *Ronnie and Jesse: A Political Odyssey* (Garden City, New York: Doubleday and Company, 1969), pp. 44–57, 91–105, *et passim*; Duane Lockard, *The Politics of State and Local Government*, 2d ed. (New York: Macmillan Company, 1969), p. 276.

3. "Legislative Committees Lean on the PUC," *California Journal* April, 1971, pp. 104–108; John R. Owens, Edmund Constantini, and Louis F. Weschler, *California Politics and Parties* (New York: Macmillan Company, 1970), pp. 246–249 *et passim*; Donald R. Hall, *Cooperative Lobbying: The Power of Pressure* (Tucson: University of Arizona Press, 1969), p. xi *et passim*; Edgar Lane, *Lobbying and the Law* (Berkeley: University of California Press, 1964), p. 8; Robert C. Fellmeth (project director), *Politics of Land: Ralph Nader's Study Group Report on Land Use in California* (New York: Grossman Publishers, 1973), pp. 457–463 *et passim*; "Lobbying the Legislature: Facts, Friendship, Favors, and Flim-Flam," *California Journal* August, 1972, pp. 212–216. See also the list of *Legislative Advocates and Organizations* published annually by the California legislature.

4. John C. Wahlke, Heinz Eulau, William Buchanan, and Leroy C. Ferguson, *The Legislative System: Explorations in Legislative Behavior* (New York: John Wiley and Sons, 1962), pp. 311–312; Owens et al., *California Politics*, pp. 256–257.

5. Philip Taft, *Labor Politics American Style: The California State Federation of Labor* (Cambridge, Massachusetts: Harvard University Press, 1968), *passim*; Frank A. Pinner, Paul Jacobs, and Philip Selznick, *Old Age and Political Behavior: A Case Study* (Berkeley: University of California Press, 1969), *passim*; Jackson K. Putnam, *Old-Age Politics in California: From Richardson to Reagan* (Stanford, California: Stanford University Press, 1970), *passim*; Daniel A. Berry, "The California Teachers Association: An Interest Group in California Politics" (unpublished M.A. thesis, University of California, Berkeley, 1958), *passim*; Robert J. Marsolais, "Forces Which Produce Educational Legislation in California: An Exploratory Study of the Miller–Unruh Basic Reading Act of 1965" (unpublished Ph.D. thesis, University of Southern California, 1969), *passim*; Eugene Bardach, *The Skill Factor in Politics: Repealing the Mental Commitment Laws in California* (Berkeley: University of California Press, 1972), *passim*; John P. Kenney, *The California Police* (Springfield, Illinois: Charles C. Thomas, 1964), pp. 123–127; Francis M. Carney, "Methods of the American Civil Liberties Union of Northern California" (unpublished M.A. thesis, Stanford University, 1949), *passim*; Corinne

L. Gilb, "Self-Regulating Professions and the Public Welfare: A Case Study of the California State Bar" (unpublished Ph.D. thesis, Radcliffe College, 1956), pp. 26–78.

6. Malcolm Jewell, *The State Legislature* (New York: Random House, 1962), pp. 101–102; Gilbert Y. Steiner and Samuel K. Grove, *Legislative Politics in Illinois* (Urbana: University of Illinois Press, 1960), pp. 62, 65, *et passim*; Dayton D. McKean, "A State Legislature and Group Pressures," *Annals of the American Academy of Political and Social Science*, Vol. 179 (May, 1935), p. 127; J. A. C. Grant, "The Introduction of Bills," *ibid.*, Vol. 195 (January, 1938), pp. 116–117; Buchanan, *Legislative Partisanship*, pp. 59–62, 98, 104, *et passim*; Wahlke *et al.*, *Legislative System*, pp. 50–51, 59–61, 145–152, *et passim*; George Goodwin, Jr., *The Little Legislatures: Committees of Congress* (University of Massachusetts Press, 1970), *passim*.

7. Buchanan, *Legislative Partisanship*, pp. 33–34; Arthur H. Samish and Bob Thomas, *The Secret Boss of California* (New York: Crown Publishers, 1971), p. 135 *et passim*; Alexander Cloner and Richard W. Gable, "The California Legislator and the Problem of Compensation," *Western Political Quarterly*, Vol. 12 (September, 1959), pp. 712–726; Cannon, *Ronnie and Jesse*, pp. 66–67, 97, 198, 203–205; Neal R. Peirce, *The Megastates of America: People, Politics, and Power in the Ten Great States* (New York: W. W. Norton, 1972), p. 595; Edward L. Barrett, Jr., *The Tenney Committee: Legislative Investigation of Subversive Activities in California* (Ithaca, New York: Cornell University Press, 1951), *passim*; Robert E. G. Harris, "The Busy Little Men in Sacramento," *Frontier*, Vol. 6 (July, 1955), p. 8; "Legislative Staff of 1500 provides Administrative Support and Professional Aid to Lawmakers," *California Journal* April, 1971, pp. 96–99, 114–115; Arthur Bolton, "Expanding the Power of State Legislatures," in *Strengthening the States: Essays on Legislative Reform*, ed. Donald G. Herzberg and Alan Rosenthal (Garden City, New York: Doubleday and Company, 1971), p. 61.

8. California State Sheriffs' Association, *Proceedings* (1949), p. 37; J. G. Woods, "The Progressives and the Police: Urban Reform and the Professionalization of the Los Angeles Police Department" (draft of unpublished Ph.D. thesis, University of California, Los Angeles, and the Institute on Law and Urban Studies, Loyola University Law School, 1973), p. 444. Samish and Thomas, *Secret Boss*, pp. 127, 179.

9. Franklin Hitchborn, "The Party, the Machine, and the Vote: The Story of Cross-Filing in California," *California Historical Society Quarterly*, Vol. 38 (December, 1959), pp. 349–359; *ibid.*, Vol. 39 (March, 1960), pp. 19–34; Charles M. Price, "Voting Alignments in the California Legislature: Roll-Call Analysis of the 1957–1959–1961 Sessions" (unpublished Ph.D. thesis, University of Southern California, 1965), *passim*; Cannon, *Ronnie and Jesse*, *passim*.

10. Melvin H. Bernstein, "Political Leadership in California: A Study of Four Governors" (unpublished Ph.D. thesis, University of California, Los Angeles, 1970), pp. 149–213.

11. Buchanan, *Legislative Partisanship*, pp. 58, 63; Royce D. Delmatier, "The Rebirth of the Democratic Party in California" (unpublished Ph.D. thesis, University of California, Berkeley, 1955), *passim*; Robert E. Burke, *Olson's New Deal for California* (Berkeley: University of California Press, 1953), *passim*; Richard B. Harvey, *Earl Warren: Governor of California* (New York: Exposition Press, 1969), *passim*.

12. Harvey, *Earl Warren*, pp. 109–111, 115, *et passim*; Wahlke *et al.*, *Legislative System*, pp. 45, 184, 356.

13. Buchanan, *Legislative Partisanship*, pp. 49–59, 61–74, *et passim*; Cannon, *Ronnie and Jesse*, pp. 94–96; *Sacramento Bee* March 10, 1955, p. 1; *ibid.*, March 28, 1955, pp. 1, 8; *ibid.*, June 9, 1955, pp. 1, 14; Friends Committee on Legislation (hereinafter FCL), *Newsletter*, February, 1955, p. 3; *ibid.*, December, 1956, p. 1; American Civil Liberties Union of South California (hereinafter ACLU of SC), *Open Forum*, March, 1955, p. 3; *ibid.*, May, 1953, p. 3; American Civil Liberties Union of Northern California (hereinafter ACLU of NC), *Union-News*, March, 1955, p. 3.

14. Robert Harris, "Busy Little Men," p. 9; *Review of Selected 1955 Code Legislation*, prepared by the Department of Continuing Education of the Bar of the University of California Extension for the Committee on Continuing Education of the Bar of the State of California (Regents of the University of California, 1955), pp. 185–187. The two bills were AB 87 and AB 1804, which became law as Chapters 1350 and 185, respectively, of the 1955 California *Statutes*.

15. *Review of Selected 1955 Code Legislation*, pp. 180–184. The four bills were (in the order in which their subject matter is mentioned in the text) AB 1224, AB 827, AB 1185, and SB 918. They became law as Chapters 873, 948, 1266, and 1862, respectively.

16. California State Peace Officers' Association (hereinafter CPOA), *California Peace Officer*, September–October, 1955, pp. 15, 48.

17. Benjamin M. Gross, *The Legislative Struggle: A Study in Social Combat* (New York: McGraw-Hill Book Company, 1953), p. 186; Buchanan, *Legislative Partisanship*, p. 145; Edwin M. Lemert, *Social Action and Legal Change: Revolution within the Juvenile Court* (Chicago: Aldine Publishing Company, 1970), p. 82.

18. Grant, "Introduction of Bills," pp. 18–19; Joseph A. Beek, *The California Legislature* (Sacramento: California State Printing Office, 1960), pp. 18–22; James D. Driscoll, *California's Legislature* (Sacramento: California State Printing Office, 1970), pp. 45–50, 80; CPOA, *California Peace Officer*, September–October, 1955, p. 15; *ibid.*, September–October, 1958), pp. C9–10; *ibid.*, September–October, 1969, p. C23.

19. *Sacramento Newsletter*, May 11, 1959, p. 1; *ibid.*, March 6, 1961, p. 1; *ibid.*, February 18, 1963, p. 1; CPOA, *California Peace Officer*, September–October, 1955, p. 15; ACLU of NC, *Union-News*, March, 1955, pp. 3–4; ACLU of SC, *Open Forum*, March, 1955, p. 3; FCL, *Newsletter*, March, 1955, pp. 2–3, 6; *Review of Selected 1955 Code Legislation*, pp. 180–187; Owens, *et al.*, *California Politics*, pp. 244–245, 346, *et passim*; Lemert, *Social Action*, pp. 108, 123.

20. For comparable figures for origination of legislation on the federal level, see: Lawrence H. Chamberlain, *The President, Congress, and Legislation* (New York: Columbia University Press, 1946), p. 453; Charles E. Lindblom, *The Policy-Making Process* (Englewood Cliffs, New Jersey: Prentice-Hall, 1968), p. 68. For executive agencies and legislative initiation in other states, see: Edwin E. Witte, "Administrative Agencies and Statute Law Making," *Public Administration Review*, Vol. 2 (Spring, 1942), p. 116 *et passim*; Elizabeth M. Scott and Belle Zeller, "State Agencies and Law Making," *ibid.*, p. 205 *et passim*.

21. Driscoll, *California's Legislature*, pp. 78–79; George S. Blair and Houston I. Flournoy, *Legislative Bodies in California* (Belmont, California: Dickenson Publishing Company, 1967), pp. 27–31; David R. Derge, "The Lawyer as Decision-

Maker in the American State Legislature," *Journal of Politics*, Vol. 21 (1959), p. 243; Corinne L. Gilb, *Hidden Hierarchies: The Professions and Government* (New York: Harper and Row, 1966), pp. 214–215.

22. Blair and Flournoy, *Legislative Bodies*, pp. 27, 31, et *passim*; Driscoll, *California's Legislature* pp. 73, 85–87, 94; California Legislature, Assembly, *Journal*, 1955, Vol. 1, p. 1176; *Sacramento Bee*, March 8, 1955, p. 16; *ibid.*, March 10, 1955, p. 10; CPOA, *California Peace Officer*, July–August, 1956, p. 53.

23. Wahlke *et al.*, p. 61.

24. California Legislature, Assembly, *Journal*, 1955–1971, *passim*; California Legislature, Senate, *Journal*, 1955–1971, *passim*. On the gradual development of partisanship, see, in addition to Buchanan's study: Robert K. Binford, "Party Cohesion in the California State Assembly, 1953–1963" (unpublished M.A. thesis, Stanford University, 1964), *passim*; Price, "Voting Alignments," *passim*.

25. AB 1857 became law as Chapter 2147 of the 1957 California *Statutes*. For the stages of its passage through the legislature see: California Legislature, Assembly, *Journal*, 1957, Vol. 4, p. 7842; and California Legislature, Senate, *Journal*, 1957, Vol. 3, p. 5291. The bill was introduced by Patrick O. McGee, a Republican lawyer–legislator from suburban Los Angeles; see the *Sacramento Bee*, August 12, 1957.

26. The fullest discussions of the evolution of AB 1857 and the implications of its provisions are: California Legislature, Senate, Interim Judiciary Committee, *Fourth Progress Report to the Legislature*, 1955–1957, *passim*; and California Legislature, Assembly, Interim Committee on Criminal Procedure, *1959–1961 Report*, *passim*.

27. California Legislature, Assembly, Interim Committee on Criminal Procedure, *1959–1961 Report*, Sections 8, 15.

28. See *ibid.*, Sections 10–11, 14; California Legislature, Senate, Interim Judiciary Committee, *Fourth Progress Report to the Legislature*, 1955–1957, Section 9.

29. For an analysis of the sections of the 1941 Uniform Arrest Act that parallel AB 1857, see Herbert L. Packer, *The Limits of the Criminal Sanction* (Stanford: Stanford University Press, 1968), pp. 182–185.

30. CPOA, *California Peace Officer*, July–August, 1956, pp. C17–18.

31. Alan F. Westin, "Bookies and 'Bugs' in California," in *The Uses of Power: Seven Case Studies in American Politics*, ed. Alan F. Westin (New York: Harcourt, Brace, and World, 1962), pp. 129–155 et *passim*; O. W. Wilson, ed., *Parker on Police* (Springfield, Illinois: Charles C. Thomas, 1957), pp. 99–131; CPOA, *California Peace Officer*, November–December, 1954, pp. 11, 21–22; *ibid.*, July–August, 1955, pp. 22–24.

32. For the range of police attitudes toward the exclusionary rule, see Jerome H. Skolnick, *Justice without Trial: Law Enforcement in Democratic Society* (New York: John Wiley and Sons, 1966), pp. 211–225. For interpretations that stress the threat posed to the professional self-image and status aspirations of the police by landmark court decisions in the due process area, see Harold E. Pepinsky, "A Theory of Police Reaction to *Miranda* v. *Arizona*," *Crime and Delinquency*, Vol. 16 (October, 1970); pp. 379–391; Albert J. Reiss, Jr., *The Police and the Public* (New Haven: Yale University Press, 1971) pp. 124–125 et *passim*. For the special sensitivity of the California police to such "symbolic" threats, see James Q. Wilson, *Varieties of Police Behavior: The Management of Law and Order in Eight Communities* (New York: Atheneum, 1970), pp. 192–193, 274–276, et *passim*; Lemert, *Social Action*, pp. 138, 140–141, 214–215. For examples of the more restrained, less denunciatory reaction to *Cahan* by California district attorneys, see: CPOA,

California Peace Officer, July–August, 1955, pp. C60–62; *ibid.*, November–December, 1955, p. 34; *ibid.*, July–August, 1957, pp. C23–24; ACLU of SC, *Open Forum*, January, 1956, p. 1. For studies of the limited and problematic character of the impact of Supreme Court decisions on the local level and especially on the police, see: Theodore Becker, ed., *The Impact of Supreme Court Decisions* (New York: Oxford University Press, 1969), *passim*; Kenneth Culp Davis, *Discretionary Justice* (Baton Rouge: Louisiana State University Press, 1969), *passim*.

33. For the limitations and qualifications of the *Cahan* decision, see Richard York Funston, "The Traynor Court and Criminal Defendants' Rights: A Case Study in Judicial Federalism" (unpublished Ph.D. thesis, University of California, Los Angeles, 1970), p. 58 *et passim*.

34. California Legislature, Senate, Interim Judiciary Committee, *Fourth Progress Report*, pp. 385, 407–408; CPOA, *California Peace Officer*, November–December, 1954, pp. 11, 21–22; *ibid.*, July–August, 1955, p. C39; California State Sheriffs' Association, *Proceedings* (1956), p. 78; William M. Turner, *The Police Establishment* (New York: G. P. Putnam's Sons, 1968), pp. 70–84. On Southern California as the special hotbed of conservative law-and-order politics, see: Seymour Martin Lipset, "Three Decades of the Radical Right: Coughlinites, McCarthyites, and Birchers," in *The Radical Right*, ed. Daniel Bell (Garden City, New York: Anchor Books, Doubleday and Company, 1964), pp. 421–439; Michael Paul Rogin and John L. Shover, *Political Change in California: Critical Elections and Social Movements, 1890–1966* (Westport, Connecticut: Greenwood Publishing Corporation, 1970), pp. 169–170 *et passim*; Kevin Phillips, *The Emerging Republican Majority* (New Rochelle, New York: Arlington House, 1969), pp. 435–449 *et passim*; James Q. Wilson, "A Guide to Reagan Country: The Political Culture of Southern California," *Commentary*, Vol. 43 (May, 1967), pp. 37–45; Lemert, *Social Action*, pp. 137, 141, 214.

35. John D. Weaver, *Warren: The Man, the Court, the Era* (Boston: Little, Brown, 1967) pp. 42–61 and 165–166; Leo Katcher, *Earl Warren: A Political Biography* (New York: McGraw-Hill, 1967), pp. 62, 68, *et passim*; Kenney, *The California Police*, pp. 23–24, 25–26, 30–39, 108, 126.

36. CPOA, *California Peace Officer*, September–October, 1955, pp. 34, 40; *ibid.*, March–April, 1956, p. 52; *ibid.*, July–August, 1956, pp. C3–4; *ibid.*, July–August, 1957, pp. 22, 43, C6–8; *Sacramento Bee*, June 4, 1957, p. A8; ACLU of NC, *Union–News*, July, 1957, pp. 2, 4.

37. Gilb, *Hidden Hierarchies*, pp. 214–221; *idem*, "Self-Regulating Professions," *Hidden Hierarchies*, pp. 135–155.

38. On group and ideological conflict within the legal profession, see Talcott Parsons, *Essays in Social Theory*, rev. ed. (New York: Free Press of Glencoe, 1954), pp. 378–379 *et passim*; David B. Truman, *The Governmental Process: Political Interests and Public Opinion* (New York: Alfred A. Knopf, 1951), pp. 94–96, 202–203; Heinz Eulau and John D. Sprague, *Lawyers in Politics: A Study in Professional Convergence* (Indianapolis: Bobbs–Merrill, 1964), pp. 20–21 *et passim*. For a model stressing the "oligarchic" characteristics of the Bar Association as political forum and its role in imposing narrow "elite" limits on both the conduct and outcomes of such conflicts, see Jack Ladinsky and Joel B. Grossman, "Organizational Consequences of Professional Consensus: Lawyers and the Selection of Judges," *Administrative Science Quarterly*, Vol. 11 (June, 1966), pp. 100–102.

39. For an acidulous sketch of Coakley, see "Metropoly," *Ramparts*, Vol. 4 (February, 1966), pp. 32–33. On his leadership during the 1950s of the law enforcement

campaign to reorient the State Bar's Committee on Criminal Law and Procedure, see CPOA, *California Peace Officer*, September–October, 1958, p. C9. For Chief Parker's outraged reaction to the State Bar's endorsement of the *Rochin* and *Irvine* decisions, see *ibid.*, November–December, 1954, p. C46. On the Bar's later backtracking, see the California State Bar (hereinafter CSB), *Journal*, Vol. 32 (July–August, 1957), p. 383.

40. CSB, *Journal*, Vol. 32 (July–August, 1957), p. 392. For a letter by Ball denouncing AB 1857 both vehemently and in detail, see California Legislature, Senate, Interim Judiciary Committee, *Fourth Progress Report*, pp. 444–447. For a more general statement of his stance toward civil liberties, see CSB, *Journal*, Vol. 34 (July–August, 1959), pp. 420–435.

41. California Legislature, Assembly, *Journal*, 1957, Vol. 2, p. 3768; *ibid.*, Vol. 3, p. 4910; Buchanan, *Legislative Partisanship*, p. 152 *et passim*.

42. CSB, *Journal*, Vol. 32 (July–August, 1957), p. 392; ACLU of NC, *Union–News*, July, 1957, p. 4; California Legislature, Senate, *Journal*, 1957, Vol. 3, pp. 4612, 4697, 4892, 4950, 5170; California Legislature, Assembly, *Journal*, 1957, Vol. 4, pp. 6951, 7331, 7334.

43. Westin, "Bookies and 'Bugs'," p. 53 *et passim*; *idem*, *Privacy and Freedom* (New York: Atheneum, 1970), pp. 189–191; Samuel Dash, Richard F. Schwartz, and Robert E. Knowlton, *The Eavesdroppers* (New Brunswick, New Jersey: Rutgers University Press, 1959), pp. 199–200. The companion Senate bill was SB 237.

44. AB 342 was enacted as Chapter 1862 of the 1959 California *Statutes*. For its legislative history, see: California Legislature, Assembly, *Journal*, 1959, Vol. 4, p. 8875; California Legislature, Senate, *Journal*, 1959, Vol. 3, p. 4325.

45. *Sacramento Newsletter*, January 5, 1959, p. 1; *ibid.*, January 19, 1959, pp. 1, 3; *ibid.*, February 9, 1959, p. 2; *ibid.*, April 13, 1959, p. 1; *ibid.*, June 22, 1959, pp. 1–3. Buchanan, *Legislative Partisanship*, pp. 123–125 *et passim*; Cannon, *Ronnie and Jesse*, p. 102 *et passim*; Totten Anderson, *California*, p. 95; *idem*, "The 1953 Election in California," *Western Political Quarterly*, Vol. 12 (March, 1959), pp. 276–300; Dick Meister, "With All Deliberate Speed: The Emergence of Liberalism at Sacramento," *Frontier*, Vol. 10 (April, 1959), pp. 16–17.

46. On the FEPC legislation and the broader civil rights–civil liberties thrust of proposed 1959 legislation, see: Cannon, *Ronnie and Jesse*, p. 102; Thomas W. Casstevens, "California's Rumford Act and Proposition 14," in *The Politics of Fair-Housing Legislation*, ed. Lynn W. Eley and Thomas W. Casstevens (San Francisco: Chandler Publishing Company, 1968), pp. 241–242; ACLU of NC, *Union-News*, March, 1959, pp. 1, 3; *ibid.*, August, 1959, p. 2.

47. For a liberal critique of Francis, which condemns him for opportunism and inconsistency, see Ed Cray, "Frantic Lou Francis: One Man's Persistent Fight against Total Obscenity," *Frontier*, Vol. 12 (June, 1951), pp. 10–12.

48. The 3-hour booking bill was AB 276; the three telephone call measure, AB 341.

49. See, for example, AB 2052 (continuing the loyalty oath requirement for property tax exemption) and AB 2249 (extending the obscenity law to cover material that the holder "should reasonably know" is obscene). The latter was one of a battery of bills that grew out of an antismut committee chaired by Francis during the interim; see California Legislature, Assembly, Subcommittee on *Pornographic Literature*, 1957–1959, *passim*. On the ill-starred antisubversive crusade that culminated Francis's political career, see: Elizabeth Poe, "The Francis Police State Amendment," *Frontier*, Vol. 13 (October, 1962), pp. 10–12; and Jenniellen A. Ferguson and Paul J. Hoffman, "Voting Behavior: The Vote on the Francis

Amendment in the 1962 California Election," *Western Political Quarterly*, Vol. 17 (December, 1964), pp. 770–776. On fluid and contradictory alignments in California politics, see: Cray, "Frantic Lou Francis,"; *idem*, "Cross-Fertilization on the Right," *Frontier*, Vol. 12 (April, 1961), pp. 11–12; Buchanan, *Legislative Partisanship*, pp. 111–117 *et passim*.

50. Gene Marine, "O'Connell for Congress: Profile of a Courageous Legislator," *Frontier*, Vol. 13 (June, 1962), pp. 9–12; California Legislature, Assembly, Interim Committee on Criminal Procedure, *1959–1961 Report*, *passim*. The Subcommittee on Constitutional Rights, for the creation of which the FCL had lobbied in order to provide civil liberties groups with a sympathetic forum before which to bring their vital concerns, was modeled on the Hennings Committee of the U.S. Senate. See: FCL, *Newsletter*, June–July 1956, p. 2; Donald J. Kemper, *Decade of Fear: Senator Hennings and Civil Liberties* (Columbia, Missouri: University of Missouri Press, 1965), *passim*.

51. *Sacramento Newsletter*, August 18, 1958, p. 3; *ibid.*, June 15, 1959, p. 2; ACLU of SC, *Open Forum*, January, 1959, p. 3; Winston W. Crouch, Dean E. McHenry, John C. Bollens, and Stanley Scott, *State and Local Government in California* (Berkeley: University of California Press, 1955), pp. 56–57; interview with former Assemblyman Charles Conrad, Sacramento, Spring, 1972.

52. CPOA, *California Peace Officer*, September–October, 1959, p. C26.

53. *Ibid.*, p. C27.

54. *Ibid.*, November–December, 1954, pp. 11, 21; *ibid.*, September–October, 1959, pp. C23–27.

55. ACLU of NC, *Union-News*, February, 1959, p. 3; *ibid.*, February, 1960, p. 4; ACLU of SC, *Open Forum*, December, 1960, p. 1; Clement E. Vose, "Interest Groups, Judicial Review, and Local Government," in *Interest Group Politics in America*, ed. Robert H. Salisbury (New York: Harper and Row, 1970), pp. 247–269; *idem*, *Caucasians Only: The Supreme Court, the NAACP, and the Restrictive Covenant Cases* (Berkeley: University of California Press, 1959), *passim*; California Legislature, Assembly, Subcommittee on Police Administration of the Interim Judiciary Committee, *Minimum Standards for Law Enforcement Personnel*, 1957–1959, passim; CPOA, *California Peace Officer*, September–October, 1959, pp. 10, 40–42. AB 2607 (the vagrancy repealer and AB 2712 (mandating the use of arrest warrants) were pocket vetoed; see California Legislature, Assembly, *Journal*, 1969, Vol. 4, p. 6206.

56. AB 874, Chapter 560, 1961 California *Statutes*; ACLU of NC, *Union-News*, July, 1961, p. 3.

57. ACLU of NC, *Union-News*, July, 1959, p. 1; *ibid.*, August, 1959, p. 4; California Legislature, Assembly, *Journal*, 1959, Vol. 3, p. 3565; *ibid.*, Vol. 4, p. 6202.

58. For Knight's reasons for pocket vetoing AB 745, Francis's 1957 three telephone call bill, see: California Legislature, Senate, Interim Judiciary Committee, *Fourth Progress Report*, p. 596; *Sacramento Bee*, May 29, 1957, p. A6. The fullest scholarly study of both the Knight and Brown Administrations is Bernstein, "Political Leadership," pp. 149–292.

59. *Sacramento Newsletter*, December 19, 1960, p. 2; *Sacramento Bee*, January 5, 1961, p. A6.

60. AB 9 became law as Chapter 274 of the 1961 California *Statutes*; SB 81, as Chapter 850. For the legislative history of the former, see: California Legislature, Assembly, *Journal*, 1961, Vol. 4, pp. 6880–6881; California Legislature, Senate, *Journal*, 1961, Vol. 3, p. 4666. For that of the latter, see: California Legislature,

Assembly, *Journal*, 1961, Vol. 3, p. 7149; and California Legislature, Senate, *Journal*, 1961, Vol. 3, p. 4579.

61. Edwin H. Sutherland, "The Diffusion of Sexual Psychopath Laws," *American Journal of Sociology*, Vol. 56 (September, 1950), pp. 142–148; Harvey, *Earl Warren*, p. 76; California Legislature, Assembly, Subcommittee of the Judiciary Committee on Capital Punishment, *Problems of the Death Penalty and Its Administration in California*, 1955–1957, *passim*; California Legislature, Senate, Committee on Judiciary, *Hearing Report and Testimony on Senate Bill No. 1, 1960 Second Extraordinary Session, Which Proposed to Abolish the Death Penalty in California, passim*.

62. CPOA, *California Peace Officer*, September–October, 1952, pp. 7, 33, 35; California Legislature, Senate, Interim Judiciary Committee, *Second Progress Report to the Legislature*, 1951–1953, pp. 82–95 *et passim*; California Legislature, Assembly, Interim Committee on Judiciary, *Report*, 1953–1955, pp. 21–28.

63. CPOA, *California Peace Officer*, March–April, 1959, p. 21; *ibid.*, March–April, 1960, p. 37; *ibid.*, May–June, 1960, p. 43; Institute of Governmental Studies, University of California, Berkeley, *Public Affairs Report* (January 2, 1959), pp. 1–2; California State Sheriffs' Association, *Proceedings* (1959), p. 21. Republican Assemblyman, Frank Luckel of San Diego was the chief sponsor of the 1959 anti-drug push. The cornerstone of Luckel's 1959 antidrug program was AB 13, imposing 30-year minimum sentences for designated narcotics offenses.

64. In 1959, AB 2727—authored, as was AB 9, by Assemblyman Clayton Dills—was the major attempt to rewrite the marijuana laws.

65. *Sacramento Newsletter*, September 1, 1959, p. 2; California Legislature, Senate, Interim Committee on Narcotics, *Report*, June 1959, p. 50; CPOA, *California Peace Officer*, July–August, 1957, p. C7; *ibid.*, May–June, 1958, p. 38; *ibid.*, September–October, 1960, p. C13; Thorwald T. Brown, *The Enigma of Drug Addiction* (Springfield, Illinois: Charles C. Thomas, 1961), pp. ix, 224; Skolnick, *Justice without Trial*, pp. 114–153; Howard S. Becker, *Outsiders: Studies in the Sociology of Deviance* (New York: Free Press, 1963), pp. 135–146, 155–162, *et passim*; Richard Blum and Associates, *Utopiates* (New York: Atherton Press, 1964), pp. 135–136; California Legislature, Assembly, Interim Committee on Criminal Procedure, *Los Angeles Narcotic Problem and Possible Use of Nalline Control Units: A Public Hearing*, May 5, 1960, p. 15; Harry J. Anslinger and J. Dennis Gregory, *The Protectors: The Heroic Story of Their Unending, Unsung Battles against Organized Crime in America and Abroad* (New York: Farrar, Strauss, 1964), pp. 217–219; Alfred R. Lindesmith, *The Addict and the Law* (New York: Vintage Books, 1965), pp. 73–77, 243–246; Ramsey Clark, *Crime in America: Observations on Its Nature, Causes, Prevention, and Control* (New York: Simon and Schuster, 1970), p. 97 *et passim*.

66. CPOA, *California Peace Officer*, September–October, 1959, pp. C2, C59. In 1959 the law enforcement–backed bills aimed at the *Cahan* and *Priestly* decisions were, respectively, SB 728 and SB 524; both were authored by Republican Donald L. Grunsky.

67. Even in Southern California, where Sheriff Peter J. Pitchess of Los Angeles County endorsed a 1959 attempt to increase penalties for marijuana possession, law enforcement support for such legislation was faltering and halfhearted. On the state level, Assemblyman John Burton, a liberal Democrat from San Francisco, scorned law enforcement spokesmen for refusing to speak out publicly against "outrageous headline hunting proposals [which] privately they [told lawmakers] would cripple law enforcement." See CPOA, *California Peace Officer*, March–April, 1959, p. 35;

ibid., March–April, 1960, p. 37; California Legislature, Assembly, Interim Committee on Criminal Procedure, *Los Angeles Narcotic Problem*, pp. 1–22.

68. CPOA, *California Peace Officer*, September–October, 1958, p. C12.

69. *Ibid.*, September–October, 1960, p. C7. The emphasis here on the "elite" law enforcement manipulation of "mass" antidrug sentiment runs parallel to the recent spurt of reinterpretations that see McCarthyism less as a spasm of popular hysteria than as the outgrowth of the structured anxieties and ambitions of political elites. See Michael Paul Rogin, *The Intellectuals and McCarthy: The Radical Specter* (Cambridge, Massachusetts: MIT Press, 1967), *passim*; Robert Griffith, *The Politics of Fear: Joseph R. McCarthy and the Senate* (New York: Hayden Book Company, 1970), *passim*; Athan Theoharis, *Seeds of Repression: Harry S. Truman and the Origins of McCarthyism* (Chicago: Quadrangle Books, 1971), *passim*; Richard M. Freeland, *The Truman Doctrine and the Origins of McCarthyism: Foreign Policy, Domestic Politics, and Internal Security, 1946–48* (New York: Alfred A. Knopf, 1972), *passim*.

70. CPOA, *California Peace Officer*, March–April, 1958, p. 41; *ibid.*, March–April, 1959, p. 36; *ibid.*, May–June, 1960, pp. 9, 52; *ibid.*, September–October, 1960, p. 2; *Los Angeles Times*, March 3, 1960, Part III, p. 2; Lindesmith, *Addict and the Law*, pp. 64–69; CPOA, *California Peace Officer*, July–August, 1962, p. 15.

71. CPOA, *California Peace Officer*, (July–August, 1962), p. 15. On the historical background of the law enforcement lobby's attempt to recruit media support, see Gene E. Carte, "August Vollmer and the Origins of Police Professionalism" (unpublished Ph.D. thesis, University of California, Berkeley, 1972), pp. 86–89.

72. Together with the *San Francisco Chronicle*, the *Los Angeles Times* and the *Oakland Tribune* formed a "political axis" that was the "bulwark" of the GOP in California during an era in which the California Republican party and the California political establishment were virtually synonymous; see Gladwin Hill, *Dancing Bear: An Inside Look at California Politics* (Cleveland: World Publishing Company, 1968), p. 96. On the origins and political evolution of these newspaper empires, see Richard C. Miller, "Otis and His Times: The Career of Harrison Gray Otis" (unpublished Ph.D. thesis, University of California, Berkeley, 1961), *passim*; James Erwin Gregg, "Newspaper Editorial Endorsements: Their Influence on California Elections, 1948–1962" (unpublished Ph.D. thesis, University of California, Santa Barbara, 1964), *passim*; John C. Merrill, *The Elite Press: Great Newspapers of the World* (New York: Pitman Publishing Corporation, 1968), pp. 254–263. On their stance toward criminal justice issues, see Eadie F. Deutsch, "Judicial Rhetoric as Persuasive Communication: A Study of Supreme Court Opinions in the *Escobedo* and *Miranda* Cases and the Responses in the California Press" (unpublished Ph.D. thesis, University of California, Los Angeles, 1970), *passim*; also, Chapter V below.

73. CPOA, *California Peace Officer*, September–October, 1958, p. C11. The State Bar strongly disapproved both the penalty increase proposals and the due-process innovations embodied in the law enforcement lobby's antidrug program; see CSB, *Journal*, Vol. 36 (July–August, 1961), pp. 481–483.

74. Loren Miller, "The Police vs. the Citizen," *Frontier*, Vol. 11 (August, 1960), p. 8; CPOA, *California Peace Officer*, September–October, 1960, p. C25.

75. For a study of a public relations firm that made its name by managing "nonpartisan" pressure campaigns for California interest groups, see Stanley Kelly, Jr., *Professional Public Relations and Political Power* (Baltimore: John Hopkins Press, 1956), the chapter "Whitaker and Baxter: Campaigns, Inc.," pp. 39–66. For the "capture" of both public relations firms and interest groups by resurgent party

organizations, see: Robert J. Pitchell, "Influence of Professional Campaign Management Firms on Partisan Elections in California," *Western Political Quarterly*, Vol. 11 (June, 1958), pp. 278-300; Joseph P. Harris, *California Politics*, 4th ed. (San Francisco: Chandler Publishing Company, 1967), p. 38 et *passim*.

76. On Allen and the Republican infusion of a partisan content into the crime and drug issues, see CPOA, *California Peace Officer*, September–October, 1959, p. C23; *ibid.*, September–October, 1961, p. A10; *Sacramento Newsletter*, March 6, 1961, p. 5; Cannon, *Ronnie and Jesse*, pp. 93-95, 107-113; Dick Meister, "Brown at the Halfway Mark," *Frontier*, Vol. 12 (March, 1961), p. 7; *idem*, "Politicians and Narcotics: Exploiting Human Misery for Political Gain," *ibid.* (April, 1961), pp. 14-15; ACLU of NC, *Union-News*, May, 1961, p. 2; Richard H. Blum and Mary Lou Funkhouser, "Legislators on Social Scientists and a Social Issue: A Report and Commentary on Some Discussions with Lawmakers about Drug Abuse," *Journal of Applied Behavioral Science*, Vol. 1 (January–March, 1965), pp. 86-89, 102-103; California Legislature, Assembly, Interim Committee on Criminal Procedure, *Indeterminate Sentence Law: A Public Hearing*, Sacramento, July 19, 1960, pp. 47-51, et *passim*.

77. California Legislature, Assembly, Interim Committee on Judiciary, Subcommittee on Rackets, *Organized Crime in California*, 1957-1958, *passim*; *Sacramento Newsletter*, March 12, 1954, p. 1; *ibid.*, January 22, 1955, p. 2; *ibid.*, June 22, 1959, pp. 2-3; *ibid.*, September 14, 1959, p. 4; *ibid.*, March 6, 1961, p. 1; Dick Meister, "End of the Beginning: The Promise of a Better Deal in California," *Frontier*, Vol. 10 (July, 1959), p. 11.

78. *Sacramento Newsletter*, June 22, 1959, p. 2; *ibid.*, September 14, 1959, p. 4; *ibid.*, May 2, 1960, p. 8; ACLU of SC, *Open Forum*, March, 1960, p. 1; "Narcotics," *Frontier*, Vol. 11 (April, 1960), p. 13; Ed Cray, "The Governor and the Police," *Frontier*, Vol. 12 (May, 1961), p. 5.

79. Bernstein, "Political Leadership," pp. 246-250; "The Governor, Chessman, and the Mob," *Frontier*, Vol. 11 (April, 1960), p. 3; CPOA, *California Peace Officer*, May–June, 1964, p. 37; Richard Milton Sax, "California Crime Commissions: A Comparative Analysis" (unpublished Ph.D. thesis, University of California, Berkeley, 1969), pp. 102-108, 274-283, et *passim*.

80. Cray, "Governor and Police," p. 5.

81. Institute of Governmental Studies, University of California, Berkeley, *Public Affairs Report* (May, 1959), p. 81; *ibid.*, (September, 1961), p. 182; Troy Duster, *The Legislation of Morality: Law, Drugs, and Moral Judgment* (New York: Free Press, 1970), pp. 133-152, et *passim*; Lindesmith, *Addict and the Law*, pp. 290-294; Packer, *Limits of Criminal Sanction*, pp. 256-257, 333-334, et *passim*; Francis A. Allen, *The Borderland of Criminal Justice* (Chicago: University of Chicago Press, 1964), pp. 14, 32-35, 134; CPOA, *California Peace Officer*, July–August, 1961, p. 38; *ibid.*, (September–October, 1961), p. C4.

82. CPOA, *California Peace Officer*, September–October, 1960, pp. C12-15; *ibid.*, September–October, 1961, pp. C2-4. For further evidence of Regan's earlier independence of the law enforcement lobby's point of view with regard to legalized wiretapping and other issues, see California Legislature, Senate, Judiciary Committee, *The Interception of Messages by the Use of Electronic and Other Devices*, 1957, pp. 24-29.

83. CPOA, *California Peace Officer*, September–October, 1961, pp. 6, C2-9. Perhaps the only major contribution that the executive branch made to the CPOA's 1961 antidrug push was the narcotics arrest statistics—compiled, beginning in 1959, by a Special Unit in the Justice Department's Bureau of Criminal Statistics—which

the advocates of harsher penalties were able to put to inflammatory use. See Institute of Governmental Studies, University of California, Berkeley, *Public Affairs Report* (January, 1961), pp. 15–16; *Sacramento Bee*, March 9, 1961, p. A1.

84. *Sacramento Bee*, January 5, 1961, p. A6; *Sacramento Newsletter*, January 9, 1961, p. 1; *ibid.*, February 27, 1961, p. 2; California Legislature, Assembly, *Journal*, 1961, Vol. 1, pp. 782–786.

85. *Sacramento Newsletter*, December 19, 1960, p. 2; California Legislature, Assembly, *Journal*, 1961, Vol. 1, pp. 729–732, 960–962; *Sacramento Bee*, February 23, 1961, pp. A1, A10; FCL, *Newsletter*, April, 1961, p. 3.

86. *Sacramento Newsletter*, February 20, 1961, p. 4.

87. *Sacramento Newsletter*, March 13, 1961, p. 3; *Sacramento Bee*, March 10, 1961, p. A4.

88. California Legislature, Senate, *Journal*, 1961, Vol. 1, pp. 1061, 1289–1291, 1367; *Sacramento Newsletter*, March 27, 1961, p. 4; *Sacramento Bee*, April 24, 1961, p. A4; *Sacramento Newsletter*, April 24, 1961, p. 2; California Legislature, Assembly, *Journal*, 1961, Vol. 2, p. 2695.

89. *Sacramento Bee*, April 27, 1961, p. A10; California Legislature, Senate, *Journal*, 1961, Vol. 2, pp. 1986, 2063; California Legislature, Assembly, *Journal*, 1961, Vol. 4, p. 6534.

90. California Legislature, Senate, *Journal*, 1961, Vol. 2, pp. 2519–2520, Vol. 3; pp. 4264, 4498, 4519; *Sacramento Bee*, March 28, 1961, pp. A1, A6; *ibid.*, April 15, 1961, p. A2; *ibid.*, April 19, 1961, pp. A6, C6; *ibid.*, April 21, 1961, p. A6; *Sacramento Newsletter*, April 3, 1961, p. 3; *ibid.*, April 24, 1961, p. 2; Meister, "Politicians and Narcotics," p. 14; CPOA, *California Peace Officer*, September–October, 1961, pp. C4, C9. The civil liberties organizations drew a distinction between the provisions of SB 81 requiring convicted addicts to register with the police, which they opposed, and the provisions requiring compulsory civil commitment and "treatment," which they either favored or maintained a benign neutrality toward. See ACLU of SC, *Open Forum*, February, 1961, p. 1; *ibid.*, March, 1961, p. 3; FCL, *Newsletter*, July, 1959, p. 2; *ibid.*, July, 1961, pp. 3–4.

91. *Sacramento Bee*, March 28, 1961, p. A6; ACLU of SC, *Open Forum*, February, 1961, p. 1; *ibid.*, March, 1961, p. 3; *Sacramento Newsletter*, August, 1961, pp. pp. 1–2.

92. Dick Meister, "The Governor Got What He Wanted," *Frontier*, Vol. 12 (August, 1961), pp. 5–8; ACLU of NC, *Union-News*, July, 1961, p. 2; ACLU of SC, *Open Forum*, June, 1961, pp. 1, 3.

93. Cray, "Governor and Police," p. 6 *et passim*.

94. G. Theodore Mitau, *Decade of Decision: The Supreme Court and the Constitutional Revolution, 1954–1964* (New York: Charles Scribner's Sons, 1967), p. 168 *et passim*; Philip B. Kurland, *Politics, the Constitution, and the Warren Court* (Chicago: University of Chicago Press, 1970), pp. 74–75 *et passim*; Clifford M. Lytle, *The Warren Court and Its Critics* (Tucson: University of Arizona Press, 1968), p. 77 *et passim*; Conrad G. Paulsen, "Criminal Law Administration: The Zero Hour Was Coming," *California Law Review*, Vol. 53 (March, 1965), pp. 103–120; Ed Cray, "The Police and Civil Rights," *Frontier*, Vol. 13 (May, 1962), pp. 5–11; CPOA, *California Peace Officer*, September–October, 1961, pp. 6, C4; FCL, *Newsletter*, July, 1961, p. 2.

95. AB 2473 became law as Chapter 1886 of the 1963 California *Statutes*. For how it wound its way through the legislature, see California Legislature, Assembly, *Journal*, 1963, Vol. 4, p. 6974; California Legislature, Senate, *Journal*, 1963, Vol. 3, p. 5033.

96. Totten J. Anderson and Eugene C. Lee, "The 1962 Election in California," *Western Political Quarterly*, Vol. 16 (June, 1963), pp. 396–420; Gordon E. Baker, *The Reapportionment Revolution: Representation, Political Power, and the Supreme Court* (New York: Random House, 1966), pp. 85–86; *Sacramento Newsletter*, November 12, 1962, pp. 2–3; Cannon, *Ronnie and Jesse*, pp. 110–112.

97. Hill, *Dancing Bear*, p. 182 *et passim*; ACLU of NC, *Union-News*, October, 1962, p. 1; *ibid.*, December, 1962, pp. 1–2; *ibid.*, February, 1963, p. 1.

98. Charles B. Saunders, Jr., *Upgrading the American Police: Education and Training for Better Law Enforcement* (Washington: Brookings Institution, 1970), p. 2; Mark Harris, *Mark the Glove Boy; Or, The Last Days of Richard Nixon* (New York: Macmillan Company, 1964), p. 65. Earl Mazo and Stephen Hess, *Nixon: A Political Portrait* (New York: Harper and Row, 1968), pp. 267–268.

99. CPOA, *California Peace Officer*, July–August, 1962, pp. 4–5; Fred P. Graham, *The Self-Inflicted Wound* (New York: Macmillan Company, 1970), pp. 79–80, 84, 339.

100. Mark Harris, *Mark the Glove Boy*, p. 71; Mazo and Hess, *Nixon*, p. 266.

101. Ferguson and Hoffman, "Voting Behavior," pp. 770–776; Poe, "Francis Amendment," pp. 10–12; FCL, *Newsletter*, May, 1962, pp. 2–3; Mazo and Hess, *Nixon*, p. 265; *Sacramento Newsletter*, June 11, 1962, pp. 1–3; Hill, *Dancing Bear*, p. 182; Bryan W. Stevens, *The John Birch Society in California Politics* (West Covina, California: Publius Society, 1966), pp. 1–27 *et passim*; Wilson, "Guide to Reagan Country"; Totten J. Anderson, "Extremism in California Politics: The Brown–Knowland and Brown–Nixon Campaigns Compared," *Western Political Quarterly* Vol. 16, pp. 371–372.

102. *Sacramento Newsletter*, May 15, 1961, p. 2; *ibid.*, June 22, 1961, p. 1; *ibid.*, July 31, 1961, p. 3; *ibid.*, October 9, 1961, p. 1; *ibid.*, November 12, 1962, pp. 2–3; *ibid.*, November 19, 1962, p. 3; *ibid.*, November 26, 1962, p. 3; *ibid.*, December 3, 1962, p. 2; *ibid.*, January 21, 1963, p. 4; *ibid.*, January 28, 1963, pp. 1–2, 4; Cannon, *Ronnie and Jesse*, pp. 118–119; Richard George Hincker, "The Speakership of the California Assembly: Jesse Unruh, Fifty-Fourth Speaker" (unpublished M.A. thesis, San Jose State College, 1966), p. 23 *et passim*; *Sacramento Bee*, January 19, 1965, p. A8.

103. Hincker, "Speakership of California Assembly," pp. 23–33; Cannon, *Ronnie and Jesse*, pp. 125–127, 171–172; *Sacramento Newsletter*, January 14, 1963, p. 3; *ibid.*, November 26, 1963, p. 3; *ibid.*, August 5, 1963, p. 3; ACLU of NC, *Union-News*, February, 1963, p. 1. On the 1963 legislature's passage of AB 1240, popularly known as the Rumford Act, see Thomas W. Casstevens, *Politics, Housing, and Race Relations: California's Rumford Act and Proposition 14* (Institute of Governmental Studies, University of California, Berkeley, 1967), *passim*. The 1963 criminal justice bills mentioned in the text were respectively, SB 73, AB 148, and AB 2242. For an overview of 1963 Penal Code legislation, see CBS, *Journal*, Vol. 38 (September–October, 1963), pp. 742–768.

104. Westin, "Bookies and 'Bugs'," pp. 125–126 *et passim*; Dash *et al.*, *The Eavesdroppers*, pp. 175, 180, *et passim*; California Legislature, Senate, *The Interception of Messages by the Use of Electronic and Other Devices*, pp. 25, 27; FCL, *Newsletter*, February, 1957, p. 3; *ibid.*, July, 1959, p. 2; Westin, *Privacy and Freedom*, pp. 199–200. AB 2293 was Burton's 1957 antisurveillance effort. His 1959 bill was AB 1669.

105. John O'Connell had to be replaced as Chairman of Criminal Procedure because he made an unsuccessful 1962 bid for Congress, rather than seek reelection to the

Assembly. See Marine, "O'Connell for Congress"; ACLU of SC, *Open Forum*, January, 1963, pp. 1–2. In its much-diluted form, the bill passed without recorded opposition. See California Legislature, Assembly, *Journal*, 1963, Vol. 3, pp. 4209, 4442.

106. FCL, *Newsletter*, July, 1963, p. 4; ACLU of SC, *Open Forum*, July, 1963, p. 2.

107. Samuel Carter McMorris, "The Decriminalization of Narcotic Addiction," *American Criminal Law Journal*, Vol. 3 (Winter, 1965), pp. 84–88; Graham, *Self-Inflicted Wound*, pp. 54–55; *Sacramento Newsletter*, July 2, 1962, pp. 2–3; *ibid.*, July 16, 1962, p. 4; *ibid.*, April 8, 1963, p. 1; FCL, *Newsletter*, March, 1963, p. 3; *ibid.*, April, 1963, p. 3. For a theoretical perspective on the range of legislative reactions to judicial innovation, see G. Thomas Dienes, "Judges, Legislators, and Social Change," *American Behavior Scientist*, Vol. 13 (January–February, 1970), pp. 511–521.

108. Cray, "Police and Civil Rights," pp. 9–10; Deutsch, "Judicial Rhetoric," pp. 161–162.

109. CPOA, *California Peace Officer*, July–August, 1962, p. 6; *Sacramento Bee*, May 25, 1963, p. A2.

110. Ed Cray, "The Politics of Blue Power," in *The Police Rebellion: A Quest for Blue Power*, ed. William J. Bopp (Springfield, Illinois: Charles C. Thomas, 1971), p. 59; CPOA, *California Peace Officer*, September–October, 1954, pp. 26–27; *ibid.*, November–December, 1956, p. 46; *ibid.*, July–August, 1959, p. 7; *ibid.*, September–October, 1961, p. 20; *ibid.*, September–October, 1962, p. 6; Turner, *Police Establishment*, pp. 104–105, 264–269, *et passim*; Bruce Clyde Bolinger, "A Report on the Political Activity of Los Angeles Voluntary Police Associations," Part I: "The Fire and Police Research Association" (unpublished study, Institute on Law and Urban Studies, Loyola University Law School, Los Angeles, 1972), *passim*. Republican Assemblyman "Chet" Wolfrum, a retired Los Angeles police captain and great friend of the law enforcement lobby, described the CPOA in a 1962 legislative hearing as

> an administrative sort of a group which is composed of high-ranking police officers. They do have right top policemen, but I think all of the officers in the association, I think, are limited to chiefs, administrative chiefs and sheriffs and this sort of things. It's the top level organization that attempts to disseminate information down through the ranks, through the use of this publication.

In the same hearings Robert Fort, legislative representative of the CPOA, admitted that though all peace officers in the state were "technically eligible for membership," its orientation was "largely . . . a product of the interest of the chief and sheriff"; see California Legislature, Assembly, *Selling Organizations Representing Themselves as Law Enforcement Agencies: A Public Hearing*, San Francisco, May 24–25, 1962, pp. 27–28.

111. AB 1920 became law as Chapter 475 of the 1965 California *Statutes*. For the stages of its passage through the legislative process, see: California Legislature, Assembly, *Journal*, 1965, Vol. 6, p. 293A; and California Legislature, Senate, *Journal*, 1965, Vol. 3, p. 4778.

112. Seymour Martin Lipset and Sheldon S. Wolin, eds., *The Berkeley Student Revolt: Facts and Interpretations* (Garden City, New York: Anchor Books, Doubleday and Company, 1965), pp. 99–200 *et passim*; *Sacramento Newsletter*, April 27, 1964, p. 2; *ibid.*, July 27, 1964, p. 2; *ibid.*, December 7, 1964, p. 1; *ibid.*,

December 28, 1964, pp. 1, 2–4; *ibid.*, January 11, 1965, pp. 3–4; *ibid.*, August 23, 1965, pp. 2–3; *ibid.*, October 11, 1965, pp. 2–3; Casstevens, *Politics, Housing, and Race Relations, passim.* Nathan Cohen, ed., *The Los Angeles Riots: A Socio-Psychological Study* (New York: Praeger Publishers, 1970), *passim.*

113. Clarence N. Stone, "Congressional Party Differences in Civil-Liberties and Crimi-nal-Procedure Issues," *Southwestern Social Science Quarterly*, Vol. 47 (Septem-ber, 1966), p. 161 *et passim;* Walter F. Murphy and Joseph Tannenhaus, "Public Opinion and the Supreme Court: The Goldwater Campaign," *Public Opinion Quarterly*, Vol. 32 (Spring, 1968), pp. 31–50; Stevens, *John Birch Society*, p. 44 *et passim;* Hill, *Dancing Bear*, p. 182; *Sacramento Bee*, April 3, 1964, pp. A1, A6; *ibid.*, September 1, 1964, pp. A1, A7; *Sacramento Newsletter*, April 6, 1964, p. 4; *ibid.*, April 27, 1964, p. 2; *ibid.*, September 7, 1964, p. 1.

114. *Sacramento Newsletter*, November 9, 1964, pp. 1–2; Phillips, *Emerging Republi-can Majority*, pp. 441–445; Rogin and Shover, *Political Change*, p. 177 *et passim;* Eugene C. Lee and Totten J. Anderson, "The 1964 Election in California," *Western Political Quarterly*, Vol. 18 (June, 1965), pp. 451–474.

115. *Sacramento Bee*, January 5, 1965, p. A9; *ibid.*, June 16, 1965, p. A6; *ibid.*, June 17, 1965, p. A6; *Sacramento Newsletter*, March 15, 1965, p. 1.

116. *Sacramento Bee*, February 14, 1965, p. B2; Bill Boyarsky, "The Big Sit-In," *Frontier*, Vol. 16 (February, 1965), pp. 5–7; Jerry Rankin, "Reapportionment in California," *ibid.*, Vol. 17 (December, 1965), pp. 5–6; Cannon, *Ronnie and Jesse*, pp. 119–127 *et passim.*

117. *Sacramento Newsletter*, November 23, 1964, p. 3; *Sacramento Bee*, May 19, 1965, pp. A1, A6; Cannon, *Ronnie and Jesse*, pp. 111, 181, 224, *et passim.* On the long-simmering political feud with Unruh, which boiled over during the 1965 speakership election, accounting for Winton's replacement by Young, see *Sacramento Bee*, January 5, 1965, p. A9; *ibid.*, January 8, 1965, p. A8; Hincker, "The Speakership," p. 53; Cannon, *Ronnie and Jesse*, pp. 107, 113, *et passim.*

118. FCL, *The Story of the 1965 California Legislature* (San Francisco: by the Com-mittee, 1965), p. 7; ACLU of SC, *Open Forum*, May, 1965, pp. 1, 4; *ibid.*, July, 1965, p. 3.

119. ACLU of SC, *Open Forum*, March, 1965, p. 4. Oakland's status as Berkeley's geographical neighbor but cultural antithesis made Mulford so acutely sensitive to the phenomenon of campus-based political and cultural radicalism, that he assumed the role of unrelenting critic of the University even before the full-fledged Berkeley Free Speech Movement erupted; see Verne A. Stadtman, *The University of California, 1868–1968* (New York: McGraw-Hill, 1970), p. 441.

120. FCL, *Newsletter*, January, 1965, p. 2; *New York Times*, January 5, 1965, p. 68. The major guns in Schrade's 1965 offensive against campus revolution were four proposed constitutional amendments: SCA 1, 2, 7, 8. For an analysis of AB 1920, see the ACLU of SC, *Open Forum*, May, 1965, p. 4; *ibid.*, June, 1965, p. 4.

121. *Sacramento Newsletter*, January 11, 1965, p. 3; *ibid.*, October 11, 1965, p. 4; Jerry Rankin, "State Senator Hugh Burns," *Frontier*, Vol. 16 (August, 1965; Lipset and Wolin, *Berkeley Student Revolt*, p. 191. *New York Times*, September 19, 1965, p. 60; Stadtman, *University of California*, pp. 379, 484–486; California Legislature, Senate Fact-Finding Subcommittee on Un-American Activities, *Thirteenth Report*, 1965, pp. 3–160; *idem, Thirteenth Report Supplement*, 1966, *passim.*

122. *Sacramento Bee*, January 7, 1965, p. A9; *ibid.*, June 17, 1963, p. A6; *ibid.*, July 14, 1963, p. A3; *Sacramento Newsletter*, January 11, 1965, p. 3; *ibid.*, May 24,

1965, Vol. 2, pp. 3690–3691; California Legislature, Senate, *Journal*, 1965, Vol. 248; Rankin, "State Senator Hugh Burns," p. 10; Arthur G. Coons, *Crises in California Higher Education: Experience Under the Master Plan and Problems of Coordination, 1958 to 1968* (Los Angeles: Ward Ritchie Press, 1968), pp. 215–230.

123. *Sacramento Newsletter*, March 15, 1965, p. 1; *New York Times*, March 10, 1966, p. 1; *ibid.*, March 11, 1965, p. 17; *Sacramento Bee*, May 19, 1965, p. A6; California Legislature, Assembly, *Journal*, 1965, Vol. 1, pp. 1579, 1967–1968; ACLU of SC, *Open Forum*, January, 1965, p. 2; *ibid.*, May, 1965, p. 4.

124. *Sacramento Bee*, May 19, 1965, p. A6; California Legislature, Assembly, *Journal*, 1965, Vol. 2, pp. 3690–3691; California Legislature, Senate, *Journal*, 1965, Vol. 2, pp. 2437–2439.

125. California Legislature, Senate, Special Committee on Pornographic Plays, *An Investigation of the Production of "The Beard" on the Campus of the California State College at Fullerton*, 1968, p. 14.

126. FCL, *Story of the 1965 Legislature, passim*; California Continuing Education of the Bar, CSB, *Review of Selected 1965 Code Legislation* (Reynard Press, 1965), pp. 174–196.

127. CPOA, *California Peace Officer*, January–February, 1957, p. 23; *idem, Proceedings: 1964–1965 Committee Reports* (May, 1965), pp. 20–24; "Metropoly," pp. 32–33; Turner, *Police Establishment*, pp. 173–175. During the 1960 demonstrations in San Francisco against the House Committee of Un-American Activities, the threat posed by "student radicalism" had evoked a brief spasm of concern on the part of California law enforcement; see *ibid.*, pp. 146–148.

128. Turner, *Police Establishment*, pp. 284–286; CPOA, *Newsletter*, Vol. 1 (September, 1965), pp. 1, 8. Gordon Winton's AB 979, enacted as Chapter 805 of the 1965 California *Statutes*, embodied the relaxation of the rules governing the disclosure of the identity of narcotics informants.

129. CPOA, *California Peace Officer*, September–October, 1963, p. 39; *ibid.*, November–December, 1963, p. 39; *ibid.*, March–April, 1965, p. 10; *idem, Newsletter*, Vol. 1 (September, 1965), pp. 1, 8.

130. SB 85–87 became law as Chapters 149–151 of the 1967 California *Statutes*. For their passage through the legislature, see: California, Legislature, Assembly, *Journal: Index*, 1967, p. 33; California Legislature, Senate, *Journal*, 1967, Vol. 3, p. 4949.

131. Cannon, *Ronnie and Jesse*, pp. 74–75, 77, 82; Hill, *Dancing Bear*, p. 209; Stevens, *John Birch Society*, pp. 44–45.

132. Cannon, *Ronnie and Jesse*, pp. 72–73, 80–81; Stevens, *John Birch Society*, pp. 41–49.

133. *Sacramento Bee*, January 5, 1966, p. A4; California Probation, Parole, and Correctional Association, *Correctional News*, Vol. 20 (February, 1966), p. 1; Ronald Reagan, *The Creative Society: Some Comments on Problems Facing America* (New York: Devin-Adair Company, 1968), p. 28. The quote is from the last. For Edmund G. "Pat" Brown's belated evaluation of Reagan's use of the law-and-order issue, see his *Reagan and Reality: Two Californias* (New York: Praeger Publishers, 1970), pp. 95–111.

134. *Sacramento Newsletter*, June 21, 1965, p. 2; *ibid.*, October 3, 1966, p. 1; *Sacramento Bee*, September 1, 1964, p. C1; CPOA, *California Peace Officer*, July–August, 1964, p. 48.

135. *New York Times*, January 10, 1965, p. 49; *ibid.*, August 30, 1965, p. 35; *Sacramento Newsletter*, December 6, 1965, p. 3; Institute of Governmental Studies,

University of California, Berkeley, *Public Affairs Report* (May–June, 1966), p. 61; James Q. Wilson, "Crime in the Streets," *Public Interest* No. 5 (Fall, 1966), pp. 31–32.

136. *New York Times*, July 27, 1966, p. 24; CPOA, *Journal of California Law Enforcement*, Vol. 1 (July, 1966), pp. 28–29; *Sacramento Newsletter*, February 14, 1966, p. 2; *ibid.*, June 6, 1966, p. 2; *ibid.*, September 27, 1966, p. 4; *ibid.*, November 7, 1966, p. 4; *Sacramento Bee*, March 9, 1966, p. A6; *ibid.*, July 21, 1966, p. A4; ACLU of SC, *Open Forum*, August, 1966, p. 3; Cannon, *Ronnie and Jesse*, p. 84; Bill Boyarsky, *The Rise of Ronald Reagan* (New York: Random House, 1968), p. 121; Joseph Lewis, *What Makes Reagan Run?* (New York: McGraw-Hill, 1968), p. 160; California Legislature, Assembly, Committee on Criminal Procedure, *Riot and the Criminal Law: A Report and Recommendations by Assemblyman Pearce Young, Chairman*, 1966, *passim*; *idem*, *Search and Seizure, Preemption, Watts, (and) Firearm Control: A Report*, 1965–1967, pp. 41–44. For the tumultuous journey of AB 201x, the 1966 antiriot statute, through the legislature, see California Legislature, Assembly, *Journal*, 1966, Vol. 1, pp. 1598–1599, 1662.

137. Cannon, *Ronnie and Jesse*, pp. 82–83; California Probation, Parole, and Correctional Association, *Correctional News*, Vol. 20 (February, 1966), p. 1; *Sacramento Newsletter*, May 30, 1966, p. 2; *ibid.*, August 15, 1966, p. 2; *ibid.*, October 3, 1966, p. 1; *Sacramento Bee*, July 24, 1966, p. A1; Boyarsky, *Rise of Ronald Reagan*, pp. 127, 194–195; Lewis, *What Makes Reagan Run?* p. 160; *New York Times*, March 18, 1966, p. 39; *ibid.*, September 30, 1966, p. 24; Joseph A. Spangler, "California's Death Penalty Dilemma," *Crime and Delinquency*, Vol. 15 (January, 1969), p. 142.

138. Graham, *Self-Inflicted Wound*, pp. 20–21; Hill, *Dancing Bear*, pp. 216–217; Weaver, *Warren*, p. 74; Funston, "The Traynor Court," pp. 4, 12–56, 167–175; Cannon, *Ronnie and Jesse*, p. 177; Reagan, *Creative Society*, p. 27; William Wingfield, "The Clean Initiative: A Cause to Match our Kooks," *Frontier*, Vol. 17 (July, 1966), pp. 12–14.

139. Eugene C. Lee and Totten J. Anderson, "The 1966 Election in California," *Western Political Quarterly*, Vol. 20 (June, 1967), pp. 535–554; Owens, *et al.*, *California Politics*, pp. 52, 149, 291; Cannon, *Ronnie and Jesse*, pp. 137, 174; Hill *Dancing Bear*, p. 232.

140. *Sacramento Newsletter*, November 21, 1966, p. 3; *Sacramento Bee*, January 17, 1967, pp. A1, A4; *ibid.*, January 24, 1967, p. A8; ACLU of NC, *Union-News*, February, 1967, p. 3; ACLU of SC, *Open Forum*, February, 1967, p. 3.

141. Cannon, *Ronnie and Jesse*, p. 175; *Sacramento Newsletter*, May 22, 1967, p. 2; ACLU of NC, *Union-News*, October, 1967, p. 3; Jerome Evans and Diane Friedman, "Criminal Justice Council: Promise vs. Performance," *California Journal*, March, 1971, pp. 64–68. The 1967 legislative proposals embodying the first four points were: Lagomarsino's SB 78–79 (pornography), Deukmejian's SB 1427 (preemption), Sherman's and Deukmejian's SR 162 (a resolution calling for an arrest records study, which, though vague enough to pass, never eventuated in the specific legislation it was intended to produce), and Grunsky's SCA 30 ("merit selection" of judges). Deukmejian's SB 84, establishing the California Council on Criminal Justice (CCCJ), was the fifth, and only unambiguously successful, proposal.

142. ACLU of SC, *Open Forum*, February, 1967, p. 3; FCL, *Newsletter*, October, 1967, Section 2, p. 6; Cannon, *Ronnie and Jesse*, p. 175; *Sacramento Newsletter*, March 20, 1967, p. 2; *Sacramento Bee*, April 19, 1967, p. A6.

143. Marine, "O'Connell for Congress," Cannon, *Ronnie and Jesse*, pp. 175–176; ACLU of NC, *Union-News*, February, 1967, p. 3; Hill, *Dancing Bear*, pp. 225, 228, 236; Bovarsky, *Rise of Ronald Reagan*, pp. 179–180; *New York Times*, November 17, 1966, p. 30.

144. Cannon, *Ronnie and Jesse*, p. 175.

145. *Sacramento Bee*, July 24, 165, p. A1; *ibid.*, April 19, 1967, p. A6; *Sacramento Newsletter*, March 20, 1967, p. 2; California Legislature, Assembly, *Journal*, 1967, Vol. 2, p. 1882–1883, 1996, 2054–2055; California Legislature, Senate, *Journal*, 1967, Vol. 2, pp. 2054–2055; Frank W. Presscoff, "The Executive Veto in American States," *Western Political Quarterly*, Vol. 3 (March, 1950), p. 98 *et passim*; Sarah P. McColly, "The Governor and His Legislative Party," *American Political Science Review*, Vol. 60 (December, 1966), pp. 923–942. For the continuation during the 1967 session of the Democrats' desperate attempts to cushion the law-and-order backlash's negative impact on their party fortunes, see the running account of the defeat of their $120 million "Law Enforcement Improvement Plan," the *Sacramento Bee*, February 28, 1967, p. A7; *ibid.*, March 21, 1967, p. A9; *ibid.*, June 8, 1967, p. A8.

146. County of Los Angeles, Sheriff's Department, "Legislative Bulletin," June 15, 1966, p. 8; *Los Angeles Times*, November 29, 1968, Part I, p. 3; *Sacramento Bee*, July 11, 1965, p. B2; *ibid.*, March 16, 1967, pp. A8, A23; Boyarsky, *Rise of Ronald Reagan*, pp. 15–16, 194–198; Cannon, *Ronnie and Jesse*, pp. 153–155, 177–178, *et passim*; Dennis Hale and Jonathan Eisen, eds., *The California Dream* (New York: Collier Books, 1968), p. 124.

147. FCL, *Newsletter*, October, 1967, Section 2, p. 6; Nathan Douthit, *Crime, The Criminal Law, and Criminal Correction: A Case for Reform* (San Francisco: Friends Committee on Legislation, n.d.), pp. 7–17, 48–49; Charles Lam Markmann, *The Noblest Cry: A History of the American Civil Liberties Union* (New York: St. Martin's Press, 1965), pp. 57, 347, 365, 379, 406.

148. Jesse Unruh, "A Reformed Legislature," *Journal of Public Law*, Vol. 16, (1967), pp. 9–15; ACLU of NC, *Union-News*, August, 1966, p. 1; *ibid.*, October, 1966, p. 1; *ibid.*, February, 1967, p. 4; ACLU of SC, *Open Forum*, September, 1966, p. 3; *Sacramento Bee*, October 18, 1966, p. A1; CBS, *Journal*, Vol. 43 (January–February, 1968), p. 41.

149. CPOA, *Newsletter*, Vol. 6 (September, 1971), pp. 1, 3; Marlise James, *The People's Lawyers* (New York: Holt, Rinehart, and Winston, 1973), pp. 175–176.

150. Enacted as Chapter 1402 of the 1968 California *Statutes*, AB 581's legislative history can be gleaned from: California Legislature, Assembly, *Journal: Index*, 1968, p. 171; California Legislature, Senate, *Journal*, 1968, Vol. 3, p. 5122.

151. California Legislature, Assembly, Committee on Criminal Procedure, *Deterrent Effects of Criminal Sanctions*, 1968; "Crime and Punishment, "*New Republic*, March 30, 1968, p. 8; W. Craig Biddle, "A Legislative Study of the Effectiveness of Criminal Penalties," *Crime and Delinquency*, Vol. 15 (July, 1969), pp. 354–358.

152. California Legislature, Assembly, Committee on Criminal Procedure, *Deterrent Effects* pp. 25–26, 35, *et passim*.

153. See the Survey of "Penal Reform Bills" and their origins in the *California Journal*, June–July, 1971, pp. 160–161, 174.

154. Edwin E. Witte, "Technical Services for State Legislators," *Annals of the American Academy of Political and Social Science*, Vol. 195 (January, 1938), p. 141 *et passim*; Alan Rosenthal, "The Consequences of Legislative Staffing," in *Strengthening the States: Essays on Legislative Reform*, ed. Donald G. Hertzberg

and Alan Rosenthal (Garden City, New York: Doubleday and Company, 1971),
p. 79; Malcolm E. Jewell and Samuel C. Patterson, *The Legislative Process in
the United States* (New York: Random House, 1966), p. 140; Hill, *Dancing
Bear*, pp. 134, 137; "Legislative Staff of 1500," p. 96; Wahlke *et al.*, *Legislative
System*, p. 51; *Sacramento Newsletter*, September 13, 1957, p. 4; Jesse M. Unruh,
"California's Legislative Internship Program: An Appraisal after Eight Years,"
State Government, Vol. 38 (Summer, 1965), pp. 154–158; Robert Seaver, "In-
ternship and Legislative Staffing," *State Legislature's Progress Reports*, Vol. 2,
(December, 1966), Supplement; Blair and Flournoy, *Legislative Bodies*, pp.
52–53.

155. "Legislative Staff of 1500," pp. 99, 114; Jesse M. Unruh, "Science in Law-
making," *National Civic Review*, Vol. 15 (October, 1965), p. 466; *idem*, "A
Reformed Legislature," p. 13; Lee Nichols, "The California Assembly Seminars,"
State Legislature's Progress Reports, Vol. 2 (November, 1966), Supplement;
Jesse Unruh, "A Talent Pool for Legislators," *ibid.*, Vol. 3 (April, 1967)
Supplement.

156. Bernard L. Hyink *et al*, *Politics and Government in California*, 3rd ed. (New
York: Thomas Y. Crowell, 1963), p. 267; *Sacramento Newsletter*, August 16,
1965, p. 2; Jesse Unruh, "Science in Lawmaking," p. 471; *idem*, "The Legislature and the Burden of Change," *Pacific Law Journal*, Vol. 1 (January, 1970),
p. 139.

157. Unruh, "The Legislature," p. 139; Albert J. Lipson, "Legislative Grantsmanship
—California Style," *State Government*, Vol. 44 (Winter, 1971), pp. 31–37;
Bolton, "Expanding the Power of State Legislature," pp. 62–72. For a critique
of this staff buildup which argues that it is still insufficient to meet "the public
interest," see Fellmeth, *Politics of Land*, pp. 463–467, 486–488.

158. Cannon, *Ronnie and Jesse*, pp. 116, 124, 244–245, 299–300; Boyarsky, *Rise of
Ronald Reagan*, pp. 181–182; Hincker, "The Speakership," pp. 76, 81; *Sacramento Newsletter*, January 3, 1966, p. 2.

159. Buchanan, *Legislative Partisanship*, pp. 144–145. For Unruh's own attempt to
place these new trends in legislative decision making within the perspective of
such a "political philosophy," see his introduction to *Attitudes, Innovation, and
Public Policy: A Symposium for the California Legislature* (Institute of Governmental Affairs, University of California, Berkeley, April, 1968).

160. Earl Latham, *The Group Basis of Politics: A Study of Basing Point Legislation*
(Ithaca, New York: Cornell University Press, 1952), p. 35; Cannon, *Ronnie
and Jesse*, pp. 124, 149, 178–182, 198–199, 244–245; Boyarsky, *Rise of Ronald
Reagan*, p. 182; Marsolais, "Educational Legislation," *passim*; Unruh, "The
Legislature," p. 240; *idem*, "From the Leader's Position," in *Strengthening the
States: Essays on Legislative Reform*, ed. Donald G. Hertzberg and Alan Rosen-
thal (Garden City, New York: Doubleday and Company, 1971), pp. 151–161;
Bolton, "Expanding the Power of State Legislature," pp. 62–72; *Sacramento
Newsletter*, June 19, 1967, p. 4; Wahlke *et al*, *Legislative System*, pp. 254–255
et passim. The true test of the durability of Unruh's legislative reforms came in
1969, after he surrendered the speakership to Robert Monagan, when the new
Republican leadership of the Assembly preserved the Unruh innovations virtually
intact, using them to push through a divorce reform act that had long been in
the works as well as to establish a high-powered Committee on Campus Disturbances that beautifully finessed the explosive issue of campus disorders. See
Cannon, *Ronnie and Jesse*, p. 99; Unruh, "The Legislature," p. 241; and Cali-

fornia Legislature, Assembly, Select Committee on Campus Disturbances, *Report,* 1969, *passim.*

161. FCL, *Story of the 1965 California Legislature,* pp. 10–11; Cannon, *Ronnie and Jesse,* p. 124; California Legislature, Assembly, Interim Committee on Criminal Procedure, *Delinquency Control: A Report,* 1967, p. 27; *idem, Parole and Probation: A Report,* 1963–1965, pp. 22–30 *et passim.*

162. California Legislature, Assembly, Interim Committee on Criminal Procedure, *Parole and Probation: A Hearing,* March 10–11, 1964, pp. 10–11. On the history and reputation of the California correctional system, see Winslow Rouse, "The Problem of Adult Corrections: A Case Study of State Penal Administration in California" (unpublished Ph.D. thesis, Claremont Graduate School, 1961), *passim;* Joseph W. Eaton *Stone Walls Not a Prison Make: The Anatomy of Planned Administrative Change* (Springfield, Illinois: Charles C. Thomas, 1962), *passim.*

163. Karl Menninger, *The Crime of Punishment* (New York: Viking Press, 1968), pp. 321–332.

164. CPOA, *California Peace Officer,* March–April, 1964, p. 7; California Probation, Parole, and Correctional Association, *Correctional News,* Vol. 17 (July, 1963), p. 1; *ibid.,* Vol. 21 (July, 1967), p. 2; California Legislature, Assembly, Select Committee on the Administration of Justice, *Parole Board Reform in California: "Order Out of Chaos,"* 1970, p. 11.

165. Clark, *Crime in America,* p. 216; Alan Evan Schenker, "When Governors Change: The Case of the California Budget" (unpublished Ph.D. thesis, University of California, Davis, 1970), pp. 64, 91, 159; *Sacramento Newsletter,* September 5, 1967, p. 4; *ibid.,* February 5, 1968, p. 3; Frank Browning, "Organizing behind Bars," *Ramparts,* Vol. 10 (February, 1972), p. 44; Ronald Goldfarb, *Problems in the Administration of Justice in California: [A Report to] the Honorable William T. Bagley, Judiciary Committee, California Assembly,* 1969, pp. 39–40; Sol Rubin, "Illusions of Treatment in Sentences and Civil Commitments,'" *Crime and Delinquency,* Vol. 16 (January, 1970), pp. 79–87; Richard McGee, "What's Past Is Prologue," *Annals of the American Academy of Political and Social Science,* Vol. 381, (January, 1969), pp. 9–10; Cannon, *Ronnie and Jesse,* p. 176; Duster, *Legislation of Morality,* p. 213; Daniel Glaser, *The Effectiveness of a Prison and Parole System* (Indianapolis: Bobbs-Merrill, 1964), p. 191 *et passim;* David Dressler, *Practice and Theory of Probation and Parole,* 2d ed. (New York: Collier Books, 1969), pp. 268–270 *et passim;* David A. Ward, "Some Implications of Negative Findings," in *Crime and Justice,* ed. Leon Radzinowicz and Marvin E. Wolfgang, Vol. 3: *The Criminal in Confinement* (New York: Basic Books, 1971), p. 198. Ward is quoted.

166. Robin Minton and Stephen Rice, "Using Racism at San Quentin," *Ramparts,* Vol. 8 (January, 1970), p. 20 *et passim.*

167. Browning, "Organizing behind Bars," pp. 41–45; *Los Angeles Times,* June 12, 1971, Part II, p. 5; ACLU of NC, *Union-News,* January, 1968, p. 4; Jessica Mitford, "Kind and Usual Punishment in California," *Atlantic Monthly,* Vol. 227 (March 1971), p. 52 *et passim;* James, *People's Lawyers,* pp. 218–219.

168. FCL, *Newsletter,* February 25, 1953, p. 3; *ibid.,* December, 1955, p. 4; *ibid.,* October, 1957, Section 1, p. 5; California Legislature, Assembly, Subcommittee of the Judiciary Committee on Capital Punishment, *Problems of the Death Penalty,* pp. 46–47.

169. American Friends Service Committee, *Struggle for Justice: A Report on Crime*

and *Punishment in America* (New York: Hill and Wang, 1971), pp. v, 8. On the historic Quaker stance toward corrections, see W. David Lewis, *From Newgate to Dannemora: The Rise of the Penitentiary in New York, 1796–1848* (Ithaca, New York: Cornell University Press, 1966), pp. 3, 20–21; David J. Rothman, *The Discovery of the Asylum: Social Order and Disorder in the New Republic* (Boston: Little, Brown and Company, 1971), p. 92 *et passim*.

170. FCL, *Newsletter*, April, 1968, p. 1; *ibid.*, July, 1968, p. 2; *ibid.*, August–September, 1968, p. 4; ACLU of NC, *Union-News* May, 1968, p. 4.

171. ACLU of NC, *Union-News*, August–September, 1968, p. 4; Peirce, *Megastates of America*, p. 603; California Board of Corrections, Human Relations Agency, *Coordinated California Corrections: The System; Correctional System Study Final Report* (July, 1971), p. 68.

172. FCL, *Newsletter*, July, 1968, p. 2; *ibid.*, August–September, 1968, pp. 1–2; ACLU of SC, *Open Forum*, January, 1970, p. 4.

173. FCL, *Newsletter*, June, 1968, p. 4; *ibid.*, August–September, 1968, pp. 2–3, 13–14; California Legislature, Assembly, *Journal*, 1968, Vol. 4, pp. 6329–6330; California Legislature, Senate, *Journal*, 1968, Vol. 3, pp. 3671–3672, 4139.

174. FCL, *Newsletter*, August–September, 1968, p. 1; Biddle, "Effectiveness of Criminal Penalties," pp. 354–358; *Los Angeles Times*, April 16, 1968, Part II, p. 6. The law enforcement lobby, after many a twist and turn, ultimately supported Biddle's marijuana law reform but not until it was amended to *stiffen penalties* for possession of "dangerous drugs." See: California State Sheriff's Association, Law and Legislative Committee, Sheriff Peter J. Pitchess, Chairman, "1968 Legislative Program—Progress Report" (February 1, 1968); *idem*, "Law and Legislative Committee Report" (April 8, 1968), p. 5; *idem*, "Subject: Legislative Digest #5" (May 27, 1968).

175. Michael Canlis, "Law Enforcement and Corrections—Allies," *Youth Authority Quarterly*, Vol. 18 (Summer, 1965), pp. 38–42; California Probation, Parole, and Correctional Association, *Correctional News*, Vol. 22 (December, 1968), p. 2; Edward L. Kimball, "Judicial Intervention in Correctional Decisions: Threat and Response," *Crime and Delinquency*, Vol. 14 (January, 1968), pp. 4–5 *et passim*; Ronald L. Goldfarb and Linda R. Singer, "Redressing Prisoners' Grievances," *George Washington Law Review*, Vol. 39 (December, 1970), pp. 175–300; Donald P. Baker, Randolph M. Blotky, Kieth M. Clemens, and Michael L. Dillard, "Judicial Intervention in Corrections: The California Experience—An Empirical Study," *UCLA Law Review*, Vol. 20 (February, 1973), pp. 453–580; Lemert, *Social Action*, pp. 214, 221.

176. For the legislative history of SB 62–63—enacted, respectively, as Chapters 248 and 249 of the California *Statutes* for 1969—see: California Legislature, Assembly, *Journal: Index*, 1969, p. 302; California Legislature, Senate, *Journal*, 1969, Vol. 3., p. 5778.

177. ACLU of SC, *Open Forum*, September, 1968, p. 4; ACLU of NC, *Union-News*, October, 1968, pp. 1–2; Hill, *Dancing Bear*, pp. 224–231. For the sometimes contradictory impact on politics of such symbolic issues as "law and order," see Murray Edelman, "Escalation and Ritualization of Political Conflict," *American Behavioral Scientist*, Vol. 13 (November–December, 1969), pp. 243–244 *et passim*.

178. *Sacramento Newsletter*, October 14, 1968, p. 3; *ibid.*, November 11, 1968, pp. 1–2; *Los Angeles Times*, October 9, 1968, Part I, p. 3; Richard M. Scammon and Benjamin J. Wattenberg, *The Real Majority* (New York: Coward-McCann,

1970), p. 39 *et passim*; Edwin M. Schur, *Our Criminal Society* (Englewood Cliffs, New Jersey: Prentice-Hall, 1969), p. 23.

179. Owens *et al.*, *California Politics*, p. 301; *Sacramento Newsletter*, January 13, 1969, p. 1; California Legislature, Assembly, *Journal*, 1969, Vol 1, p. 5.

180. *New York Times*, May 31, 1968, p. 19; *ibid.*, January 7, 1969, p. 31; *ibid.*, January 8, 1969, p. 36; *ibid.*, January 11, 1969, p. 26; *ibid.*, February 8, 1969, p. 16; *ibid.*, February 23, 1969, p. 44; *ibid.*, February 28, 1969, p. 27; *Sacramento Newsletter*, November 18, 1968, p. 1; *ibid.*, December 9, 1968, p. 1; *ibid.*, March 3, 1969, pp. 1–2; Cannon, *Ronnie and Jessie*, p. 319 *et passim*; William Barlow and Peter Shapiro, *An End to Silence: The San Francisco State College Student Movement in the 1960's* (New York: Pegasus, 1971), *passim*.

181. *Sacramento Newsletter*, November 11, 1968, p. 2; ACLU of SC, *Open Forum*, September, 1968, p. 4, *ibid.*, January, 1969, p. 2; ACLU of NC, *Union-News*, February, 1968; p. 4; FCL, *Newsletter*, February, 1968, Section 1, p. 1; Los Angeles County, Sheriff's Department, from Chief A. E. Le Bas to Sheriff Peter J. Pitchess, "Office Correspondence; Subject: Joint Law and Legislative Committee Meeting—Sacramento September 13, 1968," (September 16, 1968), p. 1. The "reform" probably most preferred by the law enforcement lobby would have been the complete abolition of Criminal Procedure in favor of a return to the old, all-purpose Assembly Judiciary Committee; see California State Sheriffs' Association, Law and Legislative Committee, Sheriff Peter J. Pitchess, Chairman, "Subject: Meeting—Combined Laws and Legislative Committees," (January 20, 1965).

182. ACLU of SC, *Open Forum*, February, 1969, p. 6.

183. *Ibid.*; *Sacramento Newsletter*, February 10, 1969, p. 2; FCL, *Newsletter*, February, 1969, p. 2. In 1970, the Republican Assembly leadership again restructured Criminal Procedure in a way that pleased the law-and-order forces. The committee's membership was reduced from nine to seven (four Republicans and three Democrats), and Alan Sieroty, the special bête noire of the law enforcement lobby, was dropped as a member. See ACLU of SC, *Open Forum*, February, 1970, p. 3.

184. CPOA, *Newsletter*, Vol. 4 (January, 1969), p. 30; ACLU of SC, *Open Forum*, February, 1969, p. 6. The quotation is from the latter.

185. *Sacramento Newsletter*, May 5, 1969, p. 2.

186. *Ibid.*, March 27, 1961, p. 2; *ibid.*, May 20, 1963, p. 3; *ibid.*, May 23, 1966, p. 2; *ibid.*, January 23, 1967, p. 2; *ibid.*, February 27, 1967, p. 3; *ibid.*, May 22, 1967, p. 3; *Sacramento Bee*, May 16, 1963, p. F8; *ibid.*, April 21, 1965, p. A6; *ibid.*, January 18, 1967, p. A11; *ibid.*, January 24, 1968, p. A8; ACLU of SC, *Open Forum*, November, 1966, p. 3; ACLU of NC, *Union-News*, May, 1961, p. 2; CPOA, *Newsletter*, Vol. 6 (November, 1970), pp. 1, 3.

187. ACLU of NC, *Union-News*, May 1965, p. 4.; *ibid.*, June, 1965, p. 4; ACLU of SC, *Open Forum*, May, 1963, p. 3; *ibid.*, March, 1965, p. 1; John E. Semonche, "Definitional and Contextual Obscenity: The Supreme Court's New and Disturbing Accommodation," *UCLA Law Review*, Vol. 13 (August, 1966), pp. 1173–1213; American Library Association, *ALA Bulletin*, Vol. 12 (December, 1968), p. 1355; Donald L. Carper, "Obscenity, 1969; Another Attempt to Define Scienter," *Pacific Law Journal*, Vol. 1 (January, 1970), pp. 364–372; Peter M. Newton, "Restricting the Pandering of Obscenity: A Case of Legislative Overkill," *ibid.*, pp. 373–388; U.S. Commission on Obscenity and Pornography, *Report* (New York: Bantam Books, 1970), pp. 360–363 *et passim*.

188. California Continuing Education of the Bar, CSB, *Review of Selected 1969 Code Legislation* (Regents of the University of California, 1969), pp. 157–158; ACLU of SC, *Open Forum*, April 1969, p. 3; California Legislature, Assembly, *Journal*, 1969, Vol. 2, pp. 2870–2871, 3637; California Legislature, Senate, *Journal*, 1969, Vol. 2, pp. 2858, 3078–3079.

189. California Continuing Education of the Bar, CSB, *Review of Selected 1969 Code Legislation*, p. 158; ACLU of SC, *Open Forum*, April, 1969, p. 3; Semonche, "Definitional Obscenity"; Newton, "Pandering of Obscenity."

190. *Sacramento Bee*, March 22, 1969, p. A6; ACLU of SC, *Open Forum*, April, 1968, p. A8; ACLU of NC, *Union News*, July 1968, p. 3; *Sacramento Newsletter*, March 24, 1969, pp. 2–3; *ibid.*, June 16, 1969, p. 4; *ibid.*, September 30, 1969, p. 3; California Legislature, Assembly, *Journal*, 1969, Vol. 2, pp. 3078–3079.

191. Peter Randolph Leigh, "The Implementation of Obscenity Decisions in the State of California" (unpublished Ph.D. thesis, University of Southern California, 1969), pp. 279, 293, 299; *Sacramento Bee*, June 12, 1968, p. A6; *ibid.*, June 13, 168, p. A8; ACLU of NC, *Union-News*, July, 168, p. 3.

192. CPOA, *Newsletter*, Vol. 5 (September, 1969), pp. 1, 3–4, 6, 12; California Legislature, Assembly, *Journal*, 1969, Vol. 4, pp. 7689–7690. The 1969 "informant protection" bill involved in the Democratic amendment debacle was SB 66.

193. CPOA, *Newsletter*, Vol. 5 (September, 1969), pp. 1, 3–4, 6, 12.

194. CPOA, *Newsletter*, Vol. 5 (September, 1969), p. 4 *et passim*.

195. ACLU of SC, *Open Forum*, September, 1969, p. 4.

196. FCL, *Newsletter*, January, 1970, p. 1; County of Los Angeles, Sheirff's Department, from Sheriff Peter J. Pitchess to All Personnel, "Office Correspondence; Subject: 1970 Legislative Program" (October 10, 1969).

197. For the legislative history of SCA 24 and SB 857, see California Legislature, Senate, *Journal*, 1970, Vol. 3, pp. 6187, 6212; California Legislature, Assembly, *Journal: Index*, 1970, p. 295.

198. ACLU of SC, *Open Forum*, October, 1969, p. 4. On the genesis and development of the Penal Law Revision Project, see Arthur H. Sherry, "Criminal Law Revision," CSB, *Journal*, Vol. 42 (May–June, 1967), pp. 379–383; *idem*, "Penal Code Revision—Progress Report," *ibid.*, Vol. 43 (November–December, 1968), pp. 900–904.

199. County of Los Angeles, Sheriff's Department, from Chief A. E. LeBas to Sheriff Peter J. Pitchess, "Office Corespondence; Subject: Joint Law and Legislative Committee Meeting—Sacramento, September 13, 1968" (September 16, 1968), p. 2; CPOA, *Newsletter*, Vol. 6 (July, 1970), p. 9; ACLU of SC, *Open Forum*, February, 1972, p. 5.

200. California Legislature, Assembly, Health and Welfare Committee, Subcommittee on Drug Abuse and Alcoholism, *Marijuana and Drug Abuse: An Interim Hearing*, Sacramento, November 10, 1969, p. 67.

201. ACLU of SC, *Open Forum*, October, 1969, p. 4.

202. California Legislature, Assembly, Ways and Means Committee, Subcommittee on Criminal Justice, *Review of Expenditure of Public Funds in the Criminal Justice System: Unedited Transcript of Hearing*, Sacramento, November 8, 1968, pp. 35–36.

203. ACLU of SC, *Open Forum*, January, 1970, p. 5.

204. Saunders, *Upgrading the American Police*, p. 26 *et passim*; Turner, *Police Estab-*

lishment, pp. 227–287; Richard Quinney, *Critique of Legal Order: Crime Control in Capitalist Society* (Boston: Little, Brown and Company, 1974), pp. 17–50.

205. Charles Foley, "Ronald Reagan's Secret 'Game Plan' for Saving America," from the *London Observer*, reprinted in *Atlas*, Vol. 19 (July, 1970), pp. 16–17; Kenneth Lamott, *Anti-California: Report from Our First Parafascist State* (Boston: Little, Brown and Company, 1971), pp. 259–260 *et passim*.

206. Lamott, *Anti-California*, pp. 259–260 *et passim*; Foley, "Reagan's Secret 'Game Plan'," pp. 16–17; ACLU of SC, *Open Forum*, May, 1969, p. 4; FCL, *Newsletter*, July, 1970, pp. 1–2.

207. Douglas Hope, "Police Are Developing New Political Muscle," in *The Police Rebellion: A Quest for Blue Power*, ed. William J. Bopp (Springfield, Illinois, Charles C. Thomas, 1971), pp. 75–78; William J. Bopp, "Incident at Vallejo," in *The Police Rebellion: A Quest for Blue Power*, ed. William J. Bopp (Springfield, Illinois: Charles C. Thomas, 1971), pp. 185–210; Jerome Skolnick, *The Politics of Protest* (New York: John Wiley and Sons, 1969), p. 271 *et passim*; Hervey Juris, "The Implications of Police Unionism," *Law and Society Review*, Vol. 6 (November, 1971), pp. 231–245.

208. Harry Kalven, Jr., and Hans Zeisel, *The American Jury* (Boston: Little, Brown, 1966), *passim*.

209. *Ibid.*, p. 461 *et passim*; CPOA and District Attorney's Association, from District Attorney J. Frank Coakley to members of the Law and Legislative Committees, "Subject: Meeting, February 5–6, 1969" (January 23, 1969), p. 2; County of Los Angeles, Sheriff's Department, from Chief A. E. LeBas to Sheriff Peter J. Pitchess, "Office Correspondence—Subject: Status of California Proposed Legislation Paralleling the Federal Omnibus Crime Control and Safe Streets Act of 1968" (July 30, 1970), p. 1; California State Sheriffs' Association, from President Michael W. Canlis to all Sheriffs, "Subject: Legislation" (September 24, 1970); *Sacramento Bee*, September 16, 1970, p. B1; California Legislature, Senate, Committee on General Research, Subcommittee on the Judiciary, *Criminal Juries— Size and Verdict: A Hearing*, Los Angeles, September 15, 1970, pp. 4–35 *et passim*; Hans Zeisel, "The Waning of the American Jury," *American Bar Association Journal*, Vol. 58 (April, 1962), pp. 367–369; Anonymous, "Case Notes," *Tennessee Law Review*, Vol. 40 (Fall, 1972), pp. 91–99; James F. Simon, *In His Own Image: The Supreme Court in Richard Nixon's America* (New York: David McKay Company, 1973), pp. 261–263.

210. California Legislature, Senate, *Journal*, 1970, Vol. 2, pp. 2681–2682, 3822; *ibid.*, Vol. 3, pp. 6028, 6026; California Legislature, Assembly, *Journal*, 1970, Vol. 4, p. 7786; CPOA, *Newsletter*, Vol. 6 (September, 1970), p. 7; *ibid.*, (November 1970), p. 4; W. Craig Biddle, "Court-Supervised Electronic Surveillance: A Proposed Statute for California," *Pacific Law Journal*, Vol. 1 (January, 1970), pp. 97–132; Walter Karabian, "The Case against Wiretapping," *ibid.*, pp. 133–145. In radically altered form, AB 857 became law as Chapter 1255 of the 1970 California *Statutes*. Killed outright was the major pretrial detention bill, SB 947, and two attempts to sanction court-authorized wiretapping, John Nejedly's SB 185 and Craig Biddle's AB 574.

211. *Sacramento Newsletter*, October 3, 1966, p. 4; CSB, *Journal*, Vol. 43 (May–June, 1968), pp. 320–322; *ibid.*, (September–October, 1968), p. 786; *ibid.*, Vol. 44 (May–June, 1969), p. 337; *ibid.* (September–October, 1969), pp. 633–642; *ibid.*, (November–December, 1971), pp. 712–717; Turner, *Police Establishment*, pp. 288–289; Reagan, *Creative Society*, p. 46; *Los Angeles Times*, October 9, 1968,

Part I, pp. 3, 27; *Sacramento Bee*, June 11, 1968, p. A6; ACLU of SC, *Open Forum*, July, 1968, p. 2; Kelly, *Professional Public Relations*, pp. 39–66. A ditty composed by a judicial balladeer of the Bar Association of the City of New York expresses criticisms of the Merit Plan that were articulated as well in California, though less poetically and without the distinctive ethnic references:

> Oh, the Old Missouri Plan
> Oh, the Old Missouri Plan
> When Wall Street lawyers all judicial candidates will scan
> If you're not from Fair Old Harvard
> They will toss you in the can . . .
> Oh, the Old Missouri Plan
> Oh, the Old Missouri Plan
> It won't be served with sauerkraut nor sauce Italian
> There'll be no corned beef and cabbage
> And spaghetti they will ban
> There'll be no such dish
> As gefilte fish
> On the Old Missouri Plan

For the quote, see Richard A. Watson and Ronald G. Downing, *The Politics of the Bench and Bar; Judicial Selection under the Missouri Nonpartisan Court Plan* (New York: John Wiley and Sons, 1969), pp. 4–5. On the politics of judicial selection in California and nationwide, see; Ladinsky and Grossman, "Professional Consensus," pp. 79–106; Joel B. Grossman, *Lawyers and Judges: The ABA and the Politics of Judicial Selection* (New York: John Wiley and Sons, 1965), *passim*; Donald Dale Jackson, *Judges* (New York: Atheneum, 1974), pp. 270–271 *et passim*.

212. Leonard Downie, Jr., *Justice Denied: The Case for Reform of the Courts* (New York: Praeger Publishers, 1971), p. 101 *et passim*; Jonathan Black, ed., *Radical Lawyers: Their Role in the Movement and in the Courts* (New York: Avon Books, 1971), *passim*; *Sacramento Newsletter*, September 15, 1969, p. 4; CPOA, *Newsletter*, Vol. 6 (July, 1970), p. 15; *ibid.* September, 1970), p. 7.

213. CPOA, *Newsletter*, Vol. 6 (July, 1970), pp. 1, 4–5, 7.

214. FCL, *Newsletter*, August–September, 1970, p. 1 *et passim*; ACLU of SC, *Open Forum*, October, 1970, p. 4; Jennie McIntyre," Public Attitudes toward Crime and Law Enforcement," *Annals of the American Academy of Political and Social Science*, Vol. 374 (November, 1967), pp. 43–44; Richard L. Block, "Fear of Crime and Fear of the Police," *Social Problems*, Vol. 19 (Summer, 1971), pp. 94, 96.

215. For contrasting perspectives on the legislature as a distinctive component of the criminal justice system, sometimes in conflict and competition with other components, see: Frank J. Remington and Victor G. Rosenblum, "The Criminal Law and the Legislative Process," College of Law, University of Illinois, *Law Forum* (Winter, 1960), pp. 481–499; Winfield Scott Bollinger, "Toward a Theory of Criminal Justice: A Comparative Systems Model" (unpublished Ph.D. thesis, Syracuse University, 1969), p. 32 *et passim*. George Deukmejian, a law-and-order conservative, felt the need to resort to very "unconservative" arguments to justify revamping the jury system, explaining that "so many things have changed since the Founding Fathers" that such traditional bulwarks against "tyranny and abuses" were no longer needed; see California Legislature, Senate, General Committee on Research, Subcommittee on Judiciary, *Criminal Juries*, p. 55.

216. CPOA, *Newsletter*, Vol. 6 (September, 1970), p. 7, William W. Turner, *Power on the Right* (Berkeley, California: Ramparts Press, 1971), pp. 226, 229.

217. For the legislative history of AB 1181; see: California Legislature, Assembly, *Journal*, 1971, Vol. 7, p. 12943; California Legislature, Senate, *Journal*, 1971, Vol. 6, p. 10146.

218. Brian Chapman, *Police State* (New York: Praeger Publishers, 1970), p. 104; James F. Ahern, *Police in Trouble* (New York: Hawthorne Books, 1972), pp. 119–120; "What is Evidence of Possible Moves toward Police State?" FCL, *Newsletter* (May, 1970), p. 7.

219. Schenker, "When Governors Change," p. 74 *et passim*. For "good elections" and their place in American political culture and mythology, see Garry Wills, *Nixon Agonistes: The Crisis of the Self-Made Man* (New York: Signet Books, 1970), pp. 397–416

220. *Sacramento Newsletter*, March 30, 1970, p. 3; *ibid.*, May 11, 1970, p. 4; *ibid.*, October 12, 1970, p. 3; *ibid.*, November 9, 1970, pp. 1–2; *ibid.*, November 16, 1970, pp. 3–4; *ibid.*, January 4, 1971, p. 1; Thomas Jesse Goff, Jr., "Republican Party: Cal Plan and Coexistence," *California Journal*, May, 1971, p. 141; Sidney Hyman, *Youth in Politics: Expectations and Realities* (New York: Basic Books, 1972), pp. 242–244, 251.

221. *Sacramento Newsletter*, November 9, 1970, pp. 1–2; January 4, 1971, p. 4; *ibid.*, May 3, 1971, p. 1; FCL, *Newsletter*, January, 1971, p. 1.

222. *Sacramento Newsletter*, January 25, 1971, p. 2; FCL, *Newsletter*, February, 1971, p. 1; *ibid.*, March, 1971, p. 4.

223. Earl Warren and Burdette J. Daniels, "California's New Penal and Correctional Law," *California Law Review*, Vol. 22 (September, 1944), p. 234; Sacramento Newsletter, May 10, 1971, p. 1; "Penal Reform Bills Offer Shorter Terms, More Rights as Rehabilitation Aid," *California Journal*, June, 1971, pp. 160–161; FCL, *Newsletter*, November, 1971, p. 2.

224. FCL, *Newsletter*, December, 1970, p. 2; Browning, "Organizing behind Bars," pp. 42–45; FCL, *Newsletter*, December 1970, p. 2.

225. FCL, *Newsletter*, August–September, 1968, p. 4; *ibid.*, August–September, 1970, p. 9; Biddle, "Effectiveness of Criminal Penalties", *The Outlaw: Journal of the Prisoners' Union*, Vol. 1 (January–February, 1972), p. 2; California Legislature, Assembly, Select Committee on the Administration of Justice, *Parole Board Reform in California*, p. 9 *et passim*; *Sacramento Bee*, March 25, 1970, p. A4.

226. FCL, *Newsletter*, January, 1970, p. 2; *ibid.*, February, 1970, p. 2; *ibid.*, March, 1970, p. 2; *ibid.*, June, 1970, p. 3; *ibid.*, August–September, 1970, p. 8; Cannon, *Ronnie and Jesse*, p. 309; Peirce *Megastates of America*, p. 603; California Board of Corrections, Human Relations Agency, *Coordinated California Corrections*, *passim*; *Sacramento Bee*, May 5, 1971, p. A4; *The Outlaw: Journal of the Prisoners' Union*, Vol. 1 (January–February, 1972), p. 10.

227. Steven Arthur Waldhorn, "Pathological Bureaucracies," in *Government Lawlessness in America*, ed. Theodore L. Becker and Vernon G. Murray (New York: Oxford University Press, 1971), pp. 224–225; Peter M. Blau, *Bureaucracy in Modern Society* (New York: Random House, 1956), pp. 96–97; Jerome C. Miller, "The Politics of Change: Correctional Reform," in *Closing Correctional Institutions* (Lexington, Massachusetts: Lexington Books, D. C. Heath and Company, 1973), pp. 3–8; David J. Rothman, "Of Prisons, Asylums, and Other Decaying Institutions," *Public Interest*, Vol. 26 (Winter, 1972), p. 14 *et passim*.

228. FCL, *Newsletter*, October, 1970, p. 2; *ibid.*, October, 1971, p. 3; *ibid.*, January, 1972, p. 2; *Sacramento Newsletter*, August 25, 1971, p. 3; *ibid.*, September 8,

1971, p. 1; *ibid.*, December 15, 1971, p. 1; "Legislative Workload Piles Up, May Force Extended Session," *California Journal*, April, 1971, p. 111.

229. FCL, *Newsletter*, December, 1970, p. 2; Timothy L. Fitzharris, *The Desirability of a Correctional Ombudsman: A Report to the Assembly Interim Committee on Criminal Procedure*, February 25, 1971, pp. 4, 8, 50; California Legislature, Assembly, Interim Committee on Criminal Procedure, *The Penal Ombudsman*, March 25, 1971, pp. 15–17 *et passim*.

230. FCL, *Newsletter*, July, 1967, p. 3; *ibid.*, January, 1972, pp. 2, 6–7; "Penal Reform Bills Offer Shorter Terms," pp. 161–162, 174; Jesse M. Unruh, "The Need for an Ombudsman," *California Law Review*, Vol. 53 (December, 1965), pp. 1212–1213; California Probation, Parole, and Correctional Association, *Correctional News*, Vol. 25 (November, 1971), pp. 2–4; "Penal Reform Bills Offer Shorter Terms," p. 174; California Legislature, Assembly, *Journal*, 1971, Vol. 7, p. 12700; Seymour Scher, "Conditions for Legislative Control," *Journal of Politics*, Vol. 25 (August, 1963), pp. 526–551.

231. CPOA, Newsletter, September, 1971, pp. 1, 3; "Attorney General Younger Gives New Direction to Justice Department," *California Journal*, April, 1971, pp. 100–101; "Attorney General Evelle J. Younger Talks about His Office and Plans," *ibid.*, pp. 102–103. The 1971 bill restricting pretrial appellate review was SB 677.

232. CPOA, *Newsletter*, Vol. 6 (April, 1971), p. 5; *Sacramento Newsletter*, May 3, 1971, p. 3; FCL, *Newsletter*, March, 1972, pp. 1–2; Carl W. Anderson, "Capital Punishment in California: Yesterday, Today, and Tomorrow," *Journal of California Law Enforcement*, Vol. 6, No. 4 (April, 1972), pp. 150–151; County of Los Angeles, Sheriff's Department, from Chief A. E. LeBas to All Division Chiefs and Staff, "Office Correspondence; Subject; 1972 Pending Legislation Digest #4" (May 22, 1972); Michael Meltsner, *Cruel and Unusual: The Supreme Court and Capital Punishment* (New York: Random House, 1973), pp. 281–285.

233. FCL, *Newsletter*, January, 1972, p. 1; "Moretti Says Legislature Provides Leadership This Year, Governor Does Not," *California Journal*, May, 1971, pp. 128–129; Peirce, *Megastates of America*, p. 598; Adam Yarmolinsky, "Responsible Law Making in a Technically Specialized Society," in the American Assembly, Columbia University, *Law in a Changing America* (Englewood Cliffs, New Jersey: Prentice-Hall, 1969), pp. 97–108; Nelson W. Polsby, "Policy Analysis and Congress," *Public Policy*, Vol. 18 (Fall, 1969), pp. 71–72 *et passim*; Richard Harris, *The Fear of Crime* (New York: Frederick A. Praeger, 1970), *passim*; *idem, Justice: The Crisis of Law, Order, and Freedom in America* (New York: E. P. Dutton and Company, 1970), *passim*; John T. Elliff, *Crime, Assent, and the Attorney General: The Justice Department in the 1960's* (Beverly Hills, California: Sage Publications, 1971), pp. 59–82 *et passim*.

III

Quantifying Legislative Change

WHILE SEVERAL ESPECIALLY VISIBLE AND controversial bills may accurately characterize salient issues in a given legislative session, they are, in fact, atypical of Penal Code revisions generally. Most changes in the Penal Code involve small alterations, often meant to clarify ambiguities without affecting broad intent. Yet, by their sheer numbers alone, these tiny increments may have significant effects. A sequential refinement in a particular definition of drug use, for example, may over several sessions gradually transform a major felony into a minor public nuisance. Further, this may occur with little public attention and perhaps even without the awareness of lawmakers. Equally important, the causal processes behind incremental changes may differ fundamentally from those of major legislative programs. Public hearings are rare, media coverage abbreviated and perfunctory, and backroom bargaining less important than technical bill drafting. In short, there seems good reason to study typical revisions as well as the dramatic revisions covered in the last chapter.

There are also important methodological justifications for studying an entire universe of revisions. First, if one could include all Penal Code changes from 1955 to 1971, sampling problems would obviously disappear. No one could challenge the research by claiming that the bills discussed were somehow unrepresentative. Second, findings might appear that were absent in a small sample. It would be very hard, for instance, to uncover subtle trends on the basis of the 20 bills discussed in Chapter II. Third, even if a subset of bills were drawn through probability procedures, a small number of cases would produce very large standard errors, making inferences to a larger population of bills inherently unstable. In other words, a replication might produce very different conclusions. Finally, by looking in detail only at a few bills, some critical enactments might be inadvertently missed and their impact neglected.

Unfortunately, developing procedures for examining many hundreds of Penal Code revisions is not an easy task. One can begin to get some sense of the problems by thinking back to the previous chapter. Especially for non-Californians, it may be difficult to keep straight whether, for example, Republicans controlled both houses during all of Reagan's first term or just the second 2 years of it. What about Jesse Unruh: In what year did he become Speaker? These and other important facts are difficult to remember, even though we have tried to summarize extensively in the text and in Table 2.3.

Chapter II discussed a small number of bills selected to highlight the critical processes of given sessions. Picture the situation had we decided to sample not one or two bills for each year but five. Our research would have been significantly complicated and readers' energies seriously taxed. In the absence of clear data reduction techniques to abstract the essentials, both parties would probably have floundered. This is why, to our knowledge, no one has tried to undertake detailed legislative histories of more than a small number of bills. There is simply too much material to digest.

This chapter describes the procedures we used to measure the legislative intent of a very large number of Penal Code revisions. Between 1955 and 1971, over 700 alterations were considered important enough to be included in the California State Bar's annual summary of "significant" Penal Code legislation. The actual revisions were the raw material with which we began. Justifications for the particular "sample" of revisions and our data reduction procedures are so critical for later analyses, that they merit the detailed discussion to follow. In essence, this chapter explains how numerous small changes in the Penal Code were each given a number (or numbers) indicating what aspect of criminal justice the revision was supposed to affect, and a number (or numbers) indicating what that intended impact was likely to be.

While our measurement procedures had apparently never been applied to legislative change, they rested on several related and widely known techniques. Probably most directly, our work builds on content analysis (see for example, North et al.[1]), in which words and phrases with certain meanings are counted and "weighted." Typically, a researcher scrutinizes some set of written material and simply tallies the number of times certain "content" appears. As a starting point, one can think of our techniques as a content analysis of Penal Code revisions in which "types" of alterations were counted. For example, we noted the number of bills in each session involving search and seizure or the number of bills criminalizing attacks on public employees (e.g., firemen). However, we wanted more than a simple tally of the number of different kinds of revisions. We wanted a number indicating the impact of each revision. Here, we borrowed from two traditions: scaling and techniques of data quality control. Psychometricians (see, for example, Guilford[2]) have a long history of methodologies that systematically transform categories of events into real numbers (or ordinal categories), and we used most directly Thurstone's work on "judges" (coders) coupled with Likert's notion that certain kinds of discrete judgments can often be literally added together to arrive at an overall measure. For data quality control we relied heavily on the insights of anthropologist Raoul Naroll[3] and his suggestions for making quantitative assessments of qualitative data.

Fortunately, we also had some previous experience with procedures closely related to the ones we ultimately employed. The senior author, in collaboration with Peter H. Rossi and Bettye K. Edison had used coding techniques to transform qualitative interviews from a large number of city officials into quantitative scales.[4] Basically, a team of judges scored the interviews for each city on a scale from 1 to 10, with the mean across all judges for each substantive issue (e.g., mayor's power) being the number used in later analyses.

Before launching into the details of our procedures, it might be helpful to provide a brief summary of how our coding scheme was implemented. (for instructions to coders, see Appendix 3.1) A group of "judges" was given copies of Penal Code changes for a given session. They independently read each revision and made three kinds of judgments. Compared to the Penal Code section before the change, they (1) selected the apparent target(s) of the legislation, (2) assessed the likely direction of the intended effect(s), and (3) evaluated how large the intended effect(s) was supposed to be. For example, a revision might be aimed at defendants, with the projected outcome a moderate increase in his/her ability to prove innocence in court (e.g., a revision supporting the exclusionary rule). Hence, under the category "defendant," each coder might independently place a "5" indicating a moderate increase in legal resources as a result of that revision. For criminalization statutes, the number would essentially specify the behavior criminalized (e.g., drug use) and the amount of activity that was being made legal or illegal. After all coders had gone through all the revisions from 1955 to 1971, various tests of reliability were applied. Reliable judgments were then aggregated and mean scores calculated for each revision. A score of 5.2 for a particular revision would represent the mean assessment of the coders and reflect an increase in the legal resources of the category identified.

Development of Coding Categories*

Commonsense characteristics of the criminal justice system provided first approximations for coding categories describing legislative targets. There were four basic types of targets:

1. Functionaries within the criminal justice system (e.g., law enforcement personnel, prosecutors, judges, corrections officials).
2. Potential and convicted offenders (e.g., suspects, defendants, appellants, prison inmates).
3. Types of criminalization: laws affecting the kinds of behavior labeled illegal (e.g., crimes against persons, crimes against property, crimes without victims).
4. Severity of penalty: changes in the fines and/or periods of incarceration for given offenses.

Initial coding procedures for the amount of impact on each target proved more difficult to develop and, more broadly, raised a fundamental methodological problem. It was clearly impossible to measure directly the actual amount of legislative effect, since the law itself was the only material to be coded. Moreover, the fit between law and actual practice could be far from perfect. Thus, our choice of legislative targets, let alone estimates of "real" impact, was to some degree suspect.

With some uneasiness, we settled on trying to code legislative intent inferred from the bill's actual content. This decision was based on the following reasoning: First, we assumed that legislative intent could be taken to an important extent on its face value. A law that defines sale of hallucinogens as a felony or limits where a police officer may search without a warrant has rather clear purposes. Though there may be a variety of hidden targets and motives, the manifest content is clear enough and important enough to warrant consideration. Further, it is unlikely that underlying targets and goals would, in general, alter the explicit content sufficiently to invalidate more superficial assessments. It is, after all, the

* We apologize to our readers in advance for any confusion that may result from our use of the verb "code" to describe our scaling procedure and the noun "code" to identify the legislative statutes which were evaluated.

written words on which actions are to be taken. Documents that are largely camouflage for their real intent would make systematic application of criminal law nearly impossible. Under such conditions, a criminal justice system would have to have the proverbial "two sets of books."

Second, we assumed that a reasonably literate person could read Penal Code revisions and specify intended targets and intended impacts. In other words, manifest content could be understood without the help of legal scholars. Tests of this assumption will be discussed later; it suffices to say that this appears to have been a sensible assumption.

Third, we assumed that understanding the intended effects was useful. The explicit content of criminal law does not detail all or even a majority of actions in the criminal justice system, but it at least identifies significant constraints on potential behavior. In short, criminal law as written has important impacts. In addition, the content of criminal laws should provide provocative insights into the concerns and goals of state legislators. Both these points can be evaluated in the data analyses presented later. Nevertheless, the reader should keep in mind that most later substantive discussions rest in part on coded legislative intent, although from here on, we shall provide only occasional reminders. (To do otherwise would be at least tedious.)

Our first approximations of target categories needed considerable elaboration. To begin, we expanded the number of targets at which legislative revisions were directed to a total of 55, based on informative and feasible refinements (see Appendix 3.1). For example, we felt that a separation between suspects and defendants was theoretically important and empirically distinct. In contrast, the difference between corrections officers in jails and corrections officers in prisons did not seem especially significant and in any case seemed too subtle to be coded from laws alone.

The codes for impact underwent similiar refinement. Through a series of pretests, a 7-point scale was developed. With 4 as the neutral, or no-change, point, the scale ranged from 1 for "large decrease" to 7 for "large increase" in impact. In cases where criminalization was the issue, the increase or decrease referred to the amount of behavior criminalized. For severity of penalty, the reference was a change in length of sentence, type of sentence, and/or amount of fine. For the various actors in the criminal justice system an increase or decrease referred to the change in the "legal rights and resources" available to the role in question. Behind this last reference was the idea that the criminal justice system produced a competitive environment, though not necessarily a zero–sum game. All actors had certain goals and means af achieving those goals. The criminal law in part defined acceptable means by which goals could be achieved. Consequently, it affected the legal rights and resources of each actor. For example, a decrease in the kinds of evidence admissable following an illegal search would increase the rights and resources of defendants and decrease the rights and resources of prosecutors. However, it should be borne in mind that these were coded as *intended* rights and resources and may not have reflected what actually occurred in court.

Before coding began in earnest, an additional clarification was needed. The degree of potential impact on a particular target was clearly a function of two underlying dimensions: degree of substantive change in the statute and the number of people affected by the change. For example, a law making the carrying of a concealed weapon a crime affects the use of several types of weapons, but relatively few people carry concealed weapons. In contrast, a law criminalizing the use of marijuana affects only one type of drug used by a relatively large number of people. Which is the more severe criminalization? In effect, the coder was asked to respond to both components before deciding on a score for a particular revision. With this issue in mind, definitions for each level of change were identified (see Table 3.1).

One important consequence of the coding scheme was the ability not only to code the degree of intended impact upon a particular target but also, if necessary, to consider the potential impact of a single revision upon a wide range of targets. For example, a single bill affecting the rights and resources of police, judges, and prosecutors would be coded in all three categories and thereby reflect a more pervasive (and important) effect than a revision affecting the rights and resources of only the police.

Since the criminal justice system involves a series of related components,

TABLE 3.1

Scale for Changes Resulting from Penal Code Revisions

Code Number	Amount of change[a]	Number of potential actions[b]
1	Large decrease	Large
2	Large decrease	Small
	Small decrease	Large
3	Small decrease	Small
4	No change in total impact of revision	
5	Small increase	Small
6	Large increase	Small
	Small increase	Large
7	Large increase	Large

[a] When criminalization is at issue, the increase or decrease refers to the amount of behavior criminalized.

For severity of penalty, the increase or decrease refers to length of sentence, type of sentence and/or fine.

For actors within the system, the increase or decrease refers to the amount of resources for the role in question.

[b] This refers to the number of people affected by the revision.

the choice of targets was more complicated than might at first appear. A law explicitly changing the rights and resources of judges could in turn alter the rights and resources of prosecutors, defendants, and ultimately, police and corrections officials. In short, because of the links between the various criminal justice institutions, a change in one place could ripple through the system. Our problem was that the different coders of a given revision might select somewhat different intended targets, depending on how thoroughly they assessed long-term ramifications. To increase coder reliability we instructed coders to take a "narrow" perspective. Rather than encouraging each coder to be an expert on the organization and functions of the criminal justice system, we asked that they select targets that were explicitly mentioned in the bill or that were clearly implied. Once again, we opted for a "superficial" approach, in order to make our techniques more reliable.

Selection of Material to Be Coded

There were several potential sources identifying legislative revisions:

1. The original Assembly or Senate bill, as amended and passed by the legislature.
2. The statute as it appears in the *California Statutes and Sessions Law,* which is published each year and identifies each Assembly and Senate bill with its appropriate chapter number and code number.
3. The Code Section as it appears in the California Penal Code, by year, as amended or newly enacted.
4. The annotated codes, such as those prepared by the publishing firms of Deering and West.
5. Various year-end reviews of selected code revisions by lobby and special interest groups.

In our pilot testing we began by coding both the actual bill (1) and the annotated code (4). Though it was possible to code with surprising reliability, we found that this procedure forced us to deal with many changes that were nonsubstantive in nature (like renumbering) and to look back constantly to original statutes to gauge change. We could have proceeded on this basis once the actual coding began, but the work would probably have been too expensive to continue. Further, though most of the law affecting the criminal justice system can be found in the Penal Codes, some of it is elsewhere (e.g., the Health and Safety Code). As a result, there is no one code that covers all bills involving criminal justice. One must look through all legislative changes to find the relevant material.

In order to cut the coding task to manageable size, three strategies were employed. First, we decided to code *only* changes in the *Penal Code*. Since most of the relevant law appeared there, we thought that should enable us to gauge the broad trends in which we were interested. Certainly some relevant and important legislative changes were excluded (e.g., some important bills on drug use were transferred to the Health and Safety Code). Our hope was that these bills were few, relative to the total number of changes, and that their alterations were consistent with those found in the Penal Code. Our findings lend credence to this hope. However, for our substantive analysis we shall refer *only* to the Penal Code.

Second, it was decided to code only changes from 1955 to 1971. This seemed a reasonable compromise between several competing factors. Most immediately, our resources were by many standards rather meager. In addition, while we wanted the most lengthy legislative time series possible, complete data on some potentially important explanatory variables were unavailable before the mid-1950s. When complete data could be obtained, changes in recording practices in certain years sometimes made subsets of the series noncomparable. Finally, it seemed critical to invest heavily in a smaller number of sessions since we hoped to ultimately disaggregate the legislative material and undertake analyses of several different kinds of Penal Code revisions. This would have been impossible unless a relatively large number of revisions were coded for each session. Therefore, although we were painfully aware of the statistical limitations our design decisions imposed, 1955 was taken as a starting point and baseline, and only revisions over the 10 following legislative sessions were coded.

Third, since the goal of the study was to assess trends in substantive penal law, elimination of minor revisions involving purely technical changes seemed sensible. Accordingly, we examined the various summaries of significant legislation and chose the California State Bar's periodic *Review of Selected Code Legislation*[5] for our coding source. Each volume of the *Review of Selected Code Legislation* included an analysis of all bills that involved substantive change during a particular legislative session. In addition to identifying change, the State Bar summary included:

1. The text of the amended sections (with italics indicating new language: brackets indicating deletions).
2. The relevant case law, the background, and the source of legislation (i.e., who sponsored the change, when this information was known).
3. A statement of the apparent effect of the change.

One obvious question these procedures raise is the relationship between the total number of bills passed, the total number of Penal Code bills passed, and the total number of Penal Code bills passed that were labeled substantively significant. For example, Penal Code revisions in 1965 numbered 275, of which the *California State Bar Review* identified 115 as significant. The pattern of these relationships can be seen in Table 3.2.

Table 3.2 indicates that a rather small fraction of bills that were passed involved the Penal Code. The fraction in 1955 is 3%, which increases gradually to 8% by 1971. Nevertheless, even 8% is not a large proportion. Of the total number of Penal Code bills, anywhere from 9% to 84% were designated significant by the California Bar Association. In total, about one-half of the Penal Code bills were analyzed in *Review of Selected Code Legislation*. However, revisions coded exceed the number of bills because each bill involves several sections. The total number of revisions coded each year can be seen in the far right-hand column. In an average year about one-third of the total revisions were considered substantively significant and as a result coded.

The preface to the *Review of Selected Code Legislation* states that "all substantive changes in the Civil Code, Code of Civil Procedure, Penal Code and Probate Code were included [in this volume]." Although "substantive" is not defined, numerous discussions with academic and practicing lawyers supported the validity of our decision to code from the State Bar summaries. Apparently for the legal profession in California, the

TABLE 3.2

Legislative Activity

Year	Total Bills	Bills Penal Code [a]	Bills CEB [b]	Penal Code Revisions Coded [e]
1955	1966	65	6	6
1957	2424	98	28	31
1959	2195	77	30	34
1961	2232	81	77	101
1963	2164	102	78	100
1965	2070	112	98	115
1967	1725	107	59	87
1968	1474	93	53	50
1969	1619	127	59	62
1970	1628	112	44 [c]	40
1971	1821	143	47 [d]	56

[a] These are the Senate and Assembly bills that revised the Penal Code.

[b] These are the Senate and Assembly bills affecting the Penal Code and identified by the California Continuing Education for the Bar (CEB) as most significant.

[c] Identified in "Review of Selected 1970 California Legislation", *Pacific Law Journal,* vol. 1 (January, 1971), p 362 ff.

[d] Identified in "Review of Selected 1971 California Legislation," *Pacific Law Journal,* vol. 3 (January, 1972), p. 191 ff.

[e] Note Penal Code revisions are different from number of bills enacted. For example, one bill enactment may result in revisions of three of four Penal Code sections.

Review of Selected Code Legislation has been an important aid in its own work and is accepted as an authoritative source on legislative change.*

To be on the safe side, however, we ran some pilot tests comparing the coding results using the *Review* with those using the actual legislation. A team of coders, which included the authors, coded a sample of revisions from both sources and found very high correlations (of the order of .80) between the two coding procedures.† We concluded that one could get virtually the same results using the *Review*, with considerably less expenditure of time and effort.

Choice of Coders

Anticipating that there could be some differences of opinion regarding the intended targets and impact for a given bill, a team of coders was used. Eight recent law school graduates with undergraduate social science majors were selected from a larger recommended group. Priority was given to those who had demonstrated a special interest in criminal law or who had law-clerking experience in criminal law. We were able to obtain such highly qualified assistance because large numbers of recent law school graduates had just taken the California State Bar Examination and were awaiting the results before making an employment commitment.

Coding Procedures and Training

Each coder was given his/her own copy of the *Review of Selected Code Legislation* and, after an initial training period, told to code independently each legislative change in the Penal Code from 1955 to 1971. Recall that each coding decision involved two kinds of judgment: choice of target(s) and type(s) of change. A revision might have several targets. The coding was done on large grids (see Appendix 3.2), with targets along the top and coder identity at the right margin. The coder placed his/her score for a particular revision in the appropriate cell. Revisions were listed by numerical sequence within each year. After the training period, there were

---

* Beginning in 1970, the *Pacific Law Journal* of the McGeorge School of Law, Sacramento, California, in cooperation with the State Bar assumed the publication of legislative summaries.[6]

† We were aware that a high correlation between codings by the *same* coder using different sources would not be persuasive evidence of a true correlation between the two sources. The correlations were, therefore, based on different coders using different sources.

no discussions about specific ratings and no opportunities for coders to change their minds once the grids were completed. However, mistakes obviously based on recording errors (like putting numbers in cells not associated with any revision) or on misunderstandings about the mechanics of the task were given back to coders for correction. By a process that is later explained in detail, the numbers assigned by the coders to each revision became the source of most of the dependent variables for this study.

Prior to beginning the coding, there was a ten-hour training period. Initially, coders were given a substantive and methodological overview of the study. It was explained that we were interested in charting changes over time in the California Penal Code, as one might chart unemployment, but specific hypotheses were not formally presented. Obviously, our methodology (e.g., measuring "increases and decreases") implied something about our substantive concerns, and the coders, who were inquiring and intelligent people, had many speculations about the kinds of trends that might appear. Yet, we tried to avoid endorsing any particular substantive perspective. Our goal, of course, was to minimize biases that might develop in reaction to the training period.

Following the introductory discussion of our study, coders spent several hours practicing the rating procedures. The year 1955 was used for training. Initially, the coding was done independently and then discussed in the group. Several minor problems in the target categories appeared, and necessary alterations were made. Problems typically involved either the need for a more specific definition or the addition of a target category not formerly included. Equally important, coders had the opportunity to become familiar with the task and to clarify through group discussion points on which they were unsure. These initial sessions brought out a number of anxieties about the coding, especially its ultimate usefulness and validity. There was a certain amount of skepticism about quantifying law. However, most doubts were sufficiently addressed so that coders undertook the rating with considerable enthusiasm and energy. Coding all of the revisions took about 6 weeks, with coders working about 15 hours a week.

Reliability and Validity of Coding

Since each coding of a penal law revision required selection of intended targets and type of change (i.e., direction and size), two types of reliability assessment were needed. The criterion for acceptable reliability in choice of target category was six of the eight coders choosing at least one particular category as applicable to a specific revision. In other words, if at least six coders could not agree on at least one target, the target selection for the particular revision was considered unreliable. For 88% of the revisions this criterion was met, and the remaining 12% were dropped from further analysis. There is nothing magical about six out of eight as a gauge of high reliability in target selection. It could have been a smaller proportion or a larger one. Nor to our knowledge is there any widely accepted technique for assessing this kind of reliability in the selection of targets. Consequently, readers anxious about 75% agreement will have to fall back on some more firmly grounded assessment. Our seat-of-the-pants justification was that if six of eight law school graduates could agree on a particular target, it was worth serious consideration. Very few group decisions in society require more than a 75% consensus.

The criteria for reliability of the quantitative ratings (degree of "increase" or "decrease") were more traditional. Acceptable consensus was indicated by very high correlations among coders (above .85) and by a large correlation ratio with associated significance tests for analyses of variance, using coder disagreements on a particular revision as the error term and differences between the means of revisions as the main effect. In *every case* where coders agreed on the category of impact, all criteria indicated acceptable consensus.* Clearly, reliability of the quantitative ratings was not a problem.

Unfortunately, validity is not so easily evaluated. What criterion exists by which to gauge the coding results? We decided that in the absence of widely accepted and firmly grounded validity criteria we would ask some "experienced professionals" to rate a sample of revisions and compare their coding with a sample of the work from our recent law school graduates. Six such professionals participated: two judges of the Los Angeles Superior Court (Criminal Division), two Deputy District Attorneys (both from the Office of Research and Training, District Attorney's Office), and two public defenders (including the Chief Deputy of the Branch and Area offices).

We selected a sample of thirty consecutive revisions from Penal Code Sections 243 through 1203, which were passed in 1965. This cluster of revisions covered various types of crimes, criminal justice procedure, and judgment. The sample was purposive and represented a good cross-section of various kinds of revision. We chose 1965 as the sample year because it fell midway in the time period of interest by being the sixth of eleven legislative sessions covered in this study (the median session).

The coding done by the "professionals" was nearly identical to that done

---

* For a given revision, only categories that had been selected by six of the eight coders were considered. In other words, if three categories had been selected for a revision, but for one of the three only four coders had marked that category, that category was not analyzed any further.

by the recent law graduates.* In more than 80% of instances, identical targets were selected by both groups,† and the correlations between the original coders and the verification coders were all above .75, most of them about .85. Clearly there was significant consensus, and if the assessments of experienced and respected legal practitioners are a sensible criterion, the validity of our coding receives considerable support.

There was also a number of less formal coding evaluations. At various times the authors and research assistants coded small samples of revisions to "get a feel" for the task and assess the results. Though no statistics were applied to these ratings, they were always very similar to the ratings done by the coders.

Transformation of the Data

For all reliable ratings of a given category for a given revision, a mean of all coder scores was calculated. For ease of reading and interpretation, 4 was subtracted from each of these means to transform the original scale of 1–7 into a scale of −3 to +3. Minuses indicated decreases in resources or in degree of criminalization, pluses indicated increases in these categories and zero indicated no change. These transformed means were then summed for each target category for each legislative year to provide an overall, "net" measure of the amount of change legislated for a particular target for each legislative session. The sums are the basic units examined in discussions to follow. One can think of these sums as the number of revisions per legislative session affecting a particular criminal justice actor or type of criminalization, weighted by the direction and degree of intended change: an indicator of net intended impact.

Conclusions

One might say that quantitative data permit a researcher to discover that something is going on, but perhaps not what that something is. Qualitative data, on the other hand, allow the researcher to learn what that something is, but perhaps not the extent to which it is happening. The former can identify patterns whose meaning may be unclear, the

---

* The coding was done independently, and each professional was individually given a brief training period. The slightly lower reliability correlations may be a result of the less intense training procedure.

† Six of the eight coders and four of the six professionals. Also, it is interesting to note that, for about 50% of the acceptably reliable selections, the proportion of coders in agreement *exceeded* the minimum criterion of six out of eight or four out of six.

latter can establish meaning whose patterns may be unclear. While such distinctions are somewhat oversimplified, the obvious implication is to work from both kinds of data.

In the pages that follow, our quantitative data will be presented. We shall be able not only to test the degree to which trends and conclusions from the narrative material seem confirmed but to undertake many important extensions. Where possible, data from both sources will be combined. We hope not only to tell an important, interesting story but to demonstrate the strength of blending methodologies that compensate for each other's weaknesses and extend each other's insights.

Appendix 3.1: Coding Documents

Background Information for Coders

Historians frequently describe enacted legislation and alterations in statutes over time. This project is also an attempt to look at patterns of legislation over time. However, the methods of analysis require that qualitative material be transformed into numerical values. We are interested in charting changes in statutes related to criminal justice from the years 1955–1971, but in order to be able to analyze such a vast amount of material, we must reduce the data into a more manageable form. The methods may seem superficial and haphazard, but such techniques are actually quite reliable and have been employed successfully by social scientists.

We will be asking for an independent judgment from each coder on a series of questions about a large number of legislative changes. Sometimes, possibly frequently, there may seem to be too little information from which to make an accurate judgment in terms of the criteria tested. However, we would like you to attempt a judgment except where you are actually guessing.

A Methodological Overview

The coders in the legislative project will be engaged in a kind of scaling. The methodology involves having a specified number of persons read identical material and then score the material through a uniform rating system. In other words, we will be asking the coders to react to identical stimuli and then specify part of their reactions.

As in all kinds of scaling, the researcher must try to maximize two kinds of conditions for the process to be of value. First, the scores that the coders specify must have high validity. By this we mean that the scores should in fact represent what the researchers and coders say they represent. Second, the scores must show high *reliability*. This means (for this kind of work) that there must be a reasonable amount of consensus among coders.

In this study we will try to maximize validity and reliability in the following ways:

1. All coders will have considerable expertise in law.

2. All coders will go through a training program in order to build up their consistency, both internally and with the other raters. Consistency through training will be improved to the degree that all raters have the same understanding of their tasks. In short, all coders will be taught to operate with the same definitions and same goals.

3. The rating scheme will have been extensively pilot tested so that it is clear.

4. The material to be coded will have also been pilot tested.

5. The material to be coded will have been drawn from sources widely recognized for their high quality.*

6. Reactions to the design of the study by experts in the fields of law, sociology, political science, and history will be solicited before coding begins.

Given that one is striving for high reliability, one must decide on criteria with which to evaluate the reliability. Two complimentary processes will be employed.

1. Initially, the project supervisor will scrutinize early coding results and where it is clear that coders are confused and the confusions rest primarily on lack of understanding of the task, give the coder additional training. After the coder has been given this additional training, he/she will begin coding again from the start.

2. After all the coding from each rater has been completed, statistical tests will be applied to discover if there is more consistency between coders than one would expect by chance. Each of the coding categories will be examined separately, and those categories which do not show statistically significant consensus will be dropped from the analysis.

Gauging validity rests on less overtly specified procedures. Essentially, the degree of validity is a result of all the operations enumerated in ponts 1–6 and the extent to which they provide a convincing case to critical readers. One would hope that, with all of the precautions taken in this study, the material will have obvious meaning and "face validity."

* *Review of Selected Code Legislation.* California Continuing Education of the Bar, Regents of the University of California; *Pacific Law Journal,* "Analysis of Significant Code Legislation," 1971, 1972.

Assuming that high reliability and validity are achieved, the scores from each coder for each legislative change in each category will be aggregated (a *mean* calculated) wherever there is statistically significant consensus. These *means* will be the fundamental data on which an analysis will be built.

The methodology described above is a variation on standard scaling procedures. Further understanding of these procedures can be found in elementary statistics books used in any of the social sciences. A good example of how this particular methodology can be usefully employed is found in the *Annals*, Fall, 1970 (Rossi and Berk, 1970).

Coding Categories

A. Criminalization re:

    1 Civil rights
    2 Consumer rights
    3 Drugs
    4 Ecological concerns
    5 Gun control
    6 Judicial system (contempt, perjury, security)
    7 Misconduct of/with gov't officials
    8 Morality/vice (except drugs)
    9 Persons (assault, etc.)
    10 Political activity
    11 Prisoner behavior
    12 Privacy (invasion of)
    13 Property rights
    14 Protection of peace officers (police, firemen, custodians, etc.)
    15 Vehicular
    16 Other
    17 Transfer from penal sanction to health and welfare concerns
    55 Felonious mischief—bombs, hijacking, explosives, etc.

B. Funtionaries within system (impact of)

    18 Administrative officials, etc.
    19 Adult Authority
    20 Correction/prison officials
    21 Judge (decision-making in a judicial capacity)
    22 Police–sheriff
    23 Probation officer
    24 Prosecution
    25 Jury
    26 Grand jury
    53 Number of persons designated as peace officers
    54 County parole board or parole officer

(*)27   Authority over public agencies (park and recreation, welfare, etc.)
(*)28   Penalty (severity of)—crime involved identified with 8
(*)29   Surveillance authority
(*)30   Technology (use of)
(*)31   Discretion—identify functionary involved with code 8

C. Subjects of the system (interest of)

    32   Defendant (after arraignment and before verdict)
    33   Appellant
    34   Ex-clients of system (ex-convicts, etc.)
    35   Insane
    36   Minor–juvenile
    37   Parolee
    38   Probationer
    39   Prisoner–convict
    40   Recidivist
    41   Suspect (prior to arraignment)
    42   Witness
    #43 Bail—own recognizance
    #44 Burden of proof (presumptions)
    #45 Constitutional protections, search and seizure, etc.
    46   Plea bargaining (encouragement of)

D. General issues

    (*)47   Efficiency: when primary intent of legislative change concerns efficiency
       48   Jurisdictional change: increase in local control to be reflected by the higher value; decrease in local control, by the lower value. If direction of shift is irrelevant or not clear, code 4
    (*)49   Public access to information re   (*)_____
       #50 Capital punishment
       51   Other
       52   Technical change, renumbering, etc.

Coding Instructions

1. After reading each statutory change, score it for the appropriate category, using the quantitative scale listed on the coding sheet.

2. Occasionally, the information available will seem incomplete for a well-measured judgment. Make an attempt to code the change anyway. If the information is inadequate, that particular revision will probably be eliminated by the researcher in his final analysis.

3. Before you can decide which categories are relevant to a particular revision, you will have to decide how narrowly to interpret the impact of

each change. In order to keep the coders consistent with one another, we would like you to code the impact *narrowly*, using the following rule of thumb: We are interested in direct and/or specified impacts. Thus, code categories that are mentioned either in the statute or its changes. Also, code categories that, if not directly mentioned, are clearly intended (in the text) to be affected by the change. Ask yourself: What was the primary intent of the legislature in passing or amending this statute?

4. Code sections followed by a dash (—) indicate the code listed in the *CEB Review* plus following adjacent sections, all of which have the same intent and are not to be distinguished for our scaling purposes. (For example, 821— refers to both 821 and 1269b for our purposes.) However, there are statutory changes that amend a code and its subsections in such a way that *all* subsections will have to be scaled separately. These we have listed separately on the coding sheets.

5. As a general rule, only one 8 (identifying number) may appear in a column. However, if there arises a situation wherein you wish to further identify categories affected by a revision, you may do so in one of the following ways:

(i) More than one 8 may be use in a column ONLY when there is one category quantified and all 8's refer to the same category. For example, a change in surveillance authority might be identified with *both* police and correction officials.

(ii) If a situation arises whereby more than one category is to be evaluated for a particular revision, an 8 may be used in that column ONLY when it is applicable to both categories. For example, if both discretion and severity of penalty are quantified and both of these quantified categories refer to the Adult Authority, then it is appropriate to use a single 8 in the same column, even though two quantified categories are involved.

(iii) Finally, to use two 8's, each applicable to a *different* quantified category, we are asking that you use the second column for the second quantified category and its appropriate 8. Obviously, since we are limited to two columns per penal code revision, the limit for which you can both evaluate and identify with an 8 is two. Again, your criterion for choice here is primary intent of the legislature.

6. (*) before a category indicates that where applicable an identifying code number (8) may be placed in the relevant category. # refers to scoring direction for these categories as follows: defendant: lower scale for decrease in resources for defendant; higher scale for increase in resources for defendant; criminalization: category 17 is to be coded with lower numbers for transfer out of penal code to health and welfare codes (decriminalization).

Appendix 3.2: Coding Grid

Coder #   Division #:   Penal code #:   Year:

Column numbers (top): 52 51 50 49 48 47 46 45 44 43 42 41 40 39 38 37 36 35 34 33 32 31 30 29 28 27 26 25 24 23 22 21 20 19 18 17 16 15 14 13 12 11 10 9 8 7 6 5 4 3 2 1

Row labels: 1, *3, 4, 5, 6, 7, 8, 9, 1, 3, 4, 5, 6, 7, 8, 9

(55 54 53)

* Coder #2 withdrew from the research after the training period, as a result of which #2 coder identification number is deleted.

REFERENCES

1. Robert Carver North, Ole R. Holsti, M. George Zaninovich, and Dina A. Zinnes, *Content Analysis: A Handbook with Applications for the Study of International Crisis* (Evanston, Illinois: Northwestern University Press, 1963).
2. Joy Paul Guilford, *Psychometric Methods*, 2nd ed. (New York: McGraw-Hill, 1954).
3. Raoul Naroll, *Data Quality Control, A New Research Technique: Prolegomena to a Cross-Cultural Study of Cultural Stress* (New York: Free Press, 1962).
4. Peter H. Rossi, Richard A. Berk, and Bettye K. Edison, *The Roots of Urban Discontent* (New York: John Wiley, 1974).
5. Committee on Continuing Education for the Bar, "Review of Selected Code Legislation." For the years 1957 through 1963, these summaries appeared in the California State Bar *Journal*, Vols. 32, 34, 36, 38. For the years 1955 and 1965 through 1969, these summaries were published in individual volumes as *Review of Selected Code Legislation, 1955, 1965, 1967, 1968, 1969* (Regents of the University of California, Reynard Press).
6. *Pacific Law Journal*, "Review of Selected 1970 California Legislation," Vol. 1 (1971), p. 362 ff. "Review of Selected 1971 California Legislation," *ibid.*, Vol. 3 (1972), p. 191 ff.

IV

Trends in the Penal Code
Affecting Actors in the
Criminal Justice System

Introduction

WHETHER THE CHARGE IS PERMISSIVENESS, repression, or something in between, it is common to hear complaints that the law of the land is changing for the worse. And, of course, if some people think the law is being subverted, there will inevitably be other people, perhaps holding different values, who arrive at precisely the opposite conclusion. Our historical analysis in Chapter II highlighted such controversies over drug use, civil unrest, and the like.

While ultimate assessments of the changing criminal law clearly rest on subjective preferences, there are prior empirical questions involving the actual direction and magnitude of Penal Code change. Is it indeed the case that legislators are "tampering" significantly with the Penal Code? Can one discern trends toward decriminalization? Are restrictions being placed on police? In other words, regardless of one's potential reactions to Penal Code alterations, one must first determine the kinds of alterations that have in fact occurred.

With the methodological discussion of Chapter III behind us, this and the next chapter will focus on quantitative trends in Penal Code revisions. The goal in these two chapters is largely descriptive, to display patterns in revisions of the code over time. Is there evidence, for example, that legislation of the late 1960s was different from legislation of the early 1960s? Or is there any evidence that some aspects of criminal justice were the targets of Penal Code revision more than others? In short, we shall be looking at the "marginals" for our dependent variables, to get a grounded sense of the data. While some potential explanations for the trends will be suggested, a thorough investigation of predictive and causal variables will be postponed until Chapter VI.

Chapter II concluded with a summary of trends in the legislature from 1955 to 1971. Table 2.3 displayed many of these trends, and its bottom line ("Outcomes") will be of special importance here, since it provides a "net" assessment of who appeared to win and who appeared to lose for a given session. Civil liberties groups were more successful before 1965 than after, while the reverse was true for law enforcement interests. In this chapter we will explore this and other leads, but to do so, we will have to be far more specific than the "bottom line" judgments of Table 2.3 in Chapter II.

To begin, we will separate various kinds of intended targets of Penal Code revisions consistent with our previous methodological considerations. This chapter will address the legislation directed at the rights and resources of actors involved in criminal justice, while in Chapter V we will examine legislation defining illegal activity. With reference to criminal justice actors, we will also distinguish criminal justice officials (police, prosecutors, corrections personnel, and the judiciary) from subjects of the criminal justice system (suspects, defendants, appellants, and convicted offenders). In Chapter V, we will separate criminalization (further subdivided) from penalty alteration. Finally, it is important to emphasize that, here, labels such as "defendant" are typically summary notations for the somewhat wider range of targets whose interests are comparable (suspects, defendants, appellants) (see Appendix 4.1). The justification for such procedures will be described later. To summarize, here we will examine trends relative to criminal justice actors, while in the next chapter, we will consider legislation affecting criminalization and penalties.

Defendants

Thinking back to Chapter II and the table in which our historical material was summarized (Table 2.3), one could visualize a bar graph showing who won and who lost over the 11 sessions. Figure 4.1 is such a bar graph, displaying the "batting average" of civil liberties interests based on

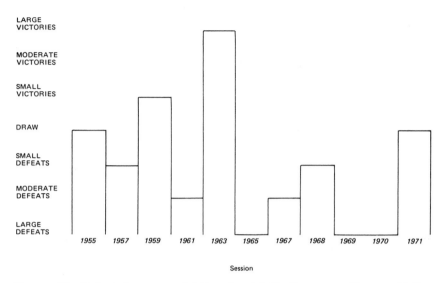

FIGURE 4.1 Estimated success and failure for civil liberties groups (from qualitative data).

the summaries in Table 2.3. Their victories represent the three highest levels in the figure. The largest victories by law enforcement interests represent the three lowest levels in the figure. A standoff is represented by "draw." Clearly, this graph assumes a zero–sum game, at least in outcomes, and while we will show later that this is far too simple a view, it provides a useful first approximation.

Figure 4.1 suggests that civil liberties groups did far better before 1965 than after. In addition, 1959 and 1963 stand out as particularly good years, and 1965, 1969, and 1970 stand out as particularly bad years. 1961 seems the best of the early years for law enforcement interests, while 1971 seems the best of the late years for civil liberties interests.

Figure 4.1 allows us to make several predictions about our quantitative analyses. One would guess that subjects of the criminal justice system would benefit most from legislation until about 1963 and less after that. In contrast, criminal justice officials would benefit after 1963, having done relatively poorly prior to that. While suspects, defendants, and convicted offenders may not have precisely the same interests as the civil liberties lobby, and police, prosecutors, and judges may not have identical interests with the law enforcement lobby, one could speculate that in both cases interests would tend to be similar. One might also like to make predictions based on year-by-year comparisons, but the somewhat impressionistic nature of the data and bar graph would seem to counsel restraint. Hence, an initial question is whether or not the broad patterns suggested by the qualitative analysis show up in the quantitaive data.

Suspects, defendants, and appellants constitute virtually the full range of people processed by police departments and the courts. Much of the criminal law has been directed at them, and from 1955 to 1971 many revisions addressed their legal rights and resources. For purposes of analysis, suspects, defendants, and appellants are collapsed into one category, "defendants,"* and, based on Figure 4.1, we would expect them to have been treated well by the legislature up to 1965.

Figures 4.2 is a graph showing the net change for each session from

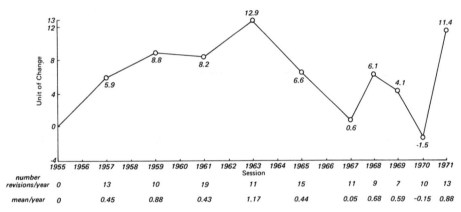

FIGURE 4.2   Net change in resources (by session) for defendants as a result of Penal Code revisions.

* There were two justifications for such decisions. First, in some cases, coders could not distinguish accurately between closely related categories. For example, legislation often blurred the difference between city police and county sheriffs. As a result, certain of the original coding categories were collapsed into broader, though still meaningful, designations. Obviously, removing such distinctions risks artificially combining categories with very different characteristics. However, where we have collapsed subgroups we will indicate the components of the grouping so that readers can evaluate the decision.

Second, our interest in identifying trends required that there be enough revisions over the 11 sessions to meaningfully plot longitudinal changes. If, for example, there were only three bills affecting the Adult Authority over the 11 sessions, it would clearly be misleading to talk about a trend. When situations like this occurred, the category was either dropped from the analysis or, more typically, it was combined with similar categories. (The Adult Authority was combined with corrections personnel.) It is important to emphasize that combining similar categories is not solely an unfortunate (though necessary) undertaking. In many cases combining related legislative targets reduced the amount of data to be interpreted and facilitated understanding.

1955 to 1971, in the intended legal rights and resources of defendants (i.e., suspects, defendants, and appellants). Recall that each coder gave each revision one number indicating the intended legislative target and another number indicating the intended direction and size of its effect. For each revision that was coded reliably (88% of the total number of revisions) we calculated the mean value of the second number (across coders): an estimate of net effect for that revision. For example, a mean of 1.1 might indicate a small increase in resources for police. Then, for each such target, the means for all revisions were *added* within each year. The final number was an estimate of *net* effect on a given target in a given session.* These are the numbers that appear at various points on the graph in Figure 4.2. The 5.9 for 1957 would be interpreted as a modest net increase in intended legal rights and resources, while the −1.5 for 1970 would be interpreted as a small net decrease.†

An examination of Figure 4.2 reveals several interesting things. First, consistent with the qualitative material, defendants did better before 1965 than after. Second, as the earlier bar graph suggested, 1963 was their best year overall and 1971 their best year in the late 1960s. Third, while the fit is far from perfect, many yearly effects are similar on both graphs, (i.e., before 1965, the years 1957 and 1961 were disappointing both for defendants and for the civil liberties lobby). In short, considering that the outcomes measured are somewhat different (civil liberties victories on the one

---

* This procedure clearly assumes that the effects of Penal Code revisions each year are additive. We shall get back to this issue shortly. It suffices to say that an additive assumption seems consistent with how one normally thinks about a body of law: one *adds* to it and *subtracts* from it. Of course, a multiplicative model might have been better. However, the additive approach is far simpler and will later show useful results. Further, to use a multiplicative model one would have to specify its functional form, and here there is little theory or data to guide us.

† Since we will not be treating this data as a probability sample, significance tests seem inappropriate and will not be used. While this may seem a somewhat unconventional decision, the use of statistical inference with historical data seems to us forced, at best. For our data, one would be hard pressed to define a meaningful population of longitudinal events from which this is a random "realization" (Box and Jenkins; Brillinger[1]) unless one wanted to make some very dubious assumptions about the nature of history (e.g., that the observed time period 1955–1971 is a random sample of all possible historical patterns that could have occurred). Similarly, while California is clearly a sample of our 50 states, it is not a random choice. Therefore, to report confidence intervals for our statistics or rigorously test various statistical hypotheses would imply properties for our data that simply are not present. (For an interesting discussion of these issues see Vic Barnett's *Comparative Statistical Inference*.[2]) In short, we will treat our data as a population. One advantage of this approach is that problems with estimation per se using time-series data (e.g., correlated disturbances) disappear.[3]

hand, the legal rights and resources of defendants on the other), the two data bases support each other remarkably well. This also suggests that many of the substantive explanations provided by the historical data should be important as explanations for the quantitative trends. For example, the poor year for defendants in 1967 occurs immediately following Reagan's election as Governor; the good year of 1963 coincides with the fact that both Unruh and Brown were at the height of their power.

In arithmetic terms, the patterns in Figure 4.2 are a function of the number of revisions passed each year and the intended effects of each. The two lines at the bottom of Figure 4.2 show the number of revisions passed each year and the mean intended effect for each year. One might wonder if in years when many revisions were passed, there also tended to be more positive impacts per revision: a sort of "one–two" punch to bring about more rapid change. There is a hint of this in the data, since the Pearson correlation between the number of revisions per year and their mean intended effect is .25. Nevertheless, this correlation is rather small and for all practical purposes the total change per year is a function of two independently varying factors: the number of revisions and the mean impact. For example, the large favorable effect in 1963 is due primarily to the high mean of 1.17 while the favorable effect in 1961 is a result primarily of the large number of revisions.

Earlier we argued that treating revisions as additive within any given year was at least a plausible first approximation of annual effects (see p. 139 footnote*). While other models were possible, the assumption that revisions either add something or take something from a body of law seemed consistent with common sense. However, one could clearly postulate more complicated effects. One might suggest, for instance, that a new revision acts like a catalyst affecting prior legislation, making an entire body of law very different. This approach would suggest a non-additive model for "interaction" effects, and one might multiply revisions rather than add them. More concretely, a strengthening of the exclusionary rule, for example, might increase by one-half the effectiveness of all laws protecting the legal rights and resources of defendants.

It should be clearer now why additivity was assumed. First, it is simpler. While it is easy to visualize a tightening in the exclusionary rule adding something to the resources of defendants overall, it is much harder to specify a multiplicative process through which other parts of the code are transformed. Second, our original scoring system had, built into it, procedures for weighing the importance of each revision *individually*. This fits nicely with an additive model but provides little help in a multiplicative one. We would have had to devise procedures to weight the effects of each revision on all others simultaneously, clearly a mind-boggling problem. In the absence of such techniques, how would one decide whether or not the catalytic effect was the same across all sections currently in the Code, and, if not, what the differential effects might be? In short, without a great deal more information from previous research or powerful theory, the additive model is the *only* model that is both consistent with common-sense notions and applicable to the data on hand.

Why this lengthy justification for the additive model? If the additive model makes sense within a given year, it should also be considered across years. That is, if one adds the revisions for 1957 to one another, should there not be some value in adding the revisions from 1957 to those of 1959? We will argue that for some purposes there is, and Figure 4.3 shows the results.

Figure 4.3 is a cumulative graph in which each year's net effects for defendants are added to those of the year before (1955 starts at zero).* The graph appears to follow a relatively straight line. While the cumulative

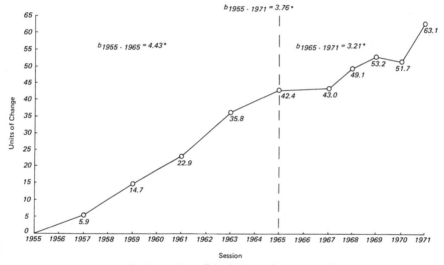

FIGURE 4.3 Cumulative net change in resources for defendants as a result of Penal Code revisions.

* There were only six substantive Penal Code revisions in 1955. We used them for training coders and, therefore, coder judgments for that year are suspect. However, when one divides the six revisions among all the target categories, most are literally unaffeceted and all are practically unaffected. Hence, there is no distortion of import in treating 1955 as a zero starting point. Further, when we examine cumulative *trends* over time, *any* starting point would do equally well as an arbitrary zero. One is only shifting the *entire* curve up or down, not changing its trend over time.

graph formally adds no new information (the data are the same as in Figure 4.2), this mode of display makes several important substantive points.*

First, it is critical to realize that all revisions are tagged on to a large body of existing law. While the fluctuations in Figure 4.2 look rather dramatic (and in many ways they are), when put in the context of the entire Penal Code, the patterns may not be quite so important. Remember that our cumulative graph reflects only the accumulated changes from 1955 to 1971. All previous law is ignored (statistically), and were it be added to the curve, one might well conclude that the Penal Code content is relatively stable.† Cumulative curves thus raise the question of how important the revisions really were. Certainly, the year-to-year fluctuations seem less dramatic when considered as part of a very large body of existing law. Even the accretion over eleven sessions is perhaps trivial. On the other hand, the criminal law may be so finely tuned that relatively subtle changes seriously affect its intent. Or, while typical Penal Code revisions might not fundamentally affect the overall intent of the criminal justice system, they might produce significant *practical* consequences. For example, if taking resources from defendants increased conviction rate by only 5%, existing prison facilities could be taxed beyond their capacity. In short, one should not be mislead by Figure 4.2 or Figure 4.3. Whether or not Penal Code revisions between 1955 and 1971 are "important" is an empirical question that we shall address in later chapters.

Second, while the cumulative curve does tend to mask year-to-year fluctuations, it is clear that, overall, defendants have been gaining resources. Indeed, 1970 is the only year in which their resources were reduced. *Therefore, the changes in fortune typically reflect different sizes of increments each year, and even in "bad" years small gains were usually made.*

Third, one can move beyond the visual picture of cumulative growth in Figure 4.3 to its statistical characteristics. Assuming that the cumulative curve is approximately linear (a valid assumption, since the Pearson correlation that assumes linearity is well over .90 for "time" against the cumulative curve),‡ a slope for the curve can be calculated. This "regression

---

* It is perhaps worth noting in passing that typically, longitudinal data is gathered in its "cumulative" form (e.g., cost of living per month, stock market prices per day) and then if necessary, "differenced" to produce a picture of the rates of change from time period to time period. Here we have done exactly the reverse since we began with coded *changes* in the Penal Code and then aggregated the changes to produce a cumulative curve.

† Also, remember that we coded overt legislative intent.

‡ Unless otherwise noted, all the cumulative plots that follow have similar correlations of over .90.

coefficient" tells the amount of change in a dependent variable for every unit of change in an independent variable. In this instance, the independent variable is the year and the dependant variable is the intended rights and resources of defendants.* For the period 1955–1971 the slope is 3.76 (b_{55-71} = 3.76), indicating that, on the average for each additional year, defendants gain 3.76 units of resources. While this number by itself is difficult to translate into substantive import, comparing it to other slopes can be quite informative.

Fourth, recall that the historical analysis, the bar graph, and Figure 4.2 all suggested that 1965 was a transition year. Fueled by Watts† and Berkeley, conservative forces seized the initiative in Sacramento. Hence on the face of it one might expect that the rate of growth of legal rights and resources for defendants would be slowed after 1965. The slope of the cumulative curve in Figure 4.3 is 4.43 up to 1965 and 3.21 after 1965. In other words, the growth rate is cut by about 25%. The drop would have been much larger had not 1971 been a year of resurgence for liberal forces.

It is important to emphasize that the two data sources essentially agree, despite the fact that for all practical purposes they were gathered *and analyzed* independently. The coders of the quantitative material were unaware that historical material was even being collected. When the senior author began analyzing the quantitative trends, the qualitative research had just begun and no results were available. Thus, the 1965 "break point" (or "regression discontinuity") in the cumulative curve was selected initially through inspection of the trend line. The decision was then more formally supported, since breaking the trend line at 1965 produced the largest difference in slopes on either side of the break point (i.e., other break points produced smaller differences in slope).‡

* Technically, this assumes that both variables are continuous. While this is true of intended impact, it is not really true of year. The legislature did not meet every year and, even if it had, we have aggregated the material year by year. However, this should not cause any interpretative errors, as long as the reader recognizes that there are no data points between legislative sessions.

† Watts: The Watts Riots took place in mid-August of 1965, too late for legislative impact during that session. Specific Penal Code revisions in response to the 1965 riots were enacted in June 1966, by the legislature meeting in Special Session. However, the term "Watts" has been used both as an event *and* as a shorthand expression for the rising tide of racial tension (as evidenced by the negation of the Rumford Fair Housing Act by referendum in 1964)—see p. 53, and the resulting political polarization that ensued.

‡ With only 11 data points, we clearly could not get very fancy. Thus, several alternative statistical approaches to the longitudinal data were immediately discarded, and even our relatively undemanding regression discontinuity approach should be interpreted very carefully. In particular, the slopes and comparisons between slopes must be placed in the historical context provided by Chapter II and be viewed primarily as

Unfortunately, the trend after 1965 is complicated for the cumulative data by the legislature's decision to meet annually after 1967. If roughly the same amount of legislation were passed each session after 1966 as had been before 1966, the cumulative curve would increase more rapidly simply because there were more sessions per unit time. In short, the slope after 1965 is "biased"* upward as a result of more frequent legislative sessions.

Figure 4.4 "controls" for frequency of sessions. Note that this reduces the overall growth of legal resources for defendants from an average of 3.76

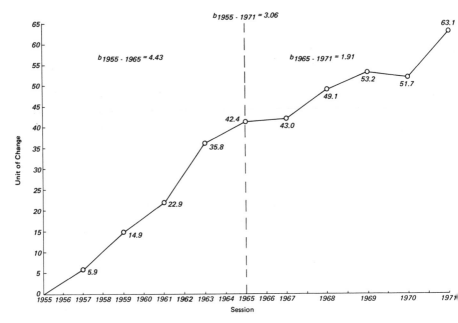

FIGURE 4.4 Cumulative net change in resources for defendants as a result of Penal Code revisions (control for frequency of sessions).

---

summary devices for trends in the data that would have had to be examined in any case. Moreover, we will always provide the graphs from which the slopes were calculated so that the reader may verify with visual inspection the credibility of our statistical coefficients. In short, our regression coefficients are heuristic devices describing patterns that are generally apparent from the graphs alone and take on special importance when they seem consistent with the qualitative historical analysis.

* We shall return to this issue later (after presenting more data) and argue that the "bias" is actually an accurate description. (The term "bias" is not technically correct, since our data represent a population and no sampling distributions are involved. By bias we simply mean a failure properly to specify the model in the population.[4])

units per session to 3.06, but, more important, it reduces the slope after 1965 from 3.21 to 1.91. In other words, holding constant how often the legislature met, the rate of growth for defendant resources was almost halved after 1965. Further, if the "rebound" year of 1971 were dropped, the slope from 1965 to 1970 would decrease to 1.45. This means that if the legislature had continued to meet every other year and everything else had remained the same, defendants would have been gaining resources at about one-half the rate after 1965 as they did before 1965. This appears entirely consistent with our conclusions in the qualitative analysis, though we now have a much more specific estimate of the change in liberal fortunes.

To summarize, the introduction of quantitative data has both complimented and extended our earlier historical analysis. Apparently, liberal, civil liberties, and defendant fortunes were intertwined, with 1965 being the critical year of transition. While defendants made gains after 1965 (and especially in 1971), these gains occurred at about three-quarters the rate of earlier years (not controlling for frequency of legislative session). It was not that defendants were losing resources, they were just gaining them less rapidly. However, it is not clear *a priori* that less successful sessions necessarily were of great practical significance to defendants. While there were some dramatic fluctuations relative to one another, the cumulative curves suggest that any facile assumptions of ultimate impact must be avoided. In later chapters, we shall address in far more detail the causes of revision fluctuations and the possible impact of those patterns.

Convicted Offenders

Persons convicted of crimes (prisoners, parolees, probationers, and ex-convicts) are also routinely processed by the criminal justice system. While largely the charge of the corrections personnel, their treatment clearly has consequences for police and the courts. Superficially, one might expect convicted offenders to have interests akin to defendants and hence to the civil liberties lobby. Yet, there are at least three *a priori* reasons why the fit may not be especially close. First, the treatment of convicted offenders was, until quite recently, a low-priority issue for the ACLU. Only in the late 1960s did the practices of the Adult Authority (the quasi-judicial body that makes parole decisions for state prisons) come under fire for due-process violations. Thus, penalties that might have been labeled earlier as "cruel and unusual punishment," took a back seat to due-process and procedural concerns. While many civil libertarians were no doubt sympathetic to the problems of prisoners, their limited resources were typically concentrated elsewhere.

Second, groups like the Friends Committee on Legislation (FCL), while involved in prisoner's rights relatively early, were not always clear on which programs to support and which to attack. The best illustration of this in the qualitative material is their initial support of the indeterminate sentence. The FCL believed that a medical model of rehabilitation, especially for drug addicts, justified programs that even Chief Parker of Los Angeles did not oppose. Consequently, the line between "liberal" prisoner programs and the "traditional" punitive approach was often blurred.

Third, the problems faced by civil liberties groups in evaluating potential programs were also faced by our coders. Like the FCL, they typically judged favorably Penal Code revisions that, *in theory*, would have given legal rights and resources to convicted offenders. For example, the bipartisan attack on the Adult Authority in 1971 was seen by all as supporting prisoners' rights. In contrast, many of the drug control programs whose *intent* was to increase prisoners' legal resources may actually have had the opposite result. Recall our coders scored revisions by legislative intent, which means that to some extent occasional errors were made in the assessment of ultimate impact.

Despite these problems, few would dispute that the interests of convicted offenders are far closer to those of the civil liberties lobby than to those of the law enforcement lobby. Further, the vast majority of Penal Code revisions were not nearly as ambiguous as some of the drug treatment bills. For example, the Sieroty Prisoner Rights Bill of 1968 could be coded without difficulty as increasing the rights and resources of convicted offenders. Hence, one might be safe to predict that, at least in broad terms, victories for convicted offenders should be modestly associated with victories for civil liberties groups. More concretely, one would predict that convicted offenders would do better before the mid-1960s than after.*

Figure 4.5 shows the yearly impact of Penal Code revisions for convicted offenders. (The "convicted offender" category includes the original coding categories of ex-convicts, parolees, probationers, prisoners, and recidivists.) At first glance, there are some similarities between the curve for defendants and the curve for convicted offenders. Both seem to do best in the early

---

* It is important, at this point, to clarify the distinction between changes in the Penal Code and changes in the Welfare and Institutions Code affecting convicted offenders. Whereas relatively fewer resources were provided the convicted by the Penal Code after 1963, significant changes were being made during this period in the Welfare and Institutions Code, which spelled out the provisions of the Probation Subsidy Program initially legislated in 1965 and expanded in 1968, 1969, and 1971. This program resulted in transferring in the first year of its operation, 1,500 state prisoners to local jurisdictions together with state subsidies to implement rehabilitative options. So, in fact, some resources of the convicted were increased in the period after 1965 but this fact is not reflected in the Penal Code.

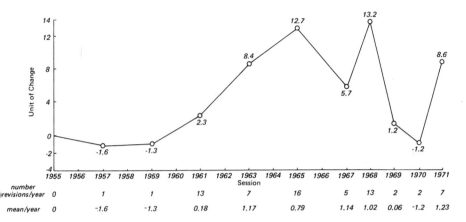

| number revisions/year | 0 | 1 | 1 | 13 | 7 | 16 | 5 | 13 | 2 | 2 | 7 |
| mean/year | 0 | -1.6 | -1.3 | 0.18 | 1.17 | 0.79 | 1.14 | 1.02 | 0.06 | -1.2 | 1.23 |

FIGURE 4.5   Net change in resources (by session) for convicted offenders as a result of Penal Code revisions.

1960s and to fare badly in 1969 and especially in 1970. Indeed, this initial assessment is supported by a Pearson correlation of .40 between the two curves. However, there are some interesting differences. The second-best year for convicted offenders was 1965, a weak year for defendants. The best year for convicted offenders was 1968, a middling year for defendants. While 1963 was the best year for defendants, it was an average year for convicted offenders.*

While this chapter will of necessity devote little time to addressing the causes of the curves, some initial observations can be made. The upswing in defendant fortunes began in 1957, two sessions before convicted offenders made substantial gains.† One might argue that this resulted from the early appearance of the due-process issues in appeals courts. Recall that the 1957 legislature was already reacting to the *Cahan* decision, which barred illegally obtained evidence. During this period, there were no such landmark court decisions concerning prisoners and no other significant irritant to bring the rights of convicted offenders per se to the attention of the legislature. By 1961, drug abuse was a controversial issue, and during 1963 bills were passed supporting a medical definition of addiction (a "liberal" reform at the time). By 1965, Watts and Berkeley had taken the steam out

---

* While the patterns for defendants were a function of the number of revisions and the mean impact acting quite independently, the patterns for convicted offenders are more a result of the two acting together. The correlation for convicted offenders between the number of revisions per year and their mean impact per year is .60.

† However, it should be pointed out that during the decade preceding 1955, California's correctional system underwent a major restructuring. As a consequence of this, in the late 1950s the state's legislators were more involved in other issues, while its correctional administrators were busy "tuning up" their new system, incorporating the legislative mandate of the early 1950s.

of legislative due-process offensives, while decriminalization of addiction managed to buck the trend. In essence, conservatives and liberals could agree on such procedures as civil commitment, since they promised rehabilitation and still kept addicts off the streets. Had not prison rebellions in the late 1960s drawn a reflex law-and-order response,* bipartisan disillusionment with an expensive and ineffective corrections system might have produced gains for convicted offenders all through the Reagan era.

Figure 4.6 shows the cumulative curve for convicted offenders. The patterns described in Figure 4.5 are highlighted and some new insights are provided. With an overall slope of 3.43 for the period 1955–1971, it seems that convicts were, on the average, gaining legal rights and resources a little less rapidly than defendants. (The slope for defendants was 3.76.) While defendants did better earlier, and convicted offenders did better later, the overall rate slightly favors defendants. This difference in growth rate translates into substantially larger total gains by 1971. Defendants had a sum of 63.1 units by 1971, convicted offenders a sum of 48.0 units. (This

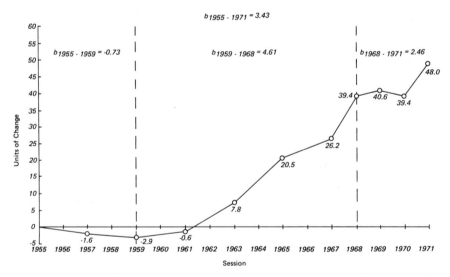

FIGURE 4.6   Cumulative net change in resources for convicted offenders as a result of Penal Code revisions.

* Ironically, the hard-line response also derived part of its force from the expansion of the Probation Subsidy Program, a "liberal" enactment of the 1965 legislature affecting the Welfare and Institutions Code. The program provided the funding for lesser offenders to remain at the local level under county supervision but thereby concentrated "hard-core offenders" in state institutions. The changing profile of this prison population may have created new problems for correctional administrators, but it also gave them potent new arguments against legislation to limit their powers.[5]

30% differential in increment for defendants is not a function of different starting points, since both began at zero in 1955.)

One might suspect that legislative reactions to the San Quentin and Folsom prison outbreaks in 1969 and 1970 had a lot to do with the disparity in gains between defendants and convicted offenders. Figure 4.6 underlines this with a discontinuity in 1968. In the period 1959–1968 convicted offenders were gaining at a rate of 4.61. After 1968 the rate dropped to 2.46. There is also a break point in 1959, which underscores the change in legislative attitude probably brought about by concern with drug abuse.*

It should be emphasized once again, that the quantitative data were collected and analyzed before the qualitative material was available. Points of discontinuity were arrived at through independent assessments of trends. That the two data bases support each other on a number of issues generates substantial credibility.

Figure 4.7 addresses the question of what the curves might have looked

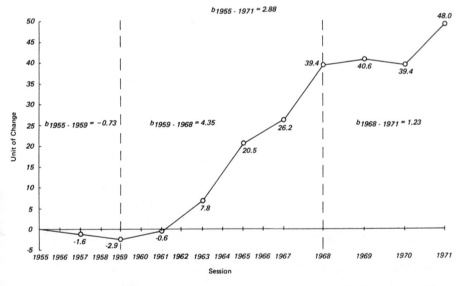

Figure 4.7 Cumulative net change in resources for convicted offenders as a result of Penal Code revisions (control for frequency of sessions).

* The slope up to 1959 must be interpreted especially cautiously. It is based on only three data points; 1955, 1957, and 1959. We could have decided not to indicate a change in slope in 1959 but concluded that even with a trend based on 3 points, the change in activity beginning in 1961 was so significant (13 revisions were passed) that it warranted emphasis in the graph. In short, there was, indeed, a significant change after 1959, though the numerical value for the 1955–1959 slope should not be taken too seriously.

like if the legislature had met every other year in the period 1967–1971. Again we are "controlling" for the switch to annual sessions and assuming that all else remains equal. Not surprisingly, the slope after 1968 is markedly decreased to 1.23. In other words, had the legislature not significantly changed its session output but continued to meet only in odd-numbered years, the reduction in rate of growth for the legal rights and resources of convicted offenders after 1968 would have been far more dramatic.

To summarize, the subjects of the criminal justice system, defendants and convicted offenders, were to some extent hurt by the law-and-order legislatures of the later 1960s. Convicted offenders managed to fight this trend more effectively because of bipartisan disillusionment with the corrections system spurred on by devastating committee reports on its performance. Had not reactions to the San Quentin and Folsom disruptions provided the corrections lobby with arguments against reform amidst crisis, the fortunes of progressive corrections legislation might have been even less affected by conservative domination. Thus, the factors affecting due-process legislation were apparently somewhat different from those affecting legislation aimed at convicted offenders.

Police

If there was one group among criminal justice personnel whose interests were anathema to the civil liberties lobby, it would probably be the police. Police priorities as defined by the California Peace Officers' Association (CPOA), were often vehemently opposed by such organizations as the FCL, and it was extremely unusual to find both sides supporting similar legislation. Looking back at the bar graph in Figure 4.1, one would predict that police interests would fare better in the late 1960s than earlier. One might also expect 1957, the year of the "Easy Arrest" Bill, to be successful for police, with 1968 and 1971 poorer years. However, one must remember that police interests were not monolithic and were often opposed by groups loosely allied within the law enforcement lobby. Recall that the crackdown on drugs in 1961 found many police professionals ambivalent about more severe penalties, and prosecutors generally in opposition. One reason was that longer sentences were thought to reduce conviction rates. In short, the very broad way in which success and failure were defined in Figure 4.1 may be insufficiently sensitive as we increasingly move to finer distinctions among types of legislation.

Figure 4.8 displays Penal Code revisions affecting the police. It appears that, consistent with expectations, police seem to do better in the later

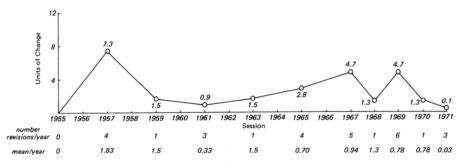

Figure 4.8 Net change in resources (by session) for police as a result of Penal Code revisions.

1960s than in the early 1960s. We also find the predicted success in 1957 and weaker showings in 1968 and 1971. Yet, we might also have thought that 1965 and 1970 would be banner years, and they are not. Recall that 1965 saw a Berkeley and Watts law-and-order offensive. 1970 found police so confident that they took on the jury system. While a more careful consideration of the qualitative material suggests reasons for the disappointing results, the essential point is that broad law enforcement offensives do not always result in concrete legislative victories.* This complexity is emphasized by the fact that the Pearson correlation between revisions affecting police and revisions affecting defendants is only −.17. The game may not be nearly as zero-sum as our earlier broad brush strokes indicated.†

The cumulative curve shown in Figure 4.9 confirms that police interests did better in the later 1960s. The break point is 1963, with the slope 1.24 before and 2.07 after. The 60% increase in slope is consistent with the bar graph reflecting the qualitative analysis though not nearly as dramatic as one might have anticipated. Nevertheless, it is important to emphasize that this is an independent verification of the qualitative data and a specific estimate of the extent to which police did better after 1963. Yet, it is also important to note that the 60% increase after 1963 was greatly affected by more frequent legislative sessions. Had the legislative output per session remained the same and had they continued to meet every other year, there would have been a negligible increase in slope, from 1.28 to 1.34 (see Figure 4.10). Of course, it is quite possible that if the legislature had contin-

* For example, the ineffective attack on the jury system in 1970 possibly diverted energies away from legislation more directly affecting day-to-day police activities.
† The correlation with revisions affecting convicted offenders is only −.22, again suggesting complexity beyond the qualitative material. Also, for police, the number of revisions per year correlates .01 with the mean for each year, indicating that the patterns are affected independently by the two factors.

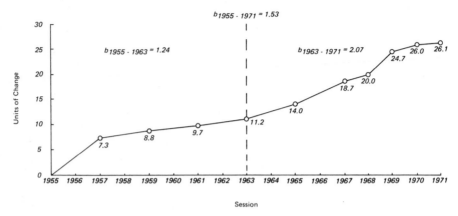

FIGURE 4.9   Cumulative net change in resources for police as a result of Penal Code revisions.

ued to meet only in odd-numbered years, they might have increased their output per session.*

Prosecutors

While the interests of police and of prosecutors sometimes differ, our qualitative analysis reveals them as members of the same coalition. In the early years of our study, the CPOA often advanced its agenda directly

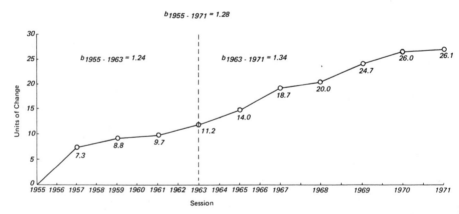

FIGURE 4.10   Cumulative net change in resources for police as a result of Penal Code revisions (control for frequency of sessions).

* While it is interesting to control for the frequency of legislative sessions, it is very difficult to say whether the resulting cumulative curve is a "better" substantive

through the Attorney General's Office, and even after the Democrats took over the executive branch, prosecutors and police typically stood shoulder to shoulder against most liberal criminal justice legislation. Hence, at first blush one would expect that good years for the law enforcement lobby would be good years not only for police but also for prosecutors. There should be a point of transition somewhere in the mid-1960s at which prosecutor fortunes markedly improve, with 1957, 1967, and 1969 proving to be especially good years. These expectations are based as much on the details of Figure 4.8, showing revisions affecting police, as on the more general bar graph derived from the qualitative material.

Revisions affecting police and revisions affecting prosecutors correlate .48, indicating that their legislative patterns tend to covary. An examination of Figure 4.11 supports this conclusion since, similarly to police, 1967 and 1969 are the best years for prosecutors, with 1957 moderately successful. Prosecutor victories in 1969 can be attributed in part to the passage of anti-pornography laws, which took advantage of U.S. Supreme Court rulings to give states new grounds for obtaining convictions. The 1967 legislature toughened up a variety of laws on crimes of violence, giving new tools to

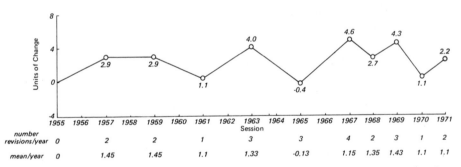

FIGURE 4.11 Net change in resources (by session) for prosecutors as a result of Penal Code revisions.

rendition. On the one hand, the more frequent sessions can be viewed as an artifact that distorts the rate of growth. In a simple arithmetic sense, more frequent sessions force the curve upward more rapidly. On the other hand, the more frequent sessions were part of the legislature's history not just an idiosyncracy biasing our arithmetic. Had the legislature continued to meet every other year, the whole pattern of events in the late 1960s would have been phased differently with sessions. The 1970 session, for example, would not have occurred, but the 1971 session would then have been the first gathering after Attica *and* the first session in which legislators could have reacted to the earlier student uprisings at San Francisco State. It is very difficult to say what this new interaction of historical events might have produced. Hence, we are predisposed to take the original unaltered cumulative graphs as a more accurate representation.

prosecutors and stiffening penalties. 1957 was the year of the "Easy Arrest" Bill as well as a Senate bill that broadened the grounds for the issuance of search warrants. While such dramatic bills determine only a portion of the legislative patterns reflected in 4.11, they are indicative of the kinds of legislation that were being passed.*

Quite surprisingly, 1965 is a bad year for prosecutors, in which legal resources were actually taken away. This is a very rare event for any actors involved in this study, since all parties tended to gain a little every session, though at different rates. Further, 1965 was one of the high-water marks of law-and-order hysteria and potentially a good year for all criminal justice personnel. This anomaly is possibly a consequence of the continued decriminalization of addiction, which took away important prosecutorial tools, while the plethora of hard-line legislation was not seen as affecting prosecutorial resources per se. Increasing the penalty for illegal assembly, for instance, does little to affect the resources available to obtain convictions.

The 1965 session being an "unsuccessful" one for prosecutors helps to explain why Figure 4.11 does not show dramatic differences before and after the mid-1960s. Still, there is a suggestion that prosecutors managed to capitalize on conservatism and law and order, since the cumulative curve in Figure 4.12 shows a distinct break point in 1965, where the slope approximately doubles (1.11 to 2.57). Recall that police showed a similar gain. Also, as with the police, controlling for frequency of session reduces the change in slope to a very small increment (see Figure 4.13). In summary,

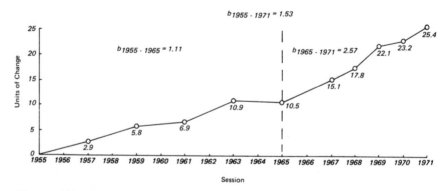

FIGURE 4.12   Cumulative net change in resources for prosecutors as a result of Penal Code revisions.

* The correlation between the number of revisions per year and their mean impact is .27, indicating only a slight tendency for them to covary. Apparently, the patterns are a result of both factors varying somewhat independently.

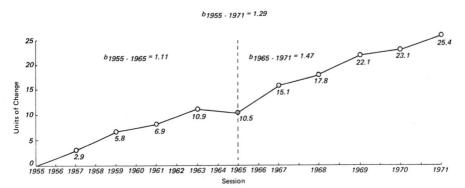

FIGURE 4.13 Cumulative net change in resources for prosecutors as a result of Penal Code revisions (control for frequency of sessions).   \

despite some important differences in the details of police and prosecutor success, the overall patterns are rather similar.

The Judiciary

Judges are the marginal men and women of the criminal justice system. As arbitrators, they ideally are supposed to be independent *a priori* of any camp and must somehow balance precedent, facts, and intuition to arrive at rulings uncompromised by politics. Clearly, this ideal is never fully achieved. But even when it is approximated, the judiciary is still criticized. Thus, from 1955 to 1971, the California judiciary was attacked at one time or another by virtually the entire political spectrum. Not only Reagan but also Brown used the courts as a scapegoat for rising crime rates. Police and prosecutors frequently attacked specific decisions and specific judges for failure to support law enforcement interests (e.g., the CPOA reaction to *Cahan*). Finally, the courts often drew fire from the public, as when the California Supreme Court invalidated the 1964 open-housing referendum in which the popular vote had gone heavily against open housing.

Given their marginal position, it is difficult to predict how Penal Code revisions affecting judges would fluctuate over the 15 years of our study. While criminal justice personnel, they were not part of the law enforcement lobby. Indeed they were often its targets. While involved in procedural matters, they certainly did not act as an arm of the ACLU. Further, it is in part just because judges were not members of a visible lobby that our earlier qualitative analysis gives us only limited insight. Nevertheless, given that it was conservatives, not liberals, who mounted statewide anticourt campaigns (e.g., the attempt in 1966 to purge the Supreme Court of Brown appointees), an initial expectation would be that judicial prerogatives should do better in years when liberal legislation did well.

Statistically our hunch is modestly supported. Judicial Penal Code revisions correlate .35 with defendant revisions and .25 with revisions affecting convicted offenders. In contrast, they correlate —.26 with police revisions and —.31 with revisions affecting prosecutors. However, correlations of this size are based on approximately 10% common variance (the square of these zero-order correlations), indicating that the curves are substantially independent of one another. This impression is underscored in Figure 4.14. The good years of 1959 and 1961 coupled with the bad years of 1967 and 1969 compare well with liberal patterns. However, the good years of 1965, 1968 (the best year), and 1970 complicate the interpretation.*

The waters are further muddied in Figure 4.15. The cumulative curve shows a substantial break point in 1967, after which the rate of growth nearly doubles (from 2.32 to 4.48). While Figure 4.16 (in which the frequency of sessions is controlled) virtually eliminates the break point, our data clearly indicate that the judiciary made more rapid gains during the law-and-order era than prior to it. Hence, the paradox. While judicial gains are modestly associated year by year with gains for defendants and convicted offenders, judicial interests were not hurt in the later 1960s. Possibly their formally nonaligned role permitted them to be seen as instruments for whatever groups were dominant. When the liberals were powerful, the courts were viewed as their allies. When conservatives took over the execu-

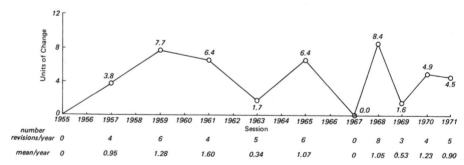

FIGURE 4.14   Net change in resources (by session) for judiciary as a result of Penal Code revisions.

* The correlation between the number of revisions per year and the mean impact per year is .71. Hence, the patterns reflected a marked tendency of these factors to covary.

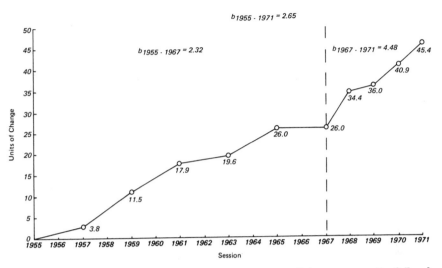

FIGURE 4.15 Cumulative net change in resources for judiciary as a result of Penal Code revisions.

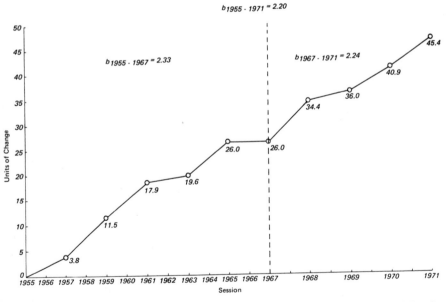

FIGURE 4.16 Cumulative net change in resources for judiciary as a result of Penal Code revisions (control for frequency of sessions).

tive and legislative branches, they may have begun to think better of the judiciary as well. To the degree that the dominant parties could pack the courts through judicial appointments, such perceptions were probably accurate.* To the extent that, in addition, court decisions were influenced by public opinion and prevailing ideologies, a more conservative bent in the late 1960s comes as no surprise. However, while this chameleonlike quality is consistent with our data, other interpretations are also plausible. In short, we have no compelling explanations within an interest group rubric for the patterns of Penal Code revisions affecting the judiciary.

Corrections Officials

Like the judiciary, corrections officials (prison personnel, administrators, and the Adult Authority) are difficult to place in a single camp. In the 1950s, the California correctional system was the darling of liberal reformers. By the late 1960s it had become a favorite whipping boy. Further, when in the late 1960s corrections officials tried to align with the law enforcement lobby, their earlier liberal ties caused uneasiness among potential allies. Even many conservative legislators could not be effectively recruited, since the corrections system appalled the fiscally orthodox by combining enormous budgets with demonstrated ineffectiveness.

Despite these complexities, one might expect that, generally, legislative patterns for corrections officials would be closer to liberal than to conservative patterns. It was not until the last several sessions covered in this study that liberals turned on the corrections system. Also, many of the early innovations took discretion away from police and prosecutors (e.g., civil commitment) and placed it in the hands of rehabilitative personnel. Finally, such reforms were often initially seen as giving more resources to prisoners.†

The pattern of correlations moderately supports such speculations. Revisions affecting corrections officials correlate positively and moderately (around .30) with revisions affecting defendants, convicted offenders, and

---

* By February 1974, Reagan (in office just over 7 years) had appointed 568 of the 1106 superior, municipal, and appellate court judges in the state. Calling the power of appointment "the single most significant power a president or a governor has in our modern society," Judge Joan Dempsey Klein of the Los Angeles Municipal Court characterized Reagan's judicial appointees as "law-and-order-oriented" in the criminal field and "defense-oriented" in the civil field.[6]

† Many of the enactments in the early and middle 1960s were directed to rehabilitation programs such as work furloughs, adult education and training, probation subsidies, and halfway houses. All of these programs, while providing increased resources for convicted offenders, at the same time augmented the authority of the corrections officials, who often recommended and initiated them.

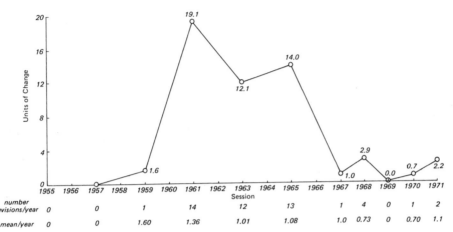

FIGURE 4.17 Net change in resources (by session) for corrections officials as a result of Penal Code revisions.

the judiciary. Negative correlations of about the same size appear for revisions affecting police and prosecutors. Figure 4.17 confirms these correlations. Corrections officials do extremely well in the period 1959–1965, which overlaps substantially with liberal dominance. In the early 1950s, the corrections system was consolidating massive changes brought about several years earlier and hence was largely ignored by the legislature. In the late 1960s, the system was under a bipartisan attack but managed to stave off wholesale dismemberment.

Figure 4.18 highlights the on-again-off-again legislative interest in the corrections system. Break points appear in 1959 and 1965, though the earlier break point is produced entirely by a transition from no activity to intense activity. While there is legislation affecting the corrections system after 1965, the revisions are not only few in number but of smaller average impact (see the two bottom lines in Figure 4.17). Controlling for the frequency of legislative sessions (Figure 4.19) underscores this later transition.

Summary and Conclusions

There seems little doubt that the broad trends revealed by our earlier qualitative analysis are supported by the quantitative material. Civil liberties victories were associated with successful legislative sessions for defendants and convicted offenders. Law enforcement victories were associated with successful legislative sessions for police and prosecutors. Further,

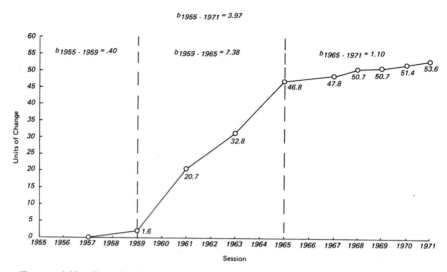

FIGURE 4.18   Cumulative net change in resources for corrections officials as a result of Penal Code revisions.

around these general patterns, many year-to-year fluctuations could be tentatively explained by historical events discussed in Chapter II. However, the quantitative material unearthed complexities not apparent earlier. First, the output of many legislative sessions was not entirely explained by broad his-

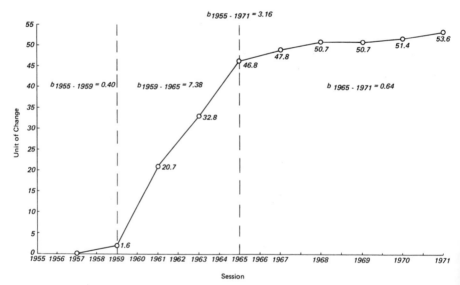

FIGURE 4.19   Cumulative net change in resources for corrections officials as a result of Penal Code revisions (control for frequency of sessions).

torical trends. Clearly, additional explanations will have to be sought. (To assist the reader in comparing the relative impact of Penal Code revisions, we have presented in Figure 4.20 a composite graph for all the actors within the criminal justice system.)

Second, the patterns for corrections officials and the judiciary, while difficult to reconcile with the qualitative data, show legislative patterns closer to defendants and convicted offenders than to their colleagues in the criminal justice system. Again, complexity is apparent which warrants further consideration.

Third, the cumulative curves reveal the critical impact of more frequent legislative sessions in the late 1960s. In the case of the judiciary, for example, output per session did not change markedly, but the cumulative effect increases more rapidly after 1967.

Fourth, the cumulative curves emphasize that change in the Penal Code is typically a slow process of accretion. Year-to-year fluctuations that appear dramatic in the disaggregated form are significantly "smoothed out" in cumulative form. Since this leveling process would be even more marked

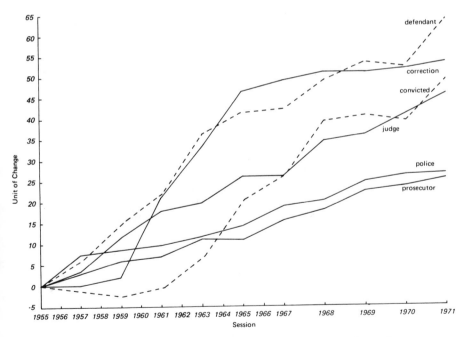

FIGURE 4.20 Composite for actors in the system: cumulative net change in resources as a result of Penal Code revisions (control for frequency of sessions). Solid lines: criminal justice officials (police, prosecutor, judge, corrections); dotted lines: subjects of the criminal justice system (defendants, convicted).

were Penal Code revisions accumulated and attached to the existing body of law, the importance of yearly changes could be questioned. We shall return to this issue later.

The basis for above conclusions is summarized in the Tables 4.1 and 4.2, in which break points and slopes are displayed. The slopes for convicted offenders, defendants, and corrections officials show the steepest rise in the period 1955–1971 (all well above 3.0). Hence, over the sessions covered by this study they have apparently made the greatest gains. To the degree that these actors are associated with civil liberties interests, the civil liberties lobby seems the overall winner in legislative combat. However, it is important to emphasize that our curves start from an arbitrary base of zero in 1955, and earlier disparities in legal rights and resources are not considered. Hence, these larger slopes may simply be allowing defendants, convicted offenders, and corrections officials to catch up with other actors. On the other hand, they may be increasing their advantages.

Liberal gains are underscored by the relatively small slopes for police and prosecutors, typically one-half of the size of the slopes for defendants, convicted offenders, and corrections officials in the 1955–1971 period. The slope for the judiciary falls in the middle. In short, the two types of criminal justice officials most closely associated with law enforcement interests appear to have been the least successful in obtaining Penal Code revisions consistent with their priorities.

Within such overall trends, there are important variations. After the early 1960s, convicted offenders, defendants, and corrections officials show substantial decreases in the rate at which they were gaining legal rights and resources. In contrast, police, prosecutors, and judges doubled their rates of growth. Were these trends to continue, there would be reason for law

TABLE 4.1

Legal Resources for Subjects of the System

| | Slopes and discontinuities for cumulative curves 1955 - 1971 | | | |
| | | | Breakpoints | |
	1955-1971	*1955-1959*	*1959-1968*	*1968-1971*
Convicted offenders	3.43	-0.73	4.61	2.46
Control[a]	2.88	-0.73	4.35	1.23
	1955-1971	*1955-1965*		*1968-1971*
Defendants	3.76	4.43		3.21
Control[a]	3.06	4.43		1.91

[a] X axis (years) is altered to control for effect of change from bi-annual to annual general sessions after 1967.

TABLE 4.2

Legal Resources for Criminal Justice Officials

	Slopes and discontinuities for cumulative curves 1955 - 1971			
		Breakpoints		
	1955-1971	1955-1965		1965-1971
Prosecution	1.53	1.11		2.57
Control[a]	1.29	1.11		1.47
	1955-1971	1955-1959	1959-1965	1965-1971
Corrections	3.97	0.40	7.38	1.11
Control[a]	3.16	0.40	7.38	0.64
	1955-1971	1955-1963		1963-1971
Police	1.53	1.24		2.07
Control[a]	1.28	1.24		1.34
	1955-1971	1955-1967		1967-1971
Judiciary	2.65	2.32		4.48
Control[a]	2.20	2.32		2.24

[a] X axis (years) is altered to control for effect of change from bi-annual to annual general sessions after 1967.

enforcement optimism. However, the 1971 legislative session suggested that liberals were beginning to counterattack effectively, and 1970 may have been a high-water mark for law and order. Further, the police growth rate after their break point *was still somewhat smaller* than the post–break point growth rates for defendants and convicted offenders.* Hence, even in the late 1960s law enforcement interests were, at best, only holding their own.

Were alterations in the legal rights and resources of actors in the criminal justice system the only means for law enforcement interests to advance their priorities, our data would seem to indicate that their attempts to shape the criminal justice system through legislative change had not been especially successful. Yet, much Penal Code activity involves not the rights and resources of actors but the definition of and sanctions for criminal behavior. Since this is the concern of our next chapter, we shall have to await this analysis of enactments involving criminalization and penalties before generalizing as to whether or not the legislature was moving significantly toward a more punitive stance in its revision of the Penal Code. We turn to that question now.

* The post–break point slope for prosecutors was larger than that for convicted offenders and smaller than that for defendants.

Appendix 4.1   Collapsed Dependent Variables

Coding categories included within dependent variables		Coding number
I. Actors in the Criminal justice system		
Corrections officials	Adult Authority	19
	Correction/prison/jail officials	20
	County parole board or parole officers	54
Judge	Judge (decision-making in judicial capacity)	21
Police	Police–sheriff	22
	Extension of peace officer designation	53
	Protection of peace officers	14
Prosecution	Prosecution	24
Convicted offenders	Ex-clients of system	34
	Parolee	37
	Probationer	38
	Prisoner	39
	Recidivist	40
Defendant	Defendant	32
	Appellant	33
	Suspect (prior to arraignment)	41
	Bail–own recognizance	43
	Burden of proof (presumptions)	44
	Constitutional protections, search and seizure, etc.	45
II. Criminalization categories		
Public interest	Civil rights	1
	Consumer rights	2
	Ecological concerns	4
	Gun control	5
Crimes against property	Property rights	13
Crimes against persons	Persons (assault, etc.)	9
Crimes without victims	Drugs	3
	Morality/vice	8
	Transfer from penal sanctions	17
Overall criminalization	All criminalization categories were included (18 categories in all)	
Severity of penalty	Severity	28

REFERENCES

1. George E. P. Box and Gwilym M. Jenkins, *Time Series Analysis* (San Francisco: Holden Day, 1970). See, for example, pp. 21–25; David R. Brillinger, *Time Series Data Analysis and Theory* (New York: Holt, Rinehart and Winston, 1975). See, for example, pp. 1–8.
2. Vic Barnett, *Comparative Statistical Inference*, (New York: John Wiley, 1973).
3. Jan Kmenta, *Elements of Econometrics* (New York: Macmillan Company, 1971), pp. 269–297.
4. Kmenta, *Elements of Econometrics*, pp. 391–405.
5. Board of Corrections of the California Human Relations Agency, *Coordinated California Corrections: Correctional System Study, Final Report*, July, 1971, p. 68.
6. *Los Angeles Daily Journal*, February 25, 1974, p. 1.

V

Trends in the Penal Code
Affecting Criminalization and
Severity of Penalties

Introduction

IN THE PREVIOUS CHAPTER WE examined Penal Code revisions
affecting actors in the criminal justice system. Our discussion emphasized
the winning and losing of legal rights and resources: rearrangements in the
balance of power among contending forces. In this chapter we move to
Penal Code revisions of a somewhat different type. Using the same techniques as in Chapter IV, we shall examine revisions affecting definitions
of criminal activity and revisions specifying severity of penalties. Caveats
discussed earlier remain, since we shall be considering only overt legislative intent.*

This chapter divides the relevant legislation into six parts. We begin with

---

* It may be useful to remind the reader of the important caveats. First, to some
degree, we have consciously traded detail for broader coverage. While not quite a
zero–sum situation, the data reduction techniques used to handle any large body of
data almost inevitably obscure some more subtle themes within smaller subsets of
material. Hence, we pay an obvious price for our quantification, but one that may
not be too dear given our ability to chart longitudinal patterns from hundreds of
revisions. Second, conceptual distinctions that could not be reliably coded were clearly
of no use in the quantification process. We would have preferred, for example, to
isolate purely procedural resources. But once one moves out of the courtroom, the
idea of procedures becomes quite muddy or, if very broadly defined, vacuous. Third,

two rather standard categories, crimes against persons and crimes against property. The next two sections involve crimes "against the public interest" (e.g., consumer protection) and "crimes without victims" (e.g., drug use). Finally, with all categories of crime aggregated, we will examine overall trends in criminalization and overall trends in severity of penalties.

There is reason to believe that Penal Code revisions of crime definition involve somewhat different processes than revisions aimed at procedural issues. If there is one lesson learned from the qualitative analysis, it is that a typical response to virtually any "crime problem" was to propose legislation making the objectionable behavior illegal. And if there already was a law, the reflex was to increase penalties. It did not matter that evidence regarding the deterrent effect of more severe sanctions was at best equivocal. Rather, a hard-line response required little consideration of the subtleties, provided a quick "answer" to the problem, and looked good for the folks back home. The old saying "there ought to be a law" could have neatly summarized the social philosophy of many a zealous legislator.

Thus, an initial expectation from the qualitative analysis is that revisions affecting crimes and penalties would be especially sensitive to short-run sentiments, and therefore the curves in this chapter should show more volatile patterns. In practice, this would mean that change would result more from immediate reactions to outside events than from persistent lobby pressures or concerted legislative programs. It would also suggest less staying power. Issues would invade Sacramento, trigger a flood of legislative proposals and enactments and then disappear, allowing the legislature to return to its "normal" business.

What were likely to be the issues? Examples include the antidrug hysteria in 1961, reactions to Berkeley, Watts, and law and order from 1965 through 1967, and the prison rebellions in the late 1960s and early 1970s. However, one would also expect that major categories of criminalization and related penalties might be differentially sensitive to such events. This will be discussed in the context of each section in the chapter.

Crimes against Persons*

Most kinds of crimes against persons were invented long before there was a state of California. Murder, rape, manslaughter, and assault and battery were thoroughly criminalized well before 1955. Yet, while these

---

we coded obvious intent and avoided more difficult assessments. Again, we would have preferred to use a more elaborate system. But, if people cannot reasonably agree on subleties, there is no point in reifying their judgments with numbers. Finally, we are not even hinting that quantification is the only way to do historical analyses of legislation. We are just suggesting that it is one way, and a useful way at that.

* Includes murder, rape, manslaughter, assault and battery, armed robbery, etc.

broad categories of crime were carefully delineated by statute, certain subsets were not. An assault on a fireman doing his duty, for instance, might
require refined definitions and refined sanctions. This suggests that a need
for more specialized categories of crimes against persons should appear in
response to new social circumstances, and our qualitative data point to the
middle and late 1960s as such a period. Urban Americans had not seen mass
disorder since the labor unrest of the 1930s and the race riots of the 1940s.
Further, Berkeley and Watts were different in many ways from earlier unrest. Berkeley found middle-class students armed with New Left ideology
challenging their university, American foreign policy, and fundamental
American values. Watts found blacks redistributing private property and
fighting police. Politics alone demanded some legislative response, and refinement of crimes against persons was a relatively simple response to make.

Figure 5.1 displays Penal Code revisions for crimes against persons. Overall, only 19 revisions affected crimes against persons, but 11 (58%) were
passed in 1965 and 1967. Much of this was a reaction to widespread disorder and sought to repress civil unrest as well as more general political
militancy among blacks and students. Attacks on police and prison guards
received special atention, along with the regulation of "paramilitary" organizations. 1969 and 1970 also saw the definition of new crimes against
persons, in response to prisoner unrest and such innovative offenses as plane
hijacking. In short, the pattern for crimes against persons seems consistent
with expectations based on our qualitative analysis.

Figure 5.2 underscores the change after 1963. A slope of virtually zero
becomes 3.31, and is reduced only to 2.12 when frequency of sessions is
controlled (Figure 5.3). There can be no doubt that revisions affecting
crimes against persons were in part a reaction to the discorders of the late
1960s.

What about the volatility dimension? Our expectations here also seem
supported. After virtually no activity, the legislature responded immedi-

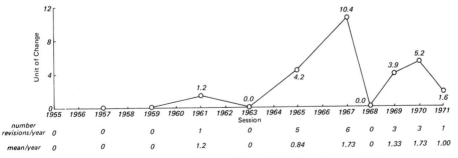

FIGURE 5.1 Net change in criminalization (by session) for crimes against persons.

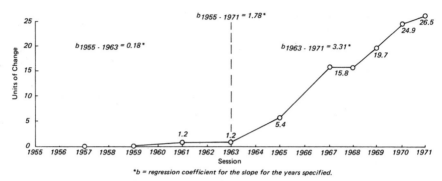

*b = regression coefficient for the slope for the years specified.

FIGURE 5.2   Cumulative net change in criminalization for crimes against persons.

ately and with vigor in 1965 and 1967. But 1968 saw not a single revision affecting crimes against persons. Berkeley and Watts were over, while San Francisco State had not yet erupted. In 1969 and 1970, the legislature again responded to a new but lesser round of unrest and then by 1971 seemed to lose interest. Such fluctuations in activity are far more dramatic than were found for revisions affecting actors in the criminal justice system (with the exception of corrections officials).

Crimes against Property*

Initially, one might expect the same kinds of reflex reaction for legislation affecting crimes against property as for that affecting crimes against persons. Certainly a society that condones shooting looters during civil

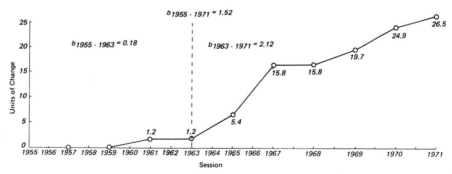

FIGURE 5.3   Cumulative net change in criminalization for crimes against persons (control for frequency of sessions).

   * Includes larceny, forgery, bribery, embezzlement, extortion, malicious mischief, burglary, etc.

disorders must hold private property sacred. Yet, the critical dimensions may have more to do with how property is appropriated than the nature of property itself. In armed robbery, for example, an emotional response may stem largely from the offender's use of force, rather than from dollar loss. In contrast, while fraud would be widely condemned, it would be unlikely to generate an immediate tidal wave of legislation.

These and other considerations lead to somewhat different expectations for longitudinal trends in property crimes as compared with trends for crimes against persons. Since the rebellions and student disorders of the 1960s involved in part attacks on private property, one would expect the legislature to respond quickly. In contrast, prisoner unrest did not endanger private property, and hence the rate of criminalization for property crimes should be less affected during the legislative sessions in which prison disorders were at issue. In addition, sessions marked by cathartic reactions to Watts and Berkeley would, perhaps, not be concerned solely with riot control. In an atmosphere where punitive measures become patriotic, legislators might try to move their legislative agenda in accordance with their particular criminal justice priorities. Thus, more liberal legislators might introduce proposals identifying new white-collar crimes or statutes aimed at police corruption, while conservative legislators might tend to be more concerned with property destruction during an illegal trespass on state property (e.g., a university). In short, our qualitative analysis leads us to expect significant property crime criminalization during sessions responding to widespread unrest, but the legislation passed may eventually reflect a broad range of concerns.

Figure 5.4 shows the revisions affecting crimes against property. Consistent with expectation, the mid-1960s show marked activity, while 1968, 1969, 1970, and 1971 do not. The mid-1960s were characterized by Berkeley

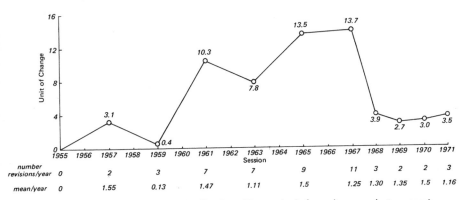

FIGURE 5.4 Net change in criminalization (by session) for crimes against property.

and Watts, while the late 1960s and early 1970s were characterized by Folsom and San Quentin.* The property crime revisions of 1961 and 1963, on the other hand, reflect legislative concern with white-collar crime (recall this is the period of liberal resurgence), and here the enactments are directed at embezzlement and false pretense such as false statements "designedly made for charitable solicitations." Of the fourteen property crime revisions in 1961 and 1963, twelve fall within this framework and have a "public interest" component.

Figures 5.5 and 5.6 show the cumulative patterns. The increase in activ-

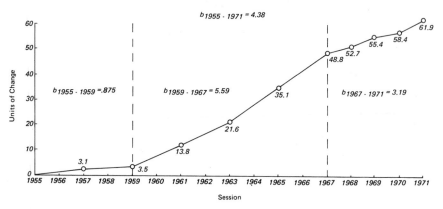

FIGURE 5.5 Cumulative net change in criminalization for crimes against property.

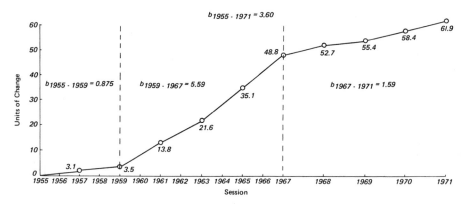

FIGURE 5.6 Cumulative net change in criminalization for crimes against property (control for frequency of sessions).

* 1969 also saw renewed student unrest, but that issue may already have been as criminalized as was politically feasible. Further, in Sacramento it showed signs of becoming a stale issue.

ity after 1959 and the decrease after 1967 are reflected in substantial disparities in slopes. The decrease is of special interest since it highlights the difference in patterns between crimes against persons and crimes against property. Recall that there was no significant discontinuity in the late 1960s (that is, no substantial decrease in growth rate) for crimes against persons (see Figure 5.2). While there was a sharp drop in Penal Code revisions for crimes against persons in 1968, such crimes again received considerable attention in 1969 and 1970. This was enough to sustain an overall picture of increased growth.

While revisions affecting crimes against property show some of the same reactivity as revisions affecting crimes against persons, the pattern is less pronounced. Two sessions accounted for 58% of the legislation involving crimes against persons, compared to only 41% for property offenses. Substantial activity in the early 1960s and reduced but continued interest in 1968 and 1971 smooth out the curves. Apparently, property crime legislation is responsive to a somewhat wider range of issues. Significantly, of the 49 enactments involving property offenses, approximately 30 were directed at white-collar crimes, such as embezzlement, fraud, and bribery, while another 10 were concerned with "malicious mischief," such as trespass, in which neither burglary nor larceny are involved.

Crimes against the Public Interest

There is a wide variety of crimes where the injured party is less likely to be an individual than a community, a neighborhood, or "the public." Such crimes would include disorderly conduct, environmental pollution, consumer protection, and gun control. Certainly these have been visible issues, especially since the late 1960s.

Our qualitative material suggest that there should be a relatively constant but low level of interest in offenses against the public interest combined with occasionally more dramatic legislative reactions to broader societal events. Hence, one would expect the 1965 and 1967 sessions to be once again unusually responsive. In addition, the 1969 session might experience a flurry of activity. Recall that this session was marked by statutes regulating obscenity and pornography. While these issues will formally appear under our category of crimes without victims their impact could easily spill over into crimes against the public interest. The use of normative standards to judge potentially objectionable materials means that justification for regulatory legislation rests in part on what is good for the morals of a community. It is in the public's interest to outlaw immoral publications. Once this principle is endorsed, it is easily generalized.

Figure 5.7 shows that once again the qualitative and quantitative data support each other. Clearly 1965 and 1967 are the busy years, with 1969 also showing well above average activity. However, the impacts of 1965 and 1967 so overshadow all other years (they are double 1969 and at least triple all other years) that Figures 5.8 and 5.9 show a break point in 1967. Ignoring frequency of sessions, the slope is cut by nearly two-thirds (6.52 to 2.52), which parallels the somewhat less dramatic post-1967 decrease in slope for property crimes. (The drop there was from 5.59 to 3.19.) Recall that crimes against persons did not show this dramatic change in slope in the late 1960s.

Somewhat surprisingly, crimes against the public interest also seem to show a volatility at least as dramatic as offenses against persons; 58% of the revisions were passed in the two years 1965 (13 revisions) and 1967 (10 revisions), while 1963 saw only 3 revisions passed, and 1968 only 1.

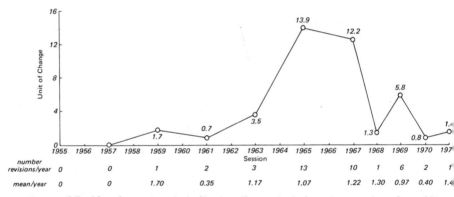

FIGURE 5.7 Net change in criminalization (by session) for crimes against the public interest.

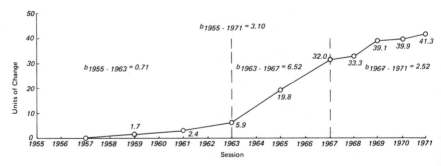

FIGURE 5.8 Cumulative net change in criminalization for crimes against the public interest.

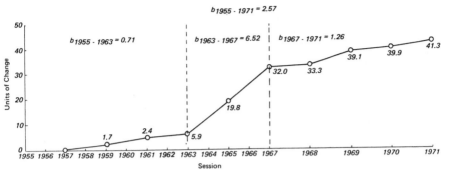

FIGURE 5.9 Cumulative net change in criminalization for crimes against the public interest (control for frequency of sessions).

This would seem to indicate the impulsive nature of a broad range of criminalization legislation.

Crimes without Victims

While it was relatively easy to link the offenses described earlier to dramatic social events, the regulation of drug and moral offenses may have more subtle causes. Certainly drug addiction of epidemic proportions can trigger legislative reactions. But epidemics do not appear all at once; they spread gradually. Hence, they may go almost unnoticed until some group decides to make drugs an issue and undertakes sustained political initiative. Similarly, moral offenses need political entrepreneurs. Our qualitative data suggest three waves of ongoing activity around such crimes. 1961 found citizen groups and narcotics officials allied against the drug "menace." The mid-1960s saw liberals supporting a medical definition of addiction that implied decriminalization. The late 1960s brought a conservative crackdown on moral offenses. With the probable exception of the 1961 anti-drug crusade, all reflect rather persistent political efforts, often well informed and clearly articulated.

Figure 5.10 confirms what the qualitative analysis suggests. The 52 revisions affecting morality and drugs are spread rather evenly over the 11 legislative sessions, with the exception of 15 revisions in 1961. Note that the 1961 session, which undertook massive criminalization, is bracketed by sessions in which decriminalization occurred. This suggests the volatility characteristic of legislative efforts linked to dramatic social events.

The 1963 and 1965 sessions were marked by the decriminalization of addiction recommended by Brown's Special Study Commission on Narcotics. Between 1961 and 1965, labels of criminality were deleted from

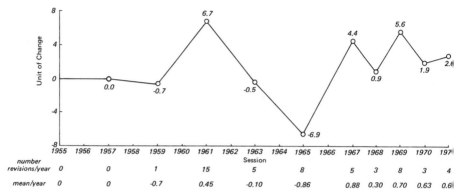

FIGURE 5.10   Net change in criminalization (by session) for crimes without victims.

commitment, release, and discharge procedures, while in 1965 the entire body of law was transferred from the Penal Code to the Health and Safety Code. As a result, where a section of the Code had previously referred to an indvidual as a "parolee," the label was now "outpatient." Recall, however, that these civil commitment procedures raised serious new problems. Many procedural safeguards available under criminal law were no longer applicable, despite the fact that the 1965 enactment provided the right to counsel at all stages of the proceedings.

While the 1965 decriminalization of addiction bucked the law-and-order trend (at least superficially), conservatives seized the initiative thereafter. Reagan's anticrime package in 1967 had some impact, culminating in the obscenity and pornography legislation of 1969.* Note that this offensive involved careful consideration of the issues, especially a series of very subtle constitutional questions. While having roots in the sentiments of law and order, the legislation was far more than an emotional reflex.

The cumulative curves in Figures 5.11 and 5.12 emphasize the transition to increased criminalization after 1965. Before 1967, the overall effects of the early antidrug legislation and the later decriminalization of addiction largely cancel each other out. The slope is virtually zero. After 1965, the slope becomes 2.66 and remains substantial even when controlled for frequency of sessions. This pattern is remarkably similar to that for revisions affecting crimes against persons, though the absence of a decrease in the late 1960s is due not to some dramatic event (e.g., a prison riot) but to a concerted political effort.

* It should be borne in mind, however, that because of the earlier transfer of much drug legislation from the Penal Code to the Health and Safety Code some late 1960s moves toward decriminalization (e.g., the softening of the marijuana laws) do not show up in our data.

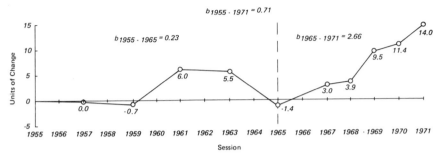

Figure 5.11   Cumulative net change in criminalization for crimes without victims.

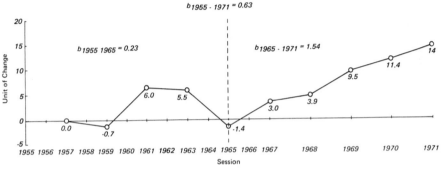

Figure 5.12   Cumulative net change in criminalization for crimes without victims (control for frequency of sessions).

Overall Criminalization

Besides examining trends for specific kinds of criminalization, one might be interested in gauging the total pattern. To this end we have constructed the category "total criminalization," which includes all the criminalization legislation discussed so far plus categories with too few revisions to merit lengthy consideration (e.g., vehicular offenses) and a miscellaneous category for revisions that did not fit into our original coding categories. While this procedure clearly obscures critical subtleties, it also allows us to assess the overall rate at which the behavior of California's citizens was being regulated by the Penal Code.

Figure 5.13 shows the patterns over time. Consistent with our earlier graphs, 1961, 1965, and 1967 are the years in which massive criminalization occurs. However, 1967 is far and away the most significant session, with nearly twice the legislative impact of the second most important session (1965). It is equally important to recognize that *in no session* is the net

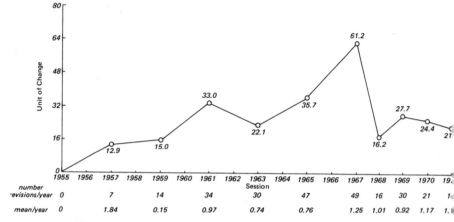

FIGURE 5.13   Net change in criminalization (by session) for all crimes.

effect to decriminalize. This is underscored in Figures 5.14 and 5.15, where cumulative curves are displayed. When frequency of session is ignored, the curve for total criminalization appears to follow some power function, in which the slope slightly increases over nearly every interval. In short, the rate of criminalization seems to be increasing a bit overall from 1955 to 1971. If a break point is calculated from the data, it occurs in 1967, after which the slope goes from 14.4 to 23.1. This further emphasizes the in-

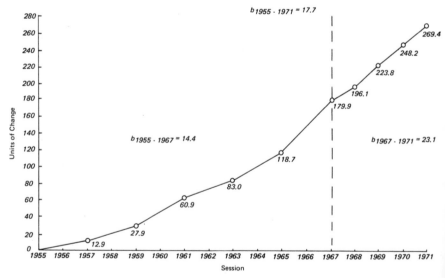

FIGURE 5.14   Cumulative net change in criminalization for all crimes.

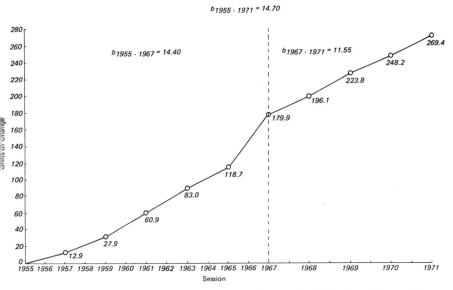

$b_{1955 - 1971} = 14.70$

$b_{1955 - 1967} = 14.40$

$b_{1967 - 1971} = 11.55$

FIGURE 5.15 Cumulative net change in criminalization for all crimes (control for frequency of sessions).

creasing rate of growth. Only when frequency of sessions is held constant (Figure 5.15) does the rate of growth taper off.

It is ultimately a political question whether increasing the rate of criminalization is worthwhile. Nevertheless, there seems adequate grounds for concern. First, a case would have to be made that the multitude of behaviors criminalized in fact represent activities not adequately covered by existing law. If such a case cannot be made, the criminalization trends represent a kind of legislative rhetoric with little import beyond public relations. Second, if the criminalization revisions are really defining new criminal behavior, it may imply growing dislocations in our society. For starters, it may be that socially unacceptable behavior is increasing at an increasing rate. If this is not the reality, it may still be true that legislators perceive it as the reality. And rather than responding to the causes of this normative breakdown, the legislative emphasis is to criminalize. Third, one must wonder if our society has the resources to invest increasing effort into the regulation of behavior. At the very least, prison sentences defined by our criminal law have taxed incarceration facilities to the breaking point. The courts are similarly burdened. Finally, there is the empirical question of whether criminalization accomplishes its manifest goals. It appears that prisons do not rehabilitate (see, for example, Lipton et al.).[1] It is doubtful that, as currently structured, the threat of sanction deters most would-be criminals (see, for example, Gibbs; and Zimring and Hawkins[2]). And it has yet to be demonstrated that people feel safer knowing that the legislature is taking a hard line on crime. Indeed, it is dubious that the public follows Penal Code legislation with sufficient awareness to know, even generally, what the legislature does in this area.

In all fairness, however, we should acknowledge the fact that few legislators fully accept the premise that increased criminalization in itself provides the total answer to antisocial behavior. At most they might agree that increased criminalization is only one response (or an important response) to the problem. However, this fails to address the more basic question of whether or not increased criminalization in itself may, in fact, be counterproductive.

Severity of Penalties

Coupled to virtually all legislation that defines criminal behavior are sections specifying penalties. In essence, penalties provide another important tool with which to change the impact of the Penal Code, and over the years covered by our study, legislators have frequently used it either in concert with criminalization revisions or alone. Occasionally penalties are reduced. Typically they are increased. To the degree that legislators sincerely believe that raising penalties is more than politics and public relations, their efficacy is usually justified through some contrived combination of retribution, deterrence, and rehabilitation.

Figure 5.16 shows the patterns affecting severity of penalties. It includes 50 revisions reflecting a cross-section of offenses. Penalty revisions were too few to warrant a breakdown of the total into subcategories for types of crime.

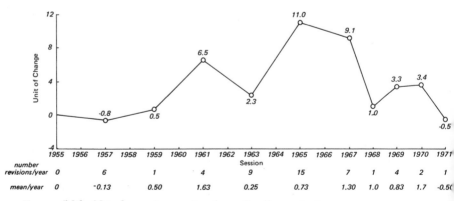

FIGURE 5.16   Net change in severity of penalty (by session).

A familiar picture appears. 1961, 1965, and 1967 are banner years, with the later two having the considerably greater impact. 1969 and 1970 also show characteristic increases. Typically, penalties are increasing, with 1957 and 1971 the only years in which net severity is reduced. The accumulation of increasingly severe penalties can be seen in Figure 5.17. As in the case of crimes against persons and crimes against the public interest, there is a reduction in slope after 1967 (from 3.60 to 2.10), suggesting that most punitive legislation was associated with the passions evoked by Berkeley and Watts. Figure 5.18, which controls for frequency of sessions further emphasizes the change after 1967. One is still struck by the overall positive slope from 1955 to 1971, possibly reflecting a legislative belief in the efficacy of punishment.*

Since increased criminalization typically implies increased penalties, the uneasiness we expressed about criminalization rates applies equally to increased penalties. There is no evidence that lengthy sentences serve any

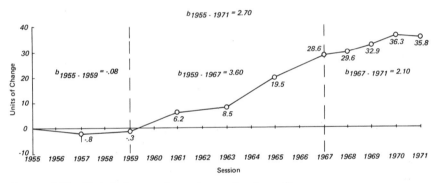

FIGURE 5.17   Cumulative net change in severity of penalty.

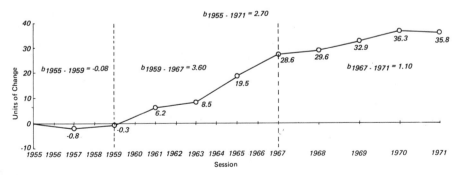

FIGURE 5.18   Cumulative net change in severity of penalty (control for frequency of sessions).

*To what extent increased penalties became operational is another matter. See Table 2.2, p. 69.

beneficial purpose for offenders and potential offenders, while the best one can say about their usefulness for the general public is that they help to keep dangerous habitual offenders off the streets.

Summary and Conclusions

While there were signs of moderation in the early 1970s, the overall patterns in our data show marked increases in criminalization and penalties. For criminalization, there is even evidence that the rate of increase has been slightly rising.

Table 5.1 summarizes the cumulative slopes and discontinuities for our four categories of crime, while Table 5.2 summarizes cumulative slopes and discontinuities for overall criminalization and severity of penalties. Crimes against the public interest, property crimes, and penalties have two break points, with the break point after 1967 showing a decrease in slope. Crimes against persons, crimes without victims, and overall criminalization have no late break point in which this occurs. However, to a greater extent than the break points might suggest, this apparent difference is more one of

TABLE 5.1

Criminalization for Specific Offenses

	Slopes and discontinuities for cumulative curves 1955 - 1971			
		Breakpoints		
	1955-1971	1955-1965		1965-1971
Crimes w/o victims	0.71[b]	0.23[b]		2.66
Control[a]	0.63[b]	0.23[b]		1.54
	1955-1971	*1955-1963*		*1963-1971*
Crimes against persons	1.78	0.18		3.31
Control[a]	1.52	0.18		2.12
	1955-1971	*1955-1963*	*1963-1967*	*1967-1971*
Crimes against public interest	3.10	0.71	6.53	2.52
Control[a]	2.57	0.71	6.53	1.26
	1955-1971	*1955-1959*	*1959-1967*	*1967-1971*
Crimes against property	4.38	0.88	5.59	3.19
Control[a]	3.60	0.88	5.59	1.59

[a] *X axis (years) is altered to control for effect of change from bi-annual to annual general sessions after 1967.*
[b] *The correlation from 1955-1967 is only .26, making use of the slope closer to an act of faith than good data analysis.*

TABLE 5.2

Overall Criminalization and Severity of Penalty

| | Slopes and discontinuities for cumulative curves 1955 - 1971 | | |
| | Breakpoints | | |
	1955-1971	*1955-1967*	*1967-1971*
Overall criminalization	17.7	14.4	23.1
Control[a]	14.7	14.4	11.55
	1955-1971	*1955-1959*	*1959-1967*	*1967-1971*
Severity of penalty	2.70	-0.08	3.60	2.10
Control[a]	2.20	-0.08	3.60	1.10

[a]*X axis (years) is altered to control for effect of change from bi-annual to annual general sessions after 1967.*

degree than of kind. Hard-line legislation across all categories declined after 1967 if one considers the impact per session. Though it declined in some cases more than in others (hence the presence or absence of 1967 discontinuities) the reduction in punitive fervor was universally evident. Nevertheless, when the legislature began meeting every year, its output accumulated more rapidly. Legislators themselves may not have been aware of this effect and may have believed that their less punitive stance was far more significant than in fact it was. Of course, it is also possible that some legislators knew exactly what was happening and were able to continue their hard-line offensive while appearing less fervent. In any case, the decrease in punitive revisions per session did not apparently translate into a significant reversal in the aggregate or in the proclivity to criminalize and increase penalties.

The slopes for the four crime categories for the period 1955–1971 reveal where the largest impacts occurred. Clearly property crimes, with a slope of 4.38 received the lion's share of attention and achieved the highest rate of criminalization. Crimes against the public interest, with a slope of 3.10, showed somewhat less criminalization; crimes against persons showed a relatively small increase (1.78), and crimes without victims showed virtually no increase. This last case may be somewhat misleading, for the decriminalization in narcotics addiction in the mid-1960s accounts for the limited growth rate and earlier we noted that procedures like civil commitment may in practice involve punitive consequences.

The uniqueness of revisions affecting drugs and morality is highlighted if one considers the pattern of correlations between its revisions and revisions for other kinds of crimes. Table 5.3 shows the zero-order Pearson correlations between revisions for all the legislation considered in this chapter and in Chapter IV. While there are high positive correlations (all

TABLE 5.3

Zero Order Correlations between Trends in Penal Code Revisions

		(1)	(2)	(3)	(4)	(5)	(6)	(7)	(8)	(9)	(10)	(11)	(12)
Defendant	(1)	X	.40	.49	.35	-.17	-.19	-.15	-.54	.08	-.13	-.19	-.13
Convicted offenders	(2)		X	.40	.25	-.22	-.04	-.35	.06	.52	.45	.35	.28
Corrections officials	(3)			X	.30	-.25	-.32	-.12	-.13	.64	.24	.54	.27
Judiciary	(4)				X	-.26	-.31	-.25	-.37	-.05	-.16	-.02	-.16
Police	(5)					X	.48	.03	.32	.20	.32	.15	.32
Prosecutor	(6)						X	.45	.22	.01	.05	-.15	.33
Crimes w/o victims	(7)							X	.22	-.07	-.26	-.10	.26
Persons	(8)								X	.58	.73	.70	.86
Property	(9)									X	.79	.89	.84
Public interest	(10)										X	.87	.78
Severity of penalty	(11)											X	.82
Overall criminalization	(12)												X

above .58) between all other types of criminalization and penalty severity, the correlations involving crimes without victims are small, with three of them actually negative. This can be most dramatically attributed to the 1965 legislative session, in which all other types of revisions showed significant increases while addiction was further decriminalized. Put another way, revisions affecting criminalization and penalties show a marked bandwagon effect, with the exception of revisions affecting drugs and morality. This lends credence to our view that most legislation defining crimes and specifying penalties is not only responsive to the same sorts of social events but often creates a punitive atmosphere, in which behavior is criminalized almost without regard to its substantive target.

The patterns among revisions affecting actors in the criminal justice system are more subtle and probably reflect more complicated processes. Recall that as defendants gained larger amounts of legal rights and resources, so did convicted offenders, corrections officials, and the judiciary. We have discussed how the ambiguous role of the latter two could produce greater legislative gains for them coupled with greater gains for defendants and convicted offenders. In contrast, police and prosecutors do well in years when defendants and convicted offenders do poorly. Our contention that these patterns reflect somewhat different processes from those for criminalization and penalties is supported through correlations between the two legislative blocks. Briefly, it is hard to find any meaningful pattern. While defendants seem to do less well in sessions marked by high criminalization, convicted offenders typically do better. While judges do less well in high criminalization sessions, corrections officials tend to make substantial gains. And while police and prosecutors tend to gain in concert with criminalization, the correlations are not large. Although the pattern is probably not random, it is unsystematic enough to suggest that there is no simple relation between the causes of criminalization revisions and revisions affecting actors in the criminal justice system. We shall return to and deal with this issue in greater depth in Chapter VI.

The apparent independence of legislative processes affecting criminal justice actors and criminalization has important political implications. Recall that Chapter IV concluded that law enforcement interests might have been the ultimate losers in the 15 years of our study; their overall rates of growth were smaller and even their post-1965 slopes at best equal to those of their political adversaries. But, we also suggested that law-and-order forces could perhaps advance their interests through another kind of legislation—that affecting crime definitions and penalties. We now see that massive amounts of criminalization occurred from 1965 to 1971, and occurred at an increasing rate. Penalties were also increased. To the degree that police and prosecutors supported such outcomes, do we alter Chapter IV's conclusions?

Recall that although police generally supported criminalization and tougher penalties,* prosecutors were often ambivalent. Longer, more flexible penalties could aid prosecutors in plea bargaining and in extracting information from informers. Yet harsher penalties per se were thought to reduce the tendency of juries to convict. Even in the case of the police, although longer mandatory sentences might get undesirables off the streets, they would make the recruiting of informers more difficult. How could police officers promise to intercede with the judge if sentences were fixed? In short, it is hard to tell if police and prosecutorial interests were really significantly advanced either in theory or in practice.

To make matters even more complicated, liberal forces were certainly not above criminalizing behavior they found objectionable. The criminalization of crimes against the public interest was often supported by the "progressive" camp, and the criminalization of many, perhaps even most, new property crimes was fully consistent with liberal ideology. Examples of such property crimes would include enactments addressed to the improper diversion of construction funds, the misuse of credit cards, and bribery of and by corporate officials. In the area of public interest are such enactments as those increasing gun and weapons control, those strengthen-

---

* Recall, however, that criminalization and increased penalties were never really the top priority for police lobbyists.

ing the eavesdropping and wiretap laws, those penalizing tampering with or removing parts from aircraft, those prohibiting the dumping of rubbish in water, and those requiring an integral lock mechanism for refrigerators and deep-freeze equipment.* Therefore, the kinds of crime with the largest slopes, crimes against property and crimes against the public interest, were a mixed array of statutes and not necessarily in the perceived interest of the law enforcement lobby.

More important, by considering who won and who lost solely in the context of small groups of partisans, a broader point is obscured. In a very significant sense, all sides seemed committed to the philosophy of controlling undesirable behavior by criminalizing it. In other words, both sides seemed enamored with the idea that active legislative intervention was a proper and useful way to regulate behavior. While they often differed on the *kinds* of behavior to be regulated, there seemed wide consensus that the State should intervene. Therefore, even if law-and-order interests did not gain, relative to civil liberties interests, one might wonder whether the conscious shaping of citizens' behavior through legislation was making the entire apparatus of criminal law an overused, possibly repressive tool.

One does not have to be an anarchist to worry about intrusion of the State into the lives of its citizens. Yet, none of the visible groups in Sacramento noted the very real implications of extending State prerogatives. Serious conservatives aggressively moved to criminalize the sale of "obscene" matter, just as thoughtful liberals actively sought the regulation of environmental quality. Perhaps legislating against undesirable behavior can become addictive. In any case, such confusions and contradictions only serve to complicate any final conclusion about which groups really benefited from Penal Code changes over the 15 years of this study. At least in terms of criminalization, perhaps the real winner was State power. Or perhaps the notion of arriving at one overall judgment about hundreds of Penal Code revisions is naive.

Thus far, we have presented the historical–qualitative analysis of Chapter II, and the quantitative trends in Penal Code change revealed in Chapters IV and V. While Chapter II emphasized the dramatic bills that were responsive to the law-and-order fury of the 1960s, the stastical assessments in Chapters IV and V have told a larger story—certainly larger than one gets from reading just about the "get tough on crime" debates in the legislative arena. But Chapter II also suggested that the political polarization result-

---

* A lock that allows refrigerator equipment to be opened from the inside by the exertion of 15 pounds of force or less against the latch edge of the closed door.

ing from the law-and-order offensive contributed more to legislative logjams than to major changes in the criminal law, and our statistical assessments seem to have borne this out.

At this point, the reader may be feeling a certain uneasiness with such historical explanations, and we shall now seek to remedy that discomfort with a more systematic consideration of the causes of Penal Code change. Thus far, it may have seemed that for almost any bump in a curve we could pull some rabbit out of the historical hat. At the very least, this suggests an atheoretical, almost *post hoc* approach to explanation, which, though often provocative, makes generalization problematic. To understand the immediate importance of Unruh's strategy of evenly dividing the Assembly's Criminal Procedure Committee between Republicans and Democrats adds little to social science knowledge without a general consideration of the role of partisanship and legislative majorities. Similarly, the CPOA attempt to recruit business support needs to be viewed more broadly in terms of what interests profit-making organizations have in Penal Code legislation. We now turn to a consideration of such questions.

REFERENCES

1. Douglas Lipton, Robert Martinson, and Judith Wilks, *The Effectiveness of Correctional Treatment* (New York: Praeger Publishers, 1975).
2. Jack P. Gibbs, *Crime, Punishment, and Deterrence* (New York: Elsevier, 1975); Franklin E. Zimring and Gordon J. Hawkins, *Deterrence* (Chicago: The University of Chicago Press, 1974).

VI

Explaining the Trends:
Zero-Order Correlations

Introduction

By THIS STAGE IN OUR analysis, broad trends in the California Penal Code between 1955 and 1971 have been identified. In addition, tentative explanations for the legislative patterns have been suggested. We have noted, for example, how law-and-order legislation seemed to be on the rise in the middle and late 1960s, perhaps in response to civil unrest, crime, and Republican resurgence. Nevertheless, we still have not considered in any depth an enormous range of factors associated with Penal Code change. Clearly, much work lies ahead of us.

Our qualitative analysis in Chapter II gives some indications of how we should proceed. There, we offered many specific, though partial, explanations for particular pieces of legislation. Thus, when the Republicans took control of the Assembly after the 1968 elections and engineered a 5 to 4 majority in the Criminal Procedure Committee, the stalemate in Penal Code legislation was broken. The attack on pornography, which followed, was in part a result of this rearrangement of power. Yet, despite those instances where cause and effect can be reasonably inferred, it is difficult to say what we know *in general* about forces shaping the Penal Code. The search for causal variables is clearly sound, but situationally specific explanations are ultimately unsatisfying. In other words, we must try to move beyond the passage of a particular statute, or even a small set of statutes. Toward this end we will now now consider additional data and the application of statistics based on the general linear model.

To begin, it is important to recognize that by developing earlier explanations almost exclusively from our qualitative data, we have skewed our conclusions toward a few dramatic events. These are, after all, what tend to be most salient and to provide the "easiest" answers. The pivotal role of Watts and Berkeley is a prominent instance, and even knowing whether or not we had analyzed it properly would leave unanswered the importance of less visible factors. Therefore, it seems critical to cast our net more widely to catch events that may have been overlooked not only by researchers but by political actors as well.

Even considering the explanatory factors we have examined, our analysis to this point provides little information about their relative importance. Consider the abortive attack on unanimous jury verdicts by the CPOA. At least two events may have hastened its defeat: a withdrawal of support by the State Bar under pressure from its more liberal elements and a reluctance by constitution-revering conservatives to "radically" alter the traditions of the jury system. However, the question remains of how to weigh the relative importance of these two forces. More generally, our historical analysis suggests that partisan control of both the Assembly and the Assembly Criminal Procedure Committee was critical in shaping the Penal Code. Yet, one might wonder if their effects were essentially redundant, complementary, or independent. If not redundant, which legislative body was more important, and how much more important? To address such issues we must move to techniques that will permit at least an ordinal assessment of the relative importance of a variety of explanations.

Our qualitative analysis also restricted the number of explanatory factors that could be considered simultaneously. Recall that we moved to a quantitative display of Penal Code trends to indicate more broadly the aggregate effects of a multitude of small changes in the Penal Code. A similar strategy could be advanced for *causes* of Penal Code alterations: namely, to utilize research techniques that can consider many more factors at once than can standard narratives.

Finally, it is important to reemphasize that the ultimate goal of social science is to generate and test theory. To explain the antidrug legislation produced by the 1961 legislative session as resulting from a petition drive by Southern California Elks clubs is less than a systematic exploration of the general importance of grass-roots citizen groups. Similarly, while the CPOA was visible in virtually every session of the period 1955–1971, its historical role does not begin to exhaust the broader importance of lobby groups. Clearly, we need to move beyond events to variables that abstract the essentials from qualitative, event-specific explanations.

In the two chapters to follow, we shall be using statistical techniques to examine various factors associated with the quantitative trends identified and described in Chapters IV and V. Our dependent variables are the 11 *noncumulative*, session-by-session net revision effects graphed for particular criminal justice categories (e.g., defendant). Recall that these were by and large positive, which means that we shall generally be analyzing patterns in the relative sizes of *increments* in rights and resources, criminalization or penalties. The independent variables will be organized into two broad types. First, we shall examine variables that operate internally on the legislature—party control of the legislature, partisanship, reactions to prior legislation, and lobby influence. Second, we shall examine variables that impinge on the legislature from outside—crime statistics, public opinion, and newspaper coverage of crime. Our analytic strategy in this chapter will be primarily to describe* the possible effects of each type of variable in isolation (zero-order effects) and then, in Chapter VII, to emphasize multivariate analyses, where simultaneous† impacts are considered. At the very least, our independent variables should be conceptualized as potential predictors of the trends, though in many cases causal explanations are plausible.‡

Effects within the Legislature

It should come as no surprise that variables describing the internal functioning of the legislature might be useful predictors of trends in the Penal Code. Apart from the our earlier findings, other researchers have empha-

---

* Since we will treat our data as a population, we will not be in the business of formally estimating population characteristics (parameters) from a sample. However, as in all empirical work, we will eventually try to say something about more general questions from our knowledge of the California scene.

† By "simultaneous" we mean in the same regression equation. For example, were we to look for the effects both of lobbies and of public opinion, together, on Penal Code revision, the effects of lobbies and public opinion would be examined "simultaneously."

‡ With our rather limited resources, we were able to consider only those independent variables whose measures were inexpensively and easily obtained. In practice, this meant relying largely on public documents with the data already available in relatively convenient form. In addition, we needed documents for variables that had been uniformly measured from 1955 to 1971. Many documents of potential use had to be excluded because material over the entire time span was not uniformly reported. One consequence is that some important independent variable may well have been omitted and that our interpretations may be vulnerable to spuriousness, even when multiple regression techniques are used.

sized such factors.* In the section that follows, we shall be looking at four independent variables associated with the internal functioning of the legislature: party composition, degree of partisanship, lobby influence, and legislative enactments of earlier sessions.

Party Composition

Our earlier analyses clearly indicated that sessions following election years were often periods of transition. Thanks to the Democrats' 1961 gerrymander and 1962 election victories, patterns of legislation became more liberal. Similarly, law-and-order legislation of 1969 and 1970 was associated with a return to Republican dominance. One obvious generalization is that the balance of power between Democrats and Republicans affects Penal Code trends. Less clear, however, is the precise nature of this relationship. Superficially, one might expect more liberal legislation with Democrats in power. Yet in 1961 much of the antidrug legislation was passed. And Democrats were still the majority when Berkeley and Watts seemed to trigger a variety of hard-line legislative responses. More generally, Democrats were not *necessarily* ideological supporters of such liberal causes as the due-process revolution, especially if they came from law-and-order constituencies.

With the above complexities in mind, we selected four measures of party control: for each session, the proportion of Democratic legislators (it could as well have been the Republican proportion) in the Senate, Assembly, Senate Judiciary Committee, and Assembly Committee on Criminal Procedure.† Our qualitative data indicate that control of these four bodies was critical for the passage of Penal Code legislation, and we shall now examine that proposition statistically.

Session by session, Democratic proportions in the four bodies are highly correlated with one another, making their empirical manifestations somewhat redundant. The Democratic proportions in the Assembly and in the Senate correlate .93; the proportions in both houses correlate above .66 with their committees. The only hint of real statistical independence is the moderate correlation of .38 between the Democratic proportions in the two committees. In brief, when Democrats constituted a high proportion in any one of these four bodies, they tended to be a high proportion

---

* See Appendix 1.1, Chapter I.

† Proposed Penal Code revisions are referred to these committees prior to floor debate or vote. The Assembly Committee on Criminal Procedure was established in 1959, when the Assembly Judiciary Committee separated itself into civil law and criminal law components. In 1970, the Assembly Committee on Criminal Procedure was renamed the Assembly Committee on Criminal Justice.

in the other three. In practice, this resulted from party control of the Assembly, and/or the Senate, typically leading to party control of that body's criminal justice committee. Recall how rapidly the Assembly's Criminal Procedure Committee came to reflect the 5 to 4 Republican majority after the 1968 elections.

Consistent with such overlapping variability, correlations for the Democratic proportions paired by session with revisions in the Penal Code (noncumulative) show roughly the same effects across all four proportions (see Table 6.1). In general, the correlations are positive, indicating that the higher the proportion of Democrats in the various bodies, the more rights and the more penalties are increased.* The few negative correlations that appear are relatively small, the largest being —.37 (or about 14% of the variance). These negative correlations occur in the middle of Table 6.1 and involve primarily legislation affecting police and victimless crimes. Here, there is a slight tendency for higher Democratic proportions to be asso-

TABLE 6.1

Zero-Order Pearson Correlations between Democratic Proportions in the Legislature and Twelve Types of Penal Code Revisions

	Independent variables			
Dependent variables	% Democrats in Assembly	% Democrats in Senate	% Democrats in Assembly Committee	% Democrats in Senate Committee
Defendant	.44	.34	.61	.66
Convicted offenders	.71	.63	.46	.30
Corrections officials	.60	.48	.38	.87
Judge	.18	.21	.31	.35
Police	-.19	-.10	-.37	-.08
Prosecution	.17	.22	.19	-.11
Crime w/o victims	-.03	-.09	-.29	-.01
Persons	.30	.16	-.02	-.13
Property	.66	.44	.26	.56
Public interest	.49	.51	.29	.11
Severity of penalty	.56	.37	.22	.36
Overall criminalization	.58	.45	.23	.29

* Recall that virtually every change in the Penal Code *added* resources, criminalized behavior, or increased penalties. Hence, regardless of the sign of the correlation, we are still analyzing Penal Code change in which very little is ever taken away. A positive correlation indicates that greater increments in the Code were associated with higher Democratic proportions. A negative correlation indicates that greater increments in the Code were associated with lower Democratic proportions. Still, the change in the Code was almost always in a positive direction.

ciated with smaller legislative increments in these categories, particularly in the Assembly Committee on Criminal Procedure. In other words, there is a hint that greater Democratic control decreases support for police interests and the criminalization of drug and morals offenses and that this effect is somewhat more pronounced in the Assembly Committee on Criminal Procedure than in the other three bodies. The latter finding is not surprising, given the committee's earlier designation as the "graveyard" of conservative criminal justice legislation. Still, the negative correlations are on the whole quite small, and no really compelling case can be made from them.

It would be hard to argue solely from the zero-order correlations in Table 6.1 that Democrats heavily favor either a law-and-order or a civil liberties position. While there are substantial positive correlations for defendants, convicted offenders, and corrections officials (whose increases in resources are often associated with such additional options for inmates as work furlough programs), there are also positive correlations for most types of criminalization and penalty increases. However, even here we must pause, since a significant portion of the criminalization of property crimes (consumer fraud, for example) and almost the entire range of public interest crimes can be associated with liberal positions. Clearly, any facile assumption that Democratic control automatically favors one or another position may be false and is certainly premature.* Table 6.1 suggests that Democratic control may stimulate legislative activism across a variety of criminal justice issues. On the other hand, perhaps the criminal lawmaking stalemates during Republican dominance mask correlations that might have been revealed had Republicans been more successful in translating their law-and-order rhetoric into legislation.

Table 6.1 was based on the assumption that effects of the Democratic proportions would be felt in the same session that bills were passed. In other words, we looked at the relationship between Democratic proportions and legislation passed in the same sessions. However, one could postulate that legislative control takes a session or two to produce results and that our analysis should "time lag" its impact. Perhaps legislative initiative in one session does not produce a statute until a later session. For example, the antibugging bill of 1963 was the product of Democratic legislative maneuvering dating back at least to 1957. The bill, which would have made

---

* Though cautioning against reading too much into his findings, in analyzing policy outcomes in the 50 states, Dye finds "higher crime rates, larger prisoner populations, and fewer pardons" associated with the "success of the Democratic party."[1] The Correlations still hold even when the effects of varying levels of state economic development are controlled for and even if the Southern states are excluded from the analysis.

unauthorized wiretapping a felony and illegally obtained evidence inadmissible, was defeated outright in 1957. It was so diluted by amendments in 1959 that it was withdrawn by its sponsor. The antidrug passions of 1961 counseled against the bill's reintroduction then, and it was only in 1963, at the liberal high-water mark, that a version of the bill managed to pass.

Pursuing the notion of lagged effects, we examined correlations between Democratic proportions and legislative activity using the proportion one and two sessions earlier in time to predict bill passage. For instance, illustrating a one-session lag, the Democratic proportion in the Assembly in 1970 was used to predict revisions passed in the 1971 session, the proportion in 1969 to predict revisions passed in 1970, and so on. The findings convincingly demonstrate that the zero-order effect of a Democratic proportion is felt more strongly when variables are paired by identical sessions. Time-lagging by one session generally cuts the correlations in half, and lagging by two sessions generally cuts the correlations by about half again. Consequently, delayed effects for Democratic proportions are not apparent.

While time-lagged effects do not seem important, there is at least one other potential complexity that we can consider with the data at hand. It appears that the effects of Democratic proportions are roughly the same in all four legislative bodies. Yet, it is possible that the correlations between the four proportions mask important processes. It may be, for example, that if one could "hold constant" the Democratic proportion in the Assembly, the effect of the Democratic proportion in the Criminal Procedure Committee would be altered. Recall that there is evidence from our qualitative analysis that in the early 1960s the Criminal Procedure Committee was especially liberal and was perhaps constrained by the Democratic Assembly majority led by Assembly Speaker Unruh and Governor Brown. To explore such complexities some preliminary multiple regression techniques were employed as a prelude to Chapter VII.

Unfortunately, since most of the correlations between our independent variables were rather high, serious multicollinearity* was a potential problem. In essence, when independent variables that are highly correlated are

---

* Multicollinearity: The term used to describe the general problem that arises when some or all of the explanatory (independent) variables in a relationship are highly correlated with one another. Small Ns tend to make partial measures from regression even more unstable when there is a multicollinearity because each zero-order correlation is based on relatively few data points. Consequently, random error that affects only one or two of the data points will have effects on the correlations large enough to alter the partial measures even when the general pattern of zero-order effects is not substantially changed. This is a simple extension of Gordon's discussion of multicollinearity.[2]

put into the same regression equation, the estimates of effect for each tend to be unstable, and misleading substantive interpretations can sometimes result. Therefore, prudence dictated that we initially consider only the simultaneous effects of the proportion of Democrats in the two legislative committees. Table 6.2 shows the result from the regression analyses using the Democratic proportions in the Assembly and Senate committees as independent variables and each type of Penal Code revision as dependent variables. The coefficients of determination (R^2) for many of the dependent variables are quite large, indicating that we are able to account for considerable quantities of variance. For example, 76% of the variance in Penal Code revisions for corrections officials can be explained by our two independent variables. In contrast, only 2% of the variance in crimes against persons is explained.

The pattern for coefficients of determination across the 12 dependent variables provides some additional information. The coefficients tend to be higher for revisions affecting criminal justice actors, suggesting that these revisions can be better explained by the proclivities of Democratic or Republican committee members. This is another indication that the processes for the two broad types of legislation are somewhat different. Revisions affecting criminal justice actors seem more likely to emerge from con-

TABLE 6.2

Regression Analyses for Democratic Proportions in Senate and Assembly Committees

			Regression coefficients[c]	
Dependent variable	R^a	R^{2b}	*% Democratic: Senate Committee*	*% Democratic: Assembly Committee*
Defendant	.77	.59	.11	.14
Convicted offenders	.48	.23	.04	.16
Corrections officials	.87	.76	.27	.03
Judge	.40	.16	.04	.05
Police	.38	.14	.01	-.07
Prosecution	.28	.08	-.02	.04
Crimes w/o victims	.31	.10	.02	-.09
Property	.56	.31	.12	.02
Persons	.13	.02	-.03	.001
Public interest	.28	.08	.00	.10
Severity of penalty	.37	.14	.05	.03
Overall criminalization	.31	.10	.17	.15

[a] *R Multiple Correlation: Measure of Association*

[b] *R^2 Coefficent of Determination: Percentage of variance explained*

[c] *Regression Coefficient: Estimated changes in Penal Code trends resulting from a change of one percent in the proportion Democratic in the Senate or Assembly*

tinuous committee activity, while legislation affecting crime definitions and penalties comes from other, possibly more volatile, sources.

The two sets of regression coefficients are a bit more complicated to interpret. In technical terms, regression coefficients show the slope of the line relating a given independent variable to a given dependent variable, with other independent variables included in the regression equation "held constant."* For example, the slope of the line between the Democratic proportion in the Senate committee and revisions affecting defendants, with Democratic proportions in the Assembly committee held constant, is .11. This means that for every percentage point of increase in Democratic proportion in the Senate committee one would expect a .11 net increment in revisions affecting defendants (i.e., .11 units more favorable). If the Democratic proportion increased 20%, that would translate into a 2.2 unit gain for defendants. A net effect of 2.2 units was well within an ordinary session's productivity for defendants, so that a 20% shift could in theory account for the relevant output of an entire session.

Looking again at Table 6.2, it is clear that by and large, the two committees have roughly the same kinds of effects. The regression coefficients are typically of the same sign for both committees and when they are not, the absolute size of both coefficients is very small. Hence, our "partial" effects show virtually the same pattern as our zero-order effects. The higher the Democratic proportion on the two criminal justice committees, the more rights and resources are typically provided, the greater the overall criminalization, and the more punitive the penalty changes. And once again, this is not likely the work of passionate civil libertarians. What our multivariate analysis does add, however, is that sometimes both committees make *independent* contributions to the passage of law and consequently both committees are at times important. Recall that our qualitative analysis often implied that only the Assembly's Criminal Procedure Committee was critical.

Given the insight from the data in Table 6.2 one might be sorely tempted to try a regression analysis with the Democratic proportions for the entire Senate and Assembly included. Against our better judgment we yielded to this temptation, and the results confirmed our earlier suspicions. While the computer program managed to run, the statistics that emerged were, to say the least, bizarre. Therefore, none of those data will be reported.†

---

* Actually, this "partial" slope is the regression coefficient between the residuals of a given independent variable and a given dependent variable when each has already had variance attributed to the control variables removed.

† The determinant of the correlation matrix was well below .01, while the standardized regression coefficients that appeared were often well above 1.0. In addition, various variance partitions that should have added up did not.

Partisanship

There can be little doubt that partisanship in the California legislature increased markedly over the years of our study. Various scholars have noted this change,[3] and our qualitative analysis highlighted growing partisanship on many occasions. By the late 1960s, party discipline had increased to such a degree that very small differences in the proportion of Democrats or Republicans could be forged into effective party control. When, for example, Speaker Unruh engineered a 5 to 5 party split in the Criminal Procedure Committee he guaranteed a virtual stalemate on much Penal Code legislation.

With this in mind, our second legislative variable is the degree of partisanship surrounding Penal Code legislation. As an indicator, we calculated the homogeneity by party in votes opposing passed legislation. Dissenting votes that were composed solely of one party were given scores of 100%, indicating complete homogeneity of dissent (i.e., high partisanship). Votes that were evenly divided by party were given scores of 50%, indicating the highest degree of nonpartisan opposition. Degrees of homogeniety in between were similarly calculated from the proportion of Democrats and Republicans casting dissenting votes. For the infrequent times (especially in the 1950s) when dissenters were formally labeled nonpartisan with a "DR" or "RD" specification, they were assigned to the party indicated by the first initial on the label.*

Our choice of partisanship measures was severely constrained by the way Penal Code legislation is typically passed. Recall that the vast majority of bills become law through the "agreed bill" process, in which formal votes on the floor of the Assembly and Senate rarely indicate any sizable opposition. Additionally, committee roll-call votes were not available. Consequently, we were limited to a single, rather weak data source, namely, the revisions wherein there was a conflict roll call in the Assembly or Senate.

Despite obvious flaws in our measure of partisanship, we applied it in three distinct ways. First, we examined zero-order correlations between partisanship and the dependent variables; the correlations clustered around zero indicating negligible effects. Second, we used partisanship as one of several variables in a regression analysis and not surprisingly found no important impact. Finally, we constructed a new variable, which was a product of a Democratic proportion times partisanship. It was hoped that partisanship would produce an "interaction effect" in which the impact of Democratic proportions would be enhanced by varying degrees of partisan

---

* Before its abolition in 1959, cross-filing allowed candidates to run in the opposition party's primary; victory in the primary in both parties obviated the necessity of facing an opponent in the general election. A candidate who cross-filed was classified as either a "DR" or "RD"—the first letter giving his "real" party affiliation.

activity. In other words, if Democratic proportions reflected party activity, then that effect should be influenced by the degree to which party membership was significant for legislative action. However, this strategy also failed, since the interaction terms in the regression equation were of little importance.* Consequently, partisanship, as reflected in roll-call data, was dropped from the analysis. Possibly, other measures of partisanship would have produced different results. For example, partisanship may have been visible in the bills that were *not* passed or in original voting patterns on the floor prior to final amendments or in roll-call votes on "critical" bills such as we discussed in Chapter II.

If, despite such measurement problems, the reader wishes to consider our partisanship indicator as at least partially valid, two substantive conclusions follow. The fact that partisanship was a poor predictor may well be a consequence of insufficient variation over the 15 years of our study. Referring back to the qualitative material, it was apparent that, once partisan politics emerged in the early 1960s, it remained at consistently high levels through 1971. Hence, for over two-thirds of the sessions we considered, partisanship did not vary significantly. And if it did not vary, it can explain no variance. On the other hand, if the small amount of variability is deemed sufficient to generate some effects, one's second conclusion must be that partisanship per se makes no direct contribution to patterns of Penal Code legislation and that it also has no potentiating effect on the Democratic proportions.

Lobby Influence

The critical role played by lobbies in shaping the Penal Code needs no introduction. Hence, we shall proceed immediately to the heart of the matter. In our qualitative material we cited numerous times the critical activities of the "law enforcement lobby" and the "civil liberties lobby." Neither was conceptualized as monolithic; rather, each was seen as a coalition of forces who, on criminal justice issues, agreed substantially more with each other than with the other camp.

In the case of the law enforcement lobby (LEL), however, one organization stands out. This is the California Peace Officers' Association (CPOA), an umbrella organization with more than 7000 members in 1971, including every district attorney, sheriff, and important police chief in the state. Founded in the 1920s by a law enforcement elite led by Earl Warren, the CPOA spearheaded the overhaul of the State Department of Justice during the interwar years. It was not until the 1950s, however, when the

---

* As will .be discussed in more detail later, the criterion for inclusion of a variable was that its increment to variance explained be at least 5%.

Attorney General's Office passed into the hands of liberal Democrats, that the CPOA began to intervene independently and on a large scale in the legislative process. As the analysis that follows reveals, victories came easiest in the area of criminalization. This has involved a frustrating irony for the peace officers because they, if not their allies among conservative legislators and citizen groups, viewed sanctions and criminalization as peripheral. The "core concerns" of the association involved procedure, and these issues have had much tougher going.

The civil liberties lobby (CLL) never enjoyed the organizational coherence that the CPOA provided for law enforcement interests. The American Civil Liberties Union (ACLU) had a California membership approaching 20,000 by 1972, but no statewide organization. Though its independent Northern and Southern California branches were founded before World War II, neither had enough interest in legislative lobbying to hire a full-time Sacramento representative before the 1960s. During the 1950s, the only civil liberties organization with a full-time lobbyist was the Friends Committee on Legislation (FCL), a group with smaller membership but a broader conception of political action. It took the due-process revolution to drive the ACLU into the legislative arena, and our quantitative analysis will reflect its success in protecting and extending procedural safeguards. However, the trends will also reveal the limitations that the ACLU placed upon itself in the area of criminal sanction, an area that until recently was beyond the bounds of its traditional procedural concerns.

When it came to operationalizing the role of criminal justice lobbies, it appeared to us that the most relevant aspect of their activities was the amount of "effective influence" they could bring to the issues year by year. This was conceptualized as the function of a lobby's skill in mobilizing the "abstract" sympathy among legislators for its organizational constituencies and programmatic goals. We identified "effective influence" in a variety of ways. The lobbyists' estimates of their own "batting averages" (and those of their opponents) were gleaned from newsletters and journals published by groups active in the criminal justice arena. These were supplemented by assessments from journalists, politicians, and professionals within the criminal justice establishment. For each lobby, an independent evaluation was made of its impact on the shaping of the Penal Code for each year of the study. A number (0 to 6, 6 being high) was assigned to the LEL and the CLL for each session, to summarize "effective influence," and these numbers were the data for statistical analysis.*

---

* The coding was done by Brackman as part of his archival research. He had no idea what the quantitative analysis might reveal, and hence his coding was totally independent of it. Similarly, Berk, who did most of the statistical analysis, did not in any way participate in the coding of "effective influence."

Table 6.3 shows the zero-order correlations between our measures of lobby influence and the 12 dependent variables. With two minor exceptions, the LEL has the opposite effect of the CLL. Column 3 shows parallel correlations using the arithmetic difference between the influence of the CLL and the LEL year by year. The pattern is virtually identical to that of the LEL.

The more influential the LEL, the larger the legislative gains for criminalization, severe penalties, police, and, to a limited extent, convicted offenders, and, conversely, the smaller the gains for defendants, the judiciary, and, to a limited extent, corrections officials. The correlation of .03 between the influence of the LEL and laws addressing prosecutory functions indicates that LEL influence has little zero-order impact on prosecutorial legislation in the Penal Code. Overall, law enforcement impacts are quite well delineated.

The influence of the CLL shows substantial positive correlations with laws more strongly favoring defendants, corrections officials, and the judiciary. Opposite effects are found for all types of criminalization (with the minor exception of crimes against property),* severity of penalties, and police. Small correlations for revisions affecting convicted offenders and prosecutors make interpretation difficult for these actors. However, CLL effects clearly differ from those of the LEL.

Differences in the relative sizes of the correlations impart some additional information. First, the LFL seems comparatively more effective than the

TABLE 6.3
Zero-Order Pearson Correlations of Lobby Variables with Dependent Variables

Dependent variable	Law enforcement lobby	Civil liberties lobby	LEL-CLL
Defendant	-.58	.67	-.64
Convicted offenders	.15	.10	.08
Corrections officials	-.12	.46	-.23
Judges	-.26	.33	-.30
Police	.28	-.52	.37
Prosecution	.03	-.10	.05
Crimes w/o victims	.15	-.06	.13
Persons	.69	-.40	.63
Property	.32	.08	.21
Public interest	.48	-.31	.46
Severity of penalty	.51	-.17	.43
Overall criminalization	.48	-.10	.39

* In this connection, it should be noted that many legislative revisions directed to crimes against property involve white-collar crime—i.e., credit card fraud, embezzlement, corporate misbehavior.

CLL in advancing its interests in areas of criminalization and penalties.*
For each dependent variable the absolute value of the correlation for the
LEL is larger than that of the CLL. Second, the CLL appears to be comparatively more effective in advancing its interests in laws that affect criminal justice actors. The absolute value of CLL correlations for defendants,
corrections officials, and police is substantially larger. Again, this reflects
the ACLU's traditional concerns with procedural safeguards and the rights
of the accused. For convicted offenders, judges, and prosecutors, both
lobbies have relatively small correlations and the differences between relative impacts are not large. However, in only one case does the LEL have a
larger correlation. Overall, one can conclude that the LEL and the CLL
are not simply mirror images of each other but seem to have some important differences regarding where they are most effective. Though the correlation between the "effective influence" of the LEL and the CLL is −.75,
there is enough residual variance to suggest that the two lobbies may have
somewhat different agenda as well as different impacts.

Column 3 of Table 6.3 was computed to test whether the relationships
between the two lobbies could be appropriately conceived as a zero-sum
game. If the two lobbies had somewhat different patterns of effective influence over the 15 years and if in most instances they had opposing goals,
a difference score of lobby impact would be a sensible independent variable.
However, the "net influence" of the LEL shows virtually the same pattern
of correlations as the gross effect of the LEL. (The correlation between
them is .98). The problem with the measure of net effect results from far
greater variability in LEL influence than CLL influence. For all practical
purposes the net measure is simply the LEL measure with a constant subtracted. We could have standardized both lobby influence measures with
"Z-scores" and then computed differences but doing this would so seriously
have violated the original intent of the measurement process (if the influence of the CLL does not vary much, so be it) that standardization was
discarded as inappropriate.

We also tried using our measures of lobby influence with one- and two-
year time lags. As in the case of Democratic proportions, it was plausible
that lobby influence would not be effective immediately. However, the
time-lagged correlations were considerably lower than the simultaneous
correlations, and the notion of delayed impact was dropped.

It should be clear from the above material, if from nothing else, that
lobby influence has critical effects on Penal Code legislation. However,
it is important to realize that we have been discussing only zero-order effects

---

* This is plausible, in view of the fact that scope and severity of penalty was of
little concern to the ACLU before the late 1960s.

and that part of apparent lobby influence may stem from other factors that covary with lobby influence. Recall that big years for the LEL were also likely to be years when Republicans were ascendant. The question is, if one were to hold the proportion of Republicans in legislative bodies constant, would lobby impact be as prominent. We will address such issues later.

Using Earlier Legislation to Predict Later Legislation

Over the 15 years covered by our study, legislation introduced by one set of interests was often vehemently opposed by other interests. Indeed, that has been the pivotal dynamic of our analysis to this point. Typically, opposition involved attempts to thwart passage of the objectionable legislation. However, it is conceivable that, rather than try to oppose certain bills directly, interest groups might choose to introduce legislation to undermine or counterbalance unacceptable revisions. For example, rather than oppose legislation favoring prosecutors, the civil liberties lobby might put its efforts behind legislation favoring defendants. While there was little evidence of such strategies in our qualitative analysis, it is plausible enough to warrant further consideration.

Basically, what we are describing is a feedback mechanism, in which legislation passed at an earlier point in time affects legislation at a later point in time. Probably the most obvious feedback model involves an equilibrium of legislative checks and balances. Legislation favoring one group is followed by legislation undercutting that group or supporting opposing groups. Statistically this would appear over sessions as a negative correlation between legislation with similar intent and a positive correlation between legislation with opposing intent. In the former case, legislation supporting police, for instance, would show an alternating longitudinal pattern, with successful sessions followed by unsuccessful sessions and vice versa. In the latter case, successful sessions for police would be followed by successful sessions for defendants and convicted offenders, and vice versa.

A competing model could be characterized as a snowball effect. When things begin to go well, they continue to go well. When things begin to go badly, they continue to go badly. The snowball model can be statistically counterposed to the equilibrium model, since they predict correlations of opposite signs. If the data is arrayed longitudinally, there should over time be positive correlations between legislation with similar intent and negative correlations with legislation of opposing intent.

While the two competing models would seem easy enough to test with our material, there are inherent problems with time series data which produce difficulties for the proposed analysis. We shall not take time to review all of these difficulties in depth,* but a brief discussion of some is necessary before we launch into a substantive examination of the data.

An initial set of problems result from the fact that, very frequently, correlations in longitudinal analyses are very high while the substantive meaning is unclear. For example, the average temperature one day may be an accurate *predictor* of the average temperature the next day. However, if one's goal is *explanation,* an interpretation that sees temperature on the first day as *causing* temperature the next day is at best incomplete and at worst misleading. Moreover, if such a variable is included with other independent variables in a multiple regression format, the effects of the other independent variables will typically be substantially altered and their potential causal impacts distorted.

A second cluster of difficulties are more purely statistical in nature and involve the accuracy of various measures produced by regression procedures when, as commonly occurs with longitudinal data, some of their underlying assumptions are violated. For our data in particular, one must treat regression results especially carefully when one of the independent variables is the same as the dependent variable, but observed at an earlier point in time. For example, if one regressed revisions affecting defendants on revisions affecting defendants one year earlier, resulting slope coefficients (or correlations) could be seriously in error. (Technically, the regression coefficient is at least biased and depending on the nature of the error term, perhaps inconsistent as well.)

A third problem is that interpretation based on longitudinal correlations are especially likely to be spurious.[5] A given association may reflect not a direct causal link but the effects of other variables. For example, in the model in Figure 6.1, the longitudinal correlation between Y_1 and Y_2 is spurious. If X is rates of reported crime and Z is the effectiveness of the law enforcement lobby, then both these variables may have important effects for Penal Code revisions (the Ys) one and two years later. If these effects are relatively consistent and powerful, Penal Code revisions at time 1 and time 2 will be associated highly but spuriously. Consequently, a *causal* interpretation involving only Penal Code revisions would be misleading.

---

* There are numerous other models one might consider, especially refinements of the ones described above. For example, for the snowball model, one might distinguish between an accelerating snowball effect and a decelerating snowball effect. Such patterns would be revealed in cumulative curves where different shapes could be plotted. However, with only 11 data points and the numerous complications, some of which are described below, these subleties seem beyond our study. (For an excellent discussion of these issues see Kmenta.[4])

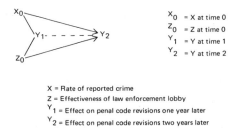

X_0 = X at time 0
Z_0 = Z at time 0
Y_1 = Y at time 1
Y_2 = Y at time 2

X = Rate of reported crime
Z = Effectiveness of law enforcement lobby
Y_1 = Effect on penal code revisions one year later
Y_2 = Effect on penal code revisions two years later

FIGURE 6.1 Model showing spurious effects.

Our data will later show several variables that at least predict changes in the Penal Code several years into the future. Hence, longitudinal correlations between Penal Code revisions are likely to have a very high spurious component.

With the above caveats in mind, let us turn to Table 6.4, which shows the matrix of zero-order correlations between different types of Penal Code revisions one session apart. Autocorrelations (correlations between the same type of revision one session apart) are boxed.* At least superficially, it is difficult to find strong support for either the snowball or the equilibrium model. The positive autocorrelations for convicted offenders, corrections officials, severity of penalties, and several kinds of criminalization suggest the snowball model for these kinds of revisions. However, the snowball model would also predict positive correlations with other legislation of similar intent, and negative correlations with legislation of opposing intent. Convicted offenders, for example, were clearly supported by liberals, yet in sessions after they did well, police (.44), prosecutors (.35), and overall criminalization (.63) did well. Defendants (−.47) and the judiciary (−.50) did poorly. The snowball model is suggested by the autocorrelations, while the equilibrium model is suggested by the longitudinal correlations with other kinds of revisions.

The equilibrium model does only slightly better. Take police as an example. The autocorrelation is negative (−.41), indicating that they did poorly following sessions in which they did well (and the reverse). The general pattern of negative correlations between police revisions in session

---

* The reader can acquire a better feel for the autocorrelations in Table 6.4 by referring back to the noncumulative graphs in Chapters IV and V. Positive auto-correlations will be reflected by good sessions following one another and bad sessions following one another. Revisions affecting corrections officials show this pattern best, with several poor sessions followed by several good sessions, which in turn are followed by several poor sessions. Negative autocorrelations will be reflected in a more zig-zag line, which is especially evident for prosecutors and police.

TABLE 6.4
Longitudinal Pearson Correlations between Penal Code Revisions One Session Apart

Earlier \ Later	Defendant	Convicted offenders	Corrections officials	Police	Prosecutor	Judge	Crimes w/o victims	Persons	Property	Public interest	Severity of penalty	Overall criminalization
Defendant	.01[a]	.14	.67	-.04	-.27	-.07	-.28	.29	.66	.65	.81	.49
Convicted offenders	-.47	.30	-.18	.44	.35	-.50	.06	.68	.42	.72	.56	.63
Corrections officials	.17	.47	.39	.09	.23	-.54	-.30	.32	.71	.62	.54	.54
Police	-.25	-.15	-.30	-.41	-.05	.52	-.09	.003	-.36	-.14	.12	-.14
Prosecutor	-.16	.19	.21	-.51	-.60	.72	-.23	-.20	-.18	-.07	.11	-.29
Judge	.19	-.13	.27	-.11	.42	-.54	.62	.25	.24	.18	.24	.45
Crimes w/o victims	.29	.12	.06	-.45	-.15	.27	-.19	-.59	-.50	-.16	-.22	-.03
Persons	-.16	.52	-.32	-.35	.09	.22	.11	.06	-.11	.48	.33	.43
Property	-.07	.71	-.02	-.06	.34	-.18	-.19	.34	.44	.48	.33	.43
Public interest	-.55	.38	-.22	.01	.23	-.12	.17	.57	.36	.34	.34	.54
Severity of penalty	-.21	.58	-.11	-.07	.38	-.32	.08	.45	.42	.32	.24	.50
Overall criminalization	-.09	.70	-.03	-.42	.13	.12	-.01	.14	.16	.11	.09	.16

[a] Auto-correlations are boxed. These are the correlations between the same variable at two points in time.

"1" and criminalization and penalties in session "2" further supports the model. However, in sessions after police did well, defendants (−.25) and convicted offenders (−.15) did somewhat more poorly, which suggests the snowball model. Probably the best case for an equilibrium model can be made for revisions affecting prosecutors, and even here there are some problems.

Not only do our models falter but even *post hoc* explanations present anomalies. While revisions favoring police are positively correlated with revisions favoring the judiciary one session later, revisions favoring the judiciary are negatively correlated with revisions favoring police one session later. One finds a similar problem for defendants and convicted offenders.

In summary, if one looks *only* at criminalization and penalties revisions, there is some evidence of snowballing forces. Yet, overall, no parsimonious patterns are revealed in Table 6.4. One almost has to develop special causal interpretations for every kind of legislation, suggesting that these data alone do not reveal important causal forces but, rather, reflect other variables and/or statistical artifacts. We experimented with different time lags and got the same sorts of confused patterns. From this we conclude that there is little compelling evidence that, by itself, legislation passed in one session has a direct causal effect on legislation passed over the next several sessions. We are not saying that predictions are impossible; rather, whatever predictions are forthcoming, the independent variables are probably not themselves direct causes but at best indirect indicators of other processes. Substantively, this seems to make sense. For the zero-order correlations in Table 6.4 to lend themselves to the feedback models we proposed (or to any other models in which direct cause is involved) legislators and/or lobbyists would have to keep track of all the day-to-day changes in the Code and then be able to change legislative output accordingly in the following sessions. This would be at least a monumental bookkeeping operation, to say nothing of mobilizing to react appropriately. Recall that our data are based on hundreds of small Penal Code alterations that may seem to the various actors to be almost as dull as they are numerous.

Of course, it is conceivable that other models and/or types of statistical analyses would reveal causal effects. For example, we briefly considered procedures in which reciprocal causation could be investigated. However, with only 11 data points, likely measurement error, and little theory to guide us, this seemed a risky fishing expedition at best. Further, our later multivariate analyses will be able to account for a large proportion of variance in the Penal Code, using far simpler models, plausible theory, and less complicated statistics.

External Factors Affecting Penal Code Revisions

In this chapter thus far we have examined the effects of four kinds of variables operating within the legislature. Clearly, a similar emphasis characterized our qualitative analysis. Both data sets have converged on a critical role for political parties and lobbies; and while the impact of neither is surprising, we have begun to unravel the details of their importance. Our identification of the eclectic impact of Democratic proportions in the legislature is but one example of the payoff.

We would be selling our qualitative analysis short, however, if we did not acknowledge evidence for factors operating on the legislature from outside. Thus we noted the impact of the Elks petition drive for a crackdown on drug use, the role of Berkeley and Watts, the repercussions of prison riots, and a general sense among legislators that public opinion could not be ignored. We will now turn to a statistical examination of these forces.

The Effects of Crime Rates

It takes no great insight to suspect that the amount of crime in California between 1955 and 1971 might have important effects on the types and amounts of Penal Code legislation passed. Certainly, "crime waves" occur periodically and may generate not only wide public concern but a variety of potential legislative remedies. When public officials and citizen leaders become involved in law-and-order issues, they often cite "frightening statistics" or unusually brutal crimes. Both Nixon and Brown, for example, addressed crime rates in their 1962 gubernatorial campaigns, and Reagan even more dramatically hitched his political wagon to soaring crime statistics.

Unfortunately, actual rates of crime are nearly impossible to come by. First, one is faced with a myriad of definitional problems in deciding when a particular action should be labeled a crime. If one tries using official legal definitions, the fit between an action and the definition is still a matter of varying opinion. In addition, definitions can change from year to year and from jurisdiction to jurisdiction. If one takes a more normative approach, there are frequently sliding definitions depending on to whom one speaks.

Second, even if there was agreement about definitions, someone must aggregate the data over time and by geographical area before rates can be gauged. Typically, this is done by official agencies like the police, which means that only crimes coming to their attention can be included. Clearly, many crimes are not reported. Further, bureaucratic procedure affects crime rates because organizational rules determine how crimes are to be detected, reported, and recorded. For example, a decision to patrol more intensively in a particular part of a city will likely produce more arrests, often mis-interpreted as an increase in crime. Indeed, official statistics sometimes tell us more about the organization producing the statistics than about the events the statistics are supposed to describe (see, for example, Cicourel and Kitsuse[6]).

Social scientists have occasionally sought to bypass the problems of official statistics by collecting their own original material with which to measure crime rates (e.g., Ennis, 1970[7]). Usually, large numbers of people are interviewed and asked if they have been crime victims. Though this leaves many definitional problems untouched, it at least avoids contamination by official bureaucracies. Results from such studies show that, with the exception of homicide, rates of victimization are often double the rates reported by official sources like the Uniform Crime Reports. (Homicide rates are about equal in the two measures.)

We did not have access to victimization data in California for the period covered by our study. Since no such material exists, we were limited to official statistics of various sorts. Yet this may not be as troublesome as first appears. It is perhaps not especially important to examine the impact of the absolute amount of crime but, rather, *changes* in the amount of crime. In other words, since we are looking at longitudinal trends, we are interested in periodic increases and decreases. A rate of 90 robberies per 100,000 citizens is probably not particularly informative unless compared to robbery rates in other years. Hence, it may not matter if the official statistics distort the absolute amount of crime; what matters is whether the distortions are consistent from year to year.

In the use of the official crime statistics that follow, we have to make an important and challengeable assumption. We must assume that there have been no serious distortions in the way the statistics were calculated for a particular set of years* If this assumption is substantially violated, then the crime rates we use as independent variables distort the picture not only of the amount of crime and the stable bureaucratic procedures but of the bureaucratic idiosyncracies of particular yearly statistics as well. In such instances, the independent variables would include events in which we are not interested.

However, even if this assumption is violated, the statistics may be of some use. Legislative activity may be in part a reaction not to any "real"

---

* The California Bureau of Criminal Statistics, the source of our data, has developed standard reporting procedures providing basic information on offenses and offenders. This information-gathering procedure via standardized format has been in effect since 1954 and is generally considered one of the most sophisticated in the country.

rate of crime but to the official statistics themselves. Crime per se may cause "crime waves" less than do crime statistics.* In other words, the fit between actual crime and crime statistics may be very poor, and still the statistics can have substantial effects.

With the above issues in mind, we examined the effects of four types of official, statewide felony-related crime statistics:† (1) felony crimes reported per year, (2) adult felony arrests per year, (3) felony complaints filed per year, and (4) felony defendants prosecuted per year. We tried two different forms of these statistics. First, we used the simple, per capita rate for each year. The assumption was that the legislature would only react to the statistics or what they reflected. Second, we used a measure of *rate of change* (in the crime rate) from year to year by calculating the percentage change in the statistic, based on the prior year. For example, if the number of felonies per 100,000 people was 1000 in 1955 and 1200 in 1956, the rate of change would be +.20.‡ This approach assumed that the legislature was reacting not to the simple crime rate but to the rate relative to the year before; in this case any important effect of crime statistics was a result of the percentage increase or decrease in its yearly rate.§ (The percentages almost always were increases.)

---

* The important consideration here is that, no matter how many limitations we can identify in crime statistics generally, they are continually used by the media, legislators, professionals, and citizens in their assessments of the crime problem. So, no matter how imprecise they may be as a measure of crime, the perception of the incidence of crime by the actors that interest us is a result to some degree of the use of these statistics.

† Felony statistics are considered a more complete and consistent measurement of crime than are statistics for less serious offenses, since all actors involved are faced with the more carefully defined screening criteria applicable in a felony offense.

‡
$$\frac{1200 - 1000}{1000} = +.20$$

§ The use of "rates" and "rates of rates" can get pretty confusing. One can begin to think of these various measures in terms of how a person decides if the number of crimes for a given year is large. First, a person may react to the raw crime rate, the number of crimes per population unit. This is what we call the "simple rate" and assumes that people "know" when a yearly crime rate is large. For example, 800 murders per 100,000 people in a city may be large while 35 may not be. Second, a person may react to the absolute increase or decrease in the crime rate from year to year. An increase from 90 to 100 robberies per 100,000 people may or may not be judged as large. We did not use this measure since, typically, change in the crime rate is not reported as the arithmetic difference but as the percentage change. This led to our third measure, which is the proportion of increase or decrease in the crime rate relative to the year before. When one sees headlines reporting crime rates as being up 15%, that number usually refers to something approximating our measure of the percentage change.

However, "percentage change" in the crime rate is also commonly called the "rate

In addition, we tried three different impact time lags: no lag, a one-year lag and a two-year lag. The rationale for the one- and two-year lags was that crime statistics are published after the year of reference and, consequently, the statistics per se could not have an impact in the same year in which they were collected. Crime statistics correlated with legislative activity in the same year might indicate that both the statistics and the legislation were a result of some mix of common prior events, such as "real" crime rates, public controversy about law and order, and/or publicity about crime in the media.

All forms of the crime statistics are highly correlated with one another. For example, the number of felonies per capita reported is correlated .62 with the percentage change in the number of felonies reported in the same year. The percentage change in number of felony complaints filed, lagged by one year, correlates .64 with the unlagged percentage change. Rather than present a very large correlation matrix with all the crime statistics correlated with one another and with the dependent variables, we initially have selected for discussion the set of crime statistics exhibiting the highest correlations with the dependent variable.

Table 6.5 shows the correlations between the four felony-related crime statistics in the *unlagged rate of change* form (i.e., unlagged percentage change) and the dependent variables. The correlations are not as large as were seen for the effects of proportion Democratic (Table 6.1) but are still of some interest. With a couple of important exceptions, the correlations are positive, indicating that the greater the percentage increase in our four measures of the crime rate, the greater the increments favoring criminalization, severity of penalties, and some criminal justice actors.

Excluding crimes without victims (and for just felonies reported), the greater the percentage increase in crime statistics, the more are various kinds of behavior criminalized through legislation. This can be seen from the positive correlation across all the types of crime (against persons, property, and public interest) and from the positive correlation with the

---

of change" in the crime rate and thus we shall use both terms to mean the same thing. Whereas "rate" in crime rate refers to standardization per units of population, "rate" in the rate of change refers to standardization based on the crime rate the year before. To make things even more complicated, when these percentage changes in the crime rate are arrayed over time, one can then speak of the rate of change per year; still another kind of "rate." In short, "rate" means that the original figures have been standardized to some common base and for our data three bases are used at various times: population, the amount of crime per units of population the year before, and the amount of time (e.g., a 10% increase *per year*). While this may all seem terribly complicated at this point, in context there should be little confusion as long as one keeps in mind that "rate" can mean several kinds of standardization.

TABLE 6.5

Zero-Order Pearson Correlations between Rate of Change in Crime Statistics and Twelve Types of Penal Code Revisions

Dependent variable	Felonies reported	Adult felony arrests	Felony complaints filed	Felony defendants prosecuted
		(No Time Lag)		
Defendant	-.11	-.28	-.15	-.08
Convicted offenders	.51	.32	.35	.03
Corrections officials	-.22	-.36	-.26	-.17
Judge	-.07	.04	.07	-.22
Police	.47	.52	.56	.54
Prosecution	.30	.48	.46	.49
Crimes w/o victims	-.07	.25	.12	.34
Persons	.30	.51	.44	.32
Property	.26	.22	.21	.09
Public interest	.25	.34	.41	.35
Severity of penalty	.09	.19	.24	.14
Overall criminalization	.27	.47	.42	.35

aggregate measure "overall criminalization." Greater positive rates of change in crime statistics are also associated with greater increases in severity of penalties, though the correlations here are a bit smaller. Apparently crime rates may affect not only what is regarded as illegal but the degree and type of punishment.

The patterns of correlations for legislation affecting the legal rights and resources of actors in the criminal justice system are a bit more complicated. Larger percentage gains in all four crime measures are linked with larger increases in the rights and resources for prosecutors, police, and convicted offenders. In contrast, larger increases in crime rates are associated with smaller increments for defendants and corrections officials. The pattern for the judiciary's rights and resources is not consistent across the crime statistics, though the largest correlation is negative.

If we accept for a moment that the correlations could involve causal mechanisms, the patterns indicate that relative increases in crime statistics may be related to a law-and-order stance in the legislature. More behavior is officially criminalized, more penalties are increased, and additional legal resources are given to police and prosecutors. Concurrently, it is less likely that legislation will be passed that gives additional legal resources to defendants and to corrections officials such as wardens and prison personnel.*

Somewhat more difficult to interpret are the patterns for convicted offen-

---

* Recall that our earlier data suggested that corrections personnel did not gain many legal rights and resources during the law-and-order era.

ders and judges. For convicted offenders, larger increases in crime rates are associated with larger increases in legal rights and resources. While at first glance this may seem a contradiction, greater resources for convicted offenders may reflect legislative concern in the mid-1960s which resulted in relatively innovative alternatives to incarceration. The pattern for judicial resources is also plausible if we remember common law-and-order assertions that judges were too lenient and insensitive to the problem of law enforcement.

While we have tentatively suggested causal interpretations for the patterns of correlations, the use of unlagged correlations indicates that the legislature could not be reacting to crime statistics per se. Possibly, the statistics are indicators of other events, such as publicity surrounding the "real" crime rate, and this may be what affects the legislature. In other words, the crime rate may be covarying with other important independent variables, and any interpretation using crime statistics directly as a cause would be spurious.*

Were we to move to lagged correlations between the various forms of our crime statistics and Penal Code legislation, it would be possible for legislators to be reacting to the actual statistics. However, both for the absolute and for the rate of change crime statistics, the correlations are difficult to interpret. In general they are smaller (compared to Table 6.5) and have perplexing sign patterns. For example, legislation criminalizing person and property offenses show negative correlations ($-.16$ and $-.22$) with felony arrests in the percentage change form one year earlier. The correlation with total criminalization is .09. Revisions favoring defendants show a positive correlation with the rate of change in felony prosecutions one year earlier and a negative correlation with this same variable two years earlier. While in each case one could probably generate a *post hoc* interpretation, we are faced with problems akin to the autocorrelations between legislative revisions. From such data we conclude that no compelling case can be made for causal effects of crime statistics per se on Penal Code legislation. We suspect that when politicians cite crime statistics they choose data that will support a position already taken. The statistics are used selectively to justify political actions and are not typically the cause of those actions.

In retrospect, the absence of an effect for crime statistics is not only con-

* It is theoretically possible and conceivably desirable to explore the independent effects of each of the felony-related crime statistics. However, we will not undertake such an elaboration here. The crime statistics are highly intercorrelated raising the problem of multicollinearity. For all practical purposes they are the same variable. And that is sensible. We would be very worried if increases in the rate of arrests, for example, were not highly associated with increases in the rate of complaints filed in courts.

sistent with our qualitative material but with common sense. To begin, while crime statistics do vary substantially over the period of our study, it would be hard to argue that the relevant actors considered the details of those changes. The overall pattern revealed that crime was increasing year to year, often at increasing rates. Lobbyists and legislators were probably aware of this, but their conclusions about crime were likely reduced to the global assertion that crime was getting worse. In other words, while the actual statistics might vary, perceptions were pretty much a constant. Were there several years in which the crime rate significantly decreased, a change in perceptions would probably have occurred. As it is, specific yearly fluctuations were pretty much ignored.

There is also evidence from our qualitative material that, while crime statistics are a year-to-year phenomenon, "crime in the streets" becomes salient more irregularly. It seemed as if a few dramatic events were needed to sensitize the public to crime before crime statistics became relevant to debate. Recall that law and order became a big issue after Berkeley and Watts. Crime statistics had been rising for some time when Brown and Nixon addressed the issue in their 1962 gubernatorial campaigns. Yet, at that time few seemed seriously interested.* In short, crime statistics may become important only *after* crime has become an issue.

Finally, it is important to emphasize again that most of the Penal Code revisions are small and undramatic, more a response to the ongoing needs of bureaucrats and professionals than to great social problems. In a sense, crime statistics may be irrelevant to typical Penal Code changes. At most, the background of rising crime may be a broad context in which to place specific rationales. One can picture prosecutors arguing that making illegally obtained evidence inadmissible would free many guilty persons, and defense lawyers arguing that to admit such evidence would encourage official lawlessness. But prosecutors could also simply claim that the exclusionary rule made their job harder, and defense lawyers that it made their job easier. In subsequent negotiations the discussions could narrowly center on details in support of either position and the potential points of compromise. The "big" questions like rising crime could be taken as "givens" or even just ignored.

The Effects of Crime Coverage in Newspapers

No study of Penal Code legislation can ignore the role of newspapers. Editorials may literally define important crime-related events, front-page coverage can unleash a "crime wave," and in-depth investigative reporting

---

* Increases in rates of crime prior to 1962 were relatively modest. The big leaps came after 1966.

may reveal the role of various underlying forces. Such importance has not been lost on social scientists, and, as early as 1932, Frank Harris in the *Presentation of Crime in Newspapers* was arguing from data that extensive crime coverage was essentially a ploy to sell newspapers and might actually trigger more violence.[8] He also demonstrated that the amount and salience of crime coverage had little to do with official crime rates. In a recent article, Danzger reviewed much of the literature on newspaper reporting and concluded there is ample evidence that editorial policy and newsroom pressures not only affect what events are reported but create biases in story content.[9] In particular, he analyzed data on civil disorders to show that public awareness of "serious" unrest may have more to do with the presence of a wire service office in the city than with the "real" severity of the disruptions. According to Danzger, where wire services are geared up to do extensive reporting, civil disorders are disproportionately characterized as violent.

Both the importance and subjectivity of news coverage was not lost on groups like the CPOA. In the early 1960s they began to court the media, holding special "forums" for reporters and even approaching publishing influentials like Chandler and Hearst. More routinely, police officers and crime reporters had always been in contact, and to some degree were dependent on one another. Reporters needed helpful police to provide newsworthy information, and the police needed a sympathetic (or at least not hostile) press to generate public support.

While it seems clear that newspapers are important in this study, less obvious is where that importance really lies. The problem centers around the way in which criminal justice news coverage translates into legislative change. Do legislators react to publicity surrounding criminal justice? Do they respond to the opinions of constituents represented in letters to the editor? Or do editorial views shape conceptions of the issues and suggest where the interests of powerful institutions lie?

To approach these questions, we began by coding samples of the *Los Angeles Times* from 1954 to 1971.* One edition was randomly selected for every 2-week period, and the following items were tabulated for the first four pages and the editorial section: (1) the number of columns of crime-related news articles, (2) the number of columns of letters to the editor about crime, (3) the number of columns of crime-related editorials, (4) the number of columns of crime-related political cartoons.† The goal was to

* The idea of coding newspapers is certainly not a new one. Besides Harris, see Davis.[10]

† We limited ourselves to the first four pages and the editorial section in order to reduce the amount of work. Remember we are interested not in absolute amounts of crime coverage but in relative changes over time.

measure not only the presence or absence of criminal justice material but also the amount of space given to crime-related items. In a sense, the number of items was weighted by the number of columns. We did not code the value positions taken in the material because this would have created a reliability problem and required many coders. Even editorials that were supposed to address a specific issue and present clear opinions often were very difficult to assess. It was easy to tell if an editorial was about crime, but the side taken was frequently ambiguous.*

The justification for selecting the *Los Angeles Times* was a combination of its wide circulation, thorough coverage, and identification with individuals who are influential in local and state politics. It would have been better had we been able to code several newspapers, but this was not possible. The coding of just the *Los Angeles Times* took several months, and we did not have the resources to extend the work. Furthermore, the findings seemed so compelling that we did not feel heavily pressured to go on.

After papers were coded, a total column figure was calculated for each newspaper variable by year. For example, the total number of columns of crime-related news articles for 1955 was 66, while for 1956 it was 72. Additionally, means and standard errors for each year were calculated. Since the coding clearly was based on a sample, we wished to gauge the stability of our yearly estimates. Fortunately, the standard errors were quite small relative to the means, indicating that from year to year the estimates are quite accurate.† In the correlational analysis and regression equations, the total numbers of columns for each newspaper variable for each year were used as independent variables.

The zero-order correlations between the four newspaper variables and the twelve dependent variables can be seen in Table 6.6. Note that the data presented are for no time lag and for a 1-year time lag. As a first approximation, the number of columns of crime-related news articles can be conceptualized as public exposure to the crime issue; letters to the editor can be interpreted partly as a measure of newspaper concern (through selection) and partly as a measure of public opinion; editorials can be conceptualized as the official position taken by the *Los Angeles Times*; and crime-related political cartoons can be seen partly as public exposure to the crime issue and partly as a reflection of the concerns of cartoonists.

Looking initially at the lower half of Table 6.6, correlations with various types of criminalization and with severity of penalties, one sees that positive signs outnumber negative signs by well over 3 to 1. The main exceptions

---

* The coding was done by Peter Li and Karen Brenner, graduate students in sociology at Northwestern University.

† Of course, this addresses only sampling error.

TABLE 6.6

Zero-Order Pearson Correlations between Newspaper Variables and Twelve Types of Penal Code Revisions

(No lag and one-year lag)

Dependent Variables	Articles no lag	Articles 1 yr lag	Letters no lag	Letters 1 yr lag	Editorials no lag	Editorials 1 yr lag	Cartoons no lag	Cartoons 1 yr lag
Defendant	-.56	-.41	-.56	.00	.15	-.70	-.13	-.27
Convicted offenders	.24	-.13	.23	.43	.64	.25	.54	.13
Corrections officials	-.62	-.72	-.35	-.15	.00	-.25	-.24	-.20
Judge	-.12	.15	-.22	.52	.18	-.25	.30	-.13
Police	.31	.07	.02	-.49	.00	.37	-.06	.20
Prosecution	.27	.09	.00	-.36	.02	.28	.24	.22
Crimes w/o victims	-.04	.27	.09	.03	-.27	.10	.05	.25
Persons	.49	.04	.83	-.21	.35	.86	.12	.17
Property	-.04	-.62	.28	-.32	.35	.51	.06	-.11
Public interest	.30	-.25	.54	-.26	.70	.68	.11	.25
Severity of penalty	.08	-.41	.44	-.27	.42	.60	.01	.13
Overall criminalization	.21	-.29	.56	-.34	.40	.77	.14	.08

are for articles and letters with a 1-year lag. What this means is that, in general, increased newspaper coverage of crime is associated with greater increments in criminalization.

Turning to the upper half of the table the pattern of correlations with the legal rights and resources of criminal justice actors is more complicated. Increased newspaper coverage appears to be associated with greater increases in resources for police, prosecutors, and convicted offenders, while inversely related to the interests of defendants and corrections officials. Patterns for the judiciary are mixed.

A tentative conclusion is that Penal Code revisions are associated with the amount of crime coverage in the *Los Angeles Times*. The question arises as to whether a general law-and-order impact by the *Los Angeles Times* might also be inferred, since it appears that the greater the crime coverage, the more law-and-order bills are likely to be passed. However, there are enough inconsistencies and ambiguities in the table to warrant a more detailed and refined analysis.

As a beginning to such an analysis, we shall address the question of causal ordering among the newspaper variables themselves. Part of the confusion in Table 6.6 may be a result of the confounded and overlapping effects of more than one newspaper variable. Table 6.7 shows the correlations between the newspaper variables with time lags of zero to 2 years,

TABLE 6.7

Intercorrelations between Newspaper Variables with Varying Time Lags

		(1)	(2)	(3)	(4)	(5)	(6)	(7)	(8)	(9)	(10)	(11)	(12)	(13)
Articles no lag	(1)	X	.62	.36	[.68]	.34	.39	[.67]	.49	.37	[.35]	.75	.67	.76
Articles 1 year lag	(2)		X	.76	.41	[.68]	.54	.38	[.60]	.51	.22	[.10]	.54	.87
Articles 2 year lag	(3)			X	.48	.29	[.74]	-.01	.28	[.71]	-.10	.11	[.34]	.61
Letters no lag	(4)				X	.29	.53	[.29]	.26	.47	[.50]	.73	.49	[.50]
Letters 1 year lag	(5)					X	.00	.51	[.33]	.26	.33	[-.09]	.58	.49
Letters 2 year lag	(6)						X	-.12	.53	[.43]	.14	.35	[.28]	.71
Cartoons no lag	(7)							X	.27	-.10	[.39]	.49	.84	[.44]
Cartoons 1 year lag	(8)								X	.27	.40	[.33]	.42	.85
Cartoons 2 year lag	(9)									X	-.34	.22	[.24]	.46
Editorials no lag	(10)										X	.33	.22	[.29]
Editorials 1 year lag	(11)											X	.57	.42
Editorials 2 year lag	(12)												X	.66
Editorials 3 year lag	(13)													X

and up to 3 years for editorials. We see immediately that there are some very large correlations, as one would expect. However, the patterns of correlation suggest that one causal ordering is far more plausible than any other.

Focusing on Columns 10–13 (showing effects of editorials), in general for each row, the correlations to the right of the diagonals (indicated by the boxed correlations) are larger than the correlations to the left. This means that the correlations between editorials and the other newspaper variables are typically higher when the editorial variables precede the other variables in time. Reversing the causal ordering or placing the variables in the same time reference shows much smaller effects.

In contrast, examination of Columns 4–9 (correlations between the three variables other than editorials) shows a very different pattern. Note that either the highest correlations tend to fall on the main diagonals (boxed correlations) or no pattern emerges. Apparently, no case for causal ordering can be made for the other three newspaper variables.

The causal ordering suggested in Table 6.7 can be used to help interpret Table 6.6. To this end we shall examine a series of postulated causal models through path analysis.[11] However, our use of causal modeling should be interpreted as merely suggestive because at least three important assumptions of path analysis are violated.[12] First, all relevant variables are not included in each model. Second, the newspaper variables are in fact estimates and are best conceptualized as having confidence intervals.* Third, the correlations between the independent variables are very high.

Figure 6.2 shows seven plausible causal models, which were selected because they seemed consistent with the nature of the variables and the correlation matrix.† The time ordering was derived from Table 6.6, while legislation was seen as a consequence (rather than a cause) because it seemed unlikely that passage of day-to-day Penal Code revisions would affect newspaper crime coverage (editorials only occasionally responded to pending or enacted bills). Statistical differences between the seven models involve the number of causal links postulated: Model V is almost fully determined (only one possible causal arrow, that between articles and letters, is missing), while Models II, VI, and VII have the fewest number of causal arrows. Substantively the seven models differ along two dimensions: First, they differ in the degree to which all three newspaper variables *directly* affect patterns of legislation: In Model I, articles and letters do, while editorials do not; in Model V, all three have direct effects. Second, models differ in the degree to which editorials have their impact on legislation *indirectly* through articles and letters. That is, editorials (or what they reflect about the newspaper's policy) determine the content of letters and articles which in turn may affect legislation: In Model I, all of the impact of editorials operates through articles and letters; in Model VI, it operates only through articles.

Through path analysis, all seven models were tested for goodness of fit for each of the dependent variables. Essentially, the fitting process involved

---

* The sampling problems actually may not be especially severe. Recall, we are treating the 11 legislative sessions as a population, and the only sample is the random sample of newspapers. Fortunately, the standard errors for each year's estimated mean were rather small. Hence, for all practical purposes we can treat these as point estimates. As for the 11 sessions, notions of bias and efficiency make little sense, since we are not engaged in statistical inference. Should we be, however, path analysis rests on ordinary least squares estimation recursive equations, which produce unbiased estimates of regression parameters, and thus does not have to rely on asymptotic sampling properties as do nonrecursive systems of equations.[13]

† We have dropped cartoons from any further analysis because the yearly estimates were based on very few cases and because the variable does not correlate especially well with the dependent variables. Further, the few substantial correlations reflect essentially redundant effects with other newspaper variables.

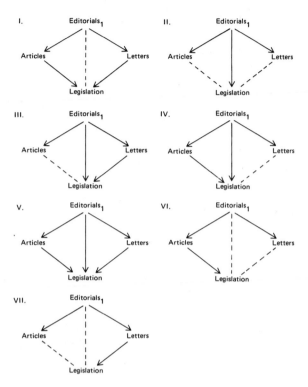

FIGURE 6.2   Possible causal models for effects of newspaper variables. Editorials$_1$ = editorials with 1-year lag effects, Articles = articles with no lag effects, Letters = letters with no lag effects, solid line = causality postulated, dotted line = causality not postulated.

testing whether observed correlations between variables having no postulated causal links could be "predicted" from the path coefficients of the included causal links. For example, if Model I of Figure 6.2 is to be accurate for a given dependent variable (e.g., revisions favoring defendants), the noncausal dotted line between editorials with a 1-year lag and legislation should reflect an actual correlation that can be totally accounted for by the causal path coefficients linking editorials to articles and letters, and the causal path coefficients linking articles and letters to legislation. Given the many high correlations between variables, we were surprisingly successful in the fitting process. Eventually, all predicted correlations were of the same sign as the actual correlations and within ±.06.

The best-fitting models are shown in Figure 6.3, with the numbers next to the causal arrows representing path coefficients (standardized regression coefficients). The coefficients must be interpreted rather cautiously because

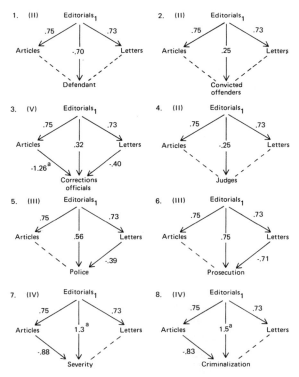

^a*Partial path coefficients greater than 1.0 are statistically permissible, through in practice rare. Here they result from the very high zero order corrlation beneath the path models.*

FIGURE 6.3   Path diagrams of best fit for newspaper variables and dependent variables. (Causal model from Figure 6.2 is identified in parentheses.) Editorials$_1$ = editorials with 1-year lag effects, Articles = articles with no lag effects, Letters = letters with no lag effects, solid line = causality postulated, dotted line = causality not postulated.

of weaknesses in the models and data noted earlier. Probably the safest approach is to take only the signs seriously, and even here these models are only suggestive.

For every type of legislation, our best-fitting models include a direct causal link between editorials and the legislation. For defendants and the judiciary, the sign of the path coefficient is negative, indicating that the greater the number of columns of crime-related editorials (lagged by 1 year), the less likely that legislation will favor defendants and judges. In all other diagrams the signs are positive. The path coefficients for defendants, police, prosecutors, severity of penalties, and overall criminalization suggest a rather traditional law-and-order stance. Interpretations for the judiciary, convicted offenders, and correction officials are less obvious.

Explanation for such patterns may lie in a more complex definition of the traditional law-and-order position, and towards this end we distinguish three important variations. The first perspective might be called vulgar law-and-orderism: a hard-line, punitive stance, in which the purpose of social control is carried to the extreme of outright repression. The aim is to get troublemakers off the streets as quickly as possible and then keep them out of circulation. Proponents would categorically support increased criminalization, longer sentences, and increased resources for police, prosecutors, judges, and corrections officials. Rights and resources for defendants and convicted offenders would be universally opposed. Sentiment behind the drug control petition drive by local Elks Lodges in 1961 is perhaps a good example of such a stance. All criminal justice officials are automatically good guys, all suspects are automatically bad guys.

A second type might be characterized as practical law-and-orderism. Here the aims are identical to vulgar law-and-orderism, but advocates give or withhold political support depending on the performance of various criminal justice officials. To the degree that particular kinds of officials further a punitive and social control perspective, they gain allies. To the degree that they thwart such aims, they lose them. Much political activity of Chief Parker's wing of the CPOA had this flavor, since they frequently tried to restrain judges and corrections officials. Judges were attacked for due-process rulings and for ineffective sentencing. Corrections officials were attacked for some of their more "liberal" programs. The important point here is that ideological aims, though not lacking, are leavened with practical exigencies.

A third type of law-and-orderism might be labeled rehabilitative. While troublemakers should be quickly identified, arrested, convicted, and sentenced, the ultimate goal is to return them to society as "productive citizens." This view often implies a medical model of criminality (i.e., prisoners as patients), in which more solely punitive corrections programs are criticized. Rehabilitation would occur to the degree that prisoners and corrections personnel could be freed from the punitive prison structure and a "therapeutic community" could be established. Sentencing is not a matter for judges to decide, but a psychiatric question best left to corrections professionals and their "patients." While many enthusiasts for this view of the California corrections system later rejected it as naive, it enjoyed widespread support in liberal circles up through the mid-1960s and still is a favorite middle-of-the-road position.*

Placing the *Times* editorials firmly within any one, let alone some combination, of these three perspectives would have required careful coding

---

* For an excellent discussion of these issues, see Kassebaum et al.[14]

of editorial content. That strategy was dismissed because of the limited resources that could be devoted to the difficult task of determining precisely where the *Times* stood in many of its editorials. Hence, from the patterns of path coefficients and our own impressionistic reading of a wide cross-section of editorials, we are able only to infer what the content might reflect. We have already noted the complex findings with regard to the path coefficients. Crime-related editorials "predict" for 1 year later: less support for defendants, more support for police and prosecutors, more criminalization, and increased penalties. These findings imply at least a practical law-and-order agenda. However, the editorials also "predicted" decreased support for the judiciary and greater support for corrections officials and convicted offenders, which *in combination* with the first set of findings suggests a rehabilitative approach. Hence, overall one might feel justified in placing the *Times* editorials within the rehabilitative law-and-order framework. It seems by far the most parsimonious way to handle the patterns of path coefficients.

Nevertheless, careful reading of many editorials covering the 15 years of our study suggests that placing the criminal justice agenda of the *Times* neatly within the rehabilitative law-and-order framework, or any other single perspective, may be an oversimplification. To make this point, and also to ground the series of critical discussions in the chapters to follow, we reproduce below seven editorials that provide a flavor of the views of the *Los Angeles Times* during these 15 years. The pivotal role of the *Times* in our later quantitative analyses requires that we start to put some meat on bare statistical bones.

Especially in the early years of our study, many editorials were as strident as any of the hard-line law-and-order pressure groups. For example, on March 3, 1960, the *Times* took a hard-line position on narcotics that combines quintessential elements of "vulgar" and "practical" law-and-orderism:

> State judges and law-enforcement officials are like deck hands working the pumps of a leaking ship. They must bend their backs and sweat—and their pumps had better be functioning efficiently—but they cure nothing; the ship's carpenters have got to go below on the double and plug the hole in the ship's side.
>
> Some suggested changes in state narcotics laws—on improvements in pumps and their management—have been sent to Sacramento. The proposed amendments to the statutes have two aims—harder penalties for narcotics violators and easier rules for the police who must catch them. . . .
>
> But proclaimed penalties do not stop the narcotics traffic; they must be imposed on the violators. The present penalties, which may be too mild, have never been tested for their full effect. Some of the recent records tend

to show that offenders are treated too leniently in the courts. The statistics suggest that judicial discretion is almost boundless.

Several undercover men of the Los Angeles Police Department were assigned last year to make narcotics purchases from pushers. They submitted their evidence to the Los Angeles County Grand Jury, which returned 90 indictments. Then the police rounded· up 79 indicated persons. This is what happened to them:

9 without prior convictions turned over to the Youth Authority.
5 without priors sentenced to prison.
14 without priors sentenced to county jail (less than a year).
1 without a prior given probation.
9 with priors sent to prison as first offenders (priors ignored).
1 with a prior sentenced to jail (less than a year).
8 with priors sent to prison (priors recognized).
47 cases disposed of with some kind of sentence.

7 acquitted.
3 dismissed.
9 identified but not apprehended.
10 not identified and not apprehended.
3 still pending.
32 cases, making a grand total of 79.

Here is justice holding not a balance but a sieve. Note that 10 defendants with prior narcotics convictions were sentenced as first offenders. Also note that while the police department made 90 cases, all with sales to police officers, only 47 resulted in prosecution (by February). The indictments were returned last August. The tabulation suggests that harsher penalties, particularly for those with prior narcotics convictions, might not make much difference in the dope trade—unless judicial discretion were circumscribed by the legislature. Perhaps it should be mandatory upon judges to recognize prior narcotics convictions in sentencing a defendant in a present narcotics case.

The record embitters zealous law enforcement officials naturally, and they have other complaints against the courts, which cut them very fine on search and seizure of narcotics cases under the so-called exclusionary rule. Police have a hard time digging into narcotics cases because violations differ from other crimes; there are no "victims" to turn in reports.

It was also during this period that the *Times* attacked Governor Brown and "the addlepates of the 'Western World'" for wanting to pardon Caryl Chessman.* Further, even as it was becoming more moderate one

* An editorial dated May 11, 1957 (Part III, p. 4), urged the State Senate to reject pending legislation that would provide a moratorium on the death penalty: "The *Times* believes that, on the whole, the argument for capital punishment is stronger

could often find significant support for a hard line on crime. For example on April 28, 1963, a *Times* editorial said:

> Each day the people of California take a gamble in which the stakes are very high and the odds are all too uncertain. In effect we bet that convicts admitted to parole won't return to crime.
>
> The parole system, however, is not a game. It places an extremely heavy responsibility upon the Adult and Youth Authorities who decide to open the gates, as well as upon parole officials who must make certain that the freedom given is not abused.
>
> The gamble is won more often than it is lost. But such a system inevitably must be judged on its failures as well as upon its successes.
>
> It was the parole failures that recently caused Gov. Brown to call a special meeting of top law enforcement officers, judges and correction officials. His particular concern, the governor told the group, was the number of violent crimes committed by individuals who have served time for other offenses.
>
> "I think the law enforcement agencies are doing an excellent job of detecting and arresting violent offenders," said Brown. But, he added, more must be done to improve parole procedures.
>
> Usually such meetings end with far more words than action. Those attending the governor's session, however, not only agreed on the problem but also agreed to do something about it.
>
> As a result, three significant steps have already been taken and further action seems certain.
>
> 1—Police Chief Parker and Walter Dunbar, director of the State Department of Corrections, have held a highly encouraging preliminary conference aimed at developing greater co-operation between police and parole officers in parolee supervision. A pilot program involving the Los Angeles Police Department and possibly the Sheriff's Department is being discussed as the first step in a statewide effort.
>
> "The best community relations we can foster," said Gov. Brown, "are to show the people we are riding herd on these parolees and keeping close tabs on them."

---

than the arguments against it, and we doubt the force of the argument that capital punishment fails as a deterrent, there is no way of knowing how many potential murderers are deterred by it." However, by 1970, a series of editorials opposing capital punishment appeared, and on February 25, 1972 (Part II, p. 6), the *Times* expressed strong support for the California Supreme Court decision to abolish the death penalty. In response to Los Angeles Police Chief Edward Davis's statement that the decision "is bound to result in the slaughter of many California citizens by an army of murderers who have been waiting for years on Death Row," the *Times* cited the Michigan experience: "Michigan abolished the death penalty 125 years ago. In the past 14 years one member of the Michigan prison system staff has been killed."

2—A high priority has been given to devising more reliable means of predicting a convict's potential of violence.

3—*At the request of the governor the Legislature now has before it a bill setting up a statewide registration of ex-convicts* [emphasis ours].

Parole will always be a gamble, but the new program of the governor and law enforcement officials seems very likely to improve society's odds.

In 1966, the *Times* supported Ronald Reagan for Governor and a year later not only endorsed the Governor's anticrime package, but pushed him to go further, at least in some areas. On April 20, 1967, the *Times* argued:

Gov. Reagan has submitted a six-point program designed to strengthen "soft spots" in state crime laws and the crime prevention program.

The objectives are laudable, and the governor has addressed himself to the popular issues, as far as crime goes, of the last election campaign. He is offering solutions to those issues in line with his pledges in that campaign.

Control or reduction of crime, however, goes far beyond the popular issues. Crime is a major problem and in his initial message to the Legislature on the subject the governor has not gone far enough. The *Times* believes that much more should be forthcoming.

The governor proposes:

Restoration to cities and counties the "ability to enact local laws designed to meet local problems." Although he mentioned specific areas, the more desirable way would be a general enactment declaring that the state would not pre-empt any field unless the Legislature specifically declared that that was its intent. In other words, the lawmakers, not the courts, would decide when the state had fully occupied any particular field.

Increased penalties for criminals who inflict bodily harm on victims in the course of a robbery, burglary or rape. Atty. Gen. Thomas Lynch supports such legislation, as he did in 1965 when similar bills were pocket-vetoed by Gov. Brown.

Comprehensive legislation on pornography with special emphasis on protection of minors and avoidance of censorship. The recommendations are in line with those of Lynch, Dist. Atty. Evelle Younger and Lt. Gov. Robert Finch.

Provide "relief" for persons arrested and later found innocent and denial of access to their records to all but law enforcement agencies and "other authorized persons." While the broad intent is commendable, it would appear that this suggestion needs clarification and refinement.

Creation of a California Crime Foundation, financed by both private and state funds, to coordinate efforts in the crime war, develop new techniques and conduct research. The *Times* shares with Atty. Gen. Lynch concern over the possibility that state funds diverted to such a project may disrupt worthwhile programs already under way in the law enforcement field.

Legislation to assure the governor opportunity to name only the most qualified attorneys to the bench. In the absence of specifics as to how that would be accomplished, we would suggest the objective might be achieved through Senate ratification of all judicial appointments.

It is to be hoped that in the future the governor will address himself to the problems of organized crime, plugging loopholes in state gambling laws and steps necessary to keep crooked money out of financial institutions and sports.

Attention should be given also to the need for additional funds to beef up law enforcement activities and to requiring cooperation in the exchange of reports and information between state agencies dealing with financial institutions.

Nonetheless, the governor's initial recommendations deserve serious and prompt consideration by the Legislature. California has more than twice its share of crime, and law enforcement officials are entitled to whatever help they can get.

Yet it was also during this period that the *Times* began to show more moderation. On March 3, 1965, it deplored Clark Kerr's resignation as president of the California University system, blaming regents, legislators, faculty, and students alike "for all that has happened in and to the university in recent months." By January 10, 1969, the *Times* was even counseling restraint in dealing with campus unrest and opposing legislative interference while calling for "maintaining and improving upon programs to provide greater educational opportunities for Negroes":

The panorama of violence and disruption so clearly in evidence at a number of state college campuses today has prompted a lot of get-tough talk by elected officials, who unquestionably are able to claim broad public support for their attitudes and their intentions.

Just what the results of this furor will be no one can yet say. At the least we probably can expect more stringent penalties against those who assault teachers and students, or who interfere with the educational process. This is Gov. Reagan's announced intention, and the Legislature appears to be with him. At the worst there is the threat of political interference and repression on the campuses which, while aimed at the dedicated troublemakers, would inevitably diminish the freedom of all.

It is not easy in the present atmosphere to think ahead to the potentially disastrous consequences of hasty punitive action, but the effort nonetheless is imperative. Passion is seldom the parent of good law, but often the incentive for an erosion of rights. The anger and disgust of the moment must not be permitted to dictate moves that could jeopardize future liberties.

At the same time it would be impossible and self-deluding to ignore the causes of the prevailing public and official mood. It is a clear response to the ruinous and arrogant attacks on the college system by a relatively small group of militants and self-proclaimed revolutionaries, who give every appearance of being unwilling to settle for anything less than complete control of the schools.

The familiar events of recent months need no rehearsing in detail. The bombings and attacks on persons and property, the refusal of the militants to enter into anything approaching reasoned discussion of their alleged grievances, the incredible abuse hurled at decent men charged with administering the colleges have cumulatively aroused the current climate of reaction.

It is all very well to try to separate and analyze the components of the campus turmoil—the struggle for black leadership, the momentum necessary to sustain any revolutionary movement and the like—but it is also of doubtful immediate relevance. For to do so is to evade the basic issues: continuing the educational process in a climate free of coercion and violence, protecting the legitimate rights of all, and maintaining and improving upon programs to provide greater educational opportunities for Negroes.

These issues are paramount. Until they are recognized as such other problems cannot be dealt with. Militant leaders may not give a damn about the fundamental issues. But the rest of the public does and it is making its views heard.

Apparently the liberal trend gathered momentum as the 1960s closed, and by the early 1970s some editorials read like literature from the ACLU. For example, on March 9, 1971, the *Times* vigorously endorsed the use of methadone for heroin addicts:

There are at least 30,000 heroin addicts in California—half of them in Los Angeles—according to latest estimates.

Experts figure that at any given time approximately half of the total are on the streets daily attempting to support their $50 a day habit. To do so they must steal at least $100 a day. That adds up to $1.5 million a day or $547 million a year in direct costs of crime to our citizenry.

In addition, state and local governments in California spend in excess of $46 million annually to support law enforcement and correctional efforts to combat heroin addiction. And in the current budget year the state will spend another $14 million for Narcotic Civil Addiction programs.

Thus the total estimated cost to Californians is more than $607.5 million yearly.

These are some of the hard economic facts—there are compelling social reasons as well—which led Assemblyman John Vasconcellos (D-San Jose) to introduce, with full support of Assembly Speaker Bob Moretti (D-Van Nuys), a series of bills designed to expand the use of methadone for treatment of heroin addiction.

Methadone maintenance of addicts has not been universally accepted. Because it is addictive, ethical, moral and medical questions have been raised. But Dr. John C. Kramer, assistant clinical professor in the College of Medicine at UC Irvine, notes that methadone's pharmacology is substantially different from that of heroin and other opiates. He insists that objections to methadone maintenance are groundless or trivial.

It would appear, then, that methadone treatment is at least worth a try.

Certainly our efforts at coping with the problem to date have been something less than a success.

Moretti points out that 85% of those voluntarily committed to the California Rehabilitation Center at Corona wind up back in our corrective system. And programs now in operation across the country are said to prove methadone maintenance 80% effective.

Vasconcellos seeks a $30 million state allocation and believes additional funds will be coming from other governmental and private sources. Where the money is to come from in a tight budgetary year is a question. Yet, if the 80% effective rate proves out, the potential saving to Californians would be more than $485 million a year.

The benefits are obvious. If hopes of proponents are realized there could be a substantial reduction in muggings, purse-snatchings, robberies and burglaries. And heroin addicts destined to become hopeless wrecks would be afforded an opportunity to become whole, healthy, fully participating members of society.

We believe, therefore, there are sound social and economic reasons why the Assembly Committee on Health should give the Vasconcellos bill a "do pass" recommendation.

On March 19, 1971, an editorial, taking a strong liberal position, suggested that prison violence is an extension in more violent form of the problems inherent in our society.

Twelve prisoners have been stabbed at San Quentin State Prison in recent weeks. One is dead, another is severely injured. Racial hatred is the cause, and more violence can be expected among the 3,200 inmates, for as one prison official said, "The veneer over racial feeling is thin. It can be pierced with a knife at any time."

Not much can be done about it. Not much, unless every prisoner is kept locked in his cell, and this would not work too effectively. Racial violence would be limited, but violence would break out in other directions. Only 10% of the prison population is involved in the present strife. Locking up the 90% along with the guilty could create more disciplinary difficulties than it would solve.

There are some basic conditions to be considered. Prisoners who are too troublesome to handle at the 12 other institutions of the California prison system are sent to San Quentin. More than half of them have a history of violent crime. The facilities at San Quentin are grossly inadequate.

But more than all this is involved. San Quentin has to deal with a problem in its most concentrated form that is racking society beyond the prison walls: racism.

"They bring the poison with them to prison," James W. L. Park, the associate warden says, adding: "There are white racists and black racists, but the problem is not really a prison problem, and it will not be solved here until a solution is found outside."

That probably is true, and it might apply as well to the whole problem of crime and punishment, its causes and cures. The current racial violence at San Quentin is only part of the larger question. The California prison system, largest in the world with 28,400 convicted felons, is widely praised as a model of humane penology. It may well be the best in the world. But is it working?

Raymond K. Procunier, director of the Department of Corrections, has doubts. Prisons, he has said, are no place to rehabilitate men. And he makes the point that Park stressed in connection with the racial tension at San Quentin. "The roots of all prison problems are to be found in society."

This points to the question of our goals, our values as a nation, and how well our society is functioning as a nation and to the effectiveness of our institutions: the schools, the police, the courts, the economic system.

The prison population may provide a clue. Today, as in the past, the prisons are filled with the poor.

Finally, on May 30, 1971, we find the *Times* vigorously criticizing the "preventive detention" provisions of Nixon's District of Columbia Anti-Crime package, calling it a "greater danger than a criminal":

The Nixon Administration persuaded Congress last year to take a nibble out of one of the basic rights of American citizens: the right not to be put in jail without a trial. Now the Administration wants Congress to take a bigger bite.

The issue is preventive detention: the holding of certain suspects up to 60 days without bail before trial. Last year Congress passed such a bill for the District of Columbia. Under the Administration's new bill, federal judges throughout the country could imprison suspects charged with loan sharking, racketeering, sale of narcotics, assault related to aircraft hijacking, bombing, kidnaping or robbery if in a detention hearing one of the following conditions was met:

The suspect has been convicted of a felony within the last 10 years; he allegedly committed a crime while on bail, probation or parole; he is a narcotics addict; or if "the government certifies" that on the basis of the person's behavior his release would threaten the safety of the community. The constitutionality of the preventive-detention measure was strongly questioned in congressional debates and is now being tested in the courts. Even the Administration concedes that there is no chance at all of congressional action on its newly proposed bill until the U.S. Supreme Court make a final determination on the legality of locking up suspects in noncapital cases before they have been convicted of anything.

This is a dangerous and frightening bill. It would permit the fundamental presumption of innocence to be abandoned in the name of unproven and unprovable speculation that someone charged with a crime might do wrong if he were allowed to remain free until such time as guilt could be determined by a jury. It would allow the government to lock up a person who may well be innocent, simply because, for one example, he may have had a prior felony conviction for which he had long since been punished.

The core of our legal system is precisely that basic right which this bill would wipe out, to be considered innocent of a crime until proof to the contrary is established in a court of law. This bill requires no proof of guilt before incarceration without the possibility of bail. It requires only that a charge has been lodged and that a judge can be persuaded of the government's suspicion that a suspect might do wrong if freed while awaiting trial.

Only one feature of this bill might call for serious consideration, that dealing with a narcotics addict who conceivably might commit a crime to support his addiction while awaiting trial on another charge. There should be room in the law to deal with such cases while still giving full protection to rights of due process. The Administration's new bill plainly is not the way to do it, however.

"The history of liberty has largely been the history of observance of procedural safeguards," said Justice Felix Frankfurter. It is specifically these safeguards which this bill would erode, and that is exactly why Congress should emphatically reject it.

While even a careful reading of the past few pages provides insufficient data to make a compelling case, these editorials do demonstrate a trend (which we sensed throughout our reading of a much larger number of editorials) from vulgar law-and-orderism to practical law-and-orderism to rehabilitative law-and-orderism. Indeed, as we have said, a few editorials in the early 1970s read somewhat like position statements from the ACLU. Perhaps, more importantly, there are hints that in some ways the *Times* anticipated important legislative trends. For instance, the tough line it took on the state narcotics laws predated by over a year the punitive 1961 antidrug legislation. Similarly, the liberalizing tendency of the late 1960s predated the more progressive legislative sessions in the early 1970s. Of course, one cannot make a rigorous case from these few editorials, but they do provide some clues to understanding the patterns of path coefficients. The path coefficients can be interpreted within the rehabilitative law-and-order framework. However, there are at least two ways in which this pattern could have emerged. First, the *Times* may have held the rehabilitative law-and-order perspective throughout the 15 years of our study. Alternatively, the *net* effect *aggregated* over the 11 legislative sessions may reflect rehabilitative law-and-order revisions, but in different periods different aspects of law-and-orderism may have been salient. In particular, the rehabilitative side may have become more prominent in the middle and late 1960s, overlaying earlier practical or perhaps even vulgar law-and-orderism. This view seems best supported by our data so far, but a full discussion of its merits will have to wait until more material is introduced. Thus far, we have been suggesting that the *Times* editorials had rather direct *causal* effects on legislative behavior. Yet, this cannot be assumed and, indeed, is problematic without further analysis, which we shall attempt in Chapter VII.

Turning now to the role of crime-related articles and letters, the picture is at least as complicated. Where causal links seem necessary, the path coefficients are negative. Increases in the number of columns of crime-related letters and/or articles are identified with a decrease in the impact of enacted legislation. Accordingly, there are smaller increments favoring corrections officials, police, prosecutors, criminalization, and severe penalties. For the last four categories, opposition to vulgar law-and-orderism, if not to the more sophisticated varieties, is suggested; while in the first, the intent is ambiguous. Yet these negative path coefficients in the face of positive zero-order correlations are perplexing, and, in every case where arrows connecting letters and/or articles are needed, they have a different sign than effects of editorials.

One possible route to an interpretation is to remember that path coefficients are partial measures and that the effects of letters and/or articles reflect impacts with editorials "held constant." Insofar as editorials indicate management policy that is implemented in the production of the newspaper, the letter and article effects may be "spillovers" once management has had its way in the initial selection of letters and news coverage.* In other words, the reversal in signs reflects the effect for letters and articles (be it overt or hidden) not determined by management policy. If this inter-

---

* In 1960, Otis Chandler became publisher of the *Los Angeles Times*. At a young 33, he seemed especially sensitive to the paper's image of "stodgy conservatism" and to the history behind that image. In an interview with Frank Riley in 1966, Chandler commented: "We tended to be very conservative, and we used to bias the news—we didn't print both sides of labor–management disputes, we wouldn't print much Democratic news, we were narrow in our religious coverage . . . ." [15]

pretation has any merit, it is important to emphasize that of the 16 opportunities that exist in the path diagrams for causal links between articles, letters, and legislation, links are needed only 6 times. This suggests that, as far as impact on legislative behavior is concerned, editorials are far more important than are crime-related news articles or letters to the editor about crime.

In summary, the most plausible interpretation of newspaper impact on Penal Code legislation at this point in our discussion may best be characterized as rehabilitative law-and-orderism. Troublemakers should be placed quickly and efficiently into a therapeutic community in which their "illness" can be cured. While crime-related articles and letters to the editor may in a few instances have altered this stance, certainly one cannot characterize the impact over the entire 15-year span as especially progressive. Assuming causality, the role of editorials seems to dominate the scene by its high correlations with Penal Code revisions. Unfortunately, this analysis still leaves unanswered exactly how editorials affect Penal Code legislation. Are they so persuasive that legislators alter their views? Or are intervening factors at work so that the legislature is not, in fact, reacting affirmatively to editorials per se? Do they affect public opinion, which in turn influences important elected officials? Or do editorials reflect the policy of corporate elites who are active behind the scenes? These and other possibilities must be considered if we are to move beyond superficial speculations. Later, both in Chapter VII and in Chapter IX, we shall return to such questions.

The Effects of Public Opinion

While various political actors periodically acknowledge the "public" and others justify their views in the context of "public opinion," our data have provided little evidence of a direct legislative role for unorganized California citizens. Occasionally grass-roots activity was visible (e.g., the Elks antidrug petition and the Chessman case), but typically the legislative process in criminal lawmaking was conducted with little public interest or participation.

Though the public may only rarely have been involved in Sacramento's day-to-day activities, one might still argue that legislators were keenly aware of their constituents and that this affected legislative behavior. Soon after citizens became more concerned about "crime in the streets," for instance, legislators would begin to support more hard-line legislation. Indeed, in general terms this is the representative model on which legislatures are supposed to operate, and on its face it seems a plausible view of the impact of public opinion. Anticipating reelection campaigns, legislators would try to respond to the views of "the folks back home."

If legislators are responding to public opinion, one would expect that change in popular moods should correlate with Penal Code trends, and shifts in public opinion should *predate* shifts in legislative behavior. In order to test this proposition, one could in theory use public opinion polls to generate independent variables and then proceed with the style of analysis we have applied to our other predictors. However, this assumes that relevant poll data are available from the early 1950s to 1971 and that comparable questions in those polls exist from year to year.

We searched the Roper files (which contain records of most of the large public polls ever taken in the United States) for questions about crime that had been asked consistently in California in the period 1950–1971. Only one question of use was found: "What are the major problems facing the country today?" This open-ended item was used by Gallup for literally decades, and fortunately there were special tabulations for California. For every 6-month period we summed the proportion of mentions received by crime-related responses and used yearly means as the independent variable predicting the passage of Penal Code legislation.*

The correlations can be seen in Table 6.8. Our measure of public opinion

TABLE 6.8

Zero-Order Pearson Correlation between Public Opinion Polls on Law and Order and Dependent Variables

Dependent variable	% Mentions[a] (no lag)	% Mentions[a] (one year lag)
Defendant	-.18	-.29
Convicted offenders	-.02	-.09
Corrections officials	-.38	-.29
Judges	-.06	.05
Police	.01	-.23
Prosecution	.18	-.13
Crimes w/o victims	.36	.17
Persons	.26	.32
Property	-.27	-.20
Public interest	-.01	-.13
Severity of penalty	-.10	-.08
Overall criminalization	.06	.06

[a] *The "% Mentions" is the sum of the percentages of crime-related responses to the Gallup Poll question: "What are the major problems facing the country today?"*

* For example, if the sum for the first half of 1970 was 20% and the sum for the second half was 22%, we used the mean of 21% for the 1970 estimate. Responses included mention of "crime," "delinquency," "drugs," "law enforcement," "unrest," and "protest."

shows no interesting patterns of association with the legislation, whether for simultaneous occurrence or with a 1-year lag. Part of the reason for the low correlations may be the small size of the California sample. With a sample in California of typically well under 100, the sampling errors are large enough in many cases to potentially overwhelm whatever "real" effects might exist. However, examination of Figure 6.4, showing public concern with crime-related issues over time, suggests consistent trends, not a random pattern. Public concern increases dramatically after 1967, but the increases appear to *follow* trends in legislation. In other words, the graph suggests that the estimates are not simply random (the graph would then show no systematic pattern) but legitimate indicators of public concern. The low correlations in Table 6.8 are a consequence of the failure of the trend to *predict* legislation.* Recall that our qualitative analysis and graphs in Chapters IV and V suggested shifts in legislative mood during the mid-1960s. Yet, Figure 6.4 indicates that it took until 1968 for the public to abstract law and order as a special and overriding problem. Ironically, 1968 is the year of Sieroty's Prisoner Rights Bill and a year when liberal forces were already beginning an effective counterattack.

It is important to emphasize what it is that the polls may be reflecting. Surveys are designed to tap broad trends in public opinion and usually do

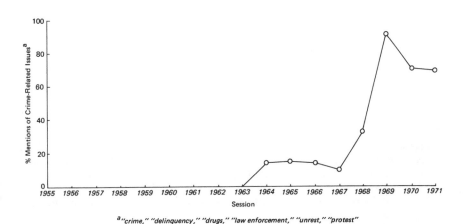

^{a}*"crime," "delinquency," "drugs," "law enforcement," "unrest," "protest"*

FIGURE 6.4 Public concern in California with crime-related issues from 1955–1971. Source: Roper Files (Gallup Polls).

* The findings of the Assembly study, *Deterrent Effects of Criminal Sanctions*,[16] underscore the public's poor comprehension both of day-to-day operations of the legislature and of the detailed provisions of criminal justice bills. This provides a partial explanation of public opinion's failure to exercise a directive influence on the evolution of the Penal Code.

not consider how strongly the opinions are held or whether they will be acted upon. Hence, a large majority might oppose (or support) a law-and-order position without their views having much impact on state politics. Similarly, a vocal minority might be extremely visible and powerful while making a negligible contribution to poll statistics. Our poll data do not address the role of vocal minorities but broad trends in the view of California citizens.

The conclusions are straightforward. Our measure of public concern about crimes shows systematic increases over time despite a small California sample for each yearly estimate. These changes in public opinion seem to lag behind changes in Penal Code legislation. At the very least there is no evidence that legislators respond to broad trends in public opinion. This does not deny a role for smaller, organized citizen groups or legislative actions based on *perceived* public positions. Still, given the prominence of lobbies and the "agreed bill" process, public input in day-to-day legislative activity is probably slight. In short, both the qualitative material and this statistical analysis have failed to uncover a salient on-going role for the public. We shall have much more to say about this in Chapter IX.

REFERENCES

1. Thomas R. Dye, *Politics, Economics, and the Public Welfare: Policy Outcomes in the American States* (New York: Rand McNally and Company, 1966), p. 234.
2. Robert Aaron Gordon, "Issues in Multiple Regression," *American Journal of Sociology*, Vol. 73 (March, 1968), pp. 592–616.
3. Robert K. Binford, "Party Cohesion in the California State Assembly, 1953–1963" (unpublished M.A. thesis, Stanford University, 1964); Charles M. Price, "Voting Alignments in the California Legislature: Roll-Call Analysis of the 1957–1959–1961 Sessions" (unpublished Ph.D. thesis, University of Southern California, 1965).
4. Jan Kmenta, *Elements of Econometrics* (New York: Macmillan Company, 1971), Sections 8-2, 11-4.
5. A. D. Miller, "Logic of Causal Analysis: From Experimental to Non-Experimental Designs," in *Causal Models in the Social Sciences*, ed. H. M. Blalock, Jr. (Chicago: Aldine Press, 1971).
6. Aaron V. Cicourel and John I. Kitsuse, *The Educational Decision-Makers* (Indianapolis: Bobbs-Merrill, 1963).
7. Phillip H. Ennis, "Crime, Victims and the Police," in *Police Encounters*, ed. Michael Lipskey (Chicago: Aldine Press, 1970).
8. Frank Harris, *Presentation of Crime in Newspapers* (Minneapolis: Sociological Press, 1932).
9. M. Herbert Danzger, "Validating Conflict Data," *American Sociological Review*, Vol. 40, No. 5 (October, 1975).
10. F. James Davis, "Crime News in Colorado Newspapers," *American Journal of Sociology*, Vol. 57, No. 4 (January, 1952).
11. Hubert M. Blalock, *Causal Inferences in Non-Experimental Research* (Chapel Hill: University of North Carolina Press, 1964); Kenneth C. Land, "Identification

Parameter Estimation and Hypothesis Testing in Recursive Sociological Models," in *Structural Equation Models in the Social Sciences*, ed. Arthur S. Goldberger and Otis Dudley Duncan (New York: Seminar Press, 1967).

12. David R. Heise, "Problems in Path Analysis and Causal Inference," in *Sociological Methodology*, ed. Edgar F. Borgatta (San Francisco: Jossey-Bass, 1967).

13. Kenneth C. Land, "Principles of Path Analysis," in *Sociological Methodology*, ed. Edgar F. Borgatta (San Francisco: Jossey-Bass, 1969).

14. Gene Kassebaum, David Ward, and Daniel Wilner, *Prison Treatment and Parole Survival* (New York: John Wiley and Sons, 1971).

15. John C. Merrill, *The Elite Press* (New York: Pitman Publishing Company, 1968), Chapter 17.

16. Criminal Procedure Committee of the California State Assembly, *Deterrent Effects of Criminal Sanctions*. (Sacramento: 1968).

VII

Explaining the Trends: Multivariate Analysis

IN CHAPTER VI WE EMPHASIZED the zero-order relationships between various independent variables and Penal Code trends. We found, for example, that a tentative interpretation can be made for the rehabilitative law-and-orderism of *Los Angeles Times* editorials. In contrast, it was difficult to explain the confused patterns for correlations involving crime statistics. Public opinion shows virtually no impact.

Despite some provocative findings such analyses are clearly incomplete. Many of the independent variables are highly correlated, suggesting that their effects may be overlapping. In other words, when we find a large impact for the proportion of Democrats on the Assembly Criminal Procedure Committee, included within that correlation may be the effects of *Times* editorials. Perhaps holding editorials constant will change or even eliminate the effects of Democratic proportions. A more thorough examination of such complexities requires statistical procedures that can partition zero-order effects into components attributable to each independent variable. Toward that end, we move to more extensive analyses using multiple regression.

Unfortunately, even for descriptive purposes and in concert with our qualitative data, a multivariate analysis with 11 data points is a risky (some might say fatuous) undertaking. High multiple correlations, for example, can be achieved simply by adding any assortment of independent variables in large numbers. Consequently, after exploring the consequences of several different statistical strategies, we decided to use no more than three independent variables simultaneously. This seemed a conservative compromise between several distinct priorities and will not seriously restrict our substantive discussion.

Another problem was created by high correlations between our independent variables. As noted earlier, to maximize the stability of the partial measures, these correlations should not be large. Consequently, we will only consider here independent variables that have correlations with one another lower than .60. There is nothing magic about .60; we could have chosen another figure. However, what little evidence exists[1] and our own attempts at simulations suggested that .60 was not too high when correlations with the dependent variable were substantial.

In order to simplify the discussion, we will restrict ourselves further to the results of multiple regression procedure in which variables failing to contribute uniquely at least 5% to variance explained are dropped from the analysis. Unfortunately, this procedure creates some difficulties when correlations between independent variables are high. Since partial measures can be unstable and the choice of variables to be included is based on partial measures, the selection of variables may be, in part, artifactual. We have attempted to minimize this difficulty with the use of a maximum intercorrelation of .60. In other words, this moderate correlation not only makes our partial measures more credible but makes the selection of included variables more credible as well.

The above discussion clearly implies that an initial screening procedure for independent variables was required, and we selected a very small number of variables from our total of more than twenty *before* applying multiple regression techniques. From the analyses presented earlier and an additional examination of the overall correlation matrix, we chose the three variables that had the highest average correlations with the dependent variables while having correlations among themselves of less than .60. Actually, the same three variables would have been chosen had the acceptable intercorrelation been as high as .70. Further, even ignoring the correlations between independent variables, the three are about the best zero-order predictors. In short, other researchers studying the correlation matrix would almost certainly have chosen the identical variables.

The three variables chosen should be immediately familiar: the Democratic proportions in the Assembly Committee on Criminal Justice, the influence of the civil liberties lobby, and *Los Angeles Times* crime-related editorials lagged by 1 year. Of the other clusters we might have used, crime statistic variables were not used because they generally showed far lower correlations with the dependent variables and moderately high correlations (around .50) with editorials. The public opinion measures showed no significant pattern of correlation with changes in Penal Code legislation. Editorials lagged by 1 year were chosen from the other newspaper variables because they were the most consistently powerful predictors. The civil liberties lobby (CLL) was chosen from the lobby variables because it had about the same size of average correlation with legislative changes while having the lowest correlation with other independent variables. The law enforcement lobby correlated .72 with crime-related editorials, higher than the maximum correlation allowed by our standards.

Multiple Regressions Results

Table 7.1 presents the results of the regression equations including all three of the independent variables finally chosen for the multivariate analysis. Reading horizontally, the slope (b) and standardized regression coefficient (β) for each dependent variable are shown. Below each slope (b) is the zero-order correlation (r) with the dependent variable. "Drop" indicates that for the given dependent variable, the independent variable in question failed to produce a 5% increment to variance explained. Also included are the multiple correlations (R) and the total variance explained (R^2).

Our analysis will rest primarily on the last three columns in Table 7.1; but before moving to these standardized measures, a brief discussion of the other measures in the table will be useful. The slope (b) measures the change in Penal Code revisions for each unit of change in the independent variable, with the other independent variables "held constant". For example, a change of 1% in the Democratic proportion in the Assembly will "cause" (or at least "predict") a change of .45 units in revisions affecting overall criminalization. We would much prefer to have undertaken our entire analysis in terms of these slopes because we could then have produced interpretations in the original measurement units. This grounding would have improved the understanding of the results. For example, since the mean change in the Democratic proportion for each session from 1955 to 1971 is 5.9, in a "typical" year the effect of Democratic proportion upon total criminalization is about 2.7 units (5.9 × .45). Additionally, since one revision usually carries a value of about .75 (a small increase) in a "typical" year, the average change in Democratic proportion will determine whether or not nearly four revisions (2.7 divided by .75) on criminalization will be passed.

Unfortunately, the use of unstandardized slopes (i.e., slopes in the orig-

TABLE 7.1

Multiple Regression Results for Percent Democratic, Editorials (one year lag), and Civil Liberties Lobby as Predictors of the Dependent Variables

Dependent variable		% Demo	ED_1	CLL	R	R^2	β	% Demo	ED_1	CLL
Overall	b	0.45	2.04	Drop	.84	.71	β	.33	.66	Drop
criminalization	r	.58	.78	-.10						
Severity of	b	0.13	0.39	Drop	.72	.52	β	.37	.50	Drop
penalty	r	.56	.63	-.17						
Public	b	0.11	0.58	Drop	.74	.55	β	.26	.60	Drop
interest	r	.49	.70	-.31						
Persons	b	Drop	0.56	Drop	.86	.75	β	Drop	.86	Drop
	r	.30	.86	-.40						
Property	b	0.22	0.37	Drop	.74	.56	β	.52	.38	Drop
	r	.66	.51	.08						
Crimes w/o	b	Drop	Drop	Drop	—	—	β	Drop	Drop	Drop
victims	r	-.03	.10	.06						
Prosecution	b	Drop	0.12	Drop	.37	.14	β	Drop	.37	Drop
	r	.17	.37	-.10						
Police	b	Drop	Drop	-1.83	.52	.27	β	Drop	Drop	-.52
	r	-.19	.36	-.52						
Judge	b	Drop	Drop	1.51	.33	.11	β	Drop	Drop	.33
	r	.18	-.25	.33						
Corrections	b	0.27	Drop	4.64	.71	.51	β	.46	Drop	.44
officials	r	.60	-.25	.46						
Convicted	b	0.34	Drop	Drop	.71	.50	β	.71	Drop	Drop
offenders	r	.71	.25	.10						
Defendants	b	0.24	-0.53	1.61	.85	.72	β	.60	-.58	.12
	r	.44	-.70	.67						

b = Slope in original units of measurement
β = Standardized regression coefficient (beta)
r = Zero order correlation
R = Multiple correlation
R^2 = Total variance explained
Drop = Increment to explained variance less than 5%. Therefore, this variable is not included in the regression equation.

inal measurement units) is most appropriate when all independent variables are in conventional units like dollars, years, or frequency counts. When some variables are measured through artificially constructed indices, such as our rating of the influence of the CLL, it is usually wiser to standardize. Slopes are greatly affected by the type and units of measurement, and one consequence is that it becomes very difficult to compare the relative important-ance of independent variables with differing units of measurement. Comparability is increased if one transforms all variables to standard scores. To this end, the standardized regression coefficients (β) indicate the slopes between independent and dependent variables, but in Z-scores. In unravel-ing the independent effects of each of the three independent variables, we shall employ these standardized measures. We gain statistical comparability between measures while losing the grounding in the original measurement units. Thus, the standardized slope indicates the number of standard deviations change in the dependent variable for every standard deviation change in the independent variable.

An initial question to ask about our attempts to predict changes in Penal Code legislation is, How accurate are the predictions? How great the amount of "error"?* Under the columns labeled R and R^2 are multiple correlations and total explained variances, respectively. With the exceptions of crimes without victims, police, prosecutors, and the judiciary, we explain at least half the variance (R^2) in every case. For police, over one-quarter of the variance is "explained" (multiple correlation of .52), while for prosecutors and the judiciary 14% and 11% are "explained," respectively.

In short, for eight of twelve dependent variables, we predict unusually well, with multiple correlations up to .86. For three of the remaining four, there is enough variance explained to warrant serious attention.†

Turning first to the pattern of β's for types of criminalization and severity of penalties, we find that two of the three variables have important impacts. The higher the proportion of Democratic legislators in the Assembly and the more columns of crime-related editorials, the more Penal Code revisions favor a hard line on crime: more behavior is criminalized and penalties are increased. The one important exception is for crimes without victims, where all variables together failed to account for 5% of the variance in that dependent variable. Despite nontrivial zero-order effects, the CLL has no important impact with the other two variables held constant.

One is tempted to speculate that, since the correlation between editorials lagged by 1 year and the "effective influence" of the CLL is −.58, somehow editorials undercut the effectiveness of CLL. This is not unreasonable, and there is some evidence that lends itself to such an interpretation. Deutsch, for instance, has pointed out in her analysis of California press coverage of the United States Supreme Court due process decisions, that of 17 articles about the *Miranda* decision appearing from June 13 to July 13, 1966, in the *Los Angeles Times*, nine were articles reporting negative assessments of *Miranda*, two were supportive, and six were nondirectional.[3] This is not to

---

* For those somewhat unfamiliar with correlational analysis, the term "error" does not mean that a mistake has been made but that some effects cannot be understood in terms of the particular independent variables included. Typically, meaningful analyses can be undertaken with as little as 10% of the variance explained (or 90% "error"). Variance explained in our data ranges from 75% for defendants and crimes against persons to 0% for crimes without victims.

† Adjusted multiple correlations for degrees of freedom are not appropriate since we are treating our data as a population.[2]

say that such coverage necessarily reflected the editorial position of the *Los Angeles Times* since recognition in this instance must be given to the highly articulated responses of organized groups opposed to the *Miranda* decision, responses that were newsworthy irrespective of *Times* editorial position. On the other hand, unanswered is the question of how deliberate the selection process was in the *Times* coverage of newsworthy reaction to *Miranda*.

Alternatively, the CLL's lack of impact may simply reflect the ACLU's traditional disinterest in penalties and definitions of criminal behavior. Were this true, no *causal* links from *Times* editorials to CLL effective influence would perhaps be required. Recall that, in fact, "cruel and unusual punishment" did not become a priority until the late 1960s. Consequently, the CLL's limited impact vis-à-vis penalties and criminalization may have less to do with thwarted influence than a deliberate choice of agenda.

Looking only at penalties and criminalization, the relative sizes of β's for the proportion of Democratic legislators and editorials indicates that, with the exception of property crimes, editorials are typically about twice as important. This pattern is to be expected, since the zero-order correlations presented in Chapter VI show approximately the same effects; also, the correlation between editorials and the proportion Democratic is too small $(-.25)$ to cause substantial alteration when multiple regression is applied. Consequently, one can reasonably conclude that for legislation affecting criminalization and severity of penalties, the most revealing independent variable is crime-related editorials.*

The patterns for Penal Code legislation affecting the intended legal rights and resources of actors in the criminal justice system are quite different from patterns for criminalization and severity of penalties. First, in four of the six cases, editorials drop out of the regression analysis. However, where editorials are important, for prosecutors and defendants, one is struck by the vulgar law-and-order implications. The relation to prosecutors is positive, to defendants negative. Second, the importance of CLL influence surfaces. For four of the six actors, the CLL has important independent effects, furthering the rights and resources of defendants, corrections officials, and judges, and opposing the rights and resources of police. Clearly, the CLL has a very different agenda from that reflected in the editorials. Finally, for the Democratic proportion in the Assembly, the greater that proportion the more likely that legislation will significantly favor corrections officials, convicted offenders, and defendants. For legislation involving *actors* in the criminal justice system, Democrats seem to support more strongly a "civil liberties" position.

---

* This assessment holds up using unstandardized slopes and predicted year-to-year changes.

Table 7.1 has a number of implications. Focusing first on the Democratic proportion in the Assembly, one finds it difficult to characterize the independent impact of this variable with a simple word or phrase. Typically, the higher the Democratic proportion, the more laws are passed. However, the evidence suggests that although laws are passed that substantially criminalize, in addition, laws are passed that appear to substantially favor civil liberties. We suggested earlier that the reason for this pattern might be a greater belief in legislative intervention on all levels—those that define criminal behavior and those that process the suspect.

Though Democrats may seem to be straddling the fence on law-and-order, there is evidence to suggest that they list toward the civil liberties side. The β's are typically about twice as large for laws about actors in the criminal justice system than for laws that criminalize and make penalties more severe. Furthermore, the criminalization effects may reflect an atypical response to vulgar law-and-order concerns. For example, β's for crimes against persons and crimes without victims are dropped for lack of impact, while Democrats apparently supported laws emphasizing public interest issues, such as consumer fraud, ecological offenses, and gun control. In addition, the so-called property crimes often involved the increased criminalization of "white-collar" offenses such as embezzlement and bribery. To characterize these crimes as responses to law-and-order is probably misleading.

We also suggested earlier that Democratic "ambivalence" on law and order had a more "political" explanation. Recall that skillful gerrymandering had allowed the Democrats to add to their legislative majorities even while law-and-order concerns were on the rise. However, it would have been foolhardy to ignore the political potential of campus unrest, crime, and white backlash, despite Democratic party dominance. Elections were on the horizon, law enforcement groups had new ammunition, and conservative Republicans were already flexing their muscles. Hence, votes favoring increases in criminalization and penalties can be seen perhaps as defensive concessions to an explosive issue. By the mid-1960s, however, increasing political defeats were suggesting that appeasement was not working. And, even before losing formal control of the legislature, Democrats began to develop an obstructionist "oppositional psychology," which freed them to "vote their consciences" and kill punitive legislation in committees. This led to the near stalemate of the first 2 years of Reagan's initial term, during which a less Democratic legislature was passing fewer law-and-order bills. The banner year for punitive legislation was 1965, just *before* Reagan became Governor. In short, one must not ignore the "realpolitik" of Sacramento.

In Chapter VI we argued that the overall *aggregate* effects of *Times* editorials might be characterized as rehabilitative law-and-orderism. While suspects would be expeditiously handled, convicted offenders would have the "benefit" of therapeutic resocialization. One might still hold to this description, but it is now clear from the multivariate analysis that far greater evidence of influence exists in the preconviction categories. The β's for convicted offenders, corrections officials, and the judiciary fail to make our cutoff point (though they each explain over 1% of the variance), and these are just the dependent variables that can distinguish vulgar and practical law-and-orderism from rehabilitative law-and-orderism. Thus, regardless of intent, the impact of the editorials may be largely punitive.*

Despite provocative statistical inferences about the impacts of crime-related editorials, our analysis remains superificial. To say that editorials have an important impact but not spell out the process by which this occurs is unsatisfying. We do know, however, that leading newspapers like the *San Francisco Chronicle, Oakland Tribune,* and *Los Angeles Times* have played an extraordinarily important role in shaping California's political culture, and that both the law enforcement lobby and civil liberties groups considered cultivating newspaper support a vital necessity. We will be far more specific about these effects in our final chapter when more basic theoretical issues are addressed.

The independent effects of the CLL are exclusively on criminal justice process: laws affecting criminal justice actors. That there should be opposition to police and support for defendants is not surprising. And CLL support for corrections officials and the judiciary makes sense, given liberal perceptions of the California corrections system. Recall that for a generation California had been a stronghold of "reform penology," winning the praises of Dr. Karl Menninger as being "far out in the lead among the states."[6] If a psychiatrist who believes punishment to be "a crime" could heap praise on this system, it is not difficult to understand liberal support for the legislation providing greater discretionary authority for the men running it—men who Menninger characterizes as a "group of idealists" providing "brilliant leadership." Disillusionment in the late 1960s led such groups to reexamine what Jessica Mitford called "pastel prisons."[7] But from 1955 to 1971 the overall pattern of support for corrections remains.

From Table 7.1 and the discussion above several conclusions emerge. First, with three variables one is able to account for very large proportions of the changes in Penal Code legislation. Besides the obvious substantive importance of such high multiple correlations, our methodology for coding

---

* Silence on the part of the liberal press has usually ensured that only punitive voices are raised when proposals to further criminalize the law are made.[4] No such "consensus by default" prevails on police power questions, however, because there are publications, especially in Northern California, vigorously committed to the due-process reforms spearheaded by the judiciary.[5]

changes in the Penal Code receives considerable validation. Apparently it is possible to quantify large amounts of legislation and meaningfully plot and analyze trends.

Second, the findings suggest that changes in criminal law occur largely through an "elite" process. The CLL is a relatively small group of persons especially interested in "due process" who have at best minimal links to the general public.* Likewise, the interests reflected in editorials consider public opinion in only the most superficial and secondary way. Recall that the poll data showed no significant effects and that letters to the editor had little impact once editorial policy was held constant. The Democratic proportion, though a result of elections, can be viewed as a response to popular sentiment only if candidates ran on their criminal justice voting records and/or on platforms that included criminal justice planks, if people voted in part on that basis, and if elected legislators altered their behavior based on expectations of constituency reactions. We suspect that these conditions were rarely met. To begin with, most bills were passed through the "agreed bill" process, in which floor votes were typically unanimous. This certainly provides no information with which voters could distinguish between candidates. Committee votes were not much help either since, until 1972, roll-call committee votes on bill passage were unavailable. In addition, committee appointments were often made from "safe" districts, that is, districts that were moderate on criminal justice, and hence less likely to react, or districts where the representative was so popular that he/she could do pretty much as he/she pleased. Finally, the vast majority of revisions were of little interest to the public. Only in times of crisis, and then only for certain bills, is it likely that California citizens were even remotely informed about criminal justice legislation.

Third, one can characterize, in general, the criminal justice agenda implied by the independent variables. The editorials up through the mid-1960s can be associated with a conservative drift in Sacramento, while the moderate-to-liberal editorials of the late 1960s and early 1970s can be associated with the return to legislative liberalism during this period. Editorials seem not to be associated with due process issues except for legislation affecting prosecutors and defendants. The highest correlations are for criminalization and severity of penalties. On the other hand, the CLL appears to have been effective in issues of due process. Their position is summarized by the label we have used for these interests. However, support for judges and corrections officials is included, which suggests that definitions of "liberal" programs can change dramatically over time. Finally, the

---

* This requires qualification only to the extent that during the 1960s the ACLU allied itself with the Democratic party which, of course, does have such links.

Democratic party has encouraged the passage of Penal Code legislation that cannot be easily characterized as either for or against law and order. With reference to Democratic support of criminalization, for example, the majority of the enactments supported by Democrats addressed a range of issues of limited interest to law enforcement. Thus, while the wider compass of the criminal sanction can, in fact, easily incorporate "liberal" enactments addressed to such issues as pollution, campaign corruption, and invasion of privacy, "law and order" in the vulgar sense refers to those punitive responses which are more narrowly concerned with street crime and violence.

Analysis of Residuals from Regression Equations

The high multiple correlations in Table 7.1 indicate that much of the variability in Penal Code revision trends can be statistically accounted for. This is especially critical, given the methodological aims of this chapter. We have argued that one could move beyond specific historical events to more abstract variables in explaining trends in the Penal Code from 1955 to 1971. In a statistical sense at least, the high multiple correlations for many of the dependent variables support our case. Nevertheless, the time has now come to reintroduce the possibility of using situation-specific historical explanations. While we shall not alter the specification of our regression equations (in part because we dare not add more variables), we shall examine the equation residuals to see if the statistical error in our equations might be the result of certain historical events.

Essentially, a residual is the difference between the actual amount of legislative change for a given year and given category and the amount of change one would predict from the simultaneous use of our independent variables. The larger the residual the less accurate the estimate. If certain years tend to have large residuals, one may be able to infer that certain important processes have been ignored. For example, if for 1965 one found large positive residuals, indicating more criminalization than had been estimated, it would suggest that the year might have special properties, which should be better understood. Or if one found large negative residuals across all criminal justice officials for a set of years, it would mean that less legislation was passed substantially favoring those actors and one might see those years as correspondingly less law-and-order oriented than had been estimated.

Analysis of residuals has another important function. If one finds serial correlations between residuals, it would suggest that an important longitudinal process might have been ignored. We raised this issue earlier, in terms of autocorrelations, and will address it again later in this section.

Table 7.2 shows the residuals for each dependent variable. In each cell is a number indicating the difference between the observed amount of change in the Penal Code for a given year and given category, and the amount predicted from the regression equation. For example, for defendants in 1955 there were 2.54 less units of legislation passed than was predicted.*

Probably the easiest way to get a feel for the meaning of Table 7.2 is to examine a few of the larger residuals. The largest is for overall criminalization in 1968, where one finds a value of −15.36. This means that after our three independent variables have accounted for all of the variability that they can in the Penal Code trends, a net impact of −15.36 remains for 1968. Since each revision has an effect of about .75 on the average, about 20 revisions less were passed than would have been expected from our linear regression equation. Thinking back to 1968, this negative residual seems sensible. Despite a law-and-order trend, obstructionist Democrats had bottled up most of Reagan's anticrime legislation, and a report on corrections from the Assembly Office of Research had stimulated significant prison reform. Indeed, both in our earlier qualitative analysis and in the graphs in Chapters IV and V, 1968 stood out as the best year for liberals after 1965. What this analysis has added, however, is that in a more fundamental way, 1968 is extremely unusual. It remains "deviant" even after we are able to explain 71% of the variance in overall criminalization through our regression equations (see Table 7.1).

The largest positive residual in Table 7.2 is for overall criminalization in 1961. The value is 12.36 (or about 16 revisions), indicating that 1961 was far more punitive than our regression equation would predict. Again this makes sense. Earlier analyses suggested that 1961 was the best year for conservative forces before 1965. A backlash against liberal attempts to abolish capital punishment, coupled with grass-roots antidrug agitation and a CPOA public relations offensive, severely challenged liberal dominance. These forces were not thoroughly considered by the variables in our regression equation, hence the large positive residual.

One could go on to examine other large residuals. However, before long one would have generated a special explanation for almost every number in Table 7.2. The problem, of course, would be that parsimony would be thrown to the winds and general interpretations would be lost. Therefore, despite the fact that most of the large residuals can be accounted for with recourse to our earlier qualitative analysis, especially the key bills passed

---

* There were only six relevant revisions in 1955. For all practical purposes, this meant a net effect of zero for all categories in 1955. Thus, we could include 1955 in the analysis giving each category a value of zero.

TABLE 7.2
Residuals of Regression Equations

Session	Defendant	Convicted offenders	Actors Corrections officials	Police	Prosecution	Judge	Crimes w/o victims	Against persons	Criminalization Against property	Public interest	Severity of penalty	Overall criminalization
1955	-2.54	2.87	2.10	-3.06	-1.62	-3.30	-1.32	0.01	0.81	-1.12	1.21	-5.12
1957	3.32	0.42	1.59	4.23	1.14	0.51	-1.38	-0.55	2.98	0.29	-0.28	4.51
1959	1.34	-2.69	-3.20	0.18	0.96	2.92	-1.94	-0.24	-3.10	1.84	-0.05	-0.93
1961	-2.06	-3.34	9.38	0.06	-0.87	0.88	5.89	0.90	4.47	-0.12	4.11	12.36
1963	1.17	-1.11	-1.14	1.05	1.72	-1.18	-1.21	-1.47	-1.10	-2.01	-2.43	-7.62
1965	0.47	3.95	5.46	0.34	-2.92	1.99	-7.90	0.76	5.13	7.02	5.21	3.58
1967	0.89	-0.59	0.53	0.65	0.61	-2.26	1.57	0.87	1.49	1.65	0.72	5.86
1968	1.58	7.41	-1.67	-1.63	0.05	4.70	-0.57	-4.05	-3.40	-4.71	-3.90	-15.36
1969	1.31	-4.12	-2.72	0.61	2.11	-1.49	4.62	0.78	-1.79	-0.46	-1.07	5.68
1970	-5.39	-5.72	-2.57	-1.73	-1.49	1.36	0.36	1.38	-3.42	-4.45	-0.82	-4.84
1971	0.87	2.97	-7.77	-0.68	0.30	-1.11	1.87	1.61	-2.06	-0.18	-2.70	1.87
Serial Correlation (1 session lag)	-.30	-.16	-.08	-.46	-.59	-.53	-.14	-.21	-.10	-.05	-.21	-.54

each year (e.g., further decriminalization of addiction in 1965), it will ultimately be more productive to broaden our use of Table 7.2. It is also important to remember that we would be studying patterns of residuals for regression equations that typically account for over one-half of the variance in Penal Code trends. By convention standards, we would be putting icing on the cake.

Looking first at the residuals on the extreme right-hand side of the table, those for overall criminalization and severity of penalties, seven of the years stand out by the consistency of the signs. The years 1959, 1963, 1968, and 1970 have negative signs, indicating that less punitive legislation was passed in those years than one would predict. It would appear that these years are less involved in criminalization processes than others, and one might be tempted to call them more liberal (after the three independent variables have explained what they could) than the equations suggested. In contrast, the years 1961, 1965, and 1967 are years with largely positive residuals, indicating more criminalization than one would predict. One might characterize these years as more law-and-order oriented than the equations suggested. That 1965 and 1967 have more criminalization than predicted makes sense, since these were the years around which we broke the single regression line into parts to take account of an apparent acceleration in the rate of criminalization. Apparently, these transition years were not as adequately explained by our independent variables. The 1965 and 1967 residuals may be in part understood through special such historical events as the Free Speech movement at Berkeley, the Watts civil disorders, and the election of Ronald Reagan. The positive residuals in 1961 reflect forces discussed above.

Looking at the left-hand side of the table, at residuals for actors in the criminal justice system, we have a more complicated picture to interpret. Though several years have large numbers of similarly signed residuals, interpretations need to consider the residuals for different actors and may suggest quite different effects. For example, a large positive residual for defendants would indicate that far more legislation significantly favoring the defendant was passed than might have been expected, reflecting a liberal climate in that year, while a positive residual for police would suggest the opposite.

1957 and 1965 were years in which one finds positive residuals across nearly all actors. For 1970, the residuals are, with one exception, negative. However, these patterns do not readily suggest a substantive interpretation beyond the simple observation that some legislative sessions tend to be more active than others across all actors, over and above what we have been able to explain with our independent variables. In contrast, 1968 which has a mixed pattern, can be characterized as having a liberal flavor. Note that the signs of the residuals are positive except for police and corrections officials. Further, the residual for prosecutors is virtually zero. Apparently, subjects of the system are being substantially favored along with the judiciary. Additional support for the liberality of 1968 on law and order comes from the right-hand side of the table, where, for all types of criminalization and for severity of penalties the residuals are negative. In short, for 1968 there was less legislation favoring criminalization, penalties, police, and corrections officials than predicted. Similarly there was more favoring defendants, convicted offenders, and judges than predicted. That 1968 was in general a more liberal year than expected may be explained by the same factors we used to interpret its large negative residual for overall criminalization.

There are several other years, such as 1971, where one might be tempted to interpret the residuals. However, with the exception of 1968 we do not find a substantively consistent pattern. In summary, for several sessions there seem to be patterns for criminalization that are interpretable in terms of a law-and-order ascendancy, but only for 1968 do the residuals suggest a swing across all categories that appears to have substantive meaning.

Besides questions involving unusual years or atypical patterns for particular legislative targets, the table of residuals can sometimes provide important information about *longitudinal* trends that the independent variables have missed. This relates to issues raised earlier, in our discussion of longitudinal correlations between Penal Code revisions. By examining the patterns of residuals for each legislative target across all legislative sessions (reading vertically on Table 7.2) and applying measures of association to the residuals, one can sometimes uncover important phenomena.*

In the last line of Table 7.2 are the serial correlations for the residuals of each column. These were calculated by taking the residual of each legislative session as a predictor for the residual in the following session. (The Durbin–Watson coefficient was inappropriate, since our data are not a sample.) The correlations are all negative, suggesting some kind of homeostatic process over and above the effects of the independent variables. In general, high residuals are followed by low residuals (or negative residuals), which are again followed by high residuals, indicating that, for each category of impact, a session of high productivity tends to be followed by a session of low productivity, which again tends to be followed by a session

---

* The patterns in the residuals are also important for improving estimation procedures when one is engaged in statistical inference. In brief, correlated residuals leave the estimates of regression coefficients unbiased, but make them inefficient and bias estimates of the standard errors. One can, however, use the information provided in the patterns among the residuals to correct these problems. Again, for our data this is not an issue since we are treating the years as a population.

of high productivity. This is precisely the equilibrium model posited earlier.

Closer inspection of the serial correlations suggests that some categories show far greater homeostatic effects than others. The correlations for police, prosecutors, judges, and overall criminalization are all above —.46.* Other correlations are typically much smaller, the average correlation being —.24. Since a variety of mechanisms could be operating to produce the homeostatic effect, it is difficult to explain why some are more negative than others. Possibly, the larger correlations reflect the more controversial legislative targets, so that legislation favoring one side of the law-and-order issues might easily generate active opposition. It is important to emphasize, however, that the correlations reflect patterns in residuals, which means that substantive interpretations must reflect operative processes other than those measured in our independent variables. One speculation is that the negative correlations indicate processes *internal* to the legislature, such as "checks and balances," ongoing compromises, or legislative moderation.

In an attempt to unravel more about the potential homeostatic effects, we ran our earlier regression equations with an additional dummy variable, alternating high and low over the legislative sessions. Though there were some promising zero-order correlations with the dependent variables (Penal Code revisions), in only two cases was the increment to variance above the inclusion level of 5%. In other words, using our conservative cutoff point,† there appeared to be no important independent homeostatic effect beyond that already absorbed by the original independent variables. The two exceptions were for prosecutors and the judiciary, where the homeostatic effect had β's of .48 and .63 respectively. We have no compelling explanation as to why independent homeostatic effects appear here and not elsewhere. Perhaps the effects result from very low multiple correlations in the original regression equations, so that any variable with even a modest zero-order correlation proves useful in prediction. The homeostatic variable might then be entered almost by default. However, judges and prosecutors also originally (Table 6.4) had the largest negative serial correlations, suggesting that the relevant legislative processes are indeed somewhat different. Perhaps legislation affecting prosecutors and the judiciary is more technical, or at least less widely of interest, leading to a less volatile pattern over time. Hence, the legislative process in this case may involve a series of compromises among courtroom experts,

---

* Recall that police, prosecutors, and the judiciary originally (Table 6.4) showed by far the largest autocorrelations: —.41, —.60, and —.54, respectively. (That is, correlations across the original data, not across residuals.)

† The conservative cutoff point is even more important here, since adding the dummy variable increases the number of independent variables by one-third.

rather than polarized, emotional conflict. From the graphs for prosecutors and the judiciary in Chapter IV, it is clear that they were little affected in an immediate sense by such events as Berkeley and Watts and, in general, the picture is a relatively stable one.

In conclusion, the zero-order correlations between residuals are suggestive of an equilibrium process in the legislature. However, if such effects exist, they appear to be of little importance for most legislative targets, both in terms of the small zero-order correlations and in terms of the lack of predictive power in the multivariate analyses. Revisions affecting prosecutors and the judiciary may well be an exception, showing a rather salient homeostatic process that may shelter these kinds revisions from more volatile forces.

Conclusions

The findings of Chapters VI and VII have two important and related consequences, which were posed as questions in the initial chapter. First, there can be no doubt that Penal Code revisions as we have coded them are associated with a large number of interesting phenomena. Hence, our quantification procedures must have been tapping rather salient and important components of legislative change. In addition, the types and directions of the associations were generally consistent with interpretations suggested by our conventional historical research techniques, indicating that the coding probably did not distort substantially the nature of the revisions. In short, our quantification procedures have taken on considerable validity.

A second consequence involves the substantive issues raised by the data. To summarize briefly:

1. The higher the proportion of Democratic legislators in the Senate, Assembly, and relevant committees, the more likely that Penal Code revisions will be passed which tend to significantly increase nearly all types of criminalization, severity of penalties, and the rights and resources of most criminal justice actors. Our measures of partisanship do not alter these findings.

2. The law enforcement lobby and the civil liberties lobby both appear to be active and effective in furthering their interests through Penal Code revisions. They seem to have somewhat different agenda: the former characterized by practical law-and-orderism and the latter by more narrow due-process concerns. Hence, their legislative game is not always zero–sum.

3. Using Penal Code revisions at one point in time to predict revisions at a later point in time (longitudinal), provides several large correlations.

However, the correlation patterns do not readily suggest an interpretation and may actually result from the effects of other variables.

4. Percentage changes in crime statistics are associated in the same sessions with Penal Code revisions. Though the correlations are not especially large there is a tendency for legislation favoring a hard line on law and order to be passed when crime statistics show substantial relative increases. However, legislators cannot be reacting to the statistics per se, so any direct causal explanation must be spurious.

5. Public opinion as measured by our poll data seems to have no relation to Penal Code legislative activity either as a predictor or as a covariant. Either this finding may be taken at face value as suggesting that the general public has little impact on Penal Code revisions (except possibly through political parties) or the power of our measures can be challenged. However, in the next chapter we will present evidence that the Gallup Poll item used does tap important public concern, but that that concern surfaces well after the Penal Code revisions have occurred.

6. Most of our measures of newspaper criminal justice coverage are associated with certain types of law-and-order Penal Code revisions. Though the pattern is not universal, the more crime-related material that appears in the newspapers (the *Los Angeles Times*), the more likely we are to find revisions favoring rehabilitative law-and-orderism. Of the cluster of variables considered, editorials with effects lagged by 1 year appear to be the most important single variable, both as a plausible cause of the other newspaper measures and as a possible cause of legislative change.

7. Our multivariate analyses indicate that a high degree of the variability in changes in the Penal Code can be statistically accounted for with three variables (editorials, percentage Democratic, and the CLL) and that while editorial response appears to be associated with law-and-order successes and the CLL with due-process victories, Democrats cannot be easily categorized as supporting one particular side. These variables are at least good predictors, and we feel that in addition plausible causal arguments can be made.

8. Analysis of the residuals from the multivariate regression equation fail to suggest any *systematic* variables we ignored, with the qualification that 1968 may have been an exceptionally "liberal" year and that judges and prosecutors may be subject to homeostatic influences over and above the effects of the three independent variables.

If there is one substantive lesson from the data it is that support and opposition for particular kinds of Penal Code legislation cannot be glibly characterized as being either for or against law and order. Our research into the Penal Code began in 1971, a period in which the Nixon–Reagan agenda appeared to dominate California politics. Thus, we expected that "repression" and "law and order" would accurately describe the major thrusts of Penal Code change. Contrary to our expectations, we found the picture much more complicated: First, because law-and-order rhetoric and the political polarization it caused often contributed more to legislative logjams than to major criminal law change. Second, because the quantitative analysis revealed trends too complex and subtle to be characterized by ideological catch phrases or a starkly simple "political" model of criminal law change responding only to law-and-order ideology. Third, we have learned, especially from the quantitative analysis, that the trends aggregate small increments in response to a whole tangle of social pressures causing legislators— not only law-and-order ideologues but also outspoken liberals—to support a range of Penal Code legislation whose ultimate impact may well be to further increase the role of the State. Revisions criminalizing behavior, increasing sanctions, and supporting police, prosecutors, judges, and corrections officials, all add to resources available for government-directed social control. In this context, trends favoring defendants and convicted offenders take on special importance both as a countervailing force and as an indicator that legislative sympathies were often focused elsewhere. Perhaps differences between liberals and conservatives were less critical than their similarities?

Finally if there is one methodological lesson it is that our quantitative procedures have produced provocative results. Our findings rest on a very large number of undramatic day-to-day changes in the Penal Code, the total consequences of which are probably unknown to the people who actually cause them. In short, we have not simply restated what knowledgeable people already understand but have begun to outline processes that, to date, have been largely inaccessible.

REFERENCES

1. Robert Aaron Gordon, "Issues in Multiple Regression," American Journal of Sociology, Vol. 73 (1968), pp. 592–616.
2. Jan Kmenta, Elements of Econometrics (New York: Macmillan Company, 1971), p. 365.
3. Eadie F. Deutsch, "Judicial Rhetoric as Persuasive Communication: A Study of Supreme Court Opinions in the Escobedo and Miranda Cases and the Responses in the California Press" (unpublished Ph.D. thesis, University of California, Los Angeles, 1970).
4. Alfred R. Lindesmith, The Addict and the Law (New York: Vintage Books, Random House, 1965).
5. Deutsch, "Judicial Rhetoric."
6. Karl Menninger, The Crime of Punishment (New York: Viking Press, 1968).
7. Jessica Mitford, "Kind and Usual Punishment in California," Atlantic Monthly, Vol. 227, 1968, pp. 45–52.

VIII

Do Penal Code Changes Matter?

W HILE IT IS CLEAR THAT lobbyists and legislators who try to influence criminal justice legislation believe that Penal Code revisions can have important effects, the validity of that belief is obviously an empirical question. Perhaps legislative change is only a well-staged but meaningless ritual with few direct consequences for the criminal justice system. Perhaps the really important decisions are made elsewhere: by wardens, judges, prosecutors, and police officers. In short, the functioning of the criminal justice system may be largely determined by administrative regulations, court decisions, and the wide use of discretion. Penal Code alterations may be at best rubber-stamp legitimation for events that have already occurred.

On the other hand, Penal Code alterations may directly affect the criminal justice system through a variety of mechanisms. By defining certain kinds of behavior as crimes and then attaching sanctions, the system differentially reinforces various behaviors. Citizens and criminal justice officials may respond to a greater or less extent to specific sanctions. Thus, pornographic book stores may close with the passage of prohibitory sanctions, police officers may respond to legislated exclusionary rules by obtaining warrants prior to all searches, and wiretapping without court order may be severely restricted through appropriate clarifications and sanctions.

Less direct influences may also occur. Penal Code revisions could shift the balance of power within the criminal justice system or between the system and the public. Thus, through a kind of domino effect, legislative change could generate a range of outcomes. For example, if sections governing release on recognizance were relaxed, defendants might be able better to hold their jobs and, therefore, to afford a good legal counsel. One consequence of this might be lower conviction rates. Or, by permitting probation for a wider range of offenses, probation officers may become overburdened and more likely to "violate" convicted offenders indiscriminately.

Finally, Penal Code alterations may serve a variety of symbolic functions by crystallizing sentiment around particular issues and/or reaffirming traditional values. Hence, the political climate surrounding criminal justice may be changed and practices be affected. Perhaps the punitive antistudent legislation of the mid-1960s implicitly encouraged police brutality on campuses. While violence directed at minorities had been common, the clubbing and gassing of students was a new development. Or perhaps, the "war on smut" of the late 1960s only served to draw attention to erotic books and movies, making them all the more enticing.

In summary, while it does not necessarily follow that Penal Code change has important effects, it is a clear possibility. One might reasonably expect that the criminal law at least places approximate boundaries between acceptable and unacceptable behavior despite the continued existence of substantial discretion. This in turn might well have important implications for the functioning of the criminal justice system. It is these kinds of questions that we now address. In this chapter, legislative change will be treated as an independent variable and we shall look for the "filtering down" of its effects. At the very least, we hope to identify those phenomena of which Penal Code revisions are predictive.

To the degree that we successfully use Penal Code change as an independent variable, two important consequences follow. First, it will demonstrate that our quantified rendition of the Penal Code has additional links to activities outside the legislature. In the last few chapters we have discussed the factors that may have brought about Penal Code change. Now a new set of associations will be introduced which should provide more support for our contention that quantifying legislation is a valid and sensible undertaking. Second, we will argue that the Penal Code may have some rather direct effects on the functioning of the criminal justice system. In short, legislative activity surrounding the Penal Code in California may be worth studying because of its important impact outside the legislature.

Unfortunately, for this chapter more than for any previous chapter, we must introduce important preliminary caveats. We began our research by focusing on predictors of Penal Code change, not its consequences. Therefore, the data we present here will be necessarily rather thin. In particular, causal interpretations are vulnerable to spuriousness. We simply do not have a wide range of variables for which accurate measures exist.

Three outcomes will be considered: legislative effects on public opinion, legislative effects on editorial crime coverage in the *Los Angeles Times*, and legislative effects on crime statistics. By selecting these three consequences, we hope to consider not only broad, amorphous changes in the political climate surrounding criminal justice but more direct impacts on the functioning of the criminal justice system.

The Effects on Public Opinion

Public concern about law and order is certainly one important aspect of the political climate in which the criminal justice system operates. Widespread fear of crime may encourage punitive excesses, while anxiety over civil liberties may place important constraints on public officials. Therefore, the ways in which Penal Code changes potentially shape public opinion is of considerable interest.

Statistical prediction of public concern about law and order is not especially difficult. Using the proportion of crime-related responses to the Gallup Poll question, "What are the major problems facing this country today?"* we find that an excellent predictor of the level of crime concern for a given year is the level of concern of the preceding year. The correlation between the two is .63. Correlations are similar using 2- and 3-year lagged effects (.62 and .73 respectively). It is important to stress that these high correlations are *not* primarily a function of the many years (1955–1964) when virtually none of the responses in the poll were crime related. Looking just at the correlations involving years when at least some of the responses were crime related, one finds the correlations reduced only about 10%. Though this suggests that public opinion may have a momentum of its own, the reader should recall the statistical problems with serial correlations discussed earlier.

One might speculate that there are more interesting and powerful predictors of public concern about law and order than the "momentum" of public opinion. Table 8.1 shows the correlations between changes in the Penal Code and public concern about law and order 1, 2, and 3 years later. The correlations for 1 and 2 years later are rather small, and the pattern is not especially suggestive. Some types of criminalization show positive cor-

---

* The sum of the proportion of responses involving "crime," "delinquency," "drugs," "law enforcement," "unrest," and "protest."

TABLE 8.1

Pearson Correlation Coefficients between Public Opinion as a Consequence and Penal Code Revisions: One, Two, and Three Years Later

Penal code revisions	Public opinion one year later	Public opinion two years later	Public opinion three years later
Defendant	-.15	-.07	-.38
Convicted offenders	.48	.38	.53
Corrections officials	-.30	-.27	-.01
Judges	.14	.12	-.35
Police	.06	.07	.28
Prosecution	.39	.39	.35
Crimes w/o victims	.25	.25	.19
Against persons	.15	.04	.98
Against property	-.08	-.19	.79
Public interest	.09	.02	.83
Severity of penalty	-.04	-.11	.78
Overall criminalization	.11	.01	.93

relations, others negative. The correlations for actors in the criminal justice system typically are small, and the moderate correlations for convicted offenders and prosecutors are not easily interpreted. Increased rights and resources for these persons are associated with public concern about lawlessness. This suggests that the public is not reacting to the legislation but, rather, that both the legislation and the concern are the result of some other set of factors. Why should there be more anxiety about crime (as measured by public opinion polls) when convicted offenders *and* prosecutors are favored by Penal Code change?

That the relationship between legislation and public concern about law and order is spurious receives some support from the correlations 3 years later. Note that while the effects for actors within the criminal justice system are about the same as 1 and 2 years later, the correlations with types of criminalization have increased markedly and now all have positive signs. Some of the variables correlate *nearly* 1.0 with public opinion. Unfortunately, we have no plausible causal explanation of these over-time patterns. Why should day-to-day changes in criminalization have such a large correlation 3 years later but not before? Why should we find no such increase for other types of change affecting the rights and resources of actors in the criminal justice system? While from changes in criminalization lagged by 3 years (that is, the period 1955–1971) one is able to predict accurately the public's concern over law and order, no persuasive causal interpretations are apparent.

In this study we are not undertaking a detailed analysis of public opinion about law and order. Our poll data are rather scanty, and we have not measured related variables of obvious importance such as letters to legislators.

TABLE 8.2

Pearson Correlation Coefficients between Public Opinion as a Consequence and Crime Statistics: One, Two, and Three Years Later

Crime statistics[a]	Public opinion one year later	Public opinion two years later	Public opinion three years later
Felonies reported	.69	.74	.87
Felony arrests	.77	.82	.89
Felony complaints filed	.80	.83	.92
Felonies prosecuted	.55	.56	.73

[a]*All crime statistics are standardized to a base of 100,000 citizens.*

However, before moving on to other issues, there are several additional correlational patterns that are of interest.

Table 8.2 shows the correlations between our four categories of crime statistics (raw rates, not percentage change form) and public concern about crime 1, 2, and 3 years later. The correlations are all positive and large, and they increase with longer lags. Apparently, crime statistics are (at the least) excellent predictors of public concern: The higher the crime statistics, the more public concern. Recall that crime statistics and public opinion were poor predictors of Penal Code revisions, which makes the correlations here all the more striking. However, we hesitate to suggest mechanisms for these relationships, since there are so many variables operating that spuriousness is a real possibility.

Table 8.3 shows correlations between our newspaper variables and public opinion 1, 2, and 3 years later. Once again there are large positive correlations, indicating that the greater the amount of crime coverage in the *Los Angeles Times*, the more the public is subsequently concerned about crime. As with crime statistics, one is tempted to postulate causal links, but the same cautions hold. With so many variables correlated so very highly with public concern about crime, unraveling mechanisms that might explain the unique impact of any single variable is impossible with these data.

Despite elusive causal interpretations, several important aspects about the role of public opinion are underscored by these data. Our measure of public concern about crime appears to be tapping something rather im-

TABLE 8.3

Pearson Correlation Coefficients between Public Opinion as a Consequence and Newspaper Variables: One, Two, and Three Years Later

Newspaper Variables	Public opinion one year later	Public opinion two years later	Public opinion three years later
Crime-related letters	.55	.77	.77
Crime-related articles	.80	.81	.80
Crime-related editorials	.26	.50	.60

portant that occurs during the 15 years covered in our study. However, as Chapter VI suggested, popular concern about crime does not precede legislative activity. Rather, as this chapter demonstrates, law-and-order anxieties can be predicted but become a public issue well after "hard-line" Penal Code revisions are passed. Though we are unable to specify what it is that causes increased concern, correlations with our one weak indicator of public opinion imply considerable measurement validity. Therefore, we can say with added confidence that unorganized *public opinion is not a cause of Penal Code revisions.* Apparently, day-to-day changes in the Penal Code reflect factors other than vagaries of actual public opinion. In short, public participation in the shaping of the Penal Code, at least as measured by polls, is nil.

The Effects on Newspaper Variables

In the last chapter, a case was made that *Los Angeles Times* editorials may have affected Penal Code revisions. The amount of crime coverage in the editorials was at least an excellent predictor of legislative change. However, one might also wonder about editorial *reactions* to criminal justice legislation. Certainly, there are editorials in response to some controversial Penal Code legislation, but the question remains of whether or not there is editorial response to day-to-day alterations involving less volatile matters. To the degree that such editorial response is found, Penal Code revisions may be viewed as affecting the political climate surrounding law and order issues.

Table 8.4 shows the correlations between Penal Code revisions and edi-

TABLE 8.4

Pearson Correlation Coefficients between Editorials as a Consequence and Penal Code Revisions: One, Two, and Three Years Later

Penal code revision[a]	Editorials one year later	Editorials two years later	Editorials three years later
Defendants	-.01	.27	.80
Convicted offenders	.72	.22	.60
Corrections officials	.42	-.13	.62
Judge	.24	-.46	.23
Police	-.17	.50	-.35
Prosecution	-.37	.46	.14
Crimes w/o victims	-.56	-.11	-.15
Against persons	.39	.39	-.32
Against property	.65	.42	.22
Public interest	.67	.49	-.05
Severity of penalty	.70	.34	.06
Overall criminalization	.43	.43	-.01

[a] *Correlations > .40 are boxed.*

torials 1, 2, and 3 years later. The correlations vary tremendously, from —.56 to .80. Looking from left to right across the table (from 1-year to 2-year to 3-year lagged effects), one finds the correlations for types of criminalization and severity of penalties decreasing. Yet two-thirds of the signs for these six variables over time are positive, indicating that, generally, the more "hard-line" the revisions, the more likely that editorials concerning law and order will appear. (The positive correlations are also typically larger.) The pattern for criminal justice actors is more complicated. Some correlations increase over time and some decrease. Further, though there are approximately the same proportion of negative correlations as for the criminalization revisions, there are often sign reversals from year to year *within* the same variable. Revisions favoring police, for example, show negative, then positive, .then negative correlations.

Parsimonious interpretations for Table 8.4 are elusive. To begin, it is not at all clear why the correlations between types of criminalization and editorials should be predominantly positive. Why should *Los Angeles Times* react with more editorial discussion about crime when the Penal Code is made more punitive? In Chapter VII we demonstrated that (with the role of the civil liberties lobby and Democratic proportion held constant), the greater the extent to which crime was addressed in editorials, the more law-and-order legislation was passed 1 year later. One explanation is that perhaps the *Times* regularly pushed for hard-line revisions. If this were true, one might interpret the positive correlations here as reflecting endorsement of law-and-order statutes after their passage. However, we still have to consider seriously the range of mechanisms through which the *Times* might be having an impact, and our examination of a series of specific editorials spaced over more than a decade indicated that the newspaper increasingly supported liberal positions. Further, our earlier assumption that the *Times* might have been law-and-order oriented does not explain why there are also positive correlations between laws favoring *defendants* and editorials 3 years later. And as if this were not making things sufficiently complicated, large positive correlations appear for convicted offenders 1 year later and for corrections officials and convicted offenders 3 years later. In short, despite some rather high correlations in Table 8.4, causal interpretations of the effects of criminalization revisions are probably spurious.

The patterns for criminal justice officials are even more confusing. Without even worrying about substantive interpretations for each type of actor, one must face the many reversals in sign for given types of actors from year to year. One way to simplify the interpretative task is to examine carefully only those correlations of at least moderate size. (We cannot screen out low correlations with significance tests because our data are not a sample.) To this end, correlations above an absolute value of .40 are boxed. The choice of .40 is rather arbitrary and the reader may wish to undertake an independent analysis using some other cutoff point.

To simplify the analysis further, we will ignore the different time-lagged effects for criminal justice actors (in part because, unlike types of criminalization, each time lag has about the same average magnitude of correlations for those boxed). However, even this attempt to transform the data into manageable patterns does not provide a vehicle for convincing analysis. With two exceptions, the boxed correlations for criminal justice actors are positive, creating much the same interpretative problems we found for criminalization, and we are left with the same post hoc speculations.

In one sense, the lack of a convincing substantive pattern in Table 8.4 should come as no surprise. First, with each successively longer time lag we necessarily lose one data point. This amounts to throwing away about 10% of the data with each yearly increase in time between the passage of revisions and the appearance of editorials. Losing that much data from correlation to correlation could account in part for the reversals in signs. In other words, with so few legislative sessions, each correlation reading from left to right has a somewhat different informational base. Second, we have been trying to understand the pattern using only the relationships between revisions and editorials appearing at some point later in time. There is good reason to believe that the correlations have large spurious components, since so many of the other variables we have examined are highly correlated with both. This is especially an important consideration for the correlations involving longer-lagged effects.

Unfortunately, Table 8.4 may raise some doubts about the validity of our earlier analysis, which suggested that crime-related editorials at the very least were a good predictor of Penal Code revisions. Table 8.5 shows correlations between Penal Code revisions and editorials 1, 2, and 3 years *earlier* than the code revisions. Comparing Table 8.4 and Table 8.5, three important differences between editorials as a consequence and editorials as a predictor are evident.

First, in Table 8.5 (editorials as a predictor, Penal Code as a consequence) the correlations generally decrease with longer-lagged effects, while in Table 8.4 (editorials as a consequence, Penal Code as a predictor) one frequently finds larger correlations associated with longer lags. In other words, Table 8.5 shows a far more plausible pattern over time with regard to the size of correlations; correlations closer in time are considerably larger.[1]

Second, Table 8.5 shows largely identical signs over time. Moving from left to right across the table, one finds very few switches from negative to positive (and vice versa). Hence, degree of consistency is another difference between Table 8.4 and Table 8.5.

TABLE 8.5

Pearson Correlation Coefficients between Penal Code Revisions as a Consequence and Editorials: One, Two, and Three Years Earlier

Penal code revision	Editorials one year earlier	Editorials two years earlier	Editorials three years earlier
Defendant	-.70	-.41	-.47
Convicted offenders	.25	.35	.01
Corrections	-.25	-.31	-.67
Police	.37	-.11	.45
Prosecutor	.28	.25	.36
Judge	-.25	-.004	-.23
Crimes w/o victims	.10	.47	.34
Against persons	.86	.32	.26
Against property	.51	.04	-.36
Public interest	.68	.02	.03
Severity of penalty	.60	.02	-.18
Overall criminalization	.77	.27	-.02

Finally, and most important, there are plausible *a priori* interpretations for Table 8.5. For these three reasons, parsimonious explanations can be developed for characterizing editorials as *predictors* of Penal Code revisions, rather than as *consequences* of Penal Code revisions. The patterns and consistency in Table 8.5 suggest underlying processes that may involve *causal* links as well. The instability of Table 8.4 suggests that many additional factors are operating and that the relationships are largely spurious.

The Effects on Crime Statistics

One might have expected that changes in the California Penal Code would have significant effects both on public concern and on the editorials of such newspapers as the *Los Angeles Times*. Legislators often play to their electorate, and alterations in the criminal law are certainly news. However, it is important to remember that our data reflect myriad small revisions of which few in themselves might seem controversial or newsworthy. Hence, it may not be surprising that we have been unable to find links between Penal Code change and our measures of public concern and editorial reaction. It is possible that better indicators might have revealed more significant effects, but, given the nature of most alterations, we remain dubious.

A *priori*, one should be more optimistic about finding effects of Penal Code changes on the criminal justice system. The criminal justice system is, after all, the special province of the Penal Code, and the manifest content of most statutes reflects attempts to "engineer" the system. Therefore, one might predict a significant "filtering down" of effects, with, for example, laws favoring police eventually producting an increase in the arrest rate. It is to these kinds of issues that we now turn.

A nearly "perfect" predictor of statewide crime statistics is those statistics 1 year earlier. Using our four crime statistics (the per capita number of felonies reported by the public, felony arrests, felony complaints filed, and felony complaints prosecuted) and using a particular statistic 1 year earlier as a predictor of itself one finds correlations of between .99 and .83. A 2-year lag produces similar results.

In this monograph, we are not especially interested in predicting per capita crime rates. The high serial correlations merely indicate that crime statistics are increasing over time as a function of many factors, neither a very interesting nor a very startling finding. Of more substantive concern are possible correlations between changes in the Penal Code and crime statistics. These correlations with a 1-year lagged effect can be seen in Table 8.6. For the criminalization categories, the correlations are small though almost exclusively positive. Possibly, greater increases in criminalization of behavior resulted in more crimes reported, more arrests made, more complaints filed, and more people prosecuted. The pattern for actors in the criminal justice system is more complicated. Greater increases in rights and resources for convicted offenders, judges, police, and prosecutors are associated (at varying magnitudes) with higher crime statistics 1 year later. Greater increases in rights and resources for defendants and corrections officials are associated with lower crime statistics 1 year later. One seductive interpretation suggested is that hard-line Penal Code changes promote more activity by citizens who report crime and by officials who at-

TABLE 8.6

Pearson Correlation Coefficients between Crime Statistics
as a Consequence and Penal Code Revisions: One Year Later

Penal code revisions	Felonies reported[a]	Felony arrests	Felony complaints filed	Felonies prosecuted
Defendants	-.41	-.48	-.48	-.30
Convicted offenders	.23	.04	.09	.25
Corrections officials	-.28	-.43	-.41	-.32
Judge	.04	.07	.06	.22
Police	.69	.09	.08	.06
Prosecution	.29	.32	.26	.28
Crimes w/o victims	.10	.27	.25	.27
Against persons	.59	.48	.46	.30
Against property	.11	.11	-.11	-.11
Public interest	.28	.08	.09	.08
Severity of penalty	.27	.07	.08	.04
Overall criminalization	.43	.28	.25	.18

[a] All crime statistics are standardized to a base of 100,000 citizens.

tempt to control it. Though the correlations involving the rights and resources of convicted offenders and corrections officials do not seem to fit
this interpretation, the others provide some tentative support. Table 8.7
shows the same variables with a 2-year lag in effect, and the pattern remains
essentially the same. (The judiciary now has negative correlations, but for
both time lags the correlations are very small.)

In order to clarify further the relationships between crime statistics and
their potential causes, one might wish to move to a multiple regression
analysis, with earlier crime statistics, Penal Code revisions, and a variety of
other variables as predictors. However, there are several constraints making
this approach impractical. The very large correlations among our four crime
statistics (lagged and unlagged) mean that, if earlier crime data were included in the model, there would be very little variance left over for other
variables to "explain." This would not be problematic were we trying solely
to forecast crime rates with the highest possible accuracy[2] or if we could
accept crime rates as a *cause* of crime rates. With regard to the former, we
are far more interested in understanding the causal processes than we are
in prediction, where these two goals are in conflict. With regard to the
latter, it is not at all clear what substantive processes serial correlations
among the crime data reflect. Crime statistics result from a composite of
very different phenomena: citizen behavior, police practices, record keeping, and a series of discretionary decisions made throughout the criminal
justice system. Each of these kinds of factors affects crime statistics, but
in a variety of ways and for a variety of reasons. Consequently, it is theoretical nonsense to say that crime statistics in one year cause crime statistics

TABLE 8.7

Pearson Correlation Coefficients between Crime Statistics
as a Consequence and Penal Code Revisions: Two Years Later

Penal code revisions	Felonies reported[a]	Felony arrests	Felony complaints filed	Felonies prosecuted
Defendants	-.20	-.34	-.35	-.35
Convicted offenders	.54	.38	.42	.50
Corrections officials	-.15	-.35	-.33	-.29
Judge	-.04	-.04	-.09	-.06
Police	.18	.22	.23	.23
Prosecution	.45	.49	.49	.50
Crimes w/o victims	.01	.06	.06	.12
Against persons	.55	.53	.54	.66
Against property	.28	.12	.14	.31
Public interest	.51	.40	.41	.52
Severity of penalty	.37	.23	.24	.36
Overall criminalization	.52	.43	.44	.59

[a] *All crime statistics are standardized to a base of 100,000 citizens.*

in the next. All one is really stating is that the processes that produce crime statistics remain rather stable in their effects from year to year.

Including the crime data as independent variables also would have produced a number of statistical distortions. Since the crime data are best understood as some unknown aggregate of many different factors, using crime rates as a summary measure necessarily would have meant that the regression equations were misspecified. The picture would have been further muddied by the fact that confounded within the relationships between crime data at different points in time are a number of spurious links. Finally, there are the statistical problems cited earlier when a variable is regressed on itself at an earlier point in time.[3] In short, statistical as well as substantive difficulties would have been produced had the crime data been used as predictors.

What follows then on Tables 8.8 and 8.9 are the results of regression analyses using three types of Penal Code revisions as independent variables and crime statistics 1 and 2 years later as dependent variables. Since there are very few data points, the number of variables included simultaneously is limited. Only three types of revisions are considered, all having relatively large zero-order correlations with the dependent variables and highlighting processes of substantive interest. Recall that criminalization is a summary measure across all types of crimes. Defendant revisions and prosecutor revisions reflect Penal Code changes for actors who are commonly in adversarial relations with one another. Typically, laws favoring the former indicate a pro–civil liberties stance in the legislature, while laws favoring the latter probably reflect a law-and-order position.

TABLE 8.8

Penal Code Revisions as a Predictor of Crime Statistics One Year Later

| Dependent variables | R | R^2 | Penal code revisions | | |
			Pro-defendant	Pro-prosecutor	Pro-criminalization
Felonies reported	.63	.40	b -84.54	b 141.62	b 14.47
			β -.44	β .29	β .29
Felony arrests	.65	.42	b -30.74	b 57.15	b 1.32
			β -.56	β .41	β .09
Felony complaints filed	.62	.38	b -22.80	b 37.29	b .79
			β -.57	β .37	β .07
Felonies prosecuted	.46	.21	b -6.97	b 16.41	b .12
			β -.37	β .34	β .02

R = Multiple correlation
R^2 = Total variance explained
b = Regression coefficient (slope) in original units of measurement
β = Standardized regression coefficent (beta)

TABLE 8.9

Penal Code Revisions as a Predictor of Crime Statistics Two Years Later

Dependent variables	R	R^2	Penal code revisions		
			Pro-defendant	Pro-prosecutor	Pro-criminalization
Felonies reported	.63	.39	b -40.24	b 161.26	b 18.11
			β -.21	β .33	β .34
Felony arrests	.67	.45	b -22.68	b 61.96	b 3.31
			β -.41	β .45	β .22
Felony complaints filed	.67	.45	b -17.22	b 46.46	b 2.54
			β -.42	β .45	β .23
Felonies prosecuted	.74	.54	b -7.18	b 18.27	b 1.97
			β -.39	β .39	β .40

R = Multiple correlation
R^2 = Total variance explained
b = Regression coefficient (slope) in original units of measurement
β = Standardized regression coefficent (beta)

The multiple correlations and total amount of variance explained are quite high. Generally, about 40% of the variance is explained by the three independent variables. Slopes for each variable in their original and standardized units can be seen in the three columns on the right-hand side of the tables. Our interpretations will emphasize slopes in original (unstandardized) units because the variables are measured in comparable ways. For example, in the table showing effects 2 years later (Table 8.9), an increment of one unit in revisions favoring defendants (a little more than a typical revision) will decrease the number of felony offenders prosecuted by 7.18 per 100,000. Since, on the average, 200 people per 100,000 were prosecuted each year, we are speaking about nontrivial effects.*

Despite the fact that the prediction is a bit better 2 years later than it is 1 year later, the patterns are esentially the same. Laws increasing criminalization and the rights and resources of the prosecutor are associated with an increase in all the crime statistics. Laws favoring the defendant are associated with a decrease in all of the crime statistics.

* The mean number of felony prosecutions from 1952 to 1971 was 210 per 100,000. Hence, a slope of −7.18 translates approximately into a yearly drop of 3.5%, and a slope of 18.27 translates into a yearly increase of 8.7%. Unfortunately, interpreting slopes in this exacting manner assumes that all relevant variables have been included in the regression equation. (This would also be true of standard measures.) Clearly, such is not the case, and so the specific size of the changes resulting from Penal Code revisions should be used very cautiously. It is probably safer to take the signs and relative sizes of the slopes seriously, remembering that they have not been standardized.

Given the units of measurement and amount of variability in the set of events we are studying here, we can make some interesting comparisons between raw slopes *across the independent variables*. First, the signs of the slopes are consistent with those of the zero-order correlations. Changes in laws more strongly favoring defendants are associated with lower crime statistics, while changes more strongly favoring prosecutors and criminalization are associated with higher crime statistics. Again, one is tempted to look on the relationships as causal, with Penal Code revisions having important direct effects on the criminal justice system. Laws favoring offenders make it more difficult for people to be processed through to conviction, while laws favoring prosecutors and criminal justice officials (such as the police) make it easier. However, such interpretations should be made very cautiously, since there are undoubtedly other variables associated with both the revisions and the crime statistics that, if included in the analysis, would alter the slopes on Tables 8.8 and 8.9 (see p. 269 footnote*). Nevertheless, one can at least see the slopes as *predictors*, with the ironic result that a law-and-order approach to Penal Code revisions foreshadows increases in crime statistics and, therefore, "increases in crime" as measured by those statistics.

A second interesting set of comparisons can be made by noting that for every independent variable in each of the tables, the order in size of unstandardized slopes is: (1) prosecutor revisions, (2) defendant revisions, and (3) criminalization revisions. Given the variance in our measures (a function of the size of the units and their variability), prosecutorial revisions predict the largest changes in crime statistics, defendant revisions the second largest changes, and criminalization the smallest changes. However, the reader should keep in mind that, typically, in each legislative session there are many more revisions involving criminalization, relative to other revisions, so that, while prosecutorial and defendant revisions predict greater amounts of change *per revision*, the *total* effects for criminalization may actually be larger. This point is underscored by the fact that the slopes in standard score form are roughly of equal size (with the exception of criminalization for 1-year lagged effects).

A third set of comparisons addresses Penal Code revisions and the size of their effects *across all crime statistics*. The unstandardized slopes suggest that in this case, statistics reflecting processes earlier in the system (such as reported felonies) are much more highly associated with revisions than those later in the system (such as offenders prosecuted). At the extremes, the slopes differ by a factor of about 10 (e.g., 1.97 to 18.11). However, one's acceptance of these interpretations depends on the kinds of generalizations one wishes to make. Because there is less variance in crime statistics as one moves down the table, the smaller unstandardized slopes do not necessarily mean a smaller *relative* effect.* Consequently, while the unstandardized slopes reflect degrees of change for our given crime statistics and from this perspective the slopes lower in the table are less impressive, a desire to look at the size of slopes (adjusting for differences in the variance of the crime statistics) requires standardization for accurate assessment. The β's provide standardization, and from these it is apparent that, holding the variance constant (at 1.0), the slopes throughout the table are roughly the same size. In other words, had the various crime measures been of the same absolute magnitude and equally variable in the real world (which they were not), the measure of effect would have been about the same. However, we prefer emphasizing the unstandardized coefficients, because differences in magnitude and variability are "real" phenomena that we wish to consider, not control.

Conclusions

There can be little doubt that Penal Code revisions are associated with important events later in time. Our data show high correlations with public concern about law and order, editorial policy, and crime statistics. Hence, our quantification of Penal Code legislation assumes increased validity. Probably more important are the possible *causal* links between Penal Code revisions and measures of activity in the criminal justice system. Correlations and slope measures suggest that laws favoring prosecutors and increasing criminalization may cause increased success in the processing of crime, while laws favoring defendants may cause a decrease. These findings could reflect important filtering down effects of changes in the California Penal Code, with the resulting irony that legislation favoring law and order may increase the rates of measured crime.

The research described in this monograph was not designed primarily to unravel the *consequences* of Penal Code revision or predict changes in crime statistics. Consequently, this chapter should be cautiously evaluated. Many of the associations are probably spurious. Indeed, the links to the number of felonies reported is particularly hard to interpret in a causal framework. Further, we have examined but a few of the kinds of phenomena that may be a function of the Penal Code, not even including all the variables for which we have measures. Our intent is to point the way toward interesting analyses that could be done in the future, while buttressing the contention that quantification of legislation is a valid and produc-

---

* In essence, the problem is that the numerator covariances in the original units will vary as a function of the variances of crime statistics, while the variances of the independent variables in the denominator do not.

tive undertaking. Still, the data do tentatively suggest that Penal Code revisions matter.

REFERENCES

1. Hubert M. Blalock, *Causal Inferences in Non-Experimental Research* (Chapel Hill: University of North Carolina Press, 1964).
2. Charles R. Nelson, *Applied Time Series Analysis for Managerial Forecasting* (San Francisco: Holden-Day, Inc., 1973).
3. J. Johnston, *Econometric Methods* (New York: McGraw-Hill, 1972), Chapter 10.

IX

Sources of the Criminal Law: Findings and Summary

AFTER MANY PAGES OF ANALYSES, tables, and graphs, we have scant empirical material left to present. The reader's head should be crammed full of details about the recent history of California's Penal Code, and it is now time to ask more generally what we have learned about the sources of criminal law. Our opening chapter raised a number of general questions, which we can review in the context of our findings.

Before launching into our rather lengthy discussion, it is important to remind the reader exactly what our data represent. We have extensive detail on 15 years of recent California history. While there were many dramatic events during this period, we clearly do not have a cross-section of time that includes a governmental overthrow, an economic catastrophe, or any massive social change. There is obviously nothing comparable to the Black Plague, the War of Independence, or the Industrial Revolution. Recall that it is precisely these kinds of events that scholars have studied most often as causes of fundamental change in the criminal law. Although the absence of analogous phenomena in our material places important restrictions on our ability to generalize, there is still good reason to look at the nature of change within this more stable historical framework.

During most periods of history, the criminal law in Western countries has changed relatively slowly. Laws are added and deleted, precedents accumulate, and legal interpretations gradually evolve. One might label this "normal" legal change, in the sense that it may be typical of most historical periods. Normal legal change does not preclude large alterations in Penal Code content, but it limits change to gradual, incremental (or decremental) steps through relatively stable procedures.

In contrast, there appear to be historical periods when massive changes in the criminal law occur much more rapidly. Recall Nelson's analysis of alterations in Massachusetts criminal law in response to postrevolutionary national consolidation.[1] National imperatives swamped local priorities, and the new nation's need for allegiance rapidly altered the entire criminal justice system. Similarly, Dubow's discussion of nation building in Tanzania[2] suggests a rather rapid and dramatic change in the basic nature of criminal law. We are tempted to call such transformations "revolutionary" legal change,* though the term is not meant to imply particular causal mechanisms; what we have in mind is that some *fundamental premises* underlying the law, or some *guiding purposes* for the law, have been rapidly and drastically altered.

One could envision two dynamics through which revolutionary legal change might occur. First, the content of criminal law might respond quickly to some critical set of events in society, such as governmental overthrow, economic disaster, or war. Second, rapid and fundamental legal change might occur after a long period of building pressure during which the law had remained unresponsive. Eventually, a "critical mass" for change might be achieved and extensive reform occur. Platt's analysis of the "invention" of juvenile delinquency[4] comes close to what we have in mind.

We would be the first to admit that the line between normal and revolutionary legal change would be hard to draw in practice and that we are probably talking about points on a continuum. In other words, we are plagued with most of the definitional problems endemic to work on social change, where the differences between "reforms" and "structural change" present serious ambiguities.[5] Clearly, much more empirical work on the sources of criminal law needs to be done before any set of definitions will gain wide acceptance. However, for our purposes, the critical point is that, despite muddy distinctions, our California material describes little that could be properly characterized as revolutionary legal change. Further, the short time period precludes an examination of massive gradual change in criminal law content. Consequently, the generalizations we hope to produce

---

* While the terms "normal" and "revolutionary" are used by Thomas S. Kuhn in talking about scientific change,[3] we are not referring to his analysis and do not mean to imply that our views on legal change necessarily parallel his on scientific change.

will refer primarily to incremental Penal Code alterations through normal legal change processes over a relatively short period.

One final introductory comment. Some of the analyses that follow will flow directly from our findings. Some will involve short leaps of inference. And occasionally, we shall take the license given to authors in their concluding chapter to speculate freely.

The Role of Societal Norms

In Chapter I, we described an incipient law perspective: Broad cultural values and societal norms become institutionalized within the content of the criminal law.* Some observers would expand this "value-consensus" view to include fundamental values of all societies. In either case, there is little evidence in our data that societal norms were an immediate and direct cause of the kind of alterations we observed. First, for the 15 years of incremental changes described, it would be difficult to argue that American culture has produced a compelling body of commonly accepted and internally consistent normative prescriptions to which the hundreds of small, often technical, Penal Code changes could specifically respond. The so-called basic values used by contending parties to justify their positions often appeared, upon close inspection, to consist of self-serving rhetoric in which words were interpreted to meet momentary political exigencies. While everyone endorsed the idea of a "fair trial," to the law enforcement lobby this often meant the admission of illegally obtained evidence, while to the ACLU it typically meant exactly the reverse. Although everyone supported "due process," due process might or might not require defense counsel, depending on which faction's viewpoint was being put forward. Everyone certainly agreed that punishment should fit the crime, yet drug offenses generated responses ranging from the imposition of capital punishment to total decriminalization. Clearly, we could expand this list for many pages, but the basic point has been made. The fundamental cultural values about which everyone could agree and which one might posit as compelling forces behind normal criminal law change seem, for our data, almost meaningless. The moment one begins to translate these "norms" into actual program, the apparent consensus evaporates. It is not as if there were wide agreement about principles and debate only over details or appropriate implementation. Rather, a flowery normative language masked different and

---

* By "norms" we simply mean understandings *shared* by broad segments of a society and typically implying prescriptions for behavior. If the understanding is not widely shared, it is not a norm.

often contradictory views of the basis for criminal law. The imprecise rhetoric of "justice" meant that virtually any Penal Code change could be easily justified. It is not just our military experts who effectively practice Orwellian obfuscation.

Second, even if in theory proposed bills were based on broad societal norms, the horse-trading endemic to the legislative process produced criminal law that at least diluted and often distorted original intent. (Indeed, the very presence of such conflict implied significant lack of consensus, at least over details.) Hence, what might have begun as incipient law soon became a hybrid whose content reflected what was politically acceptable. Politically acceptable law should not be confused with incipient law. Recall that contending parties were considering their interests not only in narrow criminal justice terms but in the context of party partisanship, bureaucratic empire building, the next election, and the earning and spending of political capital. Criminal justice proposals became law in the broader environment of state politics; and these concerns, which were at best marginally related to criminal justice, were often the principal determining factors. One is reminded of the aphorism that a camel is a horse made by committee.

Third, were cultural values an explanation for the Penal Code revisions we have examined, they would necessarily be a rather unstable phenomenon. With independent variables including the relevant lobbies, the editorials of the *Los Angeles Times*, and the party composition of the legislature, we are typically able to account for well over one-half of the variance. These variables reflect the transitory balance of power surrounding criminal justice. Unless one is prepared to argue that these factors reflect changing societal norms, it is hard to envision a direct legislative role for incipient law. On the other hand, if one grants that alterations in the relative power of these interests derive from evolving societal views on the nature of criminal justice, we would have to suggest that societal values have fluctuated rather rapidly over the 15 years described by our data (e.g., consider the rapidly shifting positions on drugs). Rapidly changing public opinion seems very unlike the fundamental consensual values identified by incipient law advocates.

Lest we sound too categorical, it should be reemphasized that we have been discussing only normal criminal law change over 15 years, not revolutionary change. In practice, this has meant incremental alterations, with advocates and opponents far less concerned about the "big" questions than how to facilitate their day-to-day activities. And even for the few groups, like the ACLU, which seem involved more saliently on principled grounds alone, there is little evidence that their views mirror societal norms. Of course, one might argue that norms act somewhat like cultural blinders, limiting people's ability to perceive certain legislative alternatives. Many potential changes are therefore systematically excluded from the consciousness of legislative actors. In addition, some changes that are proposed may be immediately dismissed as alien, utopian, or totally impractical. In either case, societal norms may restrict the range of legislative proposals that merit serious consideration and therefore place boundaries on Penal Code content. The conflict we have observed may thus reflect a kind of residual (though important) lack of consensus within the confines of broader, shared understandings. While few might agree on the proper penalty for stealing a car, for example, few would seriously propose that the offense be ignored.

Yet, even here, one must be very cautious. To begin, except for ill-defined feelings about the "seriousness" of certain specific "criminal" acts such as "armed robbery of a bank,"[6] it is unclear what the dimensions of criminal justice are on which normative consensus really exists.* This is critical, because although most people may concur on loose definitions of appropriate indignation ("murder" is worse than "robbery"), the writing of law must involve far more than catharsis. Something quite specific must be done with the offender. The doing must be accomplished by certain kinds of officials with carefully designated roles. And the process must be undertaken in prescribed ways. (This is not to say that all this happens in practice, only that the criminal law necessarily provides such guidelines.) Does one punish, rehabilitate, or return to the status quo ante? Which officials and institutions are responsible for this process? What procedures must be followed? In mapping the details implied by this necessarily organized response to "crime," cultural norms may be virtually irrelevant; there may be no value consensus on which to build. What is the consensual view on

* Perhaps an illustration will help to emphasize the point. Take the example of homicide. Every school child learns that "Thou Shalt Not Kill' has so many exceptions that its role as a cultural imperative is at best confusing. Most Americans would exempt killing in time of war (though the definition of war is itself problematic) or killing in self-defense. Perhaps a smaller number would exempt killing a convicted murderer. A considerable number might exempt killing a wife's lover. Others would exempt killing by accident, killing while insane, or killing when the perpetrator was unaware of what he/she was doing. Some would exempt the killing of a fleeing suspect or a police officer using "necessary force." Others would exempt "mercy killing" and the right to die with dignity. Some would exempt killing during riot control or to maintain order. Others would exempt suicide or killing in response to trespass, insult, injustice, or during a family feud. Some would exempt killing when a larger number of lives would thereby be saved. Finally, some would exempt killing in response to terrorism, treason, espionage, kidnapping, and plane hijacking. Note that we have chosen an issue about which consensus is supposed to exist; the choice of almost any other cultural "imperative" would reveal even greater ambiguities.

6- versus 12-person juries? What is the consensual view on preliminary hearings? What is the consensual view on representation at parole hearings?

Even where appropriate normative guidelines may exist, they may be far too blunt to determine the specific content of law in complex societies. Cultural values evolve through experiences that are shared by broad segments of a society. Since relatively few citizens interact intensively with the criminal justice system on a regular basis, their common views of its proper functioning must necessarily be rather general. Restated, the detailed operation of any criminal justice system will likely outstrip its alleged cultural base. As societies become increasingly specialized, it seems implausible that societal norms can provide useful prescriptions for *any* institutional sector. A fine-grained division of functions and responsibilities undercuts the common experiential base on which societal norms could rest. Therefore, societal norms may be far too vague to provide effective, practical guidelines.

Finally, the apparent role of normative constraints may be spurious to some substantial degree. Marcuse and Miliband are not alone in arguing that the values of most Americans are effectively shaped by the activities of a dominant economic elite.[7] To the degree that these elites also influence the content of criminal law, the link between legal content and norms may be little more than an association. Causality may play a minor role.*

In short, there seems little evidence for direct, causal normative effects on the day-to-day Penal Code alterations emphasized in this study. While societal norms may place rough boundaries on the kinds of proposals that are introduced, even here their impacts as practical guidelines may be small. Finally, perhaps during revolutionary change or over long periods, norms may be more salient to the criminal law, but, again, they seem rather blunt instruments for determining the specific content of criminal law in complex societies.

While we found little evidence for the importance of broad societal norms in the changing *content* of criminal law, there was a narrower, but substantial, agreement on the *processes* by which criminal law is enacted. Sacramento could not be fairly characterized as a Hobbesian war of all against all; it was instead a competitive game in which most of the players broadly concurred on the rules. For example, until the early 1960s, most interest groups attempted to advance their aims by lobbying with legislators, members of the executive branch, and professionals in the criminal justice

---

* An alternative though related perspective views norms and values as an intervening variable between social structure and/or economic elites on one side and criminal law content on the other. In this context, writers such as Chambliss[8] speak about the "mobilization of bias" in favor of ruling-class interests. Thus, while consensual values may be an immediate cause of important legislative change, they are not its ultimate cause.

field (e.g., the California State Bar). It would have been considered bad taste to use other channels, and rarely were appeals made to the general public. Only after landslide liberal victories did the law enforcement lobby, somewhat desperate after many defeats and tempted by the potential of wide citizen support, seriously "go public." Similarly, there were shared understandings internal to the legislature. We saw in Chapter II how Governor Brown lost some important battles when many legislators of both parties came to feel that he had exercised excessive strong-arming on several pieces of legislation. Perhaps most telling, the Penal Code was, in fact, viewed as a crucial target by all contending parties. This suggests wide agreement on the utility and legitimacy of the legislative process. Sacramento was considered the appropriate place to advance criminal justice goals.

In summary, if there is an important role over the short run for societal norms (norms shared by the vast majority of citizens) in normal criminal law change, that role may have more to do with the processes by which a law is made and the institutions in which those processes occur than with the detailed content of the law itself. Laws may often carry behavioral imperatives through consensual attachments to real or fictitious perceptions of how the laws come into being; the content may be secondary. Perhaps loyalty to a government precedes loyalty to the content of its laws.*

The Role of the Legislative Process

Our quantitative data indicated that many changes in the Penal Code from 1955 to 1971 can be partially explained by the shifting political fortunes of various interest groups and the two political parties. Recall that this is precisely what we suggested in Chapter I, when legislative process was described as the most immediate cause of changes in the criminal law.

What seems most interesting in this legislative process is the elusive role of public opinion. If one grants the validity of our one quantitative measure of public opinion and considers the qualitative material carefully, several overall findings emerge. First, certain small, but vocal, groups of citizens appear occasionally to have initiated attempts to alter the Penal Code. From time to time conservative forces from Southern California launched law-and-order offensives on such issues as drug abuse and capital punishment

---

* We fully recognize that this is a rather pregnant throw-away line. Unfortunately, a thorough consideration of the issues implied would require a careful examination of the growth and development of the state. The questions are thus extremely complex, and the literature controversial.[9] Nevertheless, we are suggesting that, perhaps for normal criminal law change, one is in essence fiddling around within the structure of basic public institutions. As long as these institutions command the loyalty of a nation's citizens, numerous small alterations in the law will be accepted almost regardless of content.

While they tended to ally with law enforcement interests, they also approached legislators directly. Somewhat in contrast, citizens endorsing civil liberties, often from Northern California, seemed more likely to work exclusively through liberal organizations like the ACLU and Friends Committee on Legislation (FCL).

Second, especially in the later years described by our study, various interest groups and partisan politicians sought to recruit citizens to their cause. Police Chief Davis of Los Angeles, for example, became a frequent talkshow guest and his regime took increasing pains to "inform" the public about "crime in the streets." With the introduction of law and order as a partisan issue in the first Reagan campaign, the attempt to mobilize public opinion became quite pronounced.

Third, despite the Watts and Berkeley disorders and increased publicity about crime, large numbers of citizens did not (according to polls) consider law and order a serious problem until the late 1960s. This suggests that wide public concern about criminal justice was probably not a stimulant to political activity but was if anything a belated response to historical events and the publicity campaigns of political parties and lobbies.

To summarize, there was occasionally some direct citizen initiative on criminal law, but typically this came from small groups having little relation to broader public opinion. There was also some indirect citizen input through political parties and organized interests. The ACLU, supported through private donations, is a prime example, but conservative forces sometimes operated through components of the law enforcement lobby. In addition, especially during the late 1960s, broader public opinion probably had an indirect impact as interest groups and legislators began to play to their perceptions of popular sentiment. In other words, when interest groups and legislators tried to anticipate popular reactions, the public perhaps had some influence. However, it seems an open question whether or not programs catering to *perceived* popular positions did in fact reflect popular opinion. Finally, given the nature of piecemeal, incremental change in the Penal Code, often based on small and somewhat technical alterations, it is difficult to link public sentiment, whatever its nature, *directly* to legislative trends. Most legislative change received no publicity precisely because it bore little relation to the interests and competence of citizens. Since the vast majority of legislation became law through the "agreed bill" process, even if there were public concern, it is unclear how the public could have participated directly. In short, it seems inescapable that criminal law in California was enacted primarily by elite actors (public officials, organizational professionals, etc.). All of our findings point to the relative impotence of public opinion and to the primary role of negotiation among special interests.

Besides the secondary role of public opinion, several other characteristics of the political process warrant brief discussion. Especially during the early years covered by our study, most of the initiative for changes in the Penal Code came from outside the legislature. There is little evidence of legislators developing their own criminal justice programs and then seeking political support. Rather, legislative actors tended to represent constituencies with special interests in the criminal justice system. Some legislators were linked to law enforcement interests, others to civil liberties interests, and still others to various agencies within the executive branch. Only after Assembly Speaker Unruh began to provide extensive resources for legislators did elected representatives begin to seize the initiative. This suggests that until rather recently the effects of public opinion were minimized not only through the mechanisms discussed above but by the relatively minor role of the legislative branch itself. Those public officials most accountable to local citizens were also the least important in the enactment process.

It is also clear that although interest groups dominated the scene, they failed to dominate each other. The quantitative trends and qualitative historical analyses indicate that no single faction was consistently able to alter the Penal Code. Although a balance of power may be responsible for this reality, there are at least three other factors undercutting the possibilities for hegemony by any single interest group. First, the issues beneath any package of Penal Code change were typically multidimensional, and the interests of contending parties were rarely in total opposition to one another: The game was usually not zero–sum. One intriguing example involved the civil liberties lobby's early support for indeterminate sentences which, while technically an effort to decriminalize, were also a challenge to "due process." Law enforcement interests did not oppose this legislation; for although they were against decriminalization, they supported the goal of getting certain kinds of offenders off the streets for extended periods of time.

Second, there were often serious divisions within each of the major lobbies. One such conflict among law enforcement lobbyists involved the use of punitive sentencing. Police generally favored harsh penalties, but prosecutors feared that severe sentences would make it far more difficult to obtain convictions. The situation was further complicated when mandatory sentences were proposed. While some criminal justice officials argued that mandatory sentences would increase deterrence, others argued that plea bargaining would be curtailed. In short, because of internal dissension, it was often difficult for any large interest group to mobilize its forces fully.

Third, both the quantitative and the qualitative data suggest that the law enforcement and civil liberties lobbies sometimes had differing agenda.

While law-and-order advocates seemed especially effective in furthering criminalization, the ACLU was far more concerned with due process. Only in the late 1960s did the ACLU reverse its earlier position and begin to consider criminalization and penalties as civil liberties issues. Given such differences in lobby priorities, any particular piece of legislation might seem satisfactory to many parties. Again the non–zero sum nature of the conflict is highlighted.

The failure of any interest group to dominate the legislative process may help explain one of the most striking findings of Chapter IV and Chapter V. Recall that laws affecting the intended rights and resources of actors within the criminal justice system rarely took anything away. At one time or another, virtually everyone gained through the making of laws. Struggles occurred more frequently over gains relative to other groups, not over the removal of previously won prerogatives. Similarly, decriminalization rarely materialized. Perhaps in a political climate where balances of power are tenuous and where negotiation and compromise are necessary, it is far easier to provide something for everyone than to deprive anyone of anything. In other words, legislative combat may be most vicious when potential resources are scarce. One way to circumvent time-consuming, overly hostile and, thus, especially disruptive conflict is to increase the pool of resources for everyone. Full-scale war may be prevented, as less intense struggles occur over who gets bigger slices of an expanding pie. One practical outcome is that, while some gain more than others, everyone can gain something. Another practical outcome is a constant pressure for growth in the power and pervasiveness of the criminal justice system. The pool of potential resources is expanded by expanding the criminal justice system itself.

The Role of Values and Beliefs

Having addressed the legislative process surrounding California's Penal Code, we are now prepared to move back along the causal chain to the role of values and beliefs. However, given the common ambiguities in these concepts, it is critical that we initially try to clarify somewhat how we hope to use them. In essence, we shall be referring to the clusters of empirical observations about criminal justice that people carry around in their heads along with attached affective reactions. Programmatic responses are typically implied as well. While the clustering inevitably has many inconsistencies, it is very far from random. Put another way, what we have in mind are the broad, somewhat integrated perspectives people may bring to their involvement with the criminal justice system: a belief in "due process," a belief in innocence until guilt is proved, and so on. This is not to argue that such catch-all phrases mean the same thing to everyone, only that most individuals usually have loosely organized views on criminal justice (whatever their labels) whose role must be considered. Note, however, that we are not talking about societal norms, which involve *widely shared* understandings at a broad cultural level.

Some people might have preferred we use the term "ideology." We have chosen to reserve that concept for a broader, more fully integrated world view. Values and beliefs about criminal justice might be seen as potentially one of the components of an ideological system. In addition, while our data often speak to perspectives on criminal justice, inferences to broader ideological positions are at best speculative.*

Given these preliminaries, it is clear that despite careless and/or manipulative rhetoric, underlying values and beliefs about criminal justice critically affected the Sacramento scene. When these views changed, so did the nature of proposed programs. Thus, in the late 1960s, after the Friends Committee on Legislation realized that penal rehabilitation in California was not working as they had anticipated, they began to lobby against programs they had originally helped to create.

The values and beliefs of different groups shaped not only the ends to be achieved but the means toward those ends. Recall the conflict between police and prosecutors over harsh sentences. Both groups were obviously committed to crime reduction, and both saw substantial merit in deterrence. Yet police often favored deterrence through severe sentences, while prosecutors thought that high conviction rates were a necessary prerequisite. Hence, while police and prosecutors agreed on ends, disagreement over means undercut support for punitive sentencing legislation.

In practice, however, the means–ends distinction was slippery, and what might have begun as means could easily evolve into ends. Initial justification for legislative programs often got lost as contending parties fought over procedural details. For example, in the late 1960s significant controversy developed over corrections. Spurred on by a devastating report from the Assembly Office of Research, the legislature proposed a monitoring system for many activities that had previously been the exclusive domain of corrections officials. Although fiscal and humanitarian considerations may have been prime movers initially, the realpolitik seemed more a question of who would exercise what sorts of power rather than for what the power would be used. In short, the evolution of legislative programs some-

---

* We fully recognize that there is a lengthy and complicated debate in the literature surrounding the differences between beliefs, values, norms, and ideology. Fortunately, a consideration of such subtleties is probably not necessary for this discussion.

times approximated an infinite regress, where means developed to further certain goals became ends. These new ends were then the subject of new means, which in turn became ends.

In addition to the elusiveness of means–ends distinctions, means and/or ends subsumed under one set of values and beliefs could often be mixed and matched with means and/or ends under another. Issue multidimensionality and non–zero sum payoffs were partly responsible for this flexibility, but it also can be explained by the loose fit between components of legislative programs. A belief in deterrence, for example, could not fully or even largely determine the content of a package of legislation. In contrast to a mathematical system in which a few axioms determine an extensive web of postulates, theorems, and proofs, proposed criminal law involves components whose relation to one another and to underlying guiding principles are usually flexible and often tenuous.

Given the flexible role of values and beliefs, it is not surprising that some groups were more bound by them than others. The effect of party membership, for instance, seemed far more a question of buying and selling influence and day-to-day realpolitik than of any principled view on criminal justice. Recall that it was difficult to interpret Democratic influence in terms of consistent perspectives on law and order. Rather, whatever values existed often were outweighed by other considerations. In contrast, the major lobbies, whose interests were less closely linked to the political process as an end in itself, could more often afford the luxury of value-laden positions.

As soon as one begins to approach values and beliefs through underlying causes, the importance of organizational attachment becomes apparent. While it is clear that the beliefs of District Attorneys helped shape the prosecutorial office, other influences may also have had an impact. Case loads, conviction rates, delays in processing defendants, and many other organizationally bound experiences clearly affected the belief systems of prosecutors. It was not simply a question of different organizational allegiances leading to different concrete interests but of a complementary shaping of attitudes as well. Policemen often become clannish not because it directly serves their interests but because their daily experience reinforces a sense of isolation from a hostile public.[10]

In short, the broad perspectives about criminal justice that helped to shape support or opposition for legislative initiatives were in part a function of the kinds of experiences advocates had with criminal justice. Clearly, when the experiences of individuals are derived from their particular location within the various parts of the criminal justice system, their beliefs must be substantially affected by the nature of the organizational context in which they serve.

The Role of Organizations

Organizational attachments can also have a rather direct effect on an individual by defining his/her specific interests in the criminal lawmaking process. We are referring here to "successful" organizational performance, almost regardless of its content. As people commit more and more of their time and energy to an organization, they develop a concrete stake in that organization, much as a stockholder does with a business investment. As stockholders hope that their companies will grow and flourish, members of organizations hope that their occupational investments will prosper. Such commitments typically generate forces for organizational growth, and our data have repeatedly revealed legislative positions determined by narrow bureaucratic interests.

Organizational ambition seemed fueled by several complementary motives. On the one hand, a motive could be purely instrumental. Police tended to feel that they were the most important factor in the battle against crime; hence, it was logical to them that police departments be given more power. California corrections officials believed that they knew the best ways to rehabilitate criminals; hence, it was logical that they should seek increased resources. In other words, power per se was less the issue than the fact that power would facilitate organizational tasks.

Other motives involved grander aspirations. Conscious and often cynical empire building was clearly prevalent, and Penal Code alteration was perceived as one route to greater power. Sometimes individuals tried to build their organizations as vehicles for personal ambition. In other cases, support for legislation was a function of power struggles within a group. Visible and effective activity on important legislation could strengthen leadership claims and undercut opposition. In both cases, power as an end in itself was the dominant goal.

Empire building was also a factor for legislators. While legislators had no immediate stake in the growth of criminal justice bureaucracies (since they were not members of them), they indulged widely in "horse-trading" to enhance their own political influence and organizational interests. It is impossible to understand the career of Jesse Unruh and the conflict between the Unruh-led Assembly and the Governor's office under both Brown and Reagan except in this context.

The coupling of organizational and personal performance produced not only motives for the acquisition of power but also a wide variety of less grandiose ambitions. Not surprisingly, nearly everyone supported legislation that could potentially help him/her work more effectively and opposed legislation with the opposite effect. Prosecutors often endorsed legislation permitting the use of "illegally" obtained evidence. Police usually supported wiretap legislation that would facilitate the apprehension of suspects and opposed efforts to limit the use of "necessary" force. Defense attorneys, on the other hand, opposed legislation that took advantage of the insecurity and confusion of newly arrested suspects. In short, the location of individuals within the criminal justice system determined the nature of their jobs, which in turn directly affected their support for legislation.

Our discussion of the roles of belief systems and organizational affiliations suggests several broad conclusions. These are not earthshaking; they are meant more as rather loose *ceteris paribus* suggestions than as detailed, rigorous hypotheses. Further, all assume that beliefs and experiences within a criminal justice bureaucracy interact in complex ways. To study either in isolation can lead to misleading conclusions. Policemen bring certain views to their jobs and then have these attitudes affected by daily, job-related experience. Conversely, the attitudes brought to the job affect the way in which the job is done.

First, other things being equal, the more general the perspective, the less it will affect job performance and the less it will be affected by job experiences. It would appear that broad views of the causes of crime, the nature of society, or the worth of "American" values are very difficult to attach to specific job experiences. In contrast, beliefs in a speedy trial, the right to have adequate defense counsel, and the efficacy of probation rather than incarceration interact far more intensely with job content. The broader ideals can support a wide (and often contradictory) variety of specific experiences.

Second, the more the content of values and beliefs relates to the content of the job, the more each will affect the other. The experience of police officers will interact more intensely with notions about the use of force than with ideas about the appropriateness of trial continuances.

Third, criminal justice perspectives will be more complex and sophisticated the more they are directly related to job experience. Police can provide detailed and subtle information about the merits or weaknesses of patrolling on foot versus in squad cars, while showing considerable naivete about the value of bench trials compared to jury trials.

Fourth, one might wonder about the comparative impact of attitudes on job performance and impact of job experience on attitudes. Our data suggest that, to the degree that important, specific, and concrete interests are involved, attitudes will be far more affected by job experience than they will shape job performance. In other words, in the light of practical job experience actors will be especially likely to alter their views to support perceptions of what in practice enhances their welfare. The more vital those interests, the more likely it is that values and beliefs will be rearranged to justify self-serving behavior. In the abstract, many prosecutors no doubt believe in stiff sentences consistently imposed as the best way to "fight crime."

In the concrete, however, their interest in obtaining sure convictions through guilty pleas may override their more general commitment to punitive orthodoxy. The proof is that, when outcomes really matter, behavior is most likely to dictate attitudes. Only when outcomes do not especially matter are attitudes more likely to dictate behavior.

We have been using criminal justice personnel to illustrate our conclusions, emphasizing the differences in job or organizational psychology within the broad category that sometimes set off prosecutors against police. So as not to overqualify the scope of our generalizations we have not drawn the even finer distinctions that could be drawn—for example, the distinction between "worker" and "management" psychology among different levels of the police. Bordua and Reiss offer an empirical warrant for downplaying this distinction by arguing that, in a "command bureaucracy" like the police, "the vertical spread of occupational culture" produces an unusually strong commonality of attitude and outlook among the different levels.[11] Yet even they admit that police "professionalization" has gone hand in hand with heightened "worker–management differences" on the order of those found in industry. The reader should bear in mind that California has always been the pacesetter when it comes to such professionalization. In Chapter II, we saw much evidence of this, and among the evidence was the presence of *two* major law enforcement organizations with statewide police membership: the California Peace Officers' Association (CPOA), preeminently the voice of chiefs of police, and the Peace Officers' Research Association of California (PORAC), which more often expressed the concerns and (not always congruent) attitudes of the rank-and-file patrolman.

Yet the broad principles we have applied to criminal justice personnel are not without their validity, and the same principles can be applied to other kinds of actors: the public, the ACLU, legislators, and members of the executive branch. In most cases, however, because their day-to-day activities do not involve close contact with the criminal justice system, the attitudes about criminal justice of these actors will be shaped largely by other factors. Hence, one would have to look elsewhere for the forces that shape their views on criminal justice: party membership, educational background, social class, exposure to publicity about lawlessness, and so on. One consequence may be that their views often do not accurately reflect the realities with which the cop on the beat must contend day in, day out. It is easy to criticize police, for instance, for using "unnecessary" force to restrain a suspect if one does not oneself have to make a living apprehending suspects.

Besides generalizations about the ways in which attitudes and job experiences within the criminal justice system interact, our data suggest several conclusions about the relative importance of each in producing support or opposition for criminal justice legislation. In other words, we have been talking about how attitudes and experiences affect each other, and we will now turn to the relative importance of each in state-level legislative intiatives.

Other things being equal, the more a group or organization is involved in the day-to-day functioning of the criminal justice system, the less salient will broad integrated beliefs and values be in *determining* positions on proposed criminal law. This means that support or opposition will be more in terms of perceived organizational interests, although ideals may be used as post hoc justifications. Further, when legislation can directly affect the details of a particular kind of criminal justice job, people in that job will be less directly motivated by broad perspectives than people whose jobs are less immediately implicated.

There are several plausible reasons for the trade-off between ideals and practicality. First, people often do not have time to worry about the big questions when their ox is about to be gored. They may readily use idealistic justifications, but the immediate motives involve "taking care of number one." Thus, prosecutors will be more worried about conviction rates than about the pursuit of justice. In addition, officials caught in the nuts and bolts of doing their jobs may be less able to step back and consider larger issues. Day-to-day exigencies may have little relation to broader questions, and, even when they do, the connections may be ambiguous. Perhaps the trees obscure the forest; it may also be that there is no forest.

In contrast, people with little firsthand experience in the jobs affected by given legislation may have *only* broad ideals on which to take positions. They may know too little about the concrete details to be more grounded. More generally, the short-term interests of the average voter are affected little by the details of how the criminal justice system operates. Their immediate experiences are relatively independent of piecemeal changes of the Penal Code, and only when the long-term trends accumulate or when a few dramatic alterations are proposed do they have something substantial to lose or gain. Therefore, with few immediate interests, their legislative positions can only be in broad, value-laden terms. Liberal middle-class support for tough exclusionary rules does not stem from disproportionately frequent criminal indictments of middle-class citizens.

A second generalization is that, other things being equal, the more multidimensional the practical interests of a given group, the less immediately relevant are general values and broad beliefs.* Since diverse and detailed practical interests are not easily subsumed under any given perspective, idealistic motives become less tenable. For example, all lawyers—

---

* This is a descriptive statement, not a prescription of what should be. Also, if the belief system is poorly articulated, almost any activity can be justified through it, and multidimensionality ceases to be a problem.

including prosecutors—might wish to support unequivocally the right to a trial for all defendants. Due process is, in theory, a cornerstone of American justice and a foundation of legal training. However, from the prosecutorial perspective, the right to trial is cross-cut by the need to convict a high proportion of defendants and the need to process criminal cases speedily. Given the complex multidimensional requirements of prosecution, due process is often compromised. In other words, the overarching belief in due process cannot accommodate these other very real pressures and, hence, is pushed into the background.

A third generalization is that the more a group emphasizes gaining and maintaining political power, the smaller the role of broad values and beliefs. While the quest for power and the presence of ideals are certainly not logically incompatible, the realities of building political capital in state politics soon tend to undercut idealistic positions. We have seen time and time again, on the international scene, political ideology distorted beyond recognition under the complex pressures of national interest. The American–Russian détente, in the face of competing world views, is testimony to the role of practical politics. In our study, no group better illustrates this process than elected officials. While some may not seek power per se, the game is played almost exclusively in those terms. Survival depends on getting things done, and, in the horse-trading process, political influence is a necessary prerequisite. This may help to explain why we were unable to trace the impact of the Democratic proportion in the legislature in terms of consistent perspectives on criminal issues. This may also in part explain why men such as Governor Brown held such inconsistent (some might say flexible) positions on law and order. Even the *Los Angeles Times* in an editorial dated June 24, 1966, faults Brown for buckling under to Mayor Yorty's cry for antiriot legislation. They pointed out that "there are already enough statutes in the Penal Code" to cover future needs. They accused Brown of responding to pure politics in trying to satisfy the 900,000 persons who supported Yorty in the gubernatorial primary.

To summarize, it is clear that organizationally shaped interests and general beliefs about criminal justice are important determinants of legislative initiatives. In addition, we have suggested some ways in which beliefs and organizational experiences interact and, under certain conditions, determine their relative importance in affecting legislative support or opposition.

Social Structure and the Puzzle of the Los Angeles Times

Throughout this chapter we have been considering citizen groups, public opinion, criminal justice lobbies, and the legislature. Yet, despite clear statistical importance, the ways in which the editorial policy of the *Los*

Angeles Times may have affected Penal Code legislation has been almost ignored. This was not accidental. Criminal justice lobbies were so directly and visibly active in the process of legislative change that our data were bound to highlight their significance. Almost as obvious was the importance of Senate and Assembly composition. Even in the case of public opinion, where the data fail to confirm popular preconceptions, there were sound a priori reasons to anticipate a substantial impact. In contrast, the importance of *Times* editorials was, and remains, a somewhat perplexing phenomenon.

Recall the nature of the findings from the multivariate analyses. A greater number of column inches in *Times* editorials devoted to crime-related issues foreshadowed by one year: greater increases in criminalization, greater increases in the severity of penalties, greater increases in the rights and resources provided for prosecutors, and smaller increases in the rights and resources provided for defendants. In addition, the effects of *Times* editorials remained even after statistical controls were introduced for the role of criminal justice lobbies and the party composition of the legislature and even after public opinion, partisanship, and official crime statistics were shown to be virtually irrelevant to the passage of Penal Code legislation. In other words, any explanation for the effects of *Times* editorials must be independent of our measures of these phenomena if it is to be consistent with the data.

As a starting point, one must at least entertain the possibility that the large standardized regression coefficients between *Times* editorials and Penal Code content 1 year later reflect spurious effects. Thus, it may be said that editorials are not directly linked to criminal justice legislation but that both editorial issues and specific bills result from some other set of external forces. However, if one accepts our measures, it is difficult to specify precisely what those forces might be, since they must have had their powerful impact independent of criminal justice lobbies, party composition of the legislature, crime statistics, partisanship, public opinion, and *all other factors highly associated with these variables*. For example, while one might cite dramatic historical events such as the Watts uprising as the underlying forces of real significance, that explanation of the apparent influence of the *Times* must also take into account why these occurrences were not immediately reflected in the measures of public opinion, why their impact was not absorbed in the legislature's party composition, and, more significantly, the effectiveness of various criminal justice lobbies. In addition, to advance this kind of explanation persuasively, one would have to make the case for each legislative session, not just the ones during which events of "obvious" import occurred. For historical events per se, our attempts were soon reduced to lengthy *post hoc* machinations that seemed more a function of our imagination than an outcome of the available data. Nevertheless, we will later return to the question of spuriousness and deal with it in greater detail.

The moment one decides at least to entertain the possibility that the *Times* effects were "real," several variations on a common theme must be considered. First, perhaps editorial comments on *specific bills* may have influenced the views of prominent legislative actors. Certainly, this is most straightforward interpretation of editorial effects. But unfortunately, this view does not square with our knowledge of editorial content. Relatively few crime-related editorials addressed themselves to particular legislation. Rather, broad social issues or immediate historical events (the latter often in the context of the former) were addressed. For example, on July 23, 1970, the *Times* discussed at length the killing of two Mexican nationals by five members of the Los Angeles Police Department and placed this violence in a set of wider concerns about police–community relations. However, except for advocating increased public support for police (with the caveat that "it is better for a guilty man to go free than for an innocent person to suffer harm"), the *Times* suggested no specific programmatic response. Commentary about specific bills was simply too infrequent to account for significant effects upon the Penal Code.

Why should this surprise us? Most revisions individually were of somewhat limited significance and of no great relevance to the larger controversial issues that usually provide the raw material for editorial comment. On the other hand, the broad brush strokes of *Times* editorials may have helped to raise wider issues and to articulate competing criminal justice perspectives. In effect, editorials may have placed certain general problems on the political agenda by affording them legitimation and wide public exposure. Even more significantly, by forcefully presenting its views, the *Times* may have helped rearrange political priorities in ways that moved the whole gamut of criminal justice issues higher up the list of legislative business. Note that these effects could be very real and yet leave the actual legislative outcome undetermined. Once the "crime problem" was raised and placed prominently on the docket, emerging statutes might reflect a wide range of political perspectives.

Of course, one cannot rule out the possibility that *Times* editorials more directly affected legislative outcomes. Though rarely venturing opinions about specific legislation, the editorials may have articulated value positions that shaped the general thrust of legislative action and thereby the content of the Penal Code. In other words, the editorial writers could have had a very clear idea of the forest despite their unconcern with individual trees; and even while keeping at a "philosophic" distance from the compromises reflected in specific bills, they may have given important ideological aid and comfort to the legislators and lobbyists more directly involved in passing legislation.

Yet, even if one assumes that the specific content of editorials was in itself having such an impact, one still faces the crucial issue of what the mechanisms were by which this was achieved. Were the legislators, lobbyists, and public officials persuaded by editorial wisdom alone? Were they, in the absence of direct political pressure, sufficiently persuaded by the sheer force of 500 to 1,000 poignant and incisive words? The alternative is, of course, that the editorials were *indicators* of positions taken by influential people whose views were taken seriously for reasons besides the eloquence of editorial writers and the wide circulation of their newspaper.* We are not suggesting that the content of editorials per se had no importance, only that other factors must also be considered.

It should come as no surprise that members of the Chandler family, which owns and operates the *Los Angeles Times*, possess considerable wealth and associate with individuals of similar visibility and prestige. Indeed, an article in the *Times* itself (December 3, 1972) documents that Norman Chandler, chairman of the executive committee of the Times–Mirror Company, was a member of the so-called Committee of 25, a sort of elite Los Angeles Chamber of Commerce which met regularly as "an informal instrument of government."† Moreover, one does not have to be a committed Marxist to recognize that any group that included such individuals as Roy Ash, president of Litton Industries; Lee Atwood, president of North American Rockwell; Fred Hartley, president of Union Oil; Louis B. Lundborg, chairman of the Bank of America; and John A. McCone, formerly of the CIA and the "McCone Commission," and then president of Hendy International could have considerable political impact, at least through the Republican Party. Finally, even if the Committee of 25 did not formally exist, these individuals either independently or in concert, are clearly a force to be reckoned with.

Thus, one might entertain the possibility that the direct impact of *Times* editorials was partly spurious and that *both* editorial content and legislative change were to some degree a product of the influence of powerful economic elites. In other words, the statistical impact of *Times* edi-

---

* Having long billed itself as "one of the world's great newspapers," the *Times* grew during the 1950s and 1960s at a rate that gave substance to its masthead boast. By 1967 its daily circulation was 850,000, topping the *Chicago Tribune* and second only to the *New York Daily News* among American dailies.[12]

† Though Norman Chandler surrendered the editor's chair to his son Otis in 1960, he continued to be "on call for consultation" when crucial questions of editorial policy were at issue.[13]

torials may reflect the concerns of powerful individuals* who also influenced the course of legislation. However, while this interpretation has perhaps some superficial validity, it is subject to a number of complications, which must be seriously addressed.

First, one must assume that these economic elites have many commitments and will necessarily (because of time constraints alone) spend a relatively small proportion of their time on criminal justice matters. This means that they will typically not be involved in the details of Penal Code change and the petty struggles (from their view) of groups whose primary concerns involve the criminal justice system itself. This leaves substantial room for narrower interest lobbies to go about their business unconcerned about what the "big boys" may be thinking.

Second, given a large number of competing commitments, one might speculate that business elites will become heavily involved in criminal jus-

---

* In the broader context of "legitimation," Miliband suggests several complementary mechanisms by which economic elites (the ruling class) can shape the content of media. Perhaps most directly, as media owners they may intervene in the selection of news stories, the writing of articles, and the formulation of editorial positions:

> However, it is not always the case that those who own or ultimately control the mass media do seek to exercise a direct and immediate control upon output. Quite commonly, editors, journalists, producers, managers, etc., are accorded a considerable degree of independence, and are even given a free hand. Even so, ideas do tend to "seep downwards," and provide an ideological and political framework which may well be broad but whose existence cannot be ignored by those who work for commercial media. They may not be *required* to take tender care of the sacred cows that are to be found in the conservative stable. But it is at least *expected* that they will spare conservative susceptibilities of the men whose employees they are, and that they will take a proper attitude to free enterprise, conflicts between capital and labour, trade unions, left-wing parties and movements, the Cold War, revolutionary movements, the role of the United States in the world, and much else besides. The existence of this framework does not require total conformity; general conformity will do. This assured, room will be found for seasoning, sometimes even seasoning with generous dissent. (emphasis the author's)[14]

Miliband then goes on to suggest other perhaps more subtle pressures from ruling-class interests: direct sanctions from advertisers or at least the exercise of self-censorship so as not to antagonize them, government regulations, civil and criminal law restricting the kinds of stories that can be published, and probably most important, the selection and socialization of newspaper personnel to increase conformity. While few could deny that such factors significantly affect newspapers and other forms of mass media, it is less clear that media positions on routine criminal justice issues will often be prominent targets. They may be relatively peripheral to ruling class interests and as we suggest below, ambiguously articulated in any case.

tice issues only if their perceived interests are immediately threatened. While the accuracy of their perceptions is often unclear and probably subject to disagreement even within relatively homogeneous groups like the Committee of 25, crime, unrest, police corruption, and crowded court dockets may thus be viewed as "social indicators" (like unemployment rates or health statistics) reflecting broad societal conditions and, hence, the business environment. Only when these suggest that social stability itself may be at stake will they reshuffle their usual priorities and turn to criminal justice. (Of course, American society—or capitalist societies in general—are not the only ones in which threats to an established order galvanize elites and cause them to change their political focus.) In addition, there may occasionally be specific criminal justice proposals especially linked to business prerogatives that warrant political initiative. Here we have in mind such topics as industrial regulation, environmental protection, use of credit cards, and advertising practices.

Third, when economic elites do occasionally become involved in criminal justice issues, their stance may often be hard to predict. Observing that societal security is a critical "ruling class" goal[15] really reveals little about elite views on detailed, often technical, criminal justice proposals. One can foster stability with a carrot, a stick, or a mixture of both, and through real or illusory (e.g., propagandistic) programs.[16] Further, if the past 20 years have taught us anything, it is that *no one* has convincing answers about how best to respond to "malfunctions" in the criminal justice system. In other words, businessmen and bankers are probably as confused as are the public, public officials, and the so-called experts. Hence, their positions may sometimes reflect inconsistencies, ambiguities, and even what occasionally seem outright contradictions of their interests. Finally, this implies that their views may change over time or may vary depending on the spokesman. In short, it was often not at all clear to us which *specific* criminal justice proposals automatically favored business interests, and we suspect that economic elites frequently confront similar complexities.

How does all this help to explain our finding that increases in crime-related editorials are associated with legislation favoring increased criminalization, penalties and prosecution coupled with smaller gains for defendants? Beginning with mechanisms involving the minimal manipulation of ultimate Penal Code content, one might speculate that on the occasions when elites do become concerned about crime and the functioning of the criminal justice system, they may act to have criminal justice issues placed higher on the political agenda. Given their large campaign contributions, economic leverage, and friends in high places, making criminal justice a salient legislative topic should not be especially difficult. Their anxieties about crime may also be expressed simultaneously in *Times* editorials. Sometimes there may be a conscious decision to coordinate a publicity offensive with a political offensive. More likely, the two occur at about the same time simply because they are both readily available means by which the same uneasiness can be expressed. Other modes are probably also used with little or no effort at orchestrating their varied effects.

A second mechanism may involve a more direct kind of intervention in the political process and may find economic elites forcing a reshuffling of legislative priorities. To the degree that minority unrest, for example, is viewed as an especially volatile circumstance, pressure may be applied to make the legislature deal immediately with civil disorders. Of course, the legislature will probably not be the only target, and public officials, groups like the NAACP, and criminal justice personnel may also be actively encouraged to move rapidly.*

It is critical to understand that both mechanisms *leave the ultimate outcome for Penal Code content undetermined.* Both raise issues, but neither attempts to resolve them in a particular direction. This means that we cannot effectively explain why editorials (as indicators of elite opinion) predict passage of legislation of any given cast. Our data reveal a specific kind of effect, while our current explanations seem to ignore the substantive content of any concrete outcome. Clearly, additional factors must be considered.

One place to begin is to remember that we have focused exclusively on the Penal Code. What can a Penal Code do in response to crime but try to control it? Thus, while some elite interests may have recognized that the Watts rebellion had roots in the life circumstances of blacks, and may even have tried to alter some of those inequalities, remedial strategies would seem very unlikely to appear in the content of the criminal law. In other words, since criminal law is designed primarily to restrain unacceptable behavior, it should not be surprising to find social control its modal response to any problem.

A second explanation for our specific editorial effects evolves from the priorities that crime and disorder typically produce. The immediate response may be to repress disruptive influences, or society itself becomes endangered. While attention may eventually be directed at alleged sources of problems, public order takes precedence over remediation. Therefore, the immediate and perhaps most dramatic outcome of raising the issue of crime and criminal justice may be automatically to increase Penal Code legislation designed to reinforce social control.

A third approach focuses on the institutions involved and the program-

---

* This is not to say that any or all of these groups always respond to the pressure. Elite businessmen and bankers are powerful, but not omnipotent.

matic responses they make. Clearly, we have a large criminal justice establishment ready to flex its muscles and justify its continued growth. The Penal Code exists precisely to deal with crime. There is also a belief (less and less tenable) that our criminal justice system works, or at least would work if given sufficient resources. In short, we have a ready made "answer" to a wide range of crime-related problems. What other institutions are there that even claim to diminish crime? If they exist, they are invisible compared to police, courts, and the law. Is it any wonder that raising the issue of crime reinforces the power of the criminal justice system?

It is also possible that once concern over crime is placed prominently on the legislative agenda, *other* political factors favor the extension of social control. In other words, once the issue has been effectively raised, the resulting balances of power in Sacramento tend to steer toward criminalization, increased penalties, and more resources for criminal justice officials. Perhaps law enforcement interests interpret the issues' renewed vitality as an opportunity to lobby aggressively. Perhaps legislators view elite anxiety over crime as a message to get tough even when the specific content of editorials is more guarded and qualified?

While these speculations seem sensible enough, there is still at least one important fact that they fail to cover. In recent years, as *Times* editorials have become more "liberal," Penal Code revisions have become somewhat less law-and-order oriented. Recall that the high water mark for hard-line legislation was about 1965 and that by the early 1970s liberal groups were effectively counterattacking. While the liberal resurgence may be partly explained by less overall concern with crime among economic elites (as measured by fewer column inches of crime-related editorials), a parallel "liberalization" should also be considered. Perhaps elites themselves were becoming more "responsible" on criminal justice matters and perhaps this affected the kinds of legislation they proposed and supported. However, the moment one begins to take this process seriously, it clearly implies that elites were doing far more than raising issues and reordering legislative agenda. They must also have been trying to shape the content of actual legislative programs. In other words, they were not leaving the ultimate Penal Code content undetermined but were directly intervening to help shape it. And if we admit this possibility for the impact of increased liberalization, we must also admit this possibility for the earlier years when their views were more hard line. We are not arguing that the mechanisms discussed above are no longer valid, but arguing that there is a possibility that on some criminal justice issues economic elites played an important role from start to finish.

What might account for a liberalizing trend among economic elites?

Perhaps, once the dramatic unrest of the mid-1960s started to subside, economic elites began to recognize that draconic legislation could itself become a stimulant to disorder. In addition, they may have felt that popular ideals describing America as a "free country" were seriously jeopardized by legislation in the style of Nixon's District of Columbia "anti-crime package." To the degree that faith in the nation's institutions and, hence, political stability were bolstered by such ideals, the negative publicity surrounding harsh and inflexible criminal justice statutes could not be ignored. The very legitimacy of the criminal justice system was perhaps being threatened, and, as a critical cog in the state's machinery, this subversion could not be tolerated.

Less Machiavellian motives may also have been involved. Since the crime rate continued to rise no matter how the Penal Code was "toughened up," economic elites may have decided that a little more carrot and a little less stick was indicated. Alternatively, they may have become disenchanted with the growing criminal justice establishment, whose huge budgets were inconsistent with conservative notions about the role of government and deficit spending. Or put most simply, they may have come to view earlier Penal Code revisions as the result of unfounded overreactions to isolated historical events.

Where does all this leave us? Perhaps most important, our data speak directly only to a large statistical effect between column inches of crime coverage and certain kinds of Penal Code revisions, holding several other factors constant. We have offered four possible interpretations for that finding: (1) editorial comment about specific bills affected legislation directly, (2) editorial comment about broader criminal justice matters affected the general thrust of criminal justice legislation, (3) both the editorials and the legislative trends reflected the impact of external historical events, and (4) the editorials were indicators of elite opinion that in turn influenced Penal Code content. Note that, in all four cases, we have at best rather indirect measures of the critical processes. Moreover, some of the speculations presented over the past few pages could apply equally well whether elites or editorial content itself initiated the controversy.

Given the current controversy over "conflict" versus "consensus" models in the criminal lawmaking process[17] and our speculations that elite interests may play some role, it is also important that our views on the role of social structure and its elites not be misunderstood. We have not been suggesting social processes that rest fundamentally on a theory of conspiracy. That would assume that dominant parties had figured out their specific criminal justice interests, secretly organized, and then effectively implemented their priorities. While a case for conspiracy might well be made for critical economic decisions at state and national levels, the day-to-day changes in the criminal law seems too peripheral and too technical to be an ongoing pivotal concern of the "ruling class" or any other economic elite. There is no comprehensive, detailed "game plan" secretly being implemented. Rather, in a broad way the social structure shapes the interests, beliefs, and resources of all citizens* who, in their routine actions and in a variety of spheres, produce consequences for the criminal justice system (which also feed back and affect the social structure). Since there is a lot of slippage between social structure and individual behavior and a lot of slippage between individual behavior and the content of the criminal law, the effects of social structure on the details of California's Penal Code are often subtle, elusive, and very far from deterministic.

This is not to argue that at a more micro level, conspiracies do not occur. Indeed, if our most compelling data are about anything, they are about conspiracies. The law enforcement lobby plots against the ACLU, who plot against punitive legislators, and so on. The point is that these conspiracies revolve around rather specific and narrow issues, changing almost from week to week. Further, they usually have to do with rather mundane concerns like conviction rates, the scope of legal searches, and how parole decisions are made. Even when groups explicitly tied to dominant class interests (like the Committee of 25) intervene, their actions generally reflect short-run measures whose links to any elaborate and coherent program for the criminal law are problematic. Economic dominance should not be confused with legislative omnipotence, and business acumen may

---

* There are several implicit ideas here that perhaps should be made manifest. First, American society is organized in such a way that different *categories* of people are necessarily placed in *inequality* relationships with one another. While disagreement exists over which categories are more "fundamental," few would deny that distinctions by sex, age, race, and social class are important. Second, this suggests that far more is involved than the obvious fact that one's location in society affects one's objective and subjective interests. Different categories of people have systematically different access to a wide variety of resources, so that some categories typically dominate others. Power generally resides in men over women, whites over blacks, parents over children, and employers over employees. Put another way, both resources available and the rules of the game are stacked in favor of certain categories of people, and which category one is in therefore affects one's life chances (in a stochastic manner) from the start. Third, given systematic differences in the power that people in various categories can wield, it should not be surprising that societal rewards cannot flow equally to all. Inequality in inputs seems inevitably to produce inequality in outcomes. Finally, and perhaps most important, these circumstances are so closely linked to, and dependent on, America's political–economic system that, in order to make great changes, the society itself would have to undergo major alterations. These circumstances are thus not simply accidents of history or consequences of the biases and prejudices of individuals (although these no doubt contribute to the situation) but are outcomes that flow necessarily from America's economic and political foundations.

have little to do with criminal justice sophistication. It is only when the outcomes of numerous and often petty squabbles, reflecting different interests and differential power, gradually accumulate that the role of social structure may become visible. In short, the long-term trends in the criminal law may be shaped more by some "unseen hand" than by the conscious will of a few powerful conspirators.

Conclusions

It should be clear by now that the content of the California Penal Code responds to a variety of forces having complex synergistic and inhibiting effects not only on changes in the criminal law but on each other. However, one's understanding of these processes depends fundamentally on the level of aggregation at which one chooses to operate.

Our qualitative material was especially useful in revealing the behavior of individuals. We saw political actors motivated by highly informed, short-run self-interest, armed with varying resources, aggressively trying to advance their agendas. Yet, few had any global perspective beyond the vague implications of elastic rhetoric and nothing approaching a detailed blueprint for the entire criminal justice system. Thus, our quantitative analyses documented how myriad compromises across a variety of issues changed the Penal Code in fits and starts with hundreds of small increments whose overall pattern seemed totally devoid of any self-contained teleological implications. While particular Penal Code alterations were certainly no accident, it is hard to see their cumulative impact except in that manner. Just as consumers rarely purchase commodities with an eye to the implications for inflation, few of the individuals whose actions we have described, seriously considered long-run consequences for Penal Code content.

Both the qualitative and quantitative data spoke to the activities of groups and organized interests. If attention is confined *solely to the legislative arena*, something approximating a pluralistic model seems applicable. Recall that for the parties and organizations that participated actively in Sacramento no single force dominated and no narrow political persuasion achieved hegemony. Moreover, differences were rarely zero sum with competing interests playing by a reasonably common set of rules. This is precisely the kind of interaction emphasized by American political science.

Moving beyond individuals and groups to societal forces, we are severely hindered by the nature of our data. Nevertheless, we would argue that societal norms played little direct role in producing the kinds of Penal Code revisions we have studied. Moreover, despite the possible existence of broad notions about the seriousness of certain kinds of crimes, the importance of even loose normative boundaries for criminal law content remains at least debatable.

Building a case solely from our data on the role of class factors affecting Penal Code revisions is even more difficult. If one interprets the impact of *Los Angeles Times* editorials as indicative of ruling-class interests, economic elites are at least an unusually powerful interest group. Yet, whether or not particular economic elites *could* effectively direct the day-to-day legislative process, it is clear that for the kinds of changes we have stressed, they do not. Short of genuine threats to the social fabric or occasional bills immediately affecting business interests, their efforts are largely directed elsewhere. Incremental Penal Code change may simply be too peripheral given their other more pressing concerns.

However, before one abandons the more provocative aspects of Conflict Theory, it may be useful to stand back a bit from the data and observe that, whether liberal or conservative, virtually all coalitions surfacing in our study were in general terms committed to current American institutions. The rhetoric of "decentralization," "deinstitutionalization," and "decontrol" was late in arriving and proved empty in practice. No one seriously proposed changing radically the State's role in regulating undesirable behavior. No one significantly challenged laws buttressing the sanctity of private property and the obvious inequalities that exist in American society. Moreover, the almost universal response to a wide spectrum of perceived social problems was increased criminalization. Similarly, over the 15 years covered by our study, there was a steady expansion in criminal sanctions. Therefore, both in ideology and deed, the range of perspectives represented in Sacramento supported a continued and widening intervention by the State in the daily affairs of its citizens. In this context, liberals and conservatives may have had far more in common than might otherwise appear.

While it is not surprising to find the influential actors surrounding criminal justice in general support of the status quo, it is difficult to say why the scope of the Penal Code has widened. Perhaps other forms of social control resting on interpersonal and normative constraints have been weakened. Perhaps legislators and partisans quickly resort to the "simple" solutions implied by legislative remedies. Perhaps an increasingly complex and technological society has no choice but to regulate behavior through the formal instrument of law. Or perhaps the society itself has increasingly produced centrifugal forces and contradictions for which change in the criminal law is seen as appropriate response. In any case, our concerns have shifted from the specter of conservative law and order to a more general anxiety over the growing power of the State. The process of Penal Code change has not favored any narrow lobby group or particular political perspective within the range represented by contending legislative factions. However, to the degree that State power has been enhanced, the larger interests it most immediately represents have new tools with which to shape society.

REFERENCES

1. William E. Nelson, "Emerging Notions of Modern Criminal Law in Revolutionary Era: An Historical Perspective," *New York University Law Review*, Vol. 42 (May, 1967) pp. 450–482.
2. Fredric Dubow, "Justice for the People: Law and Politics in Lower Courts in Tanzania" (unpublished Ph.D. thesis, University of California, Berkeley, 1973).
3. Thomas S. Kuhn, *The Structure of Scientific Revolutions* (Chicago: University of Chicago Press, 1970).
4. Anthony M. Platt, *The Child Savers* (Chicago: University of Chicago Press, 1969).
5. André Gorz, *Strategy for Labor* (Boston: Beacon Press, 1967).
6. Peter H. Rossi, Emily Waite, Christine E. Bose, and Richard A. Berk, "The Seriousness of Crimes: Normative Structure and Individual Differences," *American Sociological Review*, Vol. 39, (April, 1974), pp. 224–237.
7. Ralph Miliband, *The State in Capitalist Society* (New York: Basic Books, 1969); Herbert Marcuse, *One-Dimensional Man* (Boston: Beacon Press, 1964).
8. William J. Chambliss, "The State, the Law, and the Definition of Behavior as Criminal or Delinquent," in *The Handbook of Criminology*, ed. Daniel Glaser (Chicago: Rand McNally, 1974).
9. See, for example, *ibid*. Also Nicos Poulantzas, *Political Power and Social Classes* (London: Humanities Press, 1975).
10. See, for example, Jonathan Rubinstein, *City Police* (New York: Farrar, Strauss, and Giroux, 1973).
11. David J. Bordua and Albert J. Reiss, "Command, Control, and Charisma," *American Journal of Sociology*, Vol. 72 (July, 1966).
12. *Newsweek*, January 2, 1967.
13. *Ibid*.
14. Miliband. *The State in Capitalist Society* pp. 230–231.
15. *Ibid*; Richard Quinney, *Critique of Legal Order* (Boston: Little, Brown & Company, 1974).
16. Frank Wilkinson, "The Era of Libertarian Repression—1948 to 1973: From Congressman to President, with Substantial Support from the Liberal Establishment," *University of Akron Law Review*, Winter, 1974, pp. 280–309; Gregory Barak, "In Defense of the Rich," *Crime and Social Justice*, Vol. 3 (Summer, 1975), pp. 2–14.
17. Andrew Hopkins, "On the Sociology of Criminal Law," *Social Problems*, Vol. 22 (June, 1975), pp. 608–619.

Author Index

Subject Index

QUANTITATIVE STUDIES IN SOCIAL RELATIONS

Consulting Editor: Peter H. Rossi

UNIVERSITY OF MASSACHUSETTS
AMHERST, MASSACHUSETTS

A
B 7
C 8
D 9
E 0
F 1
G 2
H 3
I 4
J 5